SECOND EDITION

MEDICAL
LEADERSHIP

THE KEY TO MEDICAL
ENGAGEMENT AND
EFFECTIVE ORGANISATIONS

SECOND EDITION

MEDICAL LEADERSHIP

THE KEY TO MEDICAL ENGAGEMENT AND EFFECTIVE ORGANISATIONS

PETER SPURGEON
Emeritus Professor
Health Services Management Medical School
University of Warwick, UK

JOHN CLARK
Honorary Associate Professor
Warwick Medical School
University of Warwick, UK

CRC Press
Taylor & Francis Group
Boca Raton London New York

CRC Press is an imprint of the
Taylor & Francis Group, an **informa** business

CRC
Taylor Francis Group
6000 Broken Sound Parkway NW, Suite 300
Boca, FL 33487-2742

© 2018 Taylor & Francis Group, LLC
CRC is an imprint of Taylor & Francis Group, an Informa business

No claim to original U.S. Government works

Printed in Great Britain by Ashford Colour Press Ltd.

International Standard Book Number-13: 978-1-78523-161-2 (Paperback)

Library of Congress Cataloging-in-Publication Data

Names: Spurgeon, P. (Peter), author. | Clark, John, 1950 July 7- author.
Title: Medical leadership : the key to medical engagement and effective organisations / by Peter Spurgeon and John Clark.
Description: Second edition. | Boca Raton, FL : CRC Press, [2018] | Includes bibliographical references and index.
Identifiers: LCCN 2017006435| ISBN 9781785231612 (pbk. : alk. paper) | ISBN 9781138068070 (hardback : alk. paper) | ISBN 9781315158327 (ebook : alk. paper)
Subjects: | MESH: Leadership | Health Services Administration | Delivery of Health Care | Physician's Role | United Kingdom
Classification: LCC RA971 | NLM W 84 FA1 | DDC 610.68--dc23
LC record available at https://lccn.loc.gov/2017006435

Visit the Taylor & Francis Web site at
http://www.taylorandfrancis.com

and the CRC Press Web site at
http://www.crcpress.com

Contents

Foreword to the second edition

Much progress has been made in medical leadership over the past couple of decades. Gone are the days when the mantle of leadership was passed around among the most senior doctors with roles holding little or no accountability. Now, there are statutory positions achieved through increasing competition; competency frameworks, standards and specific qualifications have been developed; and accountability is significant and carries significant consequences. Medical leadership in the United Kingdom finally has a professional home—the Faculty of Medical Leadership and Management—a body of all the medical royal colleges and faculties.

While leadership development for doctors may still lack coordination and standardisation, more opportunities are now available, and there is a growing acceptance of the need to start in the training years, indeed at medical school. That said, there remains plenty to be done; for example the United Kingdom remains an outlier in the paucity of doctors who assume the most senior executive roles, which new evidence suggests may not be to the benefit of patients.

This book eloquently charts a path through recent history, providing an account of progress whilst also laying bare some of the important challenges that remain. It is no secret that the doctor–manager relationship could be better in many places, and yet there seems little positive action, plenty of prejudice and little understanding. An entire chapter looks at the underlying reasons in a helpfully analytical, dispassionate and non-accusatory way. The final chapter also helpfully adds to this by exploring the difficult challenges that doctors face in balancing their historical responsibility to the patient in front of them with a more recent responsibility to the population they serve.

Medicine relies heavily on an abundant evidence base and yet the literature surrounding medical leadership is sparse and seemingly hidden from many. Laudably, this book draws heavily throughout on research, and an interesting chapter explores the relative importance of creating an engaged medicine workforce as approved to medical leadership alone; the authors are to be congratulated on their contributions to that evidence base, which quite simply shows that a disengaged medical workforce is poor for an organisation's health but worse still for the health of its patients. It argues cogently that addressing poor medical engagement is not therefore pandering to the profession but a quality improvement issue. Helpfully, the organisational characteristics that enhance engagement are laid out and should be heeded.

General practice rightfully gets a chapter of its own, which charts, in a mine of fascinating history, the rapid rise and major change in leadership demanded within primary care. Like the rest of the book, it does not duck the perhaps difficult message that medical leaders have quite a challenge to which they must rise. But it also brings significant balance by clear enunciation as to why the task is so large and is such a seismic shift from the *modus operandi* of the relatively recent past.

In summary, this book offers a powerful blend of the recent history of medical leadership and the challenges it faces, laced with the evidence as to why it is so important to the patients and population we serve. Uncomfortable truths are highlighted, but they are balanced with powerful analyses that help to expose some of the many competing demands and accountabilities facing the medical leader. Many rightly highlight this as a time of unprecedented challenge, and the call for great leadership rolls easily off the tongue. To achieve that, we need a much deeper understanding of what we are asking of our leaders, how we can support them to be successful and how we can help them to develop. I suggest you will find many answers to this fundamental knowledge in these pages.

Peter Lees
Chief Executive and Medical Director
Faculty of Medical Leadership and Management

Foreword to the first edition

The future direction of healthcare around the world will be determined by a mix of national economics, public and professional expectations and global technology. Sometimes, these interests will be in conflict, particularly as governments increasingly focus on the economic impact of societal demands and technological growth on healthcare delivery systems. These considerations are likely to accelerate in the aftermath of the recent global financial crisis. Never before has the quality of leadership in healthcare been more important.

The quality of leadership and management defines the difference between excellence and mediocrity and success and failure for all organisations. In my view, good leaders inspire others and are able to align them towards a common goal through a clear vision. Good managers, on the other hand, simplify and streamline the way organisations work to achieve their goals and maximise potential. These are two quite different functions. Not all leaders are good managers, but most effective managers are also good leaders; the two sets of qualities are complementary to effective organisation performance.

In healthcare provider organisations, the quality of clinical leadership always underpins the difference between exceptional and adequate or pedestrian clinical services, which in aggregate determine the overall effectiveness, safety and reputation of every healthcare organisation. Similarly, effective clinical leadership in commissioning organisations brings perspective and challenge, which in turn drives up clinical quality for the whole health economy. So good clinical leadership is not an end in itself; it is a means to achieving high-performing healthcare systems.

Young doctors are inspired by good clinicians who are intellectually adept, who bring forensic scrutiny to their diagnostic and therapeutic routines, who are kind to their patients and who exhibit a comprehensive mixture of compassion and professionalism. Such doctors may have no managerial inclination, yet they are highly influential and essential leaders if our National Health Service (NHS) is to flourish.

Doctors also seek leadership from medical royal colleges and specialist associations with whom they identify on matters of clinical quality, standards of care and training of the next generation. Therefore, clinical leadership across the

NHS may take many forms, ranging from frontline leaders who provide excellent service, through a spectrum of clinical innovators and academics, to those who provide professional leadership through their professional bodies or through managerial involvement at various levels in their employing institution.

Successful medical leaders are usually, but not always, experienced and credible clinicians with good people skills, who look beyond the boundaries of their own specialty or institution, who are positive and perseverant and who are prepared to take reasonable risks to achieve their goals. Most importantly, they know how to engage their colleagues and effect change. They understand the principles of organisational performance and the balance between professional autonomy and corporate behaviour.

The problem is that over the years, we have paid too little attention to developing clinical leadership and management skills in a coherent fashion either in undergraduate or postgraduate education. This has led to an expansion of highly qualified, non-clinical, professional healthcare managers to administer an increasingly complex NHS. Inevitably, the two groups of professionals will have differing perspectives, which are addressed in Chapter 2. It seems to me that there is an enormous amount to be gained by training systems that maximise the synergy between the two professional groups, and this can be facilitated by the comprehensive application of the Medical Leadership Competency Framework across the NHS.

This book examines the historical context of how the UK NHS arrived at its current position in terms of the involvement of doctors in the wider organisational context. Lessons are drawn from comparison with systems overseas. Some exciting and critical developments are described in this text, not least the embedding of the Medical Leadership Competency Framework as a statutory element of the training and development of all doctors, evidence of the link between enhanced medical engagement and organisational performance and finally the establishment of a new Faculty of Medical Leadership and Management. The last development is a culmination of a major national project 'Enhancing Engagement in Medical Leadership' led by two of the authors (Spurgeon and Clark). The new Faculty can provide continuity from the existing project work and also give impetus to taking forward further developments in this vital sphere.

The text is a comprehensive account of the key aspects of medical leadership, but it is also readable and accessible. I can thoroughly recommend it as a read for junior and senior doctors, non-clinical and clinical managers and those taking on formal leadership roles.

Professor Sir Bruce Keogh
NHS Medical Director

1

An introduction to medical leadership and engagement: A perspective on this text

1.1 INTRODUCTION

The importance of medical leadership and engagement has become ever more evident and critical since the first edition of this book was published in 2011. This has been confirmed not only by various political and organisational initiatives but also by the increasing research and papers on the topic. There are now significantly greater national and international literature and a plethora of papers outlining different initiatives and perspectives. This has largely happened as part of a wider (and perhaps belated) recognition that health systems faced with increasing public scrutiny through a very strict regulatory approach and fiscal constraint needed to move from a heroic leadership approach based around performance targets to one where leaders are responsible for creating cultures that encourage a stronger collaborative or collective approach where all staff, but particularly doctors, act as if shareholders in the system and organisation.

As Dickinson et al. (2015) comment, 'medical engagement is a topic that has started to receive significant international attention over the last twenty years and is thought to be a helpful mechanism through which health systems can drive the efficiency of health organisations, patient experience and clinical outcomes'.

We should stress at the outset that this is a book about medical leadership and engagement. Too often, commentators use the term 'clinical leadership' when clearly meaning 'medical leadership'. We make no apology for focusing on doctors; other texts usefully cover the wider range of roles that clinical professionals play in health systems. Much of the content of policy directions and statements prefer to use the term 'clinical leadership' when all subsequent text is focused on doctors. They are, de facto, the major decision-makers regarding the use of resources. This is not to detract from the key role other clinical professionals and non-clinical managers and leaders play. Another facet of this uni-professional approach is that there has traditionally been much greater difficulty getting doctors interested in management and leadership roles. They have many other alternatives—research and education, college roles, not to mention private practice. Often, a drop in salary is involved in undertaking leadership roles. These issues do not apply to other clinical groups, where there is generally a financial incentive to undertake leadership roles and many, particularly from nursing backgrounds, readily move into these other roles. Delivery of healthcare is a team activity, with all members having a major contribution to make to improve health and the way in which services are delivered. Much of what we have to say about doctors being more involved in management, leadership and transformation can be applied to other clinical professions, but this is not the remit of this particular book. Medical leadership is a particular focus within the National Health Service (NHS) currently and indeed many other countries and, we anticipate, for the foreseeable future.

The last five years has also seen growing evidence both within the NHS and internationally that organisations with high levels of what might loosely be termed 'human resource features', for example, team working, staff (and particularly medical) engagement, clinical leadership, values-based approaches to recruitment, induction, appraisal, revalidation and training and development, coupled with a strong focus on quality improvement, delivering better clinical outcomes, higher quality of care and financial performance. Much of this evidence has been around for many years. The public exposure of many hospitals and general practices delivering poor care has served to bring politicians and policy-makers to recognise that leaders need to focus on culture as the means to achieve improvement.

There is widespread international advocacy of increasing the involvement and participation of doctors in the leadership of healthcare organisations (Darzi, 2008, in the United Kingdom; Falcone and Satiani, 2008, in the United States; and Dwyer, 2010a, 2010b; Health Workforce Australia, 2011, in Australia; Lega and Sartirana, 2015, in Italy). These are specific examples, but the viewpoint is quite widespread, and many other references will be offered throughout the book.

In the United Kingdom, most hospital chief executives are non-physicians, whilst in the United States, out of 6500 hospitals, only 235 are led by physicians (Gundesman and Kanter, 2009). Goodall (2011) reported on a study in the United States that there was a strong positive association between ranked quality of a hospital and whether the chief executive officer (CEO) is a physician. One UK newspaper even provided a headline stating that 'Doctors are the best hospital managers, study reveals'. This study is probably the first analysis of its kind, and further studies need to be undertaken to ascertain whether this association attains in the NHS. It is our contention that this is unlikely given the very small number of medically qualified chief executives, the constant churn in these roles and the greater political involvement in the way organisations in healthcare can operate. More importantly, other studies, including those by Spurgeon, support the growing view that there is also a strong association between the extent of medical engagement and clinical and organisational performance in the NHS, and this is also being seen in Australian hospitals, that is, that securing the sustained engagement of a large number of doctors is critical to high performance, irrespective of the professional background of the CEO. Veronsi et al. (2013) also found that UK trusts with a higher proportion of doctors on the board performed better.

Whilst our original motivation for the book was partly inspired by Lord Darzi's review of the health system culminating in the publication of *High Quality for All* in 2008, our enthusiasm to revise the first edition has been triggered by the increased energy for the medical leadership and engagement movement over the past five years. Policy analysts in the future may well see his strong messages about the importance of getting clinicians, and particularly doctors, more engaged in leading service improvement as a defining moment in the way in which health services are organised and led. However, in many ways, the impetus given only served to reinforce a movement that had started some 20 or more years earlier. Doctors have been involved in the running of health services, locally, nationally and internationally, since the pioneers who initiated and organised health services many centuries ago. What is new is the emerging evidence of the relationship between the extent to which doctors are engaged in the planning, prioritization and shaping of services and the wider performance of the organisation. Engagement is more than doing what the organisation wants doctors to do; it is doctors taking a leadership role in the doing.

Whilst initially increasing medical leadership and engagement made sense and was the subject of a number of past reports and initiatives, the evidence of its value is now being realised through different studies that we explore in this revised edition. It is also evident that poor clinical outcomes, patient experiences and quality of care are very much the result of poor cultures with a lack of effective engagement by clinicians in decision making and improvement.

The *Francis Report into the Mid Staffordshire Hospitals* (2013) and others related to disturbing clinical performance over the past few years have all highlighted the consequences of organisations with cultures that fail to focus on genuinely patient-orientated care. Leadership style is inevitably context based and the movement towards greater medical leadership and engagement is partly a construct of health policymakers recognising that whilst relevant performance targets have a place, they cannot be achieved and sustained without greater local ownership by clinical professionals.

The role of general practitioners (GPs) as local leaders in prioritising and commissioning services has also gained considerable momentum since the first edition. As the first edition was being published, the coalition government was establishing Clinical Commissioning Groups (CCGs) in England as part of the Health and Social Care Act 2012. Whilst GPs have had increasing influence across local health systems since the establishment of GP Fundholding in the 1990s and subsequently through Primary Care Groups and Trusts, the last few years have seen this accelerated through CCGs and emerging General Practice Federations and similar bodies.

GPs now control around 80% of health expenditure through the CCGs in England. As Douglas (2015) contends, 'these are major management roles requiring considerable expertise in management, leadership and finance, yet many of these groups have had little or no training with these vital tasks. They bring intelligence, clinical nous and goodwill to CCGs, but managing huge and limited budgets effectively needs special skills and ways need to be found to ensure all CCG members have the training and development that allows them to develop these skills'.

This edition, therefore includes a new chapter on primary care leadership, but throughout the book, we stress the need for system-wide clinical leadership and engagement. We highlight how high-performing health organisations are typified by not only high levels of internal medical engagement but also by taking a more integrated and system-wide approach based on what is best for their communities and patients and not what might be best from any individual part of the system. It is perhaps interesting to note that plans for any reconfiguration of acute hospital services 20 or more years ago might have had a token GP amongst a large number of hospital specialists on any review group. Now, GPs are very much at the helm of such reviews, seeking to secure more cost-effective and safer networks of acute services across a population.

The recognition of the growing pressure of those with chronic conditions only serves to reinforce the urgency for a stronger focus on system leadership with clinicians driving new pathways and approaches to care. We will explore this in more detail as the desire for greater medical leadership and engagement is not an isolated strategy but part of a new leadership and cultural approach that enables sustained improvements to be made to the delivery of care.

1.2 STRUCTURE OF THIS REVISED EDITION

In this revised edition, we have reduced the historical coverage of health reforms. This is not to say it is unimportant, but more of a reflection that the past five years have created a new policy context and organisational landscape for the NHS. Many of the policy initiatives are complex and interactive. They require detailed analysis, often being adopted or modified according to changing governmental priorities. This is not a text based upon policy analysis. Rather our contention is that almost any policy may founder if there is a failure to engage and obtain the support and commitment of the medical profession—a key and fundamental component of the delivery system. Understanding the current challenges requires some appreciation of past managerial, organisational and professional contexts, but the present paradigm of commissioning, targets, inspection, individual and organisational regulation, accountability and mixed economy within a harsh fiscal environment has particularly highlighted the importance of collective leadership and medical engagement. The NHS is not alone in having to face ever-increasing demands from an ageing population and higher expectations fuelled by the almost daily availability of new technologies. Most developed countries face similar challenges to the United Kingdom and all are seeking new ways of engaging doctors as one means of ensuring value. Lee and Cosgrove (2014, p. 105), writing from a mainly American perspective, sum this up well in stating that 'despite wondrous advances in medicine and technology, health care regularly fails at the fundamental job of any business: to reliably deliver what its customers need. In the face of ever-increasing complexity, the hard work and best intentions of individual physicians can no longer guarantee efficient, high quality care. Fixing health care will require a radical transformation, moving from a system organised around individual physicians to a team-based approach based on patients. Doctors, of course, must be central players in the transformation. Any ambitious strategy that they do not embrace is doomed'. The authors share this view and see some exciting organisational and system transformations both in the United Kingdom and internationally, where this philosophy has led to high performance. Alas, despite the strong evidence, too many health organisations and systems are still failing to recognise the importance of medical leadership and engagement, and poor patient care and fiscal performance are the consequences. Effective medical leadership and engagement can no longer be an optional extra but are fundamental elements of every health body and system. It is hoped that this book will contribute to the movement of medical leadership and engagement and will help policymakers, practitioners and consumers do more to make it an integral and sustained part of every health body and not just the exemplars.

We have combined the previous chapters on health system reform and a historical perspective on medical leadership into one as the medical leadership and engagement movement over the past 60 years is so entwined with successive health reforms. So, in Chapter 2, we explore the historical journey of medical leadership as responses to different reform initiatives. However, we have significantly reduced the coverage from the early decades of the NHS as the last five years have seen more significant changes and initiatives around the role of the doctor both from policy-makers and the medical profession. In the authors' leadership development activities with doctors, it is evident that many do not appreciate the extent to which the past split between general management control with a few doctors in 'leadership' roles to represent their colleagues' impacts on the current arrangements. Today's arrangements are the next stage in a journey that started from a major domination by the medical profession preceding the setting up of the NHS in 1948 through a period of disenfranchisement thereafter until perhaps the first main reorganisation of the NHS in 1974. We contend that by this time, some doctors, generally reluctantly, accepted representative roles. The Cogwheel Reports between 1967 and 1974 have had a significant impact on the way in which hospital services have been organised, that is, around specialties ever since. The Reports also started the process whereby doctors initially took on representative roles for their specialty Cogwheel Division and then assumed executive responsibility for their specialty business unit and the concept of Service Line Management increasingly being introduced into hospital Trusts in England. This historical context is important and has shaped attitudes and perspectives. However, we believe the movement towards medical leadership has reached a stage of maturity and acceptance that suggests more is to be learned (and gained) from focusing on current challenges.

This shift from representation to accountability was reinforced by the Griffiths Report published in 1983 and further endorsed by the DHSS Resource Management

Initiative in 1986 and the establishment of Clinical Directorates. The Griffiths view back in the early 1980s has continued to be stressed since then, and although new models and structures have been developed, the fundamental principle of encouraging some doctors to take on positional medical leadership positions and being accountable for clinical and business activity has been accentuated only over the past two decades. Put simply, Griffiths and later commentators could not see how a service, department or organisation could be managed effectively unless it was managed by those who commit resources.

In Chapter 3, we draw on more recent research on the historical perceived gap, or sometimes chasm, as evidenced by Mid Staffordshire Hospitals between clinicians and managers. We explore some of the factors that potentially exaggerate "the divide" but also highlight some of the ways in which high-performing health organisations nationally and internationally value the contribution of both and create leadership and management approaches and structures that are based on partnerships of mutual respect.

We also explore how the medical profession itself has changed over the same period as policy and organisational arrangements have altered. Whereas management and leadership were frequently dismissed by doctors in derogatory terms in previous eras, the medical profession is now very positively espousing the importance of doctors assuming leadership roles at all levels of training and careers and stressing their importance as being part of being a good doctor. This view is endorsed by Bohmer (2012), who argues that while individual doctor excellence is necessary, it is no longer sufficient to generate good patient outcomes. He highlights the way in which processes and micro-systems are largely controlled by practising physicians and hence the importance of their leadership skills and behaviours being exerted to improve overall health system performance.

We explore in more detail why many of the initiatives introduced over the past 65 years or so have perhaps only been partially successful. We suggest that both managers and doctors represent two very powerful groups. Unlike many other countries, the United Kingdom has experienced a very strong managerialist culture, particularly over the past 30 years, which has often led to conflict between clinicians and managers.

Trying to achieve some congruence between the individualistic nature of clinical practice and professionalism and the managers' broader population and organisational perspective is an inevitable area of potential conflict and tension. The exercise of clinical autonomy is a crucial part of the application of knowledge acquired by doctors through their medical training. As Oni (1995) suggests, at worst, some doctors will view managers as 'agents of government to control the expert power of the professional'.

In this chapter, we explore the perspective offered by organisational theorists such as Henry Mintzberg who characterise healthcare organisations as professional rather than machine (for example, government agencies) bureaucracies (Mintzberg, 1979). One of the characteristics of professional bureaucracies is that front-line staff have a large measure of control over the content of work by virtue of their training and specialist knowledge. Consequentially, hierarchical directives issued by those nominally in control have limited impact and indeed may be resisted by front-line staff. Leaders of health organisations who do not recognise and respect this perspective are unlikely to create organisations where doctors would want to be more engaged. As Ham (2012), writing in the *British Medical Journal*, summarises, 'my view...is that any leader...of any professional bureaucracy...can only succeed if they have a really strong diagnosis of how these organisations tick, where does the power and influence lie to do good or to do ill, and how do you harness that power in pursuit of the corporate good'.

The doctor–manager conflict is perhaps a stereotyped portrayal often reinforced by media coverage, including television dramas that delight in exaggerating the gap between the clinicians' desire to provide the highest quality and quantity of care unfettered by resource constraints against the managers' need to control expenditure within allocated budgets and other constraints. The demands have been accentuated in recent years by the increased pressure on managers to meet government and regulatory bodies' performance targets. It is perhaps this 'battle-zone' of the performance management philosophy inherent in the concept of managerialism that creates the real challenge for health leaders. Seeking to get some shared and balanced understandings between the individual doctor's desire to deliver high-quality care to every patient and the managers' need to deliver political and organisational imperatives has been a long-standing challenge. As we explore in later chapters, the more this potential chasm can be minimised, the more likely local communities will benefit from high-quality and efficient services. It is not an impossible dream, but understanding the different motivations and perspectives is perhaps the critical issue. Various reports where this chasm has led to disastrous consequences for patients have consistently confirmed this dysfunctionality. There can be no greater incentive or argument for seeking to reduce the divide and, as we will highlight, where there is shared respect and partnership working patients, communities, staff and the taxpayer all benefitting.

It is, as Barnett et al. (2004) contend, a need for a 'convergence of cultures' and not a contest between any perceived or real emphasised differences. Finding common ground is the challenge. Who could deny that this is around service improvement and patient safety? Throughout this book, we shall keep coming back to this need for alignment of values and aspirations.

In Chapter 4, we provide a brief chronology of different roles and models of leadership but particularly offer contemporary thinking and research into the importance of collective and system-wide leadership. We highlight how the best-performing health organisations are typified by collective leadership. We also appreciate the size of the challenge to those organisations that are still typified by heroic leadership and lack of medical and indeed staff engagement often not helped by a regulatory process that often appears to be short-term target-focused rather than supporting long-term sustained cultural change that motivates doctors and indeed all staff to be more involved.

The authors have spent over two decades being involved with the leadership development of doctors and associated research. However, much of the thinking behind this book emanates from leading a joint project between the Academy of Medical Royal Colleges and the now demised NHS Institute for Innovation and Improvement entitled 'Enhancing Engagement in Medical Leadership'. This project ran from 2006 to 2011. One key output was the development of a Medical Leadership Competency Framework (MLCF), which was first published in 2008 and has subsequently been refined and also adopted by all other clinical professional bodies as a Clinical Leadership Competency Framework (CLCF). It describes 'the leadership competences doctors need to become more actively involved in the planning, delivery and transformation of health services as a normal part of their role as doctors' (NHS Institute for Innovation and Improvement, Academy of Medical Royal Colleges, 2010, p. 6). The MLCF and CLCF subsequently formed the basis of an NHS Leadership Framework. Whilst the NHS Leadership Academy (2013) developed a Healthcare Leadership Model aimed at all those who work in health and care to become better leaders, the medical profession continues to generally adopt the MLCF as the basis for undergraduate and postgraduate medical education curricula and standards. The Faculty of Medical Leadership and Management (FMLM), which was conceived from the Enhancing Engagement in Medical Leadership Project in 2011, published a set of leadership and management standards for medical professionals in 2015 (Faculty of Medical Leadership and Management, 2015). The standards are linked to appraisal and revalidation of medical leaders. This important area of appraisal and revalidation is explored further in Chapter 8. In this regard, medicine has become the only profession to have addressed the recommendation in the Francis Report (2013) that healthcare leadership should become a profession. In Chapter 5, we explore this new framework and also review some other international models as well as provide a more detailed review of the MLCF.

In Chapter 6, we explore some of the best practice around medical leadership and engagement. An increasing number of reviews and empirical studies are underpinning the vital importance of medical engagement to organisational performance.

It is perhaps a reflection of how much more effective medical leadership and engagement has become in the NHS that in the first edition, we focused on some of the exemplars in the United States. There is no doubt that these have positively influenced many NHS organisations, but there are now many great examples in the United Kingdom and indeed other countries. There is still much to be learnt from other international examples, but now other countries are also looking at some of the best models in the NHS as well as some of the other initiatives implemented, for example, MLCF, that apply to all medical students and doctors at all levels and the growing research evidence of the strong association between medical engagement and clinical outcomes, quality and organisational performance.

We devote a new chapter to primary care medical leadership and engagement in this edition. This should be no surprise given the changing architecture of the NHS and the importance of strong leadership and engagement by primary care physicians. Chapter 7 describes the dramatic changes in the power and influence of GPs over the past 25 years. Prior to the introduction of GP Fundholding around

1990, any reviews on the provision of acute hospitals across part of a region would have had a token GP around a table of hospital executives. How this has changed with GPs through initially Primary Care Groups and Trusts and more recently CCGs having major roles in commissioning services and leading changes in the way in which health and social care is organised and delivered.

In Chapter 8, we explore the background of revalidation and how it has given a much stronger focus on the value of appraisal. It is not surprising that those hospitals or services that have high levels of medical engagement also see genuine appraisal as a key activity. Doctors are being more heavily scrutinised than perhaps any other profession. Following the Kennedy Inquiry into children's cardiac surgery at Bristol in the late 1990s and the failure of health bodies to identify the high number of deaths under Dr Shipman's (GP) care, the medical profession has been subjected to much stricter regulation, perhaps more so than in any other country. This has led to a much more systematic approach to the appraisal and revalidation of doctors to practice. We explore the drivers for this and how this is contributing to doctors in positional leadership roles accepting greater executive responsibility and accountability and more medically engaged cultures. The role of doctors reviewing other doctors' variations in practice is a crucial component of the changing landscape of the NHS and is of increasing interest internationally.

In Chapter 9, we explore some of the practical initiatives being taken in the NHS and internationally to operationalise the MLCF or similar competency frameworks and the promotion of greater medical engagement. The most exciting initiatives involve junior doctors and there appears to be a growing interest from medical students and postgraduate trainee doctors to acquire leadership skills and knowledge, particularly around service improvement. A number of Medical Royal Colleges and NHS Trusts are positively encouraging trainees to undertake a service improvement project instead of a clinical audit. We provide details of some of these initiatives, but the movement towards more effective medical engagement and leadership needs to start in medical schools. It needs to be an integral part of a doctor's education, training and development throughout his or her career, not a remedial development activity once a doctor has moved into a positional leadership role, as has been the case in the past and sadly still is in many organisations.

Ibrahim et al. (2013) suggest that it is becoming more apparent to health services internationally that junior medical staff have immense potential as contributors and drivers of service reform. Historically, they have often been ignored in any discussions around clinical reform, with their superiors stressing the need for them to totally concentrate on getting experience in their chosen specialty. Given that junior doctors are at the centre of the admission and discharge processes and diagnostic requests and in the hospital across 24-hour periods, they are in ideal positions to identify where there are inefficiencies and potential improvement processes. Furthermore, as Micallef and Straw (2014) rightly identify, their mobility across many hospitals during their rotations provides them with great opportunities to compare different practices. This has always been the case, but perhaps the difference now is that enlightened managers and leaders are recognising the value of seeking the views of junior doctors and encouraging their participation in improving services. They are, of course, tomorrow's senior doctors, and such involvement at this early stage in their careers should reap rewards for the health system at a later time.

Jorm and Parker (2015), writing from an Australian perspective, suggest that the return on investment from healthcare leadership development programmes remains largely unmeasured worldwide. There are many examples of well-designed clinical leadership development programmes, but many of these are delivered at state, regional and national levels. This has led Fulop and Day (2010) to be critical of what they term the 'sheep dipping trade', where intermittent training is divorced from daily work and is therefore more individually centred. West et al. (2015) confirm this view, suggesting that the approach to leadership development has been distorted by a preoccupation with individual leadership often provided by external providers in remote locations.

The authors agree with these views and argue for a more locally and system-based approach to leadership development. High-performing health organisations put leadership development at the very centre of their culture and ensure that all those with management and leadership responsibilities are provided with the skills and knowledge to be effective within the culture of their organisation. These are generally multi-disciplinary and based around teams tackling real improvement issues.

Finally, in Chapter 10, we explore the future and suggest that in whatever way the health system evolves over the next decade, medical leadership and engagement will be critical. We are not advocating for all senior health leaders to be doctors. Apart from the limited study by Goodall (2011), there is no evidence that doctors as CEOs are the panacea. The evidence is certainly there that those organisations who value doctors' engagement and create distributed cultures where doctors wish to contribute to decision making, priorities and improvement deliver the best outcomes for patients and the taxpayer. We hope that this book will contribute to the realisation of this philosophy.

REFERENCES

Barnett, P., Malcolm, L., Wright, L. et al. (2004) Professional leadership and organisational change: Progress towards developing a quality culture in New Zealand's health system. *New Zealand Medical Journal*, 117(1198): 1–11.

Bohmer, R. (2012) *The Instrumental Value of Medical Leadership: Engaging Doctors in Improving Services*. London: King's Fund.

Darzi, A. (2008) *High Quality Care for All: NHS Next Stage Review Final Report*. London: Department of Health.

DHSS (1986) Resource management (management budgeting) in health authorities. *Health Notice*, (86)34.

Dickinson, H., Bismark, M., Phelps, G., and Loh, E. (2015) Future of medical engagement. *Australian Health Review*, 40(4): 443–446. Available at: http://dx.doi.org/10.1071/AH14204 (accessed 8 August 2016).

Douglas, N. (2015) Setting the scene. *Future Hospital Journal*, 2(3): 182–184.

Dwyer, A.J. (2010a) Medical managers in contemporary healthcare organisations: A consideration in literature. *Australian Health Review*, 34(4): 514–522.

Dwyer, A.J. (2010b) Roles, attributes and career paths of medical administrators in public hospitals: Survey of Victorian metropolitan directors of medical services. *Australian Health Review*, 34(4): 506–513.

Faculty of Medical Leadership and Management (2015) *Leadership and Management Standards for Medical Professionals*. London: Faculty of Medical Leadership and Management.

Falcone, B.F., and Satiani, B. (2008) Physician as hospital chief executive officer. *Vascular and Endovascular Surgery*, 42(1): 88–94.

Francis, R. (2013) *Report of the Mid-Staffordshire NHS Foundation Trust Public Inquiry*. London: Stationery Office. Available at: www.midstaffspublicinquiry.com/report.

Fulop, L., and Day, G.E. (2010) From leader to leadership: Clinician managers and where to next? *Australian Health Review*, 34: 344–351. doi:10.1071/AH09763.

Goodall, A.H. (2011) Physician leaders and hospital performance: Is there an association? *Social Science and Medicine*, 73(4): 535–539.

Griffiths Report (1983) *NHS Management Inquiry*. London: HSMO.

Gundesman, R., and Kanter, S.L. (2009) Educating physicians to lead hospitals. *Academic Medicine*, 84(10): 1348–1351.

Ham, C. (2012) The management of the NHS in England. *BMJ*, 344: e928.

Health Workforce Australia (2011) *Leadership for the Sustainability of Health System*, Draft Final Report. Adelaide, Australia: Health Workforce Australia.

Ibrahim, J.E., Jeffcott, S., Davis, M.C., and Chadwick, L. (2013) Recognising junior doctors' potential contribution to patient safety and quality improvement. *Journal of Health Organisation and Management*, 27(2): 273–286.

Jorm, C., and Parker, M. (2015) Medical leadership is the New Black: Or is it? *Australian Health Review*, 39: 217–219.

Lee, T.H., and Cosgrove, T. (2014) Engaging doctors in the health care revolution. *Harvard Business Review*, pp. 105–111.

Lega, F., and Sartirana, M. (2015) An international perspective on medical leadership. *Future Hospital Journal*, 2(3): 218–220.

Micallef, J., and Straw B. (2014) Developing junior doctors as leaders of service improvement. *Leadership in Health Services*, 27(4): 316–329.

Mintzberg, H. (1979) *The Structuring of Organisations*. Englewood Cliffs, NJ: Prentice-Hall.

NHS Institute for Innovation and Improvement (2010) *Medical Leadership Competency Framework*. 3rd ed. Coventry: NHS Institute for Innovation and Improvement.

NHS Leadership Academy (2013) *The Healthcare Leadership Model*. Leeds, UK: NHS Leadership Academy.

Oni, O.O. (1995) Who should lead in the NHS? *Journal of Management in Medicines*, 9(4): 31–34.

Veronsi, G., Kirkpatrick, I., and Vallascas, F. (2013) Clinicians on the board: What difference does it make? *Social Science & Medicine*, 77: 147–155.

West, M., Armit, K., Lowenthal, L., Eckert, R., West, T., and Lee, A. (2015) *Leadership and Leadership Development in Health Care: The Evidence Base*. London: Faculty of Medical Leadership and Management.

2

A historical perspective on medical leadership

2.1 INTRODUCTION

This chapter outlines the way in which doctors have been involved in management, leadership and transformation of services over the past seven decades since the inception of the National Health Service (NHS) in 1948. It can perhaps best be summarised as a movement from major domination preceding the NHS through a period of disenfranchisement immediately thereafter, right through until closer to the 1974 reorganisation of the NHS. By this time, a few doctors, generally reluctantly, accepted representative roles. However, the latter decades of the twentieth century and the early years of this century have led to doctors playing an increasing role in management, leadership and transformation of services at all levels.

It is always tempting to analyse or assess one particular health policy announcement or intervention as a radical change from the status quo. Far more often, it is a small partial adjustment or incremental change from the current position. Nevertheless, if reviewed from a longer-term perspective, it is likely to be an important step in a more fundamental strategic journey that, over time, leads to significant change in paradigms or philosophies.

The current focus on medical leadership was particularly espoused by High Quality Care for All: Next Stage Review (Department of Health, 2008), a further step in the journey of the changing role of doctor in the NHS since its creation in 1948. This was reinforced by the Conservative-Liberal Democrat coalition government's intention to give health professionals greater decision-making powers. As the first edition of this book was going to press, the government published its White Paper 'Equity and Excellence: Liberating the NHS' (Department of Health, 2010). The new policy direction outlined in the White Paper reinforced the important role of medical leaders across the health system but particularly within the proposed general practitioner (GP) consortia.

The role of the GPs as local leaders in prioritising and commissioning services gained considerable momentum following the White Paper. Despite significant challenges and resistance, the Health and Social Care Act was introduced in 2012, and with it, Clinical Commissioning Groups (CCGs) were established in England. To a certain extent, they replaced Primary Care Trusts, although some of the staff and responsibilities moved to Local Authority Public Health teams. Each body has an accountable officer responsible for the CCG's duties, functions, finance and governance. Only about 25% of accountable officers are GPs, and the majority of the members of the CCG governing body are GPs.

Chapter 7 provides a more detailed description and analysis of primary care medical leadership.

2.2 MEDICAL DISENFRANCHISEMENT: EARLY YEARS OF THE NHS

As the NHS and many other systems internationally seek to get more doctors involved in management, it is worth reflecting that the creation of the NHS in 1948 had created a framework within which hospital medical professionals could become salaried employees whilst retaining clinical freedom. This was expressed well by Paton et al.:

> The compromise that brought medical consultants into the NHS resulted in the application of the existing consultants' contract, and the arrangement whereby medical consultants contracts were held in the 'remote filing cabinets' of Regional Hospital Boards (subsequently Regional Health Authorities). This was a clear signal to the medical profession that they were different from any other employee within the NHS, whose contract of employment was held at more local level. (Paton et al., 2005, p. 28)

This view is confirmed by Klein, who comments that:

> Implicit in the structure of the NHS was a bargain between the State and the medical profession. While central government controlled the budget, doctors controlled what happened within that budget. Financial power was concentrated at the centre; clinical power was concentrated at the periphery. Politicians in Cabinet made the decisions about how much to spend; doctors made the decision about which patient should get what kind of treatment. (Klein, 2006, p. 61)

As the independence of clinicians has eroded over the past few decades and with increasing regulation and accountability for performance, it is interesting to note that only 25 years ago, Strong and Robinson (1990) argued that, as a result of this deal, the NHS was 'fundamentally syndicalist in nature' (p. 15) in that the medical profession was able to control and regulate its own activities without interference from politicians or managers.

Whilst we believe that the power base of the medical profession is changing rapidly, the historical medicalisation of the process of healthcare has given doctors considerable power both in the doctor–patient relationship and in the relative subservience of the other healthcare professions. This imbalance has had a significant impact on the way doctors relate to their organisation and involvement in management of services.

This book provides evidence of the rapidly changing culture of NHS organisations and how the medical profession is changing. However, a number of quotes capture a sense of the medical culture during the latter years of the twentieth century, for example,

> The moment you become a consultant (in Britain), you are omnipotent. You don't have to pay attention to your colleagues; you don't have to pay attention to anybody.
> —Emeritus Professor of Surgery (in Rosenthal, 1995)

> Doctors must play a bigger part in managing the health service to protect their clinical freedom.
> —Professor Cyril Chantler (Grabham and Chantler, 1989)

> Doctors are potentially the best managers in the health service. They have the longest and the best education of all those in the hospitals, the most experience, and are responsible for most of the decisions that lead to expenditure.
> —Sir Anthony Grabham (Grabham and Chantler, 1989)

As Pollard (2001) comments, these are somewhat protective and defensive views, as if noting a threat on the horizon (as subsequently realised) but one which could be safely navigated.

As Spurgeon (2001) summarised:

> The historical precedents that created the medical power base led initially to doctors existing in a closed sub-culture cushioned from scrutiny and challenge from others within the system. The individualistic culture affirmed by doctors' training served to support and reinforce this position. The public, too, were keen to endorse such an individual focus, believing that doctors should be concerned primarily with their patients and that health care organisations had some sort of secondary existence for the purpose of facilitating medical activity.

Following the start of the NHS in July 1948, many hospitals were led by a medical superintendent supported by a matron and hospital administrator. A large number of GPs worked single-handedly. The responsibility for organising clinical services tended to reside with a plethora of local and regional medical advisory committees.

It is interesting to note that, as many hospitals now are questioning the role of medical staff committees, back in 1953, the Ministry of Health (1953) issued a circular outlining the Minister's view on the functions and constitution of Medical Staff Committees. This was an important stage in the medical engagement journey for the NHS as it provided a clear message as to the importance of engaging doctors in advising and contributing to the running of both hospitals and groups of hospitals.

This was well summarised by Merivale, who suggested that

> The detailed arrangements for these committees in the majority of hospital groups are probably more rooted in past local history and customs than in the advice given in this circular with the result that arrangements are found to vary widely from group to group. Their effectiveness and the good relations or otherwise which they induce between the authority and its medical and dental staff vary equally widely. Indeed it could be argued in this matter that success may depend as much on tradition, personalities or even chance as upon organisation. (Merivale, 1969, pp. 172–173)

Nevertheless, medical advisory and staff committees did become important forums for discussing medical matters. Lay hospital administrators quickly understood the risk of attempting to make decisions on such matters without due deference to the appropriate medical committee. Whilst the hospital administrator was generally invited (often to take minutes!), it was also not unusual for the administrator to be asked to leave the meeting whilst matters of medical sensitivity were discussed by the doctors only.

It is not the intention of this chapter to offer a detailed history lesson of the various organisational changes and their impact on managerial arrangements between 1948 and 1974. However, in terms of what was to follow from 1974, it was, in retrospect, a relatively dormant era in the policy history of the NHS. Nevertheless, the role of doctors in contributing to the running of hospitals became an increasing issue during the 1960s and early 1970s and indeed became a significant theme of the 1974 reorganisation.

2.3 MEDICAL REPRESENTATION: COGWHEEL YEARS

A Joint Working Party on the Organisation of Medical Work in Hospitals was set up in 1965 to review the progress of the NHS, particularly hospital services. The Working Party produced three reports between 1967 and 1974. Based on the design of the cover, they became known as the Cogwheel Reports. These reports have had a significant impact on the way in which hospital services are organised internally over the past 40 years. Essentially, a system involving divisions of specialities was established, with representatives of the medical staff from the various specialties with responsibility to appraise their services and methods of provision.

Most hospitals established (as a minimum) divisions of: surgery, medicine, pathology, obstetrics and gynaecology, paediatrics, radiology and anaesthetics. The chair of each of the divisions was generally elected by his or her peers for a period of two to four years. There was a tendency for the role to be given on seniority and often reluctantly undertaken on the basis of 'my turn'. There was no additional remuneration for the role and certainly no assessment of leadership capability. As Levitt et al. report:

> Most hospital groups gradually implemented this scheme and by 1972 the second report was able to identify the essential elements of an effective Cogwheel system and to report that in large acute hospitals particularly, the system had been helpful in dealing with improved communications, reductions of in-patient waiting lists and the progressive control of medical expenditure. (Levitt et al., 1999, p. 172)

Put another way, Cogwheel divisions were there to cope with the problems of management that arose in the clinical field. As we shall see later on, the Cogwheel system provided the platform for the subsequent phases of organisational arrangements within hospitals and the ways in which doctors are engaged in decision making. However, the Cogwheel system still reinforced the position that the actions of doctors could not be directly controlled by managers.

It also should be noted that, with the exception of teaching hospitals, consultants were not employed by individual hospitals or by groups of hospitals but by the regional hospital boards. This did not change until around 1990.

The Cogwheel medical structure was the embryo of the clinical directorate system that followed, but as Paton et al. (2005) argue, with one fundamental difference—they had no resources to manage. At this stage in the life of the NHS, it was not possible to apportion the global allocation into individual specialty budgets.

2.4 MEDICAL REPRESENTATION: GRIFFITHS DIRECTORATE WAY

Whilst most NHS Trusts now have directorates as business units, the development of specialty budgets began as part of a demonstration project on management budgeting and was strongly reinforced by Sir Roy Griffiths in his inquiry into the management of the NHS, which was published in October 1983 (Griffiths Report, 1983). It was further endorsed by the Resource Management Initiative in 1986.

The Griffiths Inquiry is perhaps a critical point in the modern history of doctors' greater involvement in the management and leadership of NHS hospitals at all levels. It led to the introduction of general management throughout the NHS and perhaps more significantly the start of the transition from medical representation (Cogwheel system) to one slowly but surely based on medical leadership through the emerging clinical directorate system.

As Chantler stressed,

> This involvement by clinicians in management has to embrace a contribution both to the strategic and operational management of the service, in hospital, in the community, in practice, and in the commissioning role at district and central level, rather than doctors simply seeing themselves as there to give advice. That if you like, was the old role of the Medical Advisory Committee, functioning as a sort of Greek chorus, commenting on what was going on on the stage, but not taking part in the play. (Chantler, 1994, p. 17)

Just as Lord Darzi stressed the importance of clinical leadership in his clinical visions for the NHS in High Quality Care for All (2008), so Sir Roy Griffiths some 25 years earlier had recognised that to effect real improvement in productivity and quality required greater involvement of doctors. It is also worth noting that this greater involvement of clinicians in the mid-1980s coincided with the drive for improved financial and activity information. It also came at a time when the NHS started to have a much higher political and media profile, with many of its apparent failings being vigorously highlighted to the public on a regular basis.

Paton et al. (2005) suggest that the availability of relatively good information was a major stimulus in the evolution of doctors into management. They believe that this was because it gave doctors the incentive of having resources to manage and use at a local level. As Griffiths argued, hospital doctors 'must accept the management responsibility which goes with clinical freedom' (Griffiths Report, 1983, p. 18). Most NHS hospitals began to introduce a medical management system based around clinical directorates. These tended initially to be similar specialty groupings to the previous Cogwheel divisions. Senior doctors were appointed as clinical directors responsible for leading the work of different services and specialties within the hospital. Many of the previous chairs of the Cogwheel divisions succeeded into clinical director roles. Little attention was given to the competences required of such role-holders, with more attention being given to tenure and structural arrangement. The vast majority had no prior training for the role, and indeed for many years thereafter, this continued, apart from some programmes offered by the now defunct British Association of Medical Managers (BAMM); a number of universities, for example, Birmingham, Keele and Manchester; the King's Fund and other providers. A small number of enlightened hospitals initiated in-house programmes. Overall, whatever development provided to medical leaders tended to be ad hoc, variable and remedial.

Clinical directors combined their management and leadership roles with their clinical duties. Unlike the Cogwheel chair positions, clinical directors were often paid an additional session or two; most preferring to accept this increase in pay rather than reduce their clinical commitments. Furthermore, with financial constraints impeding the appointment of new consultants during the 1990s, chief executives were happy to accept no reduction in clinical sessions as well as gaining a clinical director with responsibilities for resource management. Clinical directors usually worked with a nurse manager and business manager in a directorate team known as a tripartite team or triumvirate. Clinical directors were often part of the hospital executive team, creating a much stronger medical voice in both operational and strategic decision making.

In addition to the appointment of clinical directors, hospitals appointed a medical director. The vast majority of these were again appointed on the basis of seniority, willingness, interest etc., and not on any formal assessment of leadership competence or indeed by competition. Initially, most medical directors did not accept any reduction in clinical sessions and were offered additional sessions in recognition of their leadership activities.

The clinician prepared to accept a leadership role was therefore someone who, in effect, sat between two systems. One of these systems included the collegial and clinical professional environment, where the doctor was an advocate for his or her colleagues whilst on the other hand being required to take a wider view of the clinical specialty and organisation. In the latter role, the clinical director was involved in shaping the future direction using his or her clinical knowledge and experience with managers who were accountable, ultimately, to politicians (Simpson, 2004). As Hopkinson (2004) argued, this wearing many hats is extremely difficult, forcing a clinician, '…at one moment to represent a clinical discipline and then ten minutes later to disadvantage that discipline to the greater corporate need of another area of the Trust or NHS at large' (p. 5).

Guy's Hospital in London perhaps led the way in pioneering a new approach to medical leadership during the late 1980s and early 1990s based on the experience of the Johns Hopkins Hospital in the United States. As Chantler (1990) acknowledged, there had to be an acceptance by the clinicians of the reality of cash limits, stressing that within them, all have the ethical responsibility to ensure that resources are spent wisely to ensure effectiveness and efficiency. In a contribution to a report prepared by the Royal College of Physicians, he also espoused a new philosophy that:

> where money is limited, profligacy in the care of one patient may lead to the denial of care of another. There must be constant attention to improving efficiency in economic terms and ensuring the effectiveness of treatment to produce the best outcome. (Chantler, 1993, p. 3)

The clinical directorate model became the established internal management arrangement for hospitals in the NHS throughout the late 1980s and 1990s, particularly as the new policy strategy of the internal market became established during the latter period.

The Griffiths Report and its impact in starting a long-term process of renegotiating the role of clinicians in management and leadership and contributing to the emergence of a new definition of the medical profession cannot be under-estimated. While some hospitals made progress in using clinical directorates to engage doctors in leadership roles and to achieve improvements in perfor-mance, others experienced difficulties. These difficulties are starkly illustrated in a detailed study of leadership in an NHS hospital in the 1990s undertaken by Bate (2000).

In this hospital, consultants did not accept the legitimacy of management and as a result were able to undermine managerial power. The hospital was character-ised by sub-cultures centred on micro-systems that were isolated from each other. This was problematic when change was attempted involving more than one micro-system, as it led to tensions and, often, gridlock. Doctors held power and managers became afraid to challenge doctors lest they should face a vote of no confidence. Progress became possible only when doctors and managers agreed to establish a 'network community' (p. 504) in place of the system of clinical direc-torates which was seen to have been 'a failed experiment' (p. 509).

A more mixed picture emerged from a survey of clinical directorates in Scotland conducted by McKee and colleagues. This survey found wide variations in the way directorates were constructed and conducted their business. Three major directorates were identified (McKee et al., 1999). The dominant type, described as 'traditionalist', was characterised by a strong focus on operational issues and limited scope for innovation and change. Relationships between clini-cal directors and clinical colleagues remained embedded in a collegiate clinical network and were based on consensus building and facilitation.

The second type was described as 'managerialist' and was characterised by a business-oriented approach more in line with the philosophy of the Griffiths Report. Clinical directors in managerialist directorates had direct links with top managers in the hospital and were better placed to influence overall strategy and direction than those in traditionalist directorates. The third type was described as 'power-sharing' and involved clinical directors working across established specialty boundaries and operating as a team with the business manager and nurse manager.

McKee and colleagues note that the variability between clinical directorates shows the ability of doctors to adapt to managerial initiatives. More importantly, they emphasise the overwhelming sense of continuity rather than change, and 'few examples of trusts creating a new climate in which clinical directors of the future were being spotted, nurtured or sustained' (p. 110). Furthermore, clinical management was very thinly resourced, with many directorates run on a shoe-string. The minority of directorates that were not traditionalist held out the pros-pect that clinicians could be developed into innovative leaders, but advocated for this to happen:

> more, and more senior, doctors will have to be given the incen-tive to get involved, the relevance of management will have to be actively marketed and the clinical legitimacy of doctor-managers will have to be safeguarded. (p. 112)

In many ways, this study reaffirmed evidence from the organisational theory literature relating to the tendency of professional bureaucracies to be oriented to stability rather than change, while also underlining the limited progress in moving from professional bureaucracies to managed professional businesses.

Further confirmation of the persistence of established relationships comes from Kitchener's study of the impact of quasi-market hospitals (Kitchener, 1999). Drawing on the writing of Mintzberg (1979), Kitchener hypothesises that the NHS reforms are an attempt to replace the professional bureaucracy with the quasi-market hospital archetype. In this new archetype, the hospital is based around clinical directorates and medical cost centres, and a more business-like approach to management is adopted, centred on medical cost centres and using enhanced management information systems. Kitchener found that in practice, the impact of this new archetype was limited and warns that:

> The fact that some hospital doctors have accepted medical-manager roles within a more integrated formal structure should not be conflated with either a loss of their professional autonomy or a replacement of key elements of the PB (professional bureaucracy) interpretive scheme. (p. 197)

He concludes that the notion of the professional bureaucracy continues to provide an appropriate basis for understanding the nature of hospitals as organisations. Professional bureaucracies are characterised by dispersed or distributed leadership. In healthcare organisations, clinical micro-systems (Batalden et al., 2003) exist in many ways. Dartmouth Medical School, Hanover, New Hampshire define a healthcare clinical micro-system as a small group of people who work together on a regular basis—or as needed—to provide care. It has both clinical and business aims as part of a larger system/organisation, and clinical directorates are therefore good examples of a clinical micro-system.

The challenges facing clinical directors were highlighted in a survey of doctor–manager relationships in Great Britain by Davies and colleagues. This survey found that senior managers such as chief executives and medical directors were more positive about these relationships than managers at the directorate level. Among all the groups surveyed, clinical directors were the least impressed with management and the most dissatisfied with the role and influence of clinicians. Davies and colleagues argued that unless the divergence of views they found were addressed, it would be difficult to engage medical leaders in the government's modernisation agenda (Davies et al., 2003).

This conclusion echoes other work that concluded that clinical directors and other doctors in leadership roles occupied a 'no-man's land' between the managerial and clinical communities (Marnoch et al., 2000). It is also consistent with the research of Degeling and colleagues (2003), which has described the differences that exist among staff groups in relation to individualist versus systematised conceptions of the financial and accountability aspects of clinical work. The existence of these differences confirms the persistence of tribal relationships in hospitals and the difficulties facing staff, such as doctors, who go into management roles and must bridge different cultures.

2.5 MEDICAL LEADERSHIP: MORE PROFESSIONAL APPROACH

A major study into medical leadership arrangements in English healthcare organisations undertaken by the Universities of Birmingham and Warwick and the King's Fund. The report 'Are We There Yet? Models of Medical Leadership and Their Effectiveness' was published in 2013. The dead author, Dickinson (2013) contended that whilst some progress had been made in the development of medical leadership in the NHS in England, much remained to be done to complete the journey started with the Griffiths Report in 1983. The report concluded

> that a greater degree of professionalism needs to be bought to bear in the development of medical leadership. This includes developing career structures to make it easier for doctors to take on leadership roles; providing training, development and support in management and leadership at different stages of doctors' careers; and ensuring pay and other rewards are commensurate with the responsibilities of medical leaders.

The study also confirmed that there was wide variation in how Trusts organised their services and involved doctors in leadership roles. Three main types of unit were identified, that is, clinical directorates, divisions and service line, sometimes in combinations. What was perhaps of particular interest was the variation between Trusts included in the study of the number of doctors on the board of the directors and executive management teams. For the former, this varied between 1 and 3 and the latter between 1 and 14. This is of particular interest given the study of Veronesi et al. (2012) that confirmed the involvement of clinicians on Boards has a positive impact on a range of outcomes.

Primary care was largely bypassed by the changes that flowed from the Griffiths Report, and only recently have there been moves to strengthen management and leadership in primary care. Work by Sheaff and colleagues (2003) described the impact of these moves in primary care groups and trusts in England. Lacking any formal, hierarchical authority over GPs, primary care groups and trusts worked through GPs who took on the role of clinical governance leads, the Professional Executive Committee, medical directors and, more recently, practice-based commissioning lead roles. Medical leadership within primary care has become even more important with the establishment of CCGs, which is explored in more detail in Chapter 7. Sheaff and his co-authors argue that clinical governance leaders used a range of informal techniques to implement clinical governance in primary care, and they use the terms 'soft governance' and 'soft bureaucracy' to describe the relationships and organisations they studied.

In summary, research into medical leadership in the NHS since the Griffiths Report highlights the challenges involved in developing the role of medical managers. While progress has been made in appointing doctors as clinical directors and in establishing clinical directorates and service line business units within hospitals, the effectiveness of these arrangements is variable. If in some organisations there appears to be much greater potential for involving doctors in leading change, in most, there remain difficulties in changing established ways of doing things and in supporting medical leaders to play an effective part in bridging the divide between doctors and managers. Part of the explanation of these findings is the resourcing put into medical leadership and the limited recognition and rewards for doctors who take on leadership roles. Also important is the continuing influence of informal leaders and networks operating alongside formal management structures. Summarising the mixed experience of clinical directorates, Marnoch concluded his assessment in the following way:

> The means of controlling the operational performance of hospital doctors have advanced somewhat since the introduction of general management in the 1980s. Nevertheless, the Griffiths-inspired drive to push resource-consuming decisions down to the level where they could best be made is far from complete. A traditional centralised style of management has been used to make the internal market work. This form of control remains constrained in its influence over clinical behaviour. At worst, medical directors and clinical directors will be used as go-betweens in a familiar book-balancing exercise that involves closing wards periodically, not filling vacancies and cancelling operations. At best they are the basis for a new strategically led style of corporate management in the NHS. (Marnoch, 1996, p. 61)

2.6 MEDICAL LEADERSHIP: THE PROFESSION REDEFINES ITSELF

In conjunction with the greater involvement of doctors in service improvement initiatives, it was clear that the nature of the profession of medicine was changing in the early years of the twenty-first century. Writing from an Australian perspective, Dowton (2004) identified the traditional role of the medical profession as being defined through long-standing legislative canons coupled with the status accrued to individual doctors by society and societal contacts and deeply entrenched cultural systems arising principally from the influence of professional craft groups. Dowton identified a number of external influences that have altered doctors' autonomy and the hierarchies within which they practise. He suggests that the influences include a greater demand for accountability for the safety of patients, quality and efficacy of healthcare and public access to medical information. Dowton concludes that, despite leadership roles being critical, inadequate attention has been paid to developing individual leaders and new models of leadership within the medical profession.

The Royal College of Physicians of London has made a significant contribution to the debate on the changing nature of the medical profession. 'Doctors in society: medical professionalism in a changing world' (Royal College of Physicians, 2005) contends that the medical profession is at a turning point in its history. The report argues that

> Medicine bridges the gap between science and society. Indeed the application of scientific knowledge is a crucial aspect of clinical practice. Doctors are an important agent through which that scientific understanding is expressed. But medicine is more than that sum of our knowledge about disease. Medicine concerns the experience, feelings, and interpretation of human beings in extraordinary moments of fear, anxiety and doubt. In this extremely vulnerable position, it is medical professionalism that underpins the trust the public has in doctors. (p. 55)

The College defines medical professionalism as a set of values, behaviours and relationships that underpin this trust. Under six main themes (leadership, teams, education, appraisal, careers and research), the report offers clear, practical recommendations that should not only lead to further improvements in patient care but also offer more challenging and fulfilling lives for doctors. In particular, it recommended strengthening leadership and managerial skills and identifying young doctors with the potential to move onto medical leadership roles. Perhaps the most important message in terms of medical management and leadership is the report's recommendation that

> The complementary skills of leadership and "followership" need to be carefully documented and incorporated into a doctor's training to support professionalism. These skills argue strongly for managerial competence among doctors. An individual doctor's decisions have both clinical and managerial elements. There are signs that management skills will gradually become incorporated into fitness-to-practice requirements. (para 3.6)

Various influences have led to a marked change in the role of doctor in management, leadership and transformation of services on the last few years of the first decade of the twenty-first century. A new phenomenon has hit the NHS, with young doctors positively seeking to be involved and offered leadership development opportunities and senior medical leaders encouraging such diversions from specialty training. The journey recorded previously has clearly had some impact. Why should there be such a dramatic twist in the medical leadership story now given all the previous initiatives?

Perhaps the acknowledgement that there is a real correlation between medical engagement and leadership and quality outcomes is encouraging more doctors to move not only from the dark side but to the centre stage. Leading service improvement appears to be far more attractive to doctors than the previous resource management representative roles. Furthermore, doctors in their clinical roles have historically been influenced by evidence. Perhaps, is the increasing evidence of the relationship between medical leadership and engagement and quality of care attracting more doctors to become involved?

In response to this changing environment, the NHS Institute for Innovation and Improvement and The Academy of Medical Royal Colleges developed a joint project to enhance the engagement of doctors in management, leadership and transformation of services. Established in early 2006, it is having a profound impact on the changing nature of the doctor in the twenty-first century. The joint King's Fund and Royal College of Physicians (2008) report *Understanding Doctors: Harnessing Professionalism* contends that

> ...the world in which doctors work is changing, and changing in ways that challenge many of the assumptions on which the profession has based its practice for more than 150 years. (p. viii)

As Clark et al. argue, 'historically the medical profession in the United Kingdom has not particularly encouraged doctors to obtain competency in management and leadership. It has generally been left to individual doctors to voluntarily seek management and leadership training and development' (Clark et al., 2008, p. 3). This is explored in more detail in Chapter 9. This occurs despite the evidence that improving the health of the population and the delivery of high-quality health and social care is very dependent on the support and active engagement of all doctors, not only in their practitioner activities but also in their management and leadership roles.

Whilst healthcare has always been complex, current societal demands have accentuated this. The NHS and other international health systems require skilled and competent doctors and other clinicians to deliver high-quality clinical care whilst working as part of a multidisciplinary team in an organisation or service designed to hold staff to deliver safe and effective care. Medical training has traditionally focused on the clinical skills needed to be a safe and competent clinician. However, with the increasing trend to more team-based practice and integrated care approaches, it is important that doctors are not only competent clinicians but also have the skills to enable them to function effectively within these more complex systems. It is now recognised that being a competent clinician requires doctors to be able to manage themselves and their time, work within a team, understand when to lead and when to follow, work in a more integrated way with other clinicians and services and deliver high-quality and cost-effective best practice in a way that recognises the choices and preferences of patients.

The Final Report of the Independent Inquiry into Modernising Medical Careers (MMC Inquiry) supports this by contending that:

> The doctor's role as diagnostician and the handler of clinical uncertainty and ambiguity requires a profound educational base in science and evidence-based practice as well as research awareness. The doctor's frequent role as head of the healthcare team and commander of considerable clinical resource requires that

greater attention is paid to managerial and leadership skills irrespective of specialism. An acknowledgement of the leadership role of medicine is increasingly evident. Role acknowledgement and aspiration to enhanced roles be they in subsequently practice, management and leadership, education or research are likely to facilitate greater clinical engagement. Encouraging enhanced roles will ensure maximum return, for the benefit society will derive from the investment in medical education. (MMC Inquiry, 2008, p. 17)

2.7 MEDICAL LEADERSHIP: AN ESSENTIAL INGREDIENT FOR SERVICE IMPROVEMENT

Thus, various initiatives, studies and reports in the middle of the first decade of the twenty-first century began to have a considerable impact on the changing role of doctors and their involvement in the delivery of improved services. It is perhaps not surprising that clinicians generally and doctors in particular were widely involved in the development of High Quality Care for All: NHS Next Stage Review Final Report (2008). As an eminent surgeon, Lord Darzi, its architect and author, had been appointed by Gordon Brown, Blair's successor as Prime Minister, in 2007 as a Parliamentary Under-Secretary of State (Health).

As with the NHS Plan, leading clinicians were co-signatories to High Quality Care for All. Whereas in the former, these were national leaders, Lord Darzi secured the support of the then 10 Strategic Health Authority Clinical Leaders. Darzi acknowledged that, whilst leading the Review, he had continued his clinical practice, reinforcing very publicly that combining clinical practice and a leadership role was both feasible and perhaps to be positively encouraged.

Given his profession, it is perhaps not surprising that the new national and local clinical visions outlined in High Quality Care for All should have emerged from a wide number of local discussions involving over 2000 clinicians. High Quality Care for All is far more explicit about the role of clinicians, particularly doctors, in leading service improvement, for example,

what is clear is that this new professionalism, acknowledging clinician's roles as partners and leaders, gives them the opportunity to focus on improving not just the quality of care they provide as individuals but within their organisation and the whole NHS. We enable clinicians to be partners and leaders alongside manager colleagues. (para 5.7, p. 60)

The need for greater clinical leadership is a common theme throughout High Quality Care for All (2008). However, it recognises that it is unrealistic to expect NHS staff to take on leadership without action to make it integral to training and development. The joint NHS Institute for Innovation and Improvement and Academy of Medical Royal Colleges initiative to develop a Medical Leadership

Competency Framework for doctors at all stages of their training and careers, that is, from undergraduate through postgraduate education to continuing practice, has created a standard that can now be applied to all clinical professionals. Prior to the publication of High Quality Care for All, the Department of Health (England) appointed a medical director of the NHS for the first time. The role was conceived to give a stronger focus on medical leadership and engagement throughout the NHS.

The NHS Confederation has made a significant contribution to the debate on leadership generally and clinical leadership specifically in recent years. In acknowledging the emphasis on the leadership role of clinicians, particularly doctors, in High Quality Care for All, the NHS Confederation (2009) in its paper called the *Future of Leadership* welcomed the joint NHS Institute of Innovation and Improvement and Academy of Medical Royal Colleges initiative of integrating leadership into medical education. The NHS Confederation paper also confirms that the chief executive of the NHS in England at the time repeatedly stated that he would like to see more chief executives from a medical background and specifically at least one doctor on each chief executive short list. As the Confederation argues,

> While being a doctor can bring important insights, so can being a nurse or an accountant. The real issue is that, if doctors are effectively excluded from chief executive positions, a major pool of talent is locked away from the system and we need all the talent that is available. (NHS Confederation, 2009, pp. 4–5)

In Chapter 6, we explore in much more detail the strong evidence that exists on the relationship between engagement of doctors and organisational performance. As this chapter has shown, the NHS has historically found it difficult to encourage doctors to take up medical leadership roles, let alone chief executive positions. However, there are signs that this is changing, and indeed, there are a number of initiatives that are likely to support greater engagement. Other initiatives such as the joint NHS Institute and Academy of Medical Royal Colleges project, the Faculty of Medical Leadership and Management, the appointment of clinical fellows and similar opportunities for young doctors to lead service improvement projects (and many more) are also contributing to the newly emerging culture of enhanced medical leadership and engagement. This will be explored in Chapter 9.

NHS Improvement, the independent regulator of NHS Trusts, stresses the importance of clinicians having prominent roles in leadership, particularly in service-line management. In effect, service lines are NHS Trust's equivalent of a commercial company's business unit. An increasing number of consultants are being motivated to take up leadership roles of service lines where genuine devolution of responsibility for an integrated set of clinical, operational and financial objectives and outcomes is offered.

Hitherto, doctors have been resistant to consider such opportunities, citing the need for clearer career paths both in and out of leadership roles, lack of proper leadership roles, lack of proper leadership training and preparation, reduced pay, job insecurity and loss of links with their profession. For many doctors, the lack of access to clinical excellence awards have been cited as a further barrier, although the consultant contract does provide some flexibility, including amendments to the Clinical Excellence Awards Scheme to reflect quality improvement and clinical leadership activities.

It is evident that many of these barriers are real, but others are perhaps more a perception of the culture, which, with a few notable exceptions, has not positively encouraged doctors to make the leap into leadership roles. The current movement towards more integrated health and social care and perhaps a return to more joined up organisational approaches will stimulate patient-condition structures that cross current boundaries within health and between social care and health. System-wide leadership is clearly needed to effect change in the way that care is provided based on the patient's or client's need rather that the organisation's.

The King's Fund Report (2015), *The Practice of System Leadership: Being Comfortable with Chaos*, confirms that a critical skill for the future will be the ability to work across services and organisations to meet the growing number of people with complex medical conditions and those who rely on care and support from different agencies. Medical leaders from all parts of the current system have an important role to play to provide the clinical leadership required to ensure that a holistic approach is pursued. This will require new structures that are more patient or condition focused in the future than the current internal directorate or divisional structure is. It will also require leaders who create alliances and networks that help facilitate change through a collective leadership approach. The current model within hospitals had, in effect, been in existence for almost 50 years, starting with the Cogwheel system in the 1960s and refined with the establishment of Directorates, Divisions and Service Lines. Structural changes in NHS England over a similar period have served to separate primary, secondary and community health service and social care. There are many good examples whereby clinical pathways have been developed across organisational boundaries. In the future, this needs to be the norm, and doctors and other clinical professionals have crucial roles to play to facilitate integrated systems of care.

However, as Dickinson et al. (2014) reaffirms, medical leadership has to be taken seriously. It is not something that can be quickly brought about through a change in structure or just exhorting clinical and managerial colleagues to change. It needs to be part of a major culture change in the way in which doctors are engaged from their early days as postgraduate trainee doctors and throughout their careers.

REFERENCES

Batalden, P.B., Nelson, E., Mohr, J. et al. (2003) Microsystems in health care: Part 5. How leaders are leading. *Joint Commission Journal on Quality and Safety*, 29(6): 297–308.

Bate, P. (2000) Changing the culture of a hospital: From hierarchy to networked community. *Public Administration*, 78: 485–512.

Chantler, C. (1990) Management reform in a London hospital. In *Managing for Health Result,* edited by Carle, N. London: King Edward's Hospital Fund for London.

Chantler, C. (1993) Historical background: Where have clinical directorates come from and what is their purpose? In *The Role of Hospital Consultants in Clinical Directorates,* edited by Hopkins, A. London: Royal College of Physicians.

Chantler, C. (1994) *How to Treat Doctors: Role of Clinicians in Management (Speaking Up: Policy and Change in the NHS).* Birmingham: NAHAT.

Clark, J., Spurgeon, P., and Hamilton, P. (2008) Medical professionalism: Leadership competency—An essential ingredient. *International Journal of Clinical Leadership,* 16(1): 3–9.

Davies, H.T.O., Hodges, C., and Rundall, T. (2003) Views of doctors and managers on the doctor–manager relationship in the NHS. *BMJ,* 326: 626–628.

Degeling, P., Maxwell, S., Kennedy, J. et al. (2003) Medicine, management and modernisation: A 'danse macabre'? *BMJ,* 326: 649–652.

Department of Health (2008) *High Quality Care for All: Next Stage Review Final Report.* London: TSO.

Department of Health (2010) *Equity and Excellence: Liberating the NHS.* London: UK Stationery Office.

Dickinson, H. (2013) *Are We There Yet? Models of Medical Leadership and Their Effectiveness: An Exploratory Study.* Final Report. Southampton: NIHR Service Delivery and Organisation Programme.

Dickinson, H. et al. (2014) Medical leadership arrangements in English healthcare organisations: Findings from a national survey and case studies of NHS Trusts. *Health Service Management Research,* 26: 119–125.

Dowton, B.S. (2004) Leadership in medicine: Where are the leaders? *Medical Journal of Australia,* 181(11–12): 652–654.

Grabham, A., and Chantler, C. (1989). Doctors becoming managers: A conversation among Richard Smith, Sir Anthony Grabham and Professor Cyril Chantler [interview by Richard Smith]. *BMJ,* 298(6669): 311–314.

Griffiths Report (1983) *NHS Management Inquiry.* London: Department of Health and Social Security.

Hopkinson, R.B. (2004) Clinical leadership in practice—Wearing many hats. *Healthcare and Informatics Review Online,* 4(9). Available at: www.hinz.org .nz/journal/498 (accessed 27 May 2011).

King's Fund (2015) *The Practice of System Leadership: Being Comfortable with Chaos.* London: King's Fund.

King's Fund and Royal College of Physicians (2008) *Understanding Doctors: Harnessing Professionalism.* London: King's Fund.

Kitchener, M. (1999) 'All fur coat and no knickers: Contemporary organisational change in United Kingdom hospitals. In *Restructuring the Professional Organisation,* edited by Brock, D., Powell, M., Hinings, C. London: Routledge.

Klein, R. (2006) *The New Politics of the NHS.* 5th ed. Oxford: Radcliffe Publishing.

Levitt, R., Wall, A., and Appleby, J. (1999) *The Reorganised National Health Service*. 6th ed. Cheltenham, Great Britain: Stanley Thornes.

Marnoch, G. (1996) *Doctors and Management in the National Health Service*. Buckingham, UK: Open University Press.

Marnoch, G., McKee, L., and Dinnie, N. (2000) Between organisations and institutions: Legitimacy and medical managers. *Public Administration*, 78: 967–987.

McKee, L., Marnoch, G., and Dinnie, N. (1999) Medical managers: Puppet masters or puppets? Sources of power and influence in clinical directorates. In *Organisational Behaviour in Healthcare: The Research Agenda*, edited by Mark, A., Dopson, S. Basingstoke, UK: Macmillan.

Merivale, S.C. (1969) *Medical Organisation and Staffing in Modern Hospital Management*. London: Institute of Hospital Administrators.

Ministry of Health (1953) *Functions and Constitution of Medical Staff Committees*. London: Ministry of Health. R.H.B.(53)91/H.M.C.(53)85/B.G.(53)87.

Mintzberg, H. (1979) *The Structuring of Organisations: A Synthesis of the Research*. Englewood Cliffs, NJ: Prentice Hall.

MMC Inquiry (2008) *Aspiring to Excellence: Final Report of the Independent Enquiry into Modernising Medical Careers*. London: Aldridge Press.

NHS Confederation (Ed.) (2009) Developing NHS leadership: The role of the trust medical director. In *Future of Leadership*. London: NHS Confederation. p. 2. Available at: www.nhsconfed.org/Publications/Documents/future_leadership 020309.pdf (accessed 22 April 2011).

Paton, C., Whitney, D., and Cowpe, J. (2005) Medical leadership: Doctors, the state and prospects for improvement. In *Clinical Leadership: A Book of Readings*, edited by Edmonstone, J. Chichester, UK: Kingsham Press.

Pollard, M. (2001) On the side walk. *Health Service Journal*, pp. 22–25, November 29, 2001.

Rosenthal, M. (1995) *The Incompetent Doctor: Behind Closed Doors*. Buckingham, UK: Open University Press.

Royal College of Physicians (2005) Doctors in society: Medical professionalism in a changing world. *Clinical Medicine*, 5(6 Suppl 1): S5–S40.

Sheaff, R., Rogers, A., Pickard, S. et al. (2003) A subtle governance: 'Soft' medical leadership in English primary care. *Sociology of Health and Illness*, 25(5): 408–428.

Simpson, J. (2004) Clinical leadership in the UK. *Healthcare and Informatics Review Online*, 4(2). Available at: www.hinz.org.nz/journal/167 (accessed 27 May 2011).

Spurgeon, P. (2001) Involving clinicians in management: A challenge of perspective. *Healthcare and Informatics Review Online*, 5(4). Available at: www .hinz.org.nz/journal/546 (accessed 27 May 2011).

Strong, P., and Robinson, J. (1990) *The NHS under New Management*. Milton Keynes, UK: Open University Press.

Veronesi, G., Kirkpatrick, I., and Vallascas, F. (2012) *Clinicians in Management: Does It Make a Difference?* Leeds, UK: Leeds University Business School.

3

Doctors and managers: Differing perspectives

3.1 INTRODUCTION

Early forms of healthcare provision were typically built around the individual physician assisted by members of the emerging clinical professions. Even much later large hospitals were typically led by a medical superintendent (see Chapter 2 for a more detailed account of evolution of the medical/managerial roles). However, as with all modern organisations, healthcare saw the growth of the systems, infrastructures, management processes and managers. In the face of these developments, many doctors retreated into the delivery of individual care more detached from the organisation itself. Some retreated with a degree of hostility, resenting the apparent loss of direct control and influence. But as important as individual resentment was in terms of conflict, perhaps most critically, the positive potential contribution of the profession was rather lost to the system. It is only over the past two or three decades that there has been a strategy to reintegrate and re-establish the role of the doctor in the wider organisation. This chapter explores some of the conceptual challenges in creating greater medical involvement in the running of healthcare organisations.

There have been many attempts to encourage greater involvement of doctors in the management and leadership of the organisations in which they work. Despite the relatively high-profile nature of some of these initiatives with support from government and national leaders, the outcomes have not always been particularly successful. This suggests that structural or mechanistic approaches are not enough and that there may be a more underlying and significant difficulty. This chapter will explore what might be an important aspect of the problem: that of the differing perspectives held by doctors and managers about the focus and functioning of the health service. The National Health Service (NHS) is frequently described as comprising a series of 'tribes', and newcomers are often surprised, if not dismayed, by the strength and resilience of the different perspectives.

Degeling et al. (2001) explored the views of doctors, managers, medical managers and nurses in the context of health system reform. They point to sometimes quite subtle differences in the understanding and importance attached to common issues. These differences seem to be sustained in a range of settings and may originate from training, expectations and cultures. Degeling and his colleagues and Spurgeon and Flanagan (2000) described distinct sub-cultures within NHS organisations.

The nature and impact of sub-cultures are well documented by Powell and Davies (2012) and Davies and Mannion (2013). They suggest that sub-cultures can be key supporters and defenders of the overall organisational culture, appearing in some ways to embody just what the organisation stands for. Equally, there can be counter cultures that either overtly or covertly challenge the established organisational values. Some basic concrete factors can fuel the establishment of sub-cultures. Different departments, specialties and occupational groups have ways of working and interacting that create cultural artefacts that serve to identify particular sub-cultures. As Davies and Harrison (2003) have argued, 'Doctors and managers differ on many cultural dimensions, which can lead to misunderstandings and tensions in working relationships and approaches to improving patient care'.

Managers and doctors represent two very powerful groups, and thereby what may be matters of emphasis become important, so much so that they may lead to conflict. The situation is not new but it persists, taking on varying manifestations as particular models of organisational arrangements are put forward.

Hunter (2005) reviewed 25 years of health policy reform. He suggested that the cult of managerialism is an important contributor to this process, whether in early attempts to impose accountability on clinicians for the resources they use (early 1970 and 1980s) through to the modernisation programme initiated and continuing through the late 1990s and onwards. Hunter described the equation as increased investment but attached to a requirement to adopt major changes in working practices to promote the quality of services and patient experience. The mechanisms used to implement modernisation, targets and regulation gave rise to dysfunctional behaviour in clinicians resentful at the encroachment of managers and management onto their territory and the challenge it presented to their professionalism.

The use of the term 'territory' is instructive here as it suggests conflict, turf wars and, ultimately, a relationship between doctors and managers mediated through status and power. The dynamic interplay of power politics can manifest itself at many levels, individual and institutional. A Healthcare Commission (2009) report into the quality of care at Mid Staffordshire Hospitals NHS Foundation Trust suggested that a managerial focus upon achieving Foundation status, attaining financial balance and meeting performance targets had distracted the organisation from ensuring that quality of care to patients was the priority. If concerns were raised, it appears, at least from the outside, that the medical voice was overwhelmed by the managerial priority. At an individual level, too direct interventions by individual managers in what may be perceived as the clinical domain can spark hostilities that can be long lasting and difficult to overcome. Irrespective of the level of focus of the conflict, it is clear that such division is not good for patients. Certainly, if patient safety is compromised, then such conflicts cannot be accepted as internal squabbling. It is important then to understand better the nature of these differing perspectives.

3.2 DIFFERENT PERSPECTIVES: BASIS AND IMPLICATIONS

Numerous studies report the impact or implications of the differing perspectives, but before considering these, it may be helpful to look at two particular accounts, Thorne (2002) and Plochg and Klazinga (2005), who attempt to set out the theoretical underpinnings of the divergence in the views of managers and doctors. Thorne sets her argument within the framework of domains of jurisdiction, particularly in the workplace. Who should control and supervise work, and who is qualified to do which parts of it? A pure and typically historic jurisdiction is defined for professional bodies by knowledge and expertise. This is generally stable and changes quite slowly. However, in a workplace setting such as the NHS, there is an organisational context to these jurisdictions or boundaries. External events, like reform processes, cause disturbance and can lead to disputes between professional groups as to territory or dominance. The promotion of doctors as managers is just such a process causing managers and doctors to think about definitions of their areas. In these circumstances, many are defensive and a few see the opportunities. In a different context, these few are sometimes described as 'early adopters' but can often appear isolated and rejected by the majority. Later studies will illustrate this.

Thorne takes clinical directors as the focus of her thesis, arguing that they embody the tension between managerial and professional structures. The basis of medical power/dominance can be traced to three interlocking concepts:

- Control of the labour market (Friedson, 2001)
- Expertise expressed as clinical autonomy (Starr, 1982)
- Self-regulation

In terms of the labour market, the numbers of students entering medical school have been quite tightly controlled. Only recently has this restriction on numbers been eased by increased intakes and the establishment of new medical schools. Traditionally, the restriction on numbers has resulted in doctors having high incomes, high social status and public legitimacy. Having passed into the profession, Ackroyd (1996) described the process as being in a powerful clinical 'enclave'. This is seen in the relatively flat structure of the profession, with all consultants notionally having equal power and standing. This situation is in marked contrast to the hierarchical and accountable structures of management.

The dominance of the medical profession and its exercise of clinical autonomy are, to a large extent, based on the medicalisation of healthcare. As a consequence of this prevailing model, it is only doctors who can define 'medical work' and its diagnosis and treatment. This singular role creates a dependency for health organisations (Ackroyd, 1996) and enables doctors to determine priorities, ration care and commit scarce resources (Calman, 1994). Changes are emerging in this particular context, as resource pressures have led to a variety of role substitutions where other professions have taken over parts of what was previously the role of the doctor.

Nurse specialists, for example, have been a significant part of the approach to meeting the European Working Time Directive restriction on hours doctors can work (48 hours) by assuming some of the tasks of junior doctors. Again, as with increased entry to the medical profession, it is likely that the continuation of extended roles for other groups will have an impact upon the status of doctors. Initially, this is likely to be quite painful (as experienced by the profession) but ultimately may free doctors to become more integrated into the managed health community—those managed by it and those members of the management process.

The exercise of clinical autonomy is a crucial part of the application of the knowledge acquired through medical training. The profession's main regulatory body, the General Medical Council (GMC), acts to preserve and prescribe the boundaries to this autonomy and freedom to exercise clinical judgement. Once more, this area too is undergoing significant change, with rapidly increasing lay involvement with the GMC and also more guidelines and protocols determining the nature of care to be given to a type of patient and thus limiting individual clinical decision making. This is a sensitive and contentious area in the doctor–manager relationship. At its worst, some doctors will view managers as 'agents of government, given "structural power" to control the "expert" power of the professional' (Oni, 1995). The use of government targets and their pursuit by managers with a responsibility to achieve them have proved a major source of difficulty and conflict.

The second theoretical approach to exploring the relationship between doctors and managers comes from Plochg and Klazinga (2005) and is related to the notion of introducing clinical governance programmes. They note how many of these seem to have failed and suggest that improvement may be made through a better understanding of the perspectives of the two groups. Drawing once more on Friedson's (2001) concepts of professionalism, they suggest that doctors have the privilege of dividing and coordinating their own work processes, resulting in various specialties and subspecialties. These domains or areas are maintained and protected by a number of strategies:

- Expertise is expanded and differentiated, so only those with acknowledged competence can function in the area
- Delegation of certain tasks to non-clinicians whilst keeping overall charge of the domain
- Striving to keep their own group of patients, who thus have a dependent and particular relationship with the specialty
- Participating in specialist activities, for example, pharmaceuticals committee and guideline development

There are real benefits (to patients) of these strategies—notably, a culture of clinical excellence whereby knowledge is continuously updated to reinforce the value of the specialty. However, this drive for exclusiveness creates an inward orientation and encourages an individualistic culture. Even within the profession, therefore, there can be a disconnect from other medical colleagues, let alone from the organisational context.

In direct contrast, the 'management science' perspective endeavours to devise ways of best organising the workforce and creating procedures to ensure that the organisation meets its goals. Within these rules and structures, different staff groups will, at various times, be aligned or ill-fitting, with consequent tension and disruption. This tension is particularly acute in what Mintzberg (1983) described as 'professional bureaucracies', where knowledge and expertise are at a premium in the successful functioning of the organisation. Managers have used a range of initiatives such as guidelines, evidence-based medicine and regulation (Checkland et al., 2004) to promote standardisation of processes. Whilst it is difficult to argue against standardisation in the form of consistent treatment, it is an approach that is uncomfortable, with high levels of individually based expertise. There are issues here going far beyond this particular context of how society, in attempting to demystify and reduce the power of professions by codifying what was once discretionary decision making, may be destroying the essence of public confidence in long-standing professions and their regulatory bodies.

There are then some clear historic and underlying reasons why doctors and managers may form differing perspectives and take quite contrasting views of the same process. Numerous health service initiatives have foundered on this divide, and many studies have documented experiences of these processes and how they play out at the workplace. Before discussing approaches to overcoming the problem, it may be useful to illustrate the difficulties in context.

3.3 DOCTORS AND MANAGERS: HOW THE DIVIDE IS MANIFEST

A rather straightforward statement of the problem comes from Australia, where Jorm and Kam (2004) describe doctors as having 'their own all-pervading culture' that centres on their occupational identity, its exclusiveness and a tendency towards traditional values. From this base, Jorm and Kam argue (with some evidence) that doctors are adept at diverting the goals of many improvement initiatives that do not obviously resonate with their own position. Conflict derived from a very strong cultural identity is a source of many issues, whether with individual managers or at an organisational level. Collectively, there seem to be two main types of areas where this can be seen: (a) in the tension, ambiguity and discomfort stemming from doctors undertaking managerial and leadership roles and (b) the performance management philosophy inherent in the concept of managerialism.

3.3.1 Doctor–manager role conflict

McDermott et al. (2002) offer a study of a major reform in the Irish health system that took as a key goal the greater involvement of clinicians in management roles. Interestingly, in their conclusions, they allude to the contrast in dealing with change within a medical context as opposed to outside it. 'While scientific advances constantly drive clinicians to adopt new treatments and techniques, this capacity for change does not appear to include adaptation of the doctor's role in society'. They point also to a frequently voiced concern of having to make the transition from an independent, individually based, patient-focused decision to one that is collective and corporate.

Forbes et al. (2004) make use of the concept of the psychological contract by which employees enter into an agreed relationship with their employer. Changes in the status of the contract will have an impact upon the motivation and behaviour of the employee. Forbes and colleagues suggest that doctors enter healthcare organisations with a set of values, assumptions and ethical premises based upon their professional culture. How they experience the organisation, often as represented by managers, will make a difference to their own commitment to the psychological contract. It was to explore this experience of management that Forbes et al. conducted their study using in-depth interviews with clinicians who had undertaken management roles. They identified two distinct types of doctor–manager, which they termed the 'investors' or the 'reluctants'. The former were characterised as entering management with a specific agenda, which might include influencing health service delivery, or sometimes an escape from clinical pressures. Some members of this group saw themselves as natural leaders and innovators, taking these skills into management as a smooth transition. A key factor in defining this group was the acceptance of management, which tended to make them proactive in developing their role and management identity. Thus, they begin to acquire a new or altered identity from that with which they entered the organisation and crucially are comfortable in the role.

In contrast, the 'reluctants'—as the name suggests—tended to enter management not because of a particular desire to do so but because they felt pressured into accepting the role. They were often quite negative about management, had had poor experience of management and hence had little commitment to the role. Such individuals were clearly lacking much satisfaction from their managerial role but equally became separated from clinical colleagues because of the role and hence suffered the worst experience of this dual position. These clinical colleagues often referred to such an individual as 'having moved to the dark side'. There is a critical thread here to the entire text in that unless the role of manager/leader becomes accepted and valued by the medical profession as a whole, then the ambiguous relationship between doctors and health organisations will continue.

The cultural interplay relating to management and leadership roles has frequently focused on specific positions such as the clinical and medical director. The issues have been quite long-standing, with the difficulties seeming to continue irrespective of the particular era or initiative in question. From the outset of the 'clinical directorate' model, many authors have attempted to investigate and describe how the medical profession has responded to the desire to see them more involved in running and directing health organisations (Bruce and Hill, 1994; Buchanan et al., 1997; Smith, 2002; Davies and Harrison, 2003). The commonality in the accounts relates to a series of dilemmas for doctors as they interface with management roles which, by their persistent presence, seem to be largely unresolved.

This theme has been brought together under the generic term of 'hybrid' manager, where there is clearly a dual role with the individual having to navigate the tension between professional values (the dominant set of colleagues in their work group) and the priorities and goals of the organisation. Medical managers can find themselves at the intersection of these values and especially challenged where there is perceived conflict between the organisation and the established views of colleagues. This has perhaps been exemplified by the perceived wisdom of the new public management—prioritising cost reduction and efficiency (McLaughlin et al., 2002). Kippist and Fitzgerald (2009) also explore this concept of hybrid roles and in an unusual and interesting way. Whilst accepting that there are clearly strains for the individual in the role, they also point to some less than positive implications for the organisations and other team members. The hybrid role emerged to help align the organisation and create improvement and efficiencies. However, the reluctance of many doctors to undertake medical leadership roles suggests that not all doctors buy into the vision of this role.

They point also to other issues such as the rather individualistic orientation of doctors—largely from their training—that means they are often unaware of the contribution of other team members. Many in hybrid roles still lack appropriate training and education, and it is a moot point as to how far other team members feel about the decision making and influence of this individual—perhaps the least well equipped and prepared to take organisational decisions (as opposed to clinical ones).

McGivern et al. (2015), in a later discussion of the hybrid role, introduced greater sophistication by describing several types of hybrid role incumbents—they suggest five types, which have an implication for how the role is interpreted and enacted. The first is essentially a passive acceptance of the role, based on a sense of 'my turn'. The second is more of a temporary incumbent accepting the role to tackle a particular problem in the organisation or department. The third emphasises the representativeness of the role, which has the effect of putting the medical role first and the management/leadership aspect as very subsidiary. The fourth is a more positive perspective, where those in the role have aspired to such a role from much earlier in their career. The final and fifth type is those who come to it in mid-career, perhaps even later, but recognise that doctors can make a significant contribution to healthcare from these hybrid roles. The analysis may be helpful in understanding the diversity in the way in which doctors move into and embrace (or not) the challenges and potential of medical leadership.

As the studies previously mentioned have demonstrated, there is an overarching issue about the status (or lack of) attached to prescribed roles such as clinical director. Underlying this is the way management overall is perceived. Many doctors rapidly acquire a stereotypical view that management is the source of burdensome bureaucracy, that managers are antagonistic towards doctors and lack the commitment to the patient in the same way as doctors. Therefore, someone choosing to go into such a role is explicitly expressing preference for another group or culture. This can in itself produce alienation from the peer group. Many doctors in formal roles of management or leadership report a sense of loss and isolation from their peers and indeed a wariness from some who project a sense of disloyalty upon them. The strength of the medical community is almost palpable in these circumstances. A linked issue that emanates from the same source is that of retaining clinical credibility if one moves from full-time clinical practice. This is an extremely powerful concept and seems peculiar to doctors even in comparison with other sectors. In most industries, professional competence is assessed at entry and assumed to grow with practice; however, this experience then seems to stand one in good stead should management be the preferred career route. In medicine, this does not appear to be the case. There is an established view that even after 20 years or more of practice, this cannot confer credibility if, at any point, direct clinical contact is dropped. The NHS is probably on the cusp of confronting this position as more medical directors become full-time appointments. If these posts are successful and sought after, it may be that the acceptance of doctors in other roles (without continuing medical practice) will increase.

It is because of this credibility issue that the time allocated to medical management within a job role has been such a significant dilemma. There is no uniformity about how much time is appropriate for a role such as the clinical director—typically varying from two sessions to half the time. Virtually all part-time appointees report great pressure on time and a consequent sense of overload, perhaps also giving rise to a feeling of not being able to do the job properly.

Key principles of medical professionalism, clinical freedom and autonomy are seen by many to be in conflict with the collective ethos of management. At an individual clinician level, there may well be moral and ethical conflicts. However, a wider construct here is how far by responding to the call to become more involved in the management process the profession is also acknowledging that it too is part of the managed community of healthcare (Spurgeon, 2001).

Finally, within the realm of role pressures, it is fair to recognise the potential challenge to the individual of moving from recognised status and success in medical practice to the uncertainty that a management role represents. The majority of doctors make this transition with limited training for the role. Some would argue that the training that they have had (in the more scientific aspects of medicine) provides a particular difficulty to accepting the less precise, more interpersonally dependent outcomes attached to the managerial role. It has to date been quite unclear how the decision to accept a management role affects career prospects. There is no career structure for such roles. Merit awards do not appear to value contribution to management in the same way as they do teaching and research. There has therefore been no financial incentive to become involved.

Oc and Bashshur (2013) discuss this challenge in the context of leadership and followership, noting that the latter term is often seen as rather second rate and weak. In reality, high status followers can exercise considerable influence upon leaders. In a similar vein, Tee et al. (2013) introduce the notion of 'prototypicality', which raises the issue of how far a new role takes the individual away from their original self-identity. The more the role differs, the more distant and 'out-group' the individual (doctor) can feel from other professional medical colleagues.

It must of course be a longer-term goal that medical leadership roles become accepted as part of the medical career pathway. However, despite profound changes and improvements in the attitude of the profession, significant challenges remain. It is still the case that doctors communicate most with doctors, nurses with nurses and managers with managers (McDermott et al., 2015). The tribes are alive and well and persist. This is despite the accepted value of team-working to the quality of patient care (West et al., 2001). Fitzgerald (2015) raises a hitherto largely unrecognised issue of those doctors in medical management/leadership roles beginning to form an elite group of their own. Their knowledge and awareness of various factors affecting the organisation creating a separation from colleagues who are less informed and thus creating a further sub-culture.

3.3.2 Doctors and performance management

As discussed earlier, there are many influences of occupational socialisation that create differing perspectives on the value of management to doctors as opposed to managers. This is exacerbated or heightened by the introduction of the more specific concept of performance management, a fundamental component of the management process that exists at least in part to manage, contribute to or affect the performance of the organisation. Without this notion, management shrinks to that of administration, which is supportive of the organisation but has less direct influence over it. Chapter 4 explores the continuum of moving from administration to management, and it is no coincidence that many senior doctors hanker for the days when administrators worked to support the professionally led processes and did not challenge them. Performance management of the organisation of course involves the performance of individuals and, hence, the potential for conflict around the legitimacy of any challenge to clinical autonomy.

The same sensitivity to performance management may be seen in the way in which the appraisal system was introduced to the medical profession. In the face of a number of high-profile medical failures, the statutory and regulatory bodies could not resist the introduction of appraisal in terms of public confidence in the profession. However, in practice, there was great emphasis given to the developmental focus of the appraisal process. It was recognised that this was probably the most effective way of getting appraisal established within the profession. The more confrontational assessment component of appraisal by which areas of deficiency might be identified was largely resisted. Where attempts were made to introduce such an element, it was controversial and often undermined by attacking (not unreasonably) the quality of the data upon which an assessment might be based. Even for appraisal system purists who argue that it should be about the future and development opportunities, the lack of a proper performance management system and consequent absence of appropriate data illustrates how alien the concept is in the medical world.

The scientific aspects of medical training and the profession's broad endorsement of evidence-based medicine make it somewhat surprising that an effective performance management culture has not been established. Improvement methodologies, with some notable exceptions, have been relatively slow to gain acceptance in the profession. Improvement would require clear performance standards for each task and constant monitoring to measure improvement achieved. The imposition of external performance standards and targets has been much resisted by the medical world as not relating to appropriate clinical priorities. There is undoubtedly some substance to this point, but the real issue is why so many changes had to be imposed rather than emanating from within the profession. The reason is probably to be found within the concept of clinical autonomy and the implicit model of competence within it. The exercise of professional judgement is essential to professional work across the board, but it is heavily emphasised in medicine, with general practitioners (GPs) and consultants by dint of being GPs and consultants assumed to be competent. If everyone is competent, there would (historically) be no need for explicit standards and measurement because everyone would be doing the right thing. But is everyone doing the right things at the same level? Do we know, and how would we know? The relatively recent emergence of patient safety as a priority does suggest levels of variability in performance standards across medical practice. Many doctors are responding to this challenge with more explicit standards, measures and improvement targets developing across a wide range of procedures.

The real point of the discussion though is to illustrate how difficult it has been for managers to enter the debate about performance even when they wanted to do so. Greener (2005) suggests that managers felt inhibited about raising individual performance standards, concerned that it might provoke more generalised resistance from a profession liable to close ranks if under threat. Until quite recently, only the strongest and most confident of managers have felt it was legitimate to challenge clinical practice. This is gradually changing with better data being available more widely and with more doctors participating in the management process and feeling it an appropriate part of the role to assess the performance of colleagues. Ultimately though, it will require the medical profession to more widely recognise and accept that it is part of an integrated management system and that it does not sit slightly outside it.

3.4 RECONCILING DIFFERENT PERSPECTIVES

The chapter has made clear that by training and practice, managers and doctors often have different perspectives on a range of issues. The future enhanced involvement of doctors in the management process does require some reconciliation or coalescence of views so that both groups can work collaboratively and productively for the benefit of patients.

There is a need for a 'convergence of cultures' (Barnett et al., 2004) and as this term suggests not a dominance or sense of one prevailing over the other. It may well be that appealing to the notion of service improvement and patient safety is something around which all groups can unite. The NHS Confederation (2003) attempted to address the issue quite explicitly by promoting more shared training and development between managers and doctors. They call for more shared dialogue and engagement so that the different perspectives can be made explicit but can also be acknowledged and accepted as the basis for a positive partnership.

It may be that the concept of medical engagement (discussed fully in Chapter 6) offers a focus for greater shared purpose for doctors and managers. The link between medical engagement and organisational performance should appeal to managers attempting to create successful organisations, whilst highlighting for doctors the contribution they can make through accepting medical leadership roles.

REFERENCES

Ackroyd, S. (1996) Organisation contra organisations: Professions and organisational change in the United Kingdom. *Organisation Studies*, 17(4): 599–621.

Barnett, P., Malcolm, L., Wright, L. et al. (2004) Professional leadership and organisational change: Progress towards developing a quality culture in New Zealand's health system. *New Zealand Medical Journal*, 117(1198): 1–11.

Bruce, A., and Hill, S. (1994) Relationship between doctors and managers: The Scottish experience. *Journal of Management in Medicine*, 8(5): 49–57.

Buchanan, D., Jordan, S., Preston, D. et al. (1997) Doctors in the process: The engagement of clinical directors in hospital management. *Journal of Management in Medicine*, 11(3): 132–150.

Calman, K. (1994) The profession of medicine. *BMJ*, 309: 1140–1143.

Checkland, K., Marshall, M., and Harrison, S. (2004) Re-thinking accountability: Trust versus confidence in medical practice. *Quality and Safety in Health Care*, 13(2): 9–14.

Davies, H.T.O., and Harrison, S. (2003) Trends in doctor–manager relationships. *BMJ*, 326: 646–649.

Davies, H., and Mannion, R. (2013) Will prescription for cultural change improve the NHS? *BMJ*, 346: f1305.

Degeling, P., Kennedy, J., and Hill, M. (2001) Mediating the cultural boundaries between medicine, nursing and management—The central challenge in hospital reform. *Health Services Management Research*, 14(1): 36–48.

Fitzgerald, L. (2015) Interpersonal interactions and their impact on professional boundaries. In *The Oxford Handbook of Health Care Management* edited by Ferlie, E., Montgomery. K., and Pedersen, A.R. Oxford, UK: Oxford University Press.

Forbes, T., Hallier, J., and Calder, L. (2004) Doctors as managers: Investors and reluctants in a dual role. *Health Services Management Research*, 17(3): 1–10.

Friedson, E. (2001) *The Third Logic*. Cambridge: Policy Press/Blackwell.

Greener, I. (2005) Health management as strategic behaviour. *Public Management Review*, 7(1): 95–110.

Healthcare Commission (2009) Investigation into Mid Staffordshire NHS Foundation Trust. Available at: www.cqc.org.uk/_db/_documents /Investigation_into_Mid_Staffordshire_ NHS_Foundation_Trust.pdf (accessed 19 April 2011).

Hunter, D.J. (2005) The National Health Service 1980–2005. *Public Money and Management*, 25(4): 209–212.

Jorm, C., and Kam, P. (2004) Does medical culture limit doctors' adoption of quality improvement? Lessons from Camelot. *Journal of Health Services Research & Policy*, 9(4): 248–251.

Kippist, L., and Fitzgerald, A. (2009) Organisational professional conflict and hybrid clinician managers. *Journal of Health Organisation and Management*, 23(6): 642–655.

McDermott, R., Callanan, I., and Buttimer, A. (2002) Involving Irish clinicians in hospital management roles—Towards a functional integration model. *Clinician in Management*, 11(1): 37–46.

McDermott, A., Fitzgerald, L., Van Gestel, N., and Keating, M. (2015) From bipartite to tripartite devolved HRM in professional service contexts: Evidence from hospitals in three countries. *Human Resource Management*, 54(4): 813–831.

McGivern, G., Currie, G., Ferlie, E., Fitzgerald, L., and Waring, J. (2015) Hybrid manager—Professionals' identity work: The maintenance and hybridisation of medical professionalism in managerial contexts. *Public Administration*, 93(2): 412432.

McLaughlin, K., Osborne, S.P., and Ferlie. E. (2002) *New Public Management*. London: Routledge.

Mintzberg, H. (1983) *Structures in Fives: Designing Effective Organisations*. Englewood Cliffs, NJ: Prentice-Hall.

Oc, B., and Bashshur, M.R. (2013) Followership, leadership and social influence. *Leadership Quarterly*, 24: 919–934.

Oni, O.O. (1995) Who should lead in the NHS? *Journal of Management in Medicine*, 9(4): 31–34.

Plochg, T., and Klazinga, N.S. (2005) Talking towards excellence: A theoretical underpinning of the dialogue between doctors and managers. *Clinical Governance: An International Journal*, 10(1): 1–7.

Powell, A., and Davies, H. (2012) The struggle to improve professional boundaries. *Social Science and Medicine*, 75(5): 807–814.

Smith, D. (2002) Management and medicine: Strange bedfellows or partners in crime? *Clinician in Management*, 11(4): 159–162.

Spurgeon, P. (2001) Involving clinicians in management: A challenge of perspective. *Health Care and Informatics Online*, 5: 4. Available at: www.hinz.org.nz/journal /2001/08/Involving-Clinicians-in-Management-A-Challenge-of-Perspective/546 (accessed 27 May 2011).

Spurgeon, P., and Flanagan, H. (2000) Managerial Effectiveness. Milton Keynes, UK: Open University.

Starr, P. (1982) *The Social Transformation of American Medicine*. New York: Basic Books.

Tee, E.Y.S., Paulsen, N., and Ashkenasy, N.M. (2013) Revisiting followership through a social identity perspective: The role of collective follower emotion and action. *Leadership Quarterly*, 24: 909–918.

The NHS Confederation Medicine and Management. (2003) *Improving Relations between Doctors and Managers*. London: NHS Confederation.

Thorne, M.L. (2002) Colonizing the new world of NHS management: The shifting power of professionals. *Health Services Management Research*, 15: 14–26.

West, M.A., Borrill, C., Dawson, J., Scully, J., Carter, M., Anelay, S., Patterson, M., and Waring, J. (2001) The link between the management of employees and patient mortality in acute hospitals. *International Journal of Human Resource Management*, 13(8): 1299–1310.

Roles and models of leadership

4.1 INTRODUCTION

Many of the commentators arguing the case for enhanced medical leadership have considerable expertise in the shaping and delivery of health services at a strategic and operational level, though oddly enough, the majority do not have particular academic expertise in the study of the concept of leadership itself. As a consequence, many advocates write about leadership as if there is a single concept to which everyone adheres or alternatively without specifying any particular approach or model of leadership.

Does this rather non-specific approach to the concept of leadership matter? Probably not too much at the most general level, where there is consensus as to the need for greater positive involvement of doctors in the running and development of the organisations in which they work. However, we will see in Chapter 6— with regard to the concept of engagement—that when seeking to link particular behaviours or to develop leadership, it does become rather more important to understand and to differentiate some of the many approaches to leadership. It is not appropriate in this chapter or indeed this text to explore over a century of leadership research, but it may be helpful to discuss one or two key aspects and to see how these might relate to the possible roles of medical leaders and how doctors might be prepared for such roles. For a full discussion of approaches to leadership, the reader is referred to Northouse (2010).

4.2 LEADERSHIP—THE CONCEPT

How we talk about leadership and the language used to describe it often suggests an implicit model or concept of leadership. As Spurgeon and Cragg (2007) suggests, there is a tendency to confuse the question 'who are leaders?' with 'what do leaders do?' The former approach emphasises the notion of leadership as a personal capacity and has tended to produce an unending series of lists of personal qualities that an individual designated as a leader might possess. Inevitably, a paragon matching up to all these qualities does not exist. The lists seem to imply some kind of ideal type whereas the reality is that an individual may possess some of these personal characteristics to some degree. How much of each is needed to be a leader is never specified. As people do function as leaders, it follows that there is an almost infinite set of combinations of personal characteristics that can enable someone to be a leader, and the critical conclusion that follows is that there are lots of different ways in which leadership can be exercised.

Understanding that there is no single universal set of characteristics that define a leader goes a long way to explaining why the term leadership and all the qualities associated with it can create confusion. Also, more constructively, it suggests that many individuals can contribute as leaders, but in quite different ways, depending upon their own particular set of strengths and weaknesses.

Grint (2001) suggests that the term leadership is so 'multifaceted' and that so many constructions exist that many authors, in writing about leadership, do not really define exactly what they mean. To a large extent, this is exactly the case in the context of medical leadership.

One of the most commonly accepted definitions of leadership comes from Northouse (2010, p. 3), a major author in the field who offers 'a process whereby an individual influences a group of individuals to achieve a common goal'. Spurgeon and Klaber (2011) build on this notion, suggesting that leadership might be thought of as a 'process of influence whereby those subject to it are inspired, motivated or become willing to undertake the tasks necessary to achieve an agreed goal'. This approach has two particular and important implications in the way we think about leadership. Firstly, it is especially relevant to the concept of collective, shared or distributed leadership as it suggests that many can contribute to leadership (having influence) rather than investing all leadership power in one individual. Secondly, it enables leadership to be viewed as a set of behaviours—which influence others—and can be developed and improved. The research process in leadership work has as a consequence largely centred on identifying just what are the sources of influence enacted by the individual in the exercise of leadership.

Willcocks (2005) provides a very succinct account of the main approaches to understanding leadership and importantly attempts to relate these models in terms of their applicability to the medical world. The approaches he describes are grouped under the heading of

- Trait theory
- Leadership styles
- Contingency theory
- Transactional/transformational leadership
- Shared or distributed leadership

There is a temporal sequence to the relative standing of each of these approaches, starting with trait models dominating until the 1930s. Although each model has acquired a certain dominance at a particular period in time, the previous model has not entirely disappeared. The strands of thinking in one approach tend to re-emerge or linger and become encompassed in subsequent approaches, often reframed.

4.2.1 Trait theory

This was the earliest of the approaches and placed great emphasis upon personal characteristics possessed by eminent leaders, usually military or political leaders. Despite a great deal of research and despite a very large and long list of potential characteristics, a rather limited set of characteristics—intelligence, self-confidence, drive, integrity and achievement—have emerged. These are hardly surprising as a list and seem almost a semantic restatement of the term leadership itself. Higgs (2003) has suggested adding emotional intelligence to the list. It is perhaps not surprising that emotional intelligence, with its emphasis on reading emotions, understanding cues, social confidence and communication, is perceived as relevant to the dynamic of modern management. Jung and Sosik (2006) report that individual charismatic leaders are keen on impression management, attaining power and self-actualisation.

In order to be of practical value, the characteristics emerging as relating to leadership would need to be stable across a variety of situations, and consensus exist as to the items in the list. Unfortunately, neither position holds. The trait approach also implicitly sees leadership as an innate set of qualities possessed by some and not others, therefore negating many of the attempts to train or develop such qualities.

More recently, Alimo-Metcalfe and Alban-Metcalfe (2001) have revived interest in key characteristics and how they might enable leadership. The descriptors are more sophisticated (inspirational, integrity, genuine concern, approachable) and more accommodating of a modern context, but they remain nonetheless a list and all the caveats remain—is this the only and agreed-upon list, does a leader need all or some and how much of each, and do they apply equally in all circumstances?

The trait approach might be argued to have some resonance with the medical profession, given the emphasis placed on key personal characteristics in the undergraduate selection process. But as Willcocks (2005) points out, whilst many doctors have many qualities of leadership, not all doctors possess the same qualities. There may be a different distribution in different specialties, and moreover, the doctor may employ personal qualities in a primarily patient–doctor context and not necessarily in the dynamic group context of leadership. Although intuitively appealing, the trait approach seems of quite limited value in complex, diverse organisations and in society.

4.2.2 Leadership styles

The style approach is in part a reaction to the deficiencies of the trait approach and its failure to recognise the impact of the situation in which leadership occurred.

It is essentially a dichotomised model where leaders either focus on the task or the people involved. It is helpful to understand that leadership needs to attend to the task or relationships within the group. Implicitly attending to both simultaneously and equally is ideal, but it really depends on the situation and even more so the needs of those in followers. The notion of a choice of a style of leadership founders a little on the failure to determine whether there is a 'best' style or how one determines which style is appropriate at any one time. This same deficiency is apparent in the context of medicine, where it may be quite uncertain as to whether different specialities or groups of specialties demand particular personal characteristics, not to mention the range of follower types within teams or groups.

4.2.3 Contingency approach

Again, in a consequential development to the previously described model, this approach tries to recognise and describe the complexity of the different situations in such a way as to suggest which style may be most appropriate. Whilst an attractive model in trying to integrate style and context, it has been criticised for taking a rather narrowly defined set of situations, and as Darmer (2000) suggests, it rather depends on who defines the situation in question. The approach also demands an awareness of different models of leadership and the not inconsiderable dual skills of being able to recognise when a particular approach is required, that is, to be able to recognise the demands of the situation and also to be able to enact whatever model seems appropriate. The situational model, as endorsed by Hersey and Blanchard (1993), feels helpful again as they attempt to describe just what sort of behaviour is needed—more directive or more supportive—depending on the characteristics of followers. However, it is also this rather prescriptive approach that can be a weakness of the model in that it assumes that the components of the model are the only factors that influence leadership behaviours, ignoring a host of other factors.

In practice, in a healthcare setting, experience suggests that it is unlikely that there will exist a sufficiently wide selection of potential clinical leaders to be able to match style and context, or indeed that the context will be sufficiently amenable to adaptation should the designated leader seek to alter it. One can see here an explanation for many of the clashes between a clinical director and other clinical colleagues who either do not see the context in the same way as the leader or are unwilling to change it.

4.2.4 Transactional/transformational approach

This more recent strand of thinking about leadership derives in part from processes of globalisation provoking greater instability and turbulence in external environments. In these circumstances, being able to cope with constant change and to motivate and inspire others to see beyond the initial dislocation of change forces is seen as key, and this is the defining feature of transformational leadership. It is defined in contrast to the more traditional management focus (described as transactional), which seeks to establish order and control and is perhaps better attuned to more stable external environments. This notion of transformational leadership has proved quite attractive as it projects leaders tackling unpredictable, dynamic circumstances as opposed to the more staid, steady image of the manager. However, transformational leadership is in danger of slipping back towards the trait approach, being rather elusive to measure and appearing to emphasise the charismatic, heroic (and hence rare) nature of leadership in difficult circumstances.

There is often a desire in some to see management and leadership as quite distinct, frequently raising the question: 'But are you talking about management or leadership?' Spurgeon and Cragg (2007, p. 98) argue that this is rather a false dichotomy, seeing them as more of a dimension and having a complementary relationship. They suggest that 'delivering and maintaining change inspired by leaders requires management expertise. Thus the two functions support and complement one another. They vary in emphasis and are more or less appropriate at different times depending on circumstances. Both roles are needed but it is clear that some managers will be able to offer leadership in addition, whilst some cannot. Equally, many outstanding leaders are also very competent managers— but that is not necessarily the case for all leaders'.

Grint (2002) takes a rather wry look at the issue, noting that politicians will typically blame the ills of the National Health Service (NHS) on managers for their lack of control and on leaders for failing to give direction. If nothing else it is a convenient displacement of blame. Grint raises the fascinating question of what do leaders actually do. In exploring this, he describes the relationship between leaders and followers as crucial. The latter must actually assent to what the leader prescribes or the leader becomes powerless. The notion that there is a perfect leader who will get all the decisions correct or a perfectly managed system that will allow no errors is rather fanciful. The 50 years of leadership development programmes would surely have got this all sorted by now if we could invest this perfect expertise in one individual. It is more likely, as Grint suggests, that we recognise leadership as functioning at many levels throughout the organisation and that encouraging all to persuade and influence others to the appropriate action is the way leadership will actually be effective. This is very much the philosophy behind the emergence of the Medical Leadership Competency Framework (MLCF), described later in this text, since it sees the acquisition of basic competence in leadership skills by all doctors as a common and universal part of training and development as the way in which more effective leadership will be located in health systems (and to other professional groups as the MLCF has been extended to other clinical groups as the Clinical Leadership Competency Framework).

Transformational leadership is highly appealing, having the potential to bring about a coalescence around an idea or direction between leaders and followers. Moreover, Yuki (1999) reports evidence that transformational leadership is an effective form of leadership. The focus upon the personal characteristics of the leader has left many to critique transformational leadership as redirecting our understanding of leadership backwards towards personal traits and a notion of the 'heroic' leader—largely rejected in the context of complex organisations (King's Fund, 2012). However, Kouzes and Posner (2002) articulated transformational leadership as a set of key behaviours (Model the Way, Inspire a Shared Vision, Challenge the Process, Enable Others to Act, Encourage the Heart) that they argue can be learned and acquired—thus not dependent on outstanding personality traits.

In considering the applicability of transformational leadership to the healthcare context, there is some appeal in seeing how medical leaders with this approach might create a mood for change in their clinical colleagues. However, tension remains in that the origin of the advocated change often seems to arise from external sources and as a consequence may be viewed with suspicion by many (especially clinicians) working within the system. To be successful, transformational leadership seems to require a true commitment and passion for the goals of the change. This may not always align well when it seems that many externally inspired changes seek to direct and control the operation of previously autonomous groups.

A more recent articulation of this issue, that is, whether leaders really believe in what they are saying and doing, is in the concept of 'authentic leadership' (Northouse, 2010). As the name implies, such leaders are described as genuine, acting with conviction and very much representing their own personal values in what they do. This is a relatively new model of leadership, and whilst it has the appeal of a moral basis for leadership behaviour, it remains unclear just how values are translated into action, and of course wars have also been fought around a leader's moral conviction. Clearly, we do not all see the moral basis of actions in the same way.

Indeed, within the NHS, there are important issues around who is developing and defining the vision that the authentic leader pursues. Individuals within senior NHS roles are frequently encouraged to create excellent, inspiring cultures in their particular organisation. However, this rather assumes greater influence and control over the external context than is the case in a service so beset by intense political scrutiny and intervention.

These then are the main historical approaches both to the study and application of leadership. There are surely others that could be discussed as subtle departures from and adaptations of these main models. It is probably important to consider just one or two more, most notably shared leadership and adaptive leadership, as they are particularly relevant to the context of healthcare—one in particular that underpins the approach of the MLCF, described and advocated in this text.

4.2.5 Shared leadership

Shared leadership is a more modern conception of leadership that departs from the traditional charismatic or hierarchical models. Increasingly complex problems and organisations have seen growing reliance on multidisciplinary teams.

Shared leadership is an approach that can support and underpin this way of working. Shared leadership can be defined as a dynamic, interactive, influencing process among individuals in groups, with the objective to lead one another to the achievement of group or organisational goals. A key distinction between shared and traditional models of leadership is that the influence process involves more than just downward influence on subordinates by a positional leader. Leadership is distributed amongst a set of individuals instead of being centralised in the hands of a single individual who acts in the role of leader (Pearce and Conger, 2003). Each team member's individual experience, knowledge and capacity are valued and are used by the team to distribute or share the job of leadership through the team in response to each context and challenge being faced.

The multidisciplinary team has become the fastest growing organisational unit. It is no longer possible for one person or one discipline to have all of the knowledge and experience to solve the complexity of today's problems. For example, governments, in trying to find a solution to global warming, need to ensure that scientists, engineers, geographers, meteorologists, biologists, botanists, oceanographers, doctors, computer programmers, ecologists and manufacturers all bring their unique knowledge and experience to this complex problem. The breakthroughs are more likely to come from the interaction among all the differing disciplines rather than a single discipline working by itself.

This approach is equally relevant within a clinical setting. Clinicians are becoming more and more specialised as a direct result of breakthroughs in technology and science that enhance our medical knowledge. For example, for patients with cancer, teams from different specialties and with different areas of expertise, for example, surgeons, oncologists, anaesthetists, palliative care specialists, specialist nurses, general nurses, alternative therapists, radiologists, Macmillan nurses, general practitioners, physiotherapists and others, all have a contribution to make to the planning and delivery of care. Within a shared leadership model, leadership passes from individual to individual along the patient's pathway of care. This provides continuity of care for the patient through a key or caseworker without compromising standards of care. Supporting this clinical team are further networks including support services, laboratory services, manufacturers, administrators and managers.

Pearce et al. (2009) provide a series of examples of shared leadership success across a range of sectors. Konu and Viitanen (2008) also suggest in the Finnish health system that they saw shared leadership result in increased innovation, motivation and readiness for development. In healthcare, a shared leadership model would see the patient's care at any one point in his or her journey led by the person most able, with the key expertise to undertake the task. Shared leadership is about the quality of the interaction rather than an individual's formal position. The potential of the MLCF usage in the training of doctors to develop better communication, team working and innovation is a key reason the model is so important to the whole initiative. This emphasises the point made earlier in that using the term leadership without further explanation of the model or approach may be unhelpful. Shared or distributed leadership is the model most likely to encompass and release the considerable leadership potential of medical and clinical staff.

Serg et al. (2016) have recently developed the concept of shared leadership further by distinguishing types of shared leadership. They reaffirm that collective leadership models emerge as particularly relevant in the context of healthcare organisations as they better match these organisations' inherent complexity. But equally, they acknowledge that it is not always clear just how a shared leadership model will be enacted. They suggest two helpful dimensions to better understand that process. The first of these is built around the notion of formality—are particular individuals identified as providing leadership at particular times and in particular circumstances, or is it a role that simply emerges during the work process? These they describe as structured or emergent. The second dimension relates to who, both leaders and followers, is involved in a particular process. These they label coalitional (where a group of leaders influence a much larger group) and mutual (where members of a group agree to lead each other depending on need and requirement of the context).

It is helpful to have greater insight into the operation of shared leadership as it appears to be the favoured model in modern organisations and yet there is some uncertainty in just how it operates at any particular time. This of course is part of the challenge of leadership in recognising and adapting to the specific needs of a given situation.

Interestingly, this issue also pertains to a standard critique of competency-based leadership models. Boden and Gosling (2006) argue that competency models emphasise individual leadership, ignoring context and situation, and become static and mechanistic. This is in part a criticism of competency models based on a misuse of competencies. Firstly, they can be updated as and when required. Moreover, they represent a range of skills that all individuals can acquire, thus opening up the leadership process to all rather than a key individual. Finally, the comment that recognising the demands of particular situations is of course important, but to assume that these contextual cues can be taught and recognised so that the appropriate leadership behaviour ensues is in itself extremely mechanistic.

4.3 HOW DOES SHARED LEADERSHIP UNDERPIN MLCF?

The MLCF (see Chapter 5 for a fuller description of MLCF) is built on the concept of shared leadership where leadership is not restricted to people who hold designated leadership roles and where there is a shared sense of responsibility for the success of the organisation and its services. Acts of leadership can come from anyone in the organisation, as appropriate at different times, and are focused on the achievement of the group rather than of an individual. Therefore, shared leadership actively supports effective teamwork.

In the complex world of healthcare, the belief that a single person is the leader or manager is far from reality. Leadership is a competency-based behaviour that has to come from everyone involved in healthcare. Doctors work in multidisciplinary teams focused on the needs and safety of the patient, where leadership becomes the responsibility of the team. Whilst there is a formal leader of the team who is accountable for the performance of the team, the responsibility for identifying problems, solving them and implementing the appropriate action is shared by the team. The formal leader's role is to create the climate in which the team can flourish through team building, resolving conflicts and being clear about the vision. Evidence shows that shared leadership can increase risk taking, innovation and commitment, which should result in improved care for the patient and an organisation that is responsive, flexible and successful. The team members can demonstrate acts of leadership by challenging the team whilst the team establishes the norms and protocols in which the team works, managing differences by using all of the skills, knowledge and professional judgement of individual members for the benefit of the whole team.

4.4 HOW DOES SHARED LEADERSHIP RELATE TO POSITIONAL LEADERSHIP AND SELF-LEADERSHIP?

4.4.1 Positional leadership

Positional leadership roles are those that individuals take on within the formal structure of their organisation. Individuals are appointed to those roles on the basis of their past experience and their future potential to be part of the formal accountability structure within an organisation. The roles themselves have a set of expectations around them regardless of the individuals who occupy them. Examples of positional leadership roles within healthcare are ward managers, matrons, clinical directors, medical directors, nursing directors, finance directors, directors, chief executives, non-executive directors and chairmen. We understand in principle the responsibilities of these roles and would have little difficulty placing them in a formal diagram of the organisational hierarchy.

Shared leadership is a product of the culture of the organisation. Where an organisation is knowledge dominated and involves teams of individuals who collectively work towards a shared goal (such as the NHS), then shared leadership will flourish. Where the cultural norm is for hierarchy with power and influence coming from the top, then a more positional leader/follower norm will tend to exist.

In some ways, healthcare has led the way, incorporating more and more individuals into multidisciplinary teams for the care of patients. Children with special needs have complex care packages that rely on the knowledge and skills of a very varied team that crosses the boundaries between healthcare, social care and education. For a child with cerebral palsy, this may include specialist teachers, a special educational needs co-coordinator, physiotherapists, occupational therapists, an audiologist, an optometrist, a community paediatrician, a hospital-based general paediatrician, a paediatric surgeon, a neurologist, community and hospital nursing teams, respite carers, social workers and others. Different events will influence and change the key issues for the child and his or her family, so the main focus of care will need to move accordingly. A shared leadership approach is the model that best supports this.

The MLCF provides a helpful means to integrate shared leadership in practice. For example, if the team providing care for children with complex needs was asked to review its current service by the positional leader (in this instance the clinical director), they might start by setting out the direction of the service; they would then look at ways they could improve the service through their experience of managing the service. They would examine how they worked as a team and the personal qualities of all the team members. No individual could hold the knowledge and experience to incorporate all the dimensions, so they would use shared leadership to incorporate all the team members' views and use the interrelationship to innovate new solutions.

Hartley and Benington (2010) recently looked at leadership specifically in the context of healthcare. It is interesting to note from their analysis of changes in healthcare provision why they see an increased demand for new and better healthcare leadership. Changing patterns of disease with greater emphasis upon prevention, lifestyle changes, community-based interventions and a more educated, demanding public will require a more outward-facing form of leadership response. Similarly, they suggest that the need for greater team-working in the way care is delivered, the pace of innovation and change and the demand for continuous service improvement, especially with respect to patient safety, will place tremendous demands on professional leaders working in healthcare environments.

4.4.2 Self-leadership

Self-leadership is at the heart of shared leadership. Leaders need to be effective self-leaders understanding themselves and their impact on others through self-regulation, self-management and self-control. To be self-aware is to ask: 'What impact am I having?' Who is better at this than me?' and 'This is not working, what do I need to change? Self-leaders need to learn to lead themselves before they can lead others in the team or organisation (Houghton et al., 2002, pp. 126–132). Self-leadership and shared leadership are complementary, and self-leaders will willingly and enthusiastically accept shared leadership roles and responsibilities, as this may be the only way to get the job done in complex organisations.

The MLCF recognises that self-leadership is a building block for leadership, and this is articulated within the domain of Demonstrating Personal Qualities (see Chapter 5).

The MLCF also recognises within its domain of Working with Others that, whilst some doctors will take on positional leadership roles, all doctors will, as individuals, be leaders through working with others in multidisciplinary teams, making decisions about patient care, as well as being members of organisational teams making decisions about resources, people and strategy.

4.5 ADAPTIVE LEADERSHIP

This model described by Heifetz (1994) may resonate with those struggling with apparently intractable problems in the NHS and also with the debate surrounding management and leadership. Heifetz suggests that there is a distinction to be made between largely technical problems for which there is a general agreement about what needs to be done as opposed to adaptive problems where there is uncertainty and disagreement about what needs to be done.

In order to tackle adaptive problems, Heifetz outlines a framework or set of processes that essentially involve the team or community where the problem is based and providing a safe yet challenging environment where people are encouraged to focus on creating a solution to the 'wicked' problem. There are clearly aspects of the approach that lend themselves to promoting innovation and as such may be useful to the challenges facing many health systems. Although not yet a major force in leadership terms, the approach may provide useful principles in terms of the 'debate' many have called for in respect of the future of the NHS and its level of funding.

4.6 KEY ROLES OF MEDICAL LEADERS

Over the past decade, there has been a steady growth in the number of designated medical leadership roles. We have discussed already how these roles have evolved, moving from a rather stuttering position where there was uncertainty about value of the roles and limited enthusiasm from those taking up these positions. Today, effective performers in these roles are critical to system and organisational change.

Interestingly, despite the criticality of these roles, it is probable that most incumbents would have little direct relationship with the earlier debate about leadership models. Therefore, success (or otherwise) in the exercise of the roles has thus far been heavily dependent upon the personal qualities that individuals bring to the position. It is vital for the future that a more professional approach to preparation is adopted involving systematic and sustained training for all clinicians in management and leadership. In this way, the entire level of service delivery, change and innovation can be improved to meet the challenges ahead.

4.7 LEADERSHIP AND MEDICAL EDUCATION

Angood and Shannon (2014), writing in the context of the American health system, endorse the view that in challenging financial times, there will be an increasing demand for physician leaders. They elaborate their position to suggest that physicians are uniquely qualified for the role—as professionals with a natural orientation to evidence-based medicine and a focus on the best care for the patient. They also provide a crucial interface between management and medicine with direct experience of how organisational pressures and decisions impact upon frontline delivery.

However, they also point to a significant gap in the provision of training for physicians to acquire the necessary leadership competencies. This process they believe should be available throughout the medical career stages—as illustrated in the MLCF implementation (see Chapter 9). McKimm and O'Sullivan (2016), in a recent edited text, provided various useful perspectives on clinical leadership. Not the least is the contribution from Burr and Leung (2016), who, supporting the importance of leadership, also see the role as crucial to creating the level of engagement in the medical workforce that creates improved quality of care. The text overall retains some problematic elements. Its title is clinical leadership, but nearly all the individual separate chapters refer to doctors. Also, the editors themselves conclude that the MLCF is likely to be replaced by the Healthcare Leadership Model. This comment ignores the fact that the latter model has no curriculum, essential for undergraduate and postgraduate education. It is also associated with learning material and courses that have a significant cost and will therefore almost certainly never be available to all doctors in training. The comment represents a rather historic view that if some doctors go on some courses, leadership provision is made. The past four decades clearly indicate that this won't work and that a consistent provision of a model of leadership within the medical education framework is essential to provide development for all within a profession.

An NHS Leadership Review led by Lord Rose (2015) reflects this type of thinking when reporting a lack of good, clear leadership especially in clinical staff. The model of implementation of leadership training (in Chapter 9) based on the MLCF represents an approach that incorporates all staff in a professional group and is also cost neutral and so realistically achievable.

The introduction and implementation of the MLCF for all doctors will provide a basic platform of management and leadership skills although further specific training will be required as individuals move on to more formal leadership positions.

REFERENCES

Alimo-Metcalfe, B., and Alban-Metcalfe, T. (2001) The development of a new transformational leadership questionnaire. *Journal of Occupational and Organisational Psychology*, 74: 1–27.

Angood, P., and Shannon, D. (2014) Unique benefits of physician leadership—An American perspective. *Leadership in Health Services*, 27(4): 272–282.

Boden, R., and Gosling, J. (2006) Leadership competency: Time to change the tune? *Leadership*, 2(2): 147–163.

Burr, S.A., and Leung, Y.L. (2016) Towards a better understanding of clinical leadership. In *Clinical Leadership Made Easy: Integrating Theory and Practice*, edited by McKimm, J., O'Sullivan, H. London: Quay Books.

Darmer, P. (2000) The subjectivity of management. *Journal of Organisational Change Management*, 13(4): 1–15.

Grint, K. (2001) *Literature Review on Leadership*. London: Cabinet Office.

Grint, K. (2002) Management or leadership? *Journal of Health Services Research & Policy*, 7(4): 248–51.

Hartley, J., and Benington, J. (2010) *Leadership for Healthcare*. Bristol, UK: The Policy Press.

Heifetz, R. (1994) *Leadership without East Answers*. Cambridge, MA: Belknapp Press.

Hersey, P., and Blanchard, K.H. (1993) *Management of Organisational Behaviour: Utilising Human Resources*, 6th ed. Englewood Cliffs, NJ: Prentice Hall.

Higgs, M. (2003) How can we make sense of leadership in the 21st century? *Leadership and Organisational Development Journal*, 24(5): 1–17.

Houghton, J.D., Neck, C.P., and Manz, C.C. (2002) Self-leadership and super-leadership: The heart and art of creating shared leadership in Pearce. In *Shared Leadership: Reframing the Hows and Whys of Leadership*, edited by Pearce, C.L., Conger, J.A. Thousand Oaks, CA: Sage Publications; 126–132.

Jung, D., and Sosik, J.J. (2006) Who are the spellbinders? Identifying personal attributes of charismatic leaders. *Journal of Leadership and Organisational Studies*, 12: 12–27.

King's Fund (2012) *The Future of Leadership and Management in the NHS: No More Heroes*. London: King's Fund.

Konu, A., and Viitanen, E. (2008) Shared leadership in Finnish social and health care. *Leadership in Health Services*, 21(1): 28–40.

Kouzes, J.M., and Posner, B.Z. (2002) *The Leadership Challenge,* 3rd ed. San Francisco, CA: Jossey-Bass.

McKimm, J., and O'Sullivan, H. (2016) *Clinical Leadership Made Easy: Integrating Theory and Practice*. London: Quay Books.

Northouse, P.G. (2010) *Leadership: Theory and Practice*. London: Sage.

Pearce, C.L., and Conger, J.A. (2003) All those years ago: The historical under-pinnings of shared leadership. In *Shared Leadership: Reframing the Hows and Whys of Leadership*, edited by Pearce, C.L., Conger, J.A. Thousand Oaks, CA: Sage; 1–18.

Pearce, C.L., Manz, C.C., and Sims Jr, H.P. (2009) Is shared leadership the key to team success? *Organisational Dynamics*, 38(3): 234–238.

Rose, L. (2015) Better leadership for tomorrow. NHS Leadership Review. Available at: www.gov.uk/government/publications/better-leadership-for-tomorrow-nhs-leadership-review (accessed November 2015).

Serg, V., Comeau-Vallee, M., Lusiani, M., Denis, J.-L., and Langley, A. (2016) Plural leadership in health care organisations in *The Oxford Handbook of Health Care Management*, edited by Ferlie, E., Montgomery, K.Q., Petersen, A.R. Oxford, UK: Oxford University Press.

Spurgeon, P., and Cragg, R. (2007) Is it management or leadership? In *How to Succeed as a Leader,* edited by Chambers, R., Mohanna, K., Spurgeon, P. et al. Oxford, UK: Radcliffe Publishing.

Spurgeon, P., and Klaber, R. (2011) *Medical Leadership: A Practical Guide for Doctors and Trainers*. London: BPP Learning Media.

Willcocks, S. (2005) Doctors and leadership in the UK National Health Service. *Clinician in Management*, 13: 11–21.

Yuki, G.A. (1999) An evaluation of conceptual weaknesses in transformational and charismatic leadership theories. *Leadership Quarterly*, 10(2); 285–305.

Medical leadership competency approaches

5.1 INTRODUCTION

As we have argued in earlier chapters, there is a clear link between effective medical leadership and engagement and clinical outcomes and organisational performance. As Jagger (2015, p. 211) confirms, 'leadership competences are not only required by senior clinicians or trainees who aspire to positional leadership roles; leadership is an integral component of everyday clinical practice and is essential to the delivery of high quality, continually improving, compassionate, patient-centred-care'. This coincides with the authors' view that trainee doctors require a range of leadership and management competences, which become more significant as they progress throughout their careers. We contend that all doctors, as practitioners, have management, leadership and service improvement responsibilities, and thus, attaining competence in them should not be optional but an integral element of being a good doctor.

The first edition of this book was published not long after the acceptance by all the medical regulatory, professional and educational bodies of the Medical Leadership Competency Framework (MLCF). This was developed by a joint project between the Academy of Medical Royal Colleges and the National Health Service (NHS) Institute for Innovation and Improvement. Both authors were very heavily involved in this work, which included a highly inclusive approach involving all the key medical bodies as well as service organisations. It was adopted by the General Medical Council (GMC) in Tomorrows' Doctors. Since then, other leadership frameworks have been promulgated by the NHS Leadership Academy, but to date, the MLCF remains the endorsed framework by the GMC, and most medical colleges and other medical bodies continue to use this as the basis for curricula and development programmes.

To some extent, leadership competency frameworks can be seen to be somewhat bureaucratic. We have some sympathy with this view and would not seek to be prescriptive about any particular framework, but we would argue that the

NHS, like private companies, should clearly determine which one properly reflects the preferred leadership style. What is important is that doctors, along with all other clinical professionals, develop relevant management, leadership and service improvement competences and that this should start with undergraduate or pre-registration education and training and continue through postgraduate or post-registration training and development. We would argue that all health systems need all doctors to be more engaged in the running and improvement of services, and thus, attainment of these competences should not be an optional extra. Since the first edition, there have been some great initiatives around leadership competency frameworks for doctors in positional leadership roles. This includes initiatives from Canada, Australia and the United Kingdom. The Royal Australasian College of Medical Administrators (RACMA) and the Faculty of Medical Leadership and Management (FMLM) in the United Kingdom have developed some important new frameworks for those doctors in, or aspiring to, positional leadership roles. In this revised edition, we incorporate some of this useful addition to the movement but also reinforce the importance of management, leadership and service improvement competences in medical education, training and practice. It should be noted that the review is not comprehensive or representative but a selective account of relevant and topical models.

As Douglas (2015) suggests, positional medical management roles are not much sought after. He reflects that such positions are often filled with little or no competition, and particularly at clinical director level, by candidates with little leadership experience or proven track record in management. He goes on to argue that the best medical graduates tend to target roles as stellar academics, leading clinicians or private practitioners rather than seeing their future in improving the broader delivery of healthcare by focusing on medical management. The future depends on training doctors who have attained competence in relevant management competences at an early stage of their careers and thus stimulate a wider and more experienced pool of candidates for positional leadership roles in the future.

As Jagger (2015) confirms, the FMLM has built on the MLCF and developed the first ever UK Leadership and Management Standards for medical professionals. As she suggests, these standards provide a benchmark against which trainees can assess their skills, experience and impact as a medical leader; measure their leadership development; and gain certification for their leadership competences. We will summarise this very useful addition to the medical leadership and engagement movement along with a number of other international frameworks later in this chapter.

5.2 COMPETENCES AS A BASIS FOR MEDICAL TRAINING

Rapid change in the healthcare environment has pressured healthcare organisations and medical professional, regulatory and educational bodies to begin examining more carefully what it means to be a fully competent doctor. As a result, interest in developing and using competences to influence how healthcare professionals are educated, trained and work has increased over the past few decades. Of particular interest is the emphasis on management and leadership competences.

There are various definitions of competency, although all are broadly similar and mainly focused in the workplace situation/job. From a human resources perspective, competency could be defined as the knowledge, skills and attitudes that

1. Affect a major part of one's job (role or responsibility)
2. Correlate with performance on the job
3. Are measured against well-accepted standards
4. Are improved by training and development (Lucia and Lepsinger, 1999, p. 5)

Wass and van der Vleuten (2009), in Carter and Jackson, define competency in the clinical context as 'the ability to handle a complex professional task by integrating the relevant cognitive, psychomotor and affective skills' (p. 105).

Prior to the introduction and widespread use of competences, intelligence and aptitude tests were commonly used to determine an individual's suitability for particular roles and responsibilities. McClelland (1973) suggested that such measurements were unsuitable due to their poor relationship to practical outcomes and proposed that competences would be a more useful approach. Competences have many advantages in that they 'include a broad range of knowledge, attitudes, and observable patterns of behaviour which together account for the ability to deliver a specified professional service' (McGaghie et al., 1978, p. 19) and can be used to apply to a range of professions and career levels or stages.

In 2002, the first competency-based curriculums were published by the three Royal Colleges of Physicians in the United Kingdom (Joint Committee for Higher Medical Training). These represented a restructuring of training and assessment for specialist registrars. The curricula were based on achieving a range of competences considered necessary for doctors to work as independent consultants. Knowledge, skills and attitudes required for each competency were described. Assessment for each competency was also defined and was to be continuous, on the job, with tutors cross-checking knowledge and experience (Mayor, 2002).

The process of acquiring or developing competence or defining the different levels of competence development can be described using Miller's pyramid (Miller, 1990) or Bloom's seminal taxonomy (Bloom, 1956).

For Miller's pyramid, from the base of the pyramid upwards, *knows* indicates basic knowledge, *knows how* is applied knowledge (highlighting that there is more to clinical competence than knowledge alone), *shows how* represents a behavioural function and *does* tests performance. This system is often used in assessment of skills and performance in medicine. Bloom's (1956) original taxonomy, however, focuses more on cognitive knowledge than performance. This framework has six major categories or levels consisting of knowledge, comprehension, application, analysis, synthesis and evaluation. With the exception of 'knowledge', the other five categories were presented as skills and abilities. Bloom recognised that these were required to transfer knowledge into practice.

In developing core competences that apply to healthcare professionals, Shewcuk et al. (2005) highlight several important factors worthy of consideration. Firstly, there are often numerous organisational settings in terms of focus and mission; for example, doctors can work in many different settings from primary care to acute, mental health, third sector etc.

Secondly, in healthcare, there are multiple professions with their own knowledge and skills based on numerous disciplines and specialties. For doctors in the United Kingdom, there is a choice of 57 different specialties! That said, in many cases, more than one profession and more than one specialty will have or use some of the same body of knowledge in a particular field.

Thirdly, different competences may emerge at different points along a career trajectory. For a medical student, opportunities to develop and demonstrate particular competences will be different from those of a doctor in training or a consultant or general practitioner (GP); therefore, they will develop over time through their education, training and practice.

Fourthly, healthcare is a context-specific field. If competences are removed from specific contexts and actual behaviours have almost no meaning in terms of how they relate to important outcomes and objectives of training, they are unlikely to have value. Furthermore, Shewcuk et al. (2005) contend that competences not embedded in a framework are likely to be of little lasting value.

5.3 COMPETENCY FRAMEWORKS IN THE UNITED KINGDOM

Historically, there have been a number of reviews and publications from within the medical profession, for example, the British Medical Association (2004), GMC (2006) and the Royal College of Surgeons of England (2007), that focus on non-clinical competences, the managerial role of doctors and the effective management of doctors by doctors (Davies et al., 2003). Later in the chapter, we will review the updated version of the GMC's Good Medical Practice (2013a).

In addition, there have been multiple studies that have developed generic competency frameworks for all levels of doctors in training, those at the consultant level and for senior clinical manager–leader roles, for example, clinical and medical directors. The essential message from these studies is that sufficient clinical knowledge and skill are the baseline; however, for a doctor to be an effective and safe practitioner in a complex health system, an additional range of non-clinical competences, including management and leadership, is required.

In the United Kingdom, management and leadership were not generally considered part of the core undergraduate curriculum (medical school) as the focus has been on the clinical skills necessary to become a competent doctor. However, many elements of what could be considered management and leadership, for example, communication, teamwork and self-awareness, have historically been taught under different headings such as professionalism or personal and professional development. Some student-selected modules introduce the concepts of leadership and management outside the core curriculum. However, until recently, there has been a lack of a comprehensive and common framework for these competences.

At foundation stage, most training has been through in-house arrangements with postgraduate deaneries and their successor bodies and NHS trusts. The Foundation Programme (www.foundationprogramme.nhs.uk/pages) details a series of core professional competences that cover 12 areas:

1. Professionalism
2. Relationship and communication with patients
3. Safety and clinical governance
4. Ethical and legal issues
5. Teaching and training
6. Maintaining good medical practice
7. Good clinical care
8. Recognition and management
9. Resuscitation and end-of-life care
10. Patients with long-term conditions
11. Investigations
12. Procedures

Leadership is explicitly mentioned under 'professionalism', which also includes behaviour in the workplace, time management and team working.

During the postgraduate or specialty training stage, the emphasis historically was on developing doctors for the future. While there were some specific programmes on management and leadership offered by some deaneries locally, many doctors did not access these programmes until the final six months of their specialty training in preparation for appointment to a GP or consultant post.

Currently, development and assessment of generic skills have not been robust or consistent enough throughout this stage, and there is general agreement by medical leadership and health policymakers that all doctors, regardless of specialty, should have a minimum set of management and leadership skills to be able to fulfil their practitioner roles more effectively.

Once a doctor is appointed to a consultant or GP position in the United Kingdom, they ipso facto become leaders within the health system—not necessarily in formal leadership roles but as professionals who are expected to give a lead both by the health and wider community. Over the past decade, there has been a much clearer understanding and acceptance of the need for qualified doctors to have developed, or to rapidly acquire, a range of leadership and managerial competences.

In the United Kingdom, until 2008, there was no one common and recognised management and leadership competency framework for doctors, although a number of papers and frameworks have been published in recent years by a variety of medical and non-medical organisations.

The GMC initially published *Management for Doctors* in February 2006 (GMC, 2006), which set out the competences and standards that define a good medical manager. This was superseded by new guidance from the GMC in 2012 entitled *Leadership and Management for All Doctors* (GMC, 2012), raising and acting on concerns about patient safety and writing references. This guidance provides more detailed advice on how the principles in 'Good Medical Practice', the GMC's core guidance to doctors, apply in the context of the doctors' role in the workplace. These include responsibilities relating to employment issues, teaching and training, planning, using and managing resources, raising and acting on concerns and helping to develop and improve services. It supports our view that being a good doctor means more than simply being a good clinical expert.

The guidance covers a wide range of duties, but in essence, doctors, whatever their role, must do the following:

1. Engage with colleagues to maintain and improve the safety and quality of patient care
2. Contribute to discussions and decisions about improving the quality of service and outcomes
3. Raise and act on concerns about patient safety
4. Demonstrate effective team working and leadership
5. Promote a working environment free from unfair discrimination, bullying and harassment, bearing in mind that colleagues and patients come from diverse backgrounds
6. Contribute to teaching and training of doctors and other healthcare professionals, including by acting as a positive role model
7. Use resources effectively for the benefit of patients and the public

5.4 COMPETENCY APPROACHES IN OTHER COUNTRIES

Other countries with similar histories of low medical engagement in planning, delivery and transformation of services are also recognising that improvements to the health system are unlikely to be realised without creating organisational cultures that encourage doctors to want to be involved. This requires a paradigm shift in how the medical profession sees the future role of the doctor and, thus, how they are trained in the future. Both Denmark and Canada stand out in their approach to defining the role of a doctor and the competences required, including management and leadership, to be effective practitioners.

The Royal College of Physicians and Surgeons of Canada developed the CanMEDS Roles Framework and associated competences. CanMEDS 'is a competency framework, a guide to the essential abilities physicians need for optimal patient outcomes' (Frank, 2005, p. 1). It 'forms the basis of the standards of the educational mission of the Royal College and has been incorporated into accreditation, evaluation and examinations, as well as objectives of training and standards for continuing professional development' (Frank, 2005, p. 1). It can be used by educators, teachers, trainees, practising physicians, researchers and other healthcare professionals. Importantly, it can be used as the 'basis for medical curricula and throughout the physician's learning continuum, beginning at undergraduate level, during residency and continuing professional development' (Frank, 2005, p. v).

These are six roles with associated competences that combine to provide a central role of 'medical expert'. These roles are in effect what is expected of a good doctor; that is, in addition to being a medical expert, a doctor should be a

- Professional
- Communicator
- Collaborator
- Manager
- Health advocate
- Scholar

Interestingly, since the original framework, 'manager' has been changed to 'leader'. CanMEDS stresses that physicians engage with others to contribute to a vision of a higher-quality healthcare system and take responsibility for the delivery of excellent patient care through their activities as clinicians, administrators, scholars or teachers. The CanMEDS model has been adapted by a wide number of countries.

CanMEDS is not a medical management and leadership group of competences. It is set at a high level of description and implies a range of underlying subsets of competences in terms of how these would actually be achieved in practice through the application of specific skills and knowledge to particular situations.

The Board of the National Union of Consultants in the Danish Medical Association developed a model of leadership, which included five leadership core competences:

- Personal leadership
- Leadership in a political context
- Leading quality
- Leading change
- Leading professionals

They also included eight roles for the consultant as a professional leader (these are similar to the CanMEDS roles):

- Medical expert
- Professional
- Leader/administrator
- Academic
- Collaborator
- Communicator

- Promoter of health
- Adviser (Danish Medical Association, 2006).

These roles are part of the Danish medical culture and influence behaviours and curriculum and also form appointment criteria. The curricula at both undergraduate and postgraduate levels are based around these eight roles. This includes mandatory training in management and leadership before the equivalent of a Certificate of Completion of Training (CCT) is awarded, providing access to apply for consultant and GP positions. Immediately after appointment, all new hospital consultants are expected, as part of their continuous professional development, to participate in further leadership development programmes jointly run by the Association of County Councils in Denmark and the Danish Medical Association, for example, 'You are a good clinician—are you a good leader too?'

The RACMA is one of a few medical colleges in the world accredited to offer medical administration as a specialty. The College was established in 1963 in response to the need for a professional association dealing with the speciality of medical administration. Unlike other countries, trainee doctors can opt to pursue the specialty of medical administration. The RACMA training programme aims to develop doctors able to lead from senior and executive management roles. A significant number of Directors of Clinical Services in Australia and New Zealand are RACMA fellows.

RACMA Fellows have therefore experienced the clinical world as students and postgraduate trainees before deciding that medical administration is their interest. The RACMA Medical Leadership and Management Curriculum defines the capabilities and competencies for training, attaining and enhancing of the skills of the specialist medical administrator. The curriculum is accredited by the Australian Medical Council. Doctors who satisfactorily complete the training programme are eligible to join RACMA as Fellows.

MacCarrick (2014) confirms that RACMA has adapted the CanMEDS framework conceptualising leadership as the principle buttress underpinning all seven CanMEDS competencies, that is, medical expert, communicator, advocate, scholar, professional, collaborator and manager/leader.

Figure 5.1 summaries these seven role competencies and the competency theme of each one. Within each of the role competency themes, the curriculum defines a set of goals that are clarified through a set of enabling competencies and objectives.

CanMEDS has had a significant impact on medical curricula in many parts of the world. It influenced the development of the Canadian *LEADS in a Caring Environment* (Canadian College of Health Leaders, 2013). As Sebastian et al. (2014) confirm, Health LEADS Australia, a national health leadership framework, was developed by the new demised Health Workforce Australia based on the Canadian framework. As part of the development of Health LEADS Australia, medical educationalists were consulted, and it was hoped that the framework might be incorporated into all postgraduate specialty and medical school curricula, but, alas, there is little evidence of it having any impact at this time.

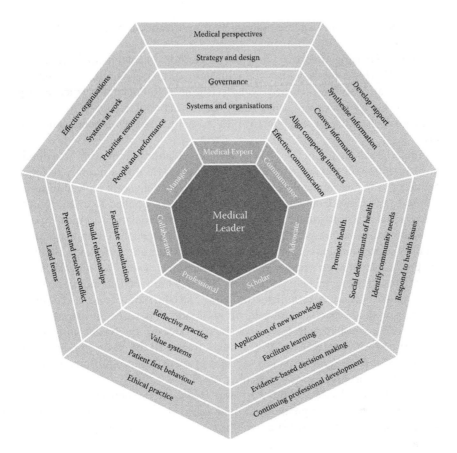

Figure 5.1 RACMA medical leadership and management curriculum framework. (Copyright the Royal Australasian College of Medical Administration, 2011.)

In the United Kingdom, the FMLM (2015) has developed and published Leadership and Management Standards for Medical Professionals (2015). The FMLM standards are designed specifically for medical professionals working in the United Kingdom, from all specialities, career stages and across all sectors involving healthcare. They are derived from, and build upon, earlier work including the GMC's guidance *Leadership and Management for All Doctors*, UK national leadership frameworks and models and research on medical leadership, management and engagement. The standards set a common expectation of medical professionals and can be used to support personal and professional development of self and colleagues, as well as recruitment, commissioning and guiding leadership development, informing education and training interventions and organisational development. The initiative by the FMLM was influenced by the *Report of the Mid Staffordshire NHS Foundation Trust Public Inquiry* (UK Government, 2013), which called for stronger healthcare leadership and for healthcare management and leadership to be treated as a profession.

In the NHS (England), there have been a plethora of leadership frameworks. As the NHS (England) redefines and relocates national leadership development on a regular basis, so each new body feels a need to create a new leadership framework. To some extent, this need reflects the changing context for leaders, but with each change, new opportunities are created but other benefits may be lost.

The original version of the NHS Leadership Qualities Framework was developed in 2002 and was widely adopted across the NHS and a number of other countries. The development of the MLCF, which subsequently evolved into the Clinical Leadership Competency Framework (CLCF), applied to every clinical professional as a practitioner recognising that every clinician has some management and leadership responsibilities as soon as they graduate. Given that a large number of positional management and leadership roles are undertaken by clinical professionals, a few years after graduating, much of their training for these roles is undertaken after being appointed. The NHS Leadership Framework (NHS Leadership Academy, 2011) built on the MLCF and CLCF and provided a common and consistent approach to professionals and leadership, based on shared values and beliefs, consistent with the principles and values of the NHS Constitution. This framework was developed in conjunction with all the clinical professional, regulatory and educational bodies as well as patient groups and some progress made with incorporation into curricula.

The NHS Leadership Framework was based on the concept that leadership is not restricted to people who hold designated roles and where there is shared responsibility for the success of the organisation, services or care being delivered.

The Framework incorporates the five domains for the MLCF and CLCF (see later in this chapter), which apply to all staff in health and care irrespective of discipline, role or function and represents the foundation of leadership behaviour. Two additional domains were added to reflect those competencies expected of those in positional leadership roles, that is,

- Creating the vision
- Delivering the strategy

The NHS Leadership Academy produced a new Healthcare Leadership Model (2013) to help staff become better leaders in their day-to-day role, irrespective of whether in a clinical or non-clinical setting.

It comprises nine dimensions:

- Inspiring shared purpose
- Leading with care
- Evaluating information
- Connecting our service

- Sharing the vision
- Engaging the team
- Holding to account
- Developing capability
- Influencing for results

As Spurgeon and Klaber (2016) highlight, it is different in style and focus from the MLCF as it is intended primarily as a basis for the provision of leadership training programmes offered by the Academy. As they also comment, crucially, it has not been endorsed by the GMC or other clinical bodies as the basis for leadership development for clinicians in training.

There appears to be a diversity of models and approaches to medical leadership and management in the United States, which may be a reflection of the variety of organisations and systems of provision. However, 'competency or outcome based education has been increasingly examined and endorsed by many educational accreditation and professional certification bodies across the health professions' (Calhoun et al., 2008, p. 376). A study in 2004 of the development of physician leadership competences, conducted by McKenna et al. (2004), identified nine competences of high importance for physician leaders. In rank order these were the following:

interpersonal and communication skills professional ethics and social responsibility continuous learning and improvement ability to build coalitions and support for change clinical excellence ability to convey a clear compelling vision system based decision making/ problem solving ability to address needs of multiple stakeholders financial acumen and resource management. (p. 348)

In terms of how competence is developed, Mayo Clinic found, through a needs survey of managing and consulting staff physicians and external survey of other organisations and programmes, that a combination of traditional academic approaches and contextually embedded, personally relevant, behaviourally based experiential learning is essential for the successful development of physician leadership competences (Tangalos et al., 1998).

All the approaches, frameworks and research mentioned broadly focus on competence that contributes to leadership ability and success in healthcare at the individual level, for example, communication; management skills; engaging, working with and leading others; being a role model and analysing and strategic thinking. Those that are particularly aimed at doctors also recognise the professional role of the doctor as medical expert or in terms of clinical excellence.

Until recently, there was clearly no one framework that addressed the undergraduate, postgraduate and continuing practice management and leadership areas of a doctor's practitioner role either in the United Kingdom or internationally. The MLCF, developed by the Academy of Medical Royal Colleges, and the NHS

Institute is the first management and leadership competency framework that the writers know to be applicable to all stages of a doctor's training and career. Several of the frameworks mentioned previously were influential in the development of the MLCF.

5.5 MEDICAL LEADERSHIP COMPETENCY FRAMEWORK

The MLCF was first published in 2008 and has subsequently been refined. The MLCF describes 'the leadership competences doctors need to become more actively involved in the planning, delivery and transformation of health services as a normal part of their role as doctors' (NHS Institute for Innovation and Improvement, Academy of Medical Royal Colleges, 2010, p. 6).

The purpose of the MLCF was to provide the medical profession, health service and individual doctors with the key management and leadership competences expected of doctors. Although some of these competences may have been previously implicit in medical education and training, the MLCF aims to make them explicit and reduce the variability between medical schools and specialties in how much emphasis these are given.

It was proposed that the MLCF could help inform the design of education and training curricula and development programmes, enable doctors to identify individual strengths and development areas through self-assessment and structured feedback from colleagues and assist with personal development planning and career progression.

The document was designed to complement and build on a range of existing standards and frameworks published by the Department of Health and key medical organisations such as the GMC.

A significant aspect of the MLCF is that it is based on the concept of shared leadership 'where leadership is not restricted to people who hold designated leadership roles, and where there is a shared sense of responsibility for the success of the organisation and its services' (NHS Institute for Innovation and Improvement, Academy of Medical Royal Colleges, 2010, p. 6).

How the MLCF was developed is also an important contributor to the wide acceptance and use that it has gained in the United Kingdom and interest received internationally. The highly inclusive nature by which it was developed involved extensive consultation with key members of the medical and wider NHS community through interviews, reference groups, focus groups, patient groups and a steering group of the top leaders from a wide range of medical bodies. It was also informed by a literature review, comparative analysis of existing leadership competency frameworks and specialty curricula (the latter to identify current provision and any variations or gaps) and review of key medical professional documents. In addition, the developing framework was tested in a variety of medical and service communities. These processes have ensured that the leadership competences were positioned within the reality of working in healthcare in the United Kingdom today. It also ensured that the language used is appropriate and meaningful to the medical profession.

Delivering services to patients, service users, carers and the public is at the heart of the MLCF. There are five domains of the MLCF (Figure 5.2), and it is considered essential that every doctor is competent in each domain to deliver appropriate, safe and effective services. Within each domain, there are four elements (Table 5.1), and each of these is further divided into four competency outcomes.

The competences in the MLCF are supported by examples and scenarios that demonstrate how competence can be developed through everyday training and clinical practice at each stage of a doctor's career—undergraduate education, post graduate training and within the first five years of a doctor becoming a consultant or GP (continuing practice). The MLCF emphasises that the way a doctor demonstrates competence and ability will vary according to the career path chosen and his or her level of experience and training. An important distinction with other existing frameworks discussed in the previous section is that the MLCF applies to all medical students and doctors as practitioners.

At the *undergraduate* stage (medical school), all medical students are expected to attain learning outcomes as defined by the medical school curriculum (based on the GMC's *Tomorrow's Doctors*). During their medical school training,

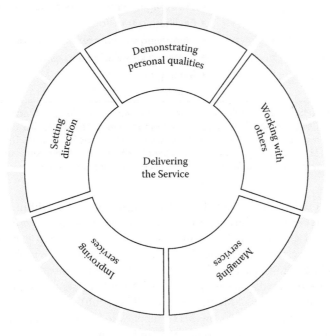

Figure 5.2 Medical Leadership Competency Framework. (From the NHS Institute for Innovation and Improvement, Academy of Medical Royal Colleges, *Medical Leadership Competency Framework*, 3rd ed., NHS Institute for Innovation and Improvement, Coventry, 2010, p. 6. The MLCF and associated graphics are copyright of the NHS Leadership Academy and Academy of Medical Royal Colleges. All rights reserved.)

Table 5.1 MLCF domains and elements

Domain	Elements
Demonstrating personal qualities	• Developing self-awareness • Managing yourself • Continuing personal development • Acting with integrity
Working with others	• Developing networks • Building and maintaining relationships • Encouraging contribution • Working within teams
Managing services	• Planning • Managing resources • Managing people • Managing performance
Improving services	• Ensuring patient safety • Critically evaluating • Encouraging improvement and innovation • Facilitating transformation
Setting direction	• Identifying the contexts for change • Applying knowledge and evidence • Making decisions • Evaluating impact

Source: NHS Institute for Innovation and Improvement, Academy of Medical Royal Colleges, *Medical Leadership Competency Framework,* 3rd ed., NHS Institute for Innovation and Improvement, Coventry, 2010, p. 11. The MLCF and associated graphics are copyright of the NHS Leadership Academy and Academy of Medical Royal Colleges. All rights reserved.

students should have access to relevant learning opportunities within a variety of situations, for example, during peer interaction, group learning or clinical placements, which can provide opportunities to develop leadership experience, to develop their personal styles and abilities and to understand how effective leadership will have an impact on the system and benefit patients as students move from learner to practitioner on graduating (NHS Institute for Innovation and Improvement, Academy of Medical Royal Colleges, 2010, p. 8).

At the *postgraduate* stage, the MLCF applies to all doctors in training and practice, that is during foundation years and for those in specialty training—where specialty curriculum was approved by the former Postgraduate Medical Education and Training Board (PMETB)—and in non-specialist training posts, that is, staff grade and associate specialist doctors.

As doctors train and consolidate their skills and knowledge in everyday practice, they are very often the key medical person relating with other staff and experiencing how day-to-day healthcare works in action. They are therefore uniquely placed to develop experience in management and leadership through relationships with other people, departments and ways of working and to understand how the patient experiences healthcare and how the processes and systems of delivering care can be improved. Specific activities such as clinical audit and research also offer the opportunity to learn management and leadership skills. With all this comes the need to understand how their specialty and focus of care contributes to the wider healthcare system (NHS Institute for Innovation and Improvement, Academy of Medical Royal Colleges, 2010, p. 8).

Continuing practice describes the stage of post-specialist certification, or the time during the first years of practice after training. The MLCF applies to all consultants and GPs. It also applies to doctors who do not have specialist or generalist registration but who work as staff or associate specialist grade or as trust doctors in non-career grade posts in hospitals (NHS Institute for Innovation and Improvement, Academy of Medical Royal Colleges, 2010, p. 9).

The end of the formal training period brings with it roles and responsibilities within the team delivering patient care, as well as in the wider healthcare system. Doctors require an understanding of the need for each area to play its part. Experienced doctors develop their abilities in leadership within their departments and practices and by working with colleagues in other settings and on projects. Familiarity with their specific focus of care enables them to work outside their immediate setting and to look further at ways to improve the experience of healthcare for patients and colleagues. As established members of staff or partners, they are able to develop further their leadership abilities by actively contributing to the running of the organisation and to the way care is generally provided (NHS Institute for Innovation and Improvement, Academy of Medical Royal Colleges, 2010, p. 9).

Figure 5.3 shows the emphasis that is likely to be given to the MLCF domains at each stage of career progression.

By the end of the undergraduate stage, it is expected that competence should have been developed in all aspects of Demonstrating Personal Qualities and Working with Others. There will have been less opportunity for undergraduates to demonstrate competence in all aspects of the other three domains, particularly Setting Direction. However, they should at least have developed the underpinning knowledge and skills as a foundation for future competence in these areas (NHS Institute for Innovation and Improvement, Academy of Medical Royal Colleges, 2010, pp. 8–9).

Integrating the MLCF into curricula at undergraduate and postgraduate levels will ensure medical students and doctors are developing competence in management and leadership early in their career and make it compulsory, rather than an optional extra. The implication of this is that a medical student or doctor will not be able to progress to the next career stage without demonstrating competence in management and leadership.

As mentioned previously, the GMC document *Tomorrow's Doctors* now incorporates all competences of the MLCF, albeit in slightly different language, and makes the requirement of developing management and leadership skills more

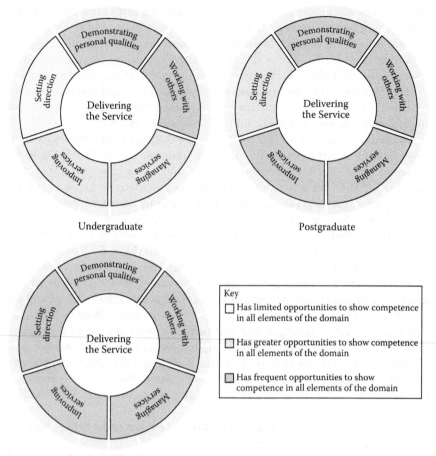

Undergraduate

Postgraduate

Continuing Practice

Key

☐ Has limited opportunities to show competence in all elements of the domain

▨ Has greater opportunities to show competence in all elements of the domain

▨ Has frequent opportunities to show competence in all elements of the domain

Figure 5.3 Application of MLCF. (From the NHS Institute for Innovation and Improvement, Academy of Medical Royal Colleges, *Medical Leadership Competency Framework*, 3rd ed., NHS Institute for Innovation and Improvement, Coventry, 2010, pp. 8–9. The MLCF and associated graphics are copyright of the NHS Leadership Academy and Academy of Medical Royal Colleges. All rights reserved.)

explicit for undergraduates. This requires all medical schools in the United Kingdom to demonstrate that the competences are included and assessed in their undergraduate curricula.

The competences have also been incorporated into each Medical Royal College's specialty curriculum. The specialty curriculum outlines the competences trainees need to attain in order to secure a CCT. As the regulatory body responsible at the time for approving curricula, PMETB (and now the GMC) stated that they would expect to see the MLCF competences and appropriate assessment methods, for example, multisource feedback and case-based discussion, integrated into specialty curricula.

One of the implications of integration into curricula is that those responsible for medical education and training will be required to deliver the management and leadership element of the curriculum and assess management and leadership competence in medical students and doctors in training. The ability and competence of clinical tutors and medical educationalists are crucial to ensuring that doctors learn management and leadership in the context of their everyday clinical practice. Furthermore, doctors learn from other doctors and the importance of role models should not be underestimated.

As the MLCF competences are embedded in undergraduate and postgraduate curricula, there will be a stronger expectation over the coming years that when doctors apply for consultant or GP posts, they will be able to demonstrate competence in management and leadership. Indeed, there is an expectation now that doctors can demonstrate such competence. However, organisations are likely to consider this a key part of recruitment decisions in the future, particularly as organisations know that they are recruiting a consultant or GP for many years and want to ensure they are getting the right person, with the right skills and drive to develop and improve services for patients and enhance organisational performance.

Management and leadership competences are also likely to be given more emphasis during annual appraisal so doctors continue to demonstrate how their management and leadership skills are contributing to patient services, the organisation and system within which they work.

As we explore in Chapter 8, the UK medical profession has now introduced revalidation, whereby doctors need to demonstrate on a regular basis that they practice in accordance with GMC's generic standards and they meet the standards appropriate to their specialty (see www.gmc-uk.org/doctors/revalidation .asp). As the competences are integrated into specialty curriculum and into the GMC's core guidance for doctors, *Good Medical Practice*, it is likely that competence in management and leadership will need to be demonstrated as part of revalidation.

Healthcare organisations may also explore more joint management and leadership development opportunities for doctors and managers. This will help facilitate the process of cultural change and may also be of benefit to other clinical professions. Indeed, the successful introduction and application of competency-based leadership and management education and training in the United Kingdom may provide a useful model for other countries to adopt elsewhere. This is explored further in Chapter 9.

The implementation of the MLCF in education, training and practice will help support the development of learning opportunities that are timely and relevant to all medical students and doctors. In accepting that the acquisition of leadership and management skills are core for all doctors, the MLCF affords the possibility to deliver appropriate learning outcomes within core clinical training, rather than as a peripheral or extracurricular activity.

5.6 GENERIC PROFESSIONAL CAPABILITIES

The development of the MLCF and its acceptance and endorsement by the profession and by the GMC were very significant steps in highlighting a wider set of skills required for excellent medical practice. The focus of the MLCF was of course management and leadership competence, and whilst implementation at all stages of the medical career path remains uneven, it set an important trajectory for further developments in the area of non-clinical skills for doctors.

Perhaps the most significant culmination of this direction is the emergence from the GMC of the document developing Generic Professional Capabilities (GPC). It was highlighted as an area of concern by the Shape of Training review (2013b) which suggested that 'across all speciality training doctors will develop generic capabilities that reinforce professionalism in their medical practice'. These professional skills are common to all medical practitioners and too often are areas of practice which most challenge doctors, which most trouble patients and which are often the focus of complaint or litigation. The GMC has taken this forward in a consultation document released in 2015, and remarkably receiving overwhelming support, with 97% of all respondents confirming the need for the framework. GPCs are wider than the focus of the MLCF being based on the professional responsibilities outlined in Good Medical Practice (GMC, 2013a), but they parallel the MLCF process as being required as part of core medical training from medical school through postgraduate training to continuing professional development. The MLCF is incorporated as domain 5 in the full set of 9 domains comprising GPC:

1. Professional values and behaviour
2. Professional skills
3. Professional knowledge
4. Health promotion and illness prevention
5. Leadership and team working
6. Patient safety and quality improvement
7. Safeguarding vulnerable groups
8. Education and training
9. Research and scholarship

Each domain is made up of several components too lengthy to list here, but they constitute the core educational outcomes that doctors need to demonstrate to achieve a UK CCT and are essential to delivering safe, effective and high-quality care.

The domains are interdependent, but each one is important in its own right. The development of the GPCs also involves a significant collaboration and joint working between the GMC and the Academy of Medical Royal Colleges. At the time this book went to press, there is a joint GPC Working Group—Peter Spurgeon, one of the authors of this book, was on the group—which is deliberating how best to advise and support the respective colleges that incorporate GPCs into their curriculum and assessment processes.

Clearly, many organisations in the United Kingdom and elsewhere have gone to great effort to develop their own leadership framework despite a degree of similarity with others that already existed. This probably indicates that the process by which a framework is developed, as well as the resulting buy-in and ownership from key players that comes from a highly inclusive approach, is what is important.

Improving the health of the population, as well as the delivery and effectiveness of health and social care services, depends heavily on the support and active engagement of all doctors, not only in their practitioner activities but also in their managerial and leadership roles.

Embedding management and leadership competences in curricula and learning pathways will enable all clinicians to actively contribute to the planning, delivery and transformation of health services for patients.

As the development of management and leadership competence becomes an integral part of doctors' training and learning, all doctors will have a minimum set of management and leadership competence in the future, thereby enhancing their effectiveness. Although not all doctors will want to move into formal leadership positions (for example clinical director or medical director), it will provide a basic leadership toolkit to enable all doctors to develop further if they wish. On the other hand, it may stimulate more doctors to take on service improvement and executive leadership roles. Hopefully, it will also encourage more non-clinical leaders to recognise the importance of real engagement and to be involved in creating cultures and incentives that value the contribution of all doctors.

It is important to recognise that attainment of leadership competence will span across 15+ years of doctors' training and that leadership competences developed for doctors are now likely to be applied to other clinical professionals.

The integration and application of the MLCF into undergraduate and postgraduate curricula, health service organisations and revalidation will require further development of appropriate assessment methodologies and an ongoing commitment by the medical education community and regulatory bodies to pursue a competency-based approach to examination and accreditation of leadership skills for all doctors. It will also have a long-term and significant impact on the way in which doctors are trained and recruited in the twenty-first century. To be deemed an effective and safe doctor, all doctors in the United Kingdom will be required to attain competence in clinical as well as management and leadership skills.

REFERENCES

Bloom, B.S. (1956) *Taxonomy of Educational Objectives*. New York: Longman.
British Medical Association. (2004) Developing the doctor–manager leadership role. Available at: www.bma.org.uk/images/Drmanager_tcm41-20460.pdf (accessed 1 April 2009).

Calhoun, J.G., Dollet, L., Sinioris, M.E. et al. (2008) Development of inter-professional competency model for healthcare leadership. *Journal of Healthcare Management*, 53(6): 375–390.

Canadian College of Health Leaders (2013) Leads collaborative. Canadian College of Health Leaders. Available at: http://leads.cchl.ca (accessed 28 March 2017).

Danish Medical Association (2006) *Education for Physician Leadership and Management in Denmark—OLAU*. Copenhagen: Danish Medical Association.

Davies, H.T., Hodges, C.L., Rundall, T.G. et al. (2003) Views of doctors and managers on the doctor–manager relationship in the NHS. *BMJ*, 326(7390): 626–628.

Douglas, N. (2015) Setting the scene. *Future Hospital Journal*, 2(3): 182–184.

Faculty of Medical Leadership and Management (2015) Leadership and management standards for medical professionals. Available at: https://www.fmlm.ac.uk/themes/standards (accessed 28 March 2017).

Frank, J.R., editor (2005) *The CanMEDS Physician Competency Framework. Better Standards. Better Physicians. Better Care*. Ottawa, ON: Royal College of Physicians and Surgeons of Canada.

General Medical Council (2006) *Management for Doctors*. Manchester: General Medical Council. Available at: www.gmc-uk.org/guidance/current/library/management_for_ doctors.asp (accessed 1 April 2009).

General Medical Council (2012) *Leadership and Management for All Doctors*. Manchester: General Medical Council. Available at: www.gmc-uk/Leadership_and_management_for_all_doctors (accessed 28 March 2017).

General Medical Council (2013a) *Good Medical Practice*. Manchester: General Medical Council. Available at: www.gmc-uk.org/guidance (accessed 28 March 2017).

General Medical Council (2013b) *Shape of Training: Securing the Future of Excellent Care*. London: GMC.

Jagger, O. (2015) Supporting and driving trainee-led leadership. *Future Hospital Journal*, 2(3): 211–217.

Lucia, A.D., and Lepsinger, R. (1999) *The Art and Science of Competency Models: Pinpointing Critical Success Factors in Organisations*. San Francisco, CA: Jossey-Bass/Pfeiffer.

MacCarrick, G. (2014) Professional medical leadership: A relational training model. *Leadership in Health Services*, 27(4): 343–354.

Mayor, S. (2002) UK Royal Colleges publish competency based curriculums. *BMJ*, 325(7377): 1378.

McClelland, D.C. (1973) Testing for competence rather than 'intelligence'. *American Psychologists*, 28(1): 1–14.

McGaghie, W.C., Miller, G.E., Sajid, A.W. et al. (1978) *Competency-Based Curriculum Development in Medical Education: An Introduction* [Public Health Papers No. 68]. Geneva, Switzerland: World Health Organization.

McKenna, M., Gartland, P., and Pugno, P. (2004) Development of physician leadership competencies: Perceptions of physician leaders, physician educators and medical students. *Journal of Health Administration Education*, 21(3): 343–354.

Miller, G.E. (1990) The assessment of clinical skills/competence/performance. *Academic Medicine*, 65(9): s63–s67.

NHS Institute for Innovation and Improvement, Academy of Medical Royal Colleges (2010) *Medical Leadership Competency Framework*, 3rd ed. Coventry: NHS Institute for Innovation and Improvement.

NHS Leadership Academy (2011) *NHS Leadership Framework*. Leeds: NHS Leadership Academy.

NHS Leadership Academy (2013) *The Healthcare Leadership Model*. Leeds: NHS Leadership Academy.

Royal College of Surgeons of England (2007) *The Leadership and Management of Surgical Team*. England: Royal College of Surgeons of England.

Sebastian, A., Fulop, L., Dadich, A., Fitzgerald, A., Kippist, L., and Smyth, A. (2014) Health LEADS Australia and implications for medical leadership. *Leadership in Health Service*, 27(4): 355–370.

Shewcuk, R.M., O'Connor, S.J., and Fine, D.J. (2005) Building an understanding of the competencies needed for health administration practice. *Journal of Healthcare Management*, 50: 32–49. Available at: www.entrepreneur.com /tradejournals/article/128166399.html (accessed 14 April 2010).

Spurgeon, P., and Klaber, B. (2016) *Medical Leadership: A Practical Guide for Tutors and Trainees*. London: BPP Learning Media Ltd.

Tangalos, E.G., Bloomberg, R.A., Hicks, S.S. et al. (1998) Mayo leadership programs for physicians. *Mayo Clinic Proceedings*, 73(3): 279–284.

UK Government (2013) *Report of the Mid-Staffordshore NHS Foundation Trust Public Inquiry*. Volume 3: P1553, 24.184. London: Stationery Office.

Wass, V., and van der Vleuten, C. (2009) Assessment in medical education and training. In *Medical Education and Training: From Theory to Delivery*, edited by Carter, Y., Jackson, N. Oxford, UK: Oxford University Press.

6

Why does it matter?
Medical engagement and
organisational performance

6.1 INTRODUCTION

Earlier chapters have illustrated the vital role of leadership and, in particular, medical leadership in the process of creating sustained system reform. Ham (2003) summarises key aspects of this context of change. He points to the distance between policy initiatives, whether managed competition or integrated care, and the day-to-day delivery of care by health professionals. Over the past 30 years, the National Health Service (NHS) in the United Kingdom has acquired an unenviable reputation for the frequency with which it undertakes organisational restructuring. The cynicism of many doctors has been fuelled by their observation of this process and the contrasting reality of their own practice, where they will typically say: patients just keep turning up whatever politicians do with the system. It is surely the direct experience of patients in receiving treatment and the outcomes achieved that represent the true focus of system reform.

Policymakers must therefore, in designing changes or reforms, recognise that in order to be implemented successfully, the impact on patients must be apparent to those who have to enact the new system. Consultation with and involvement of clinical staff is therefore crucial to system reform. However, there is, as Ham points out, a reciprocal requirement on doctors in particular to recognise that politicians represent the public and that their attempts at reform (whether sound or not) are often well-intentioned attempts to achieve improvements for the user, the patient. Inevitably, some system changes will impinge upon the work of frontline staff, notably the setting of targets and formulation of priorities. At times, such policy initiatives have been resented by doctors as limitations upon their autonomy and professional discretion in the discharge of their practice. However, society has changed dramatically in terms of levels of education, accountability and the relative power of professional elites. Political initiatives empowering the

81

public/patient and the erosion of traditional medical power bases is a manifestation of this change. The focus of change may occur at various levels within the system. Indeed, policy initiatives such as those directed towards greater integration of care are explicitly trying to address historic boundaries within the system that have come to hamper improvements. However, for the majority of health professionals and indeed for patients, it is at the organisational level that the impact of change seems most real. Our advocacy of medical leadership and engagement is in some ways driven by the belief that medical leadership, by supporting innovation and improvement in service delivery, is at its most crucial. The remainder of this chapter will therefore explore the inter-related concepts of organisational performance, medical leadership and engagement.

6.2 ORGANISATIONAL PERFORMANCE

There can be no doubt that healthcare providers have come under increasing scrutiny in the last two or three decades. There has been a tremendous increase not only in the number of performance metrics but also in the number of institutions and public bodies to whom this data flow or are reported. And yet in the midst of the growth of this 'performance industry', the United Kingdom experienced the disastrous breakdown of care at Mid Staffordshire NHS Trust. How did this happen, which of the various bodies should have looked at the data and done something and what does it say about performance measurement? Lewis (2016) rather neatly characterises this as a performance measurement paradox, meaning that we seem to have more and more measures but potentially less of a sense of accountability and action. It has been argued that this is the consequence of the 'new public management', which, as Hood (1991) described, was particularly focused on saving money, reducing input and cutting waste. It was felt by advocates and supporters of this approach that the existence of performance measurement was almost in itself a solution to how to improve services. This is similar to Walshe's (2011) analysis, who sees performance management as particularly concerned to address economy, efficiency, effectiveness and equity.

The potential for performance measures to distort behaviour and produce unintended consequences is well documented (Hood and Margetts, 2010). These are often dismissed by supporters as minor technical deficiencies that will be overcome by modifying or amending particular performance targets. However, the highly rationalist underlying assumption behind performance management—identify a measured deficiency and the organisation will mechanistically respond and improve—is really much more challenging and at odds with the prevailing culture of health organisations. Klein (2010) sees health organisations as much more a dynamic, negotiated and flexible set of arrangements, while Collier (2008) sees professional values of autonomy and discretion as in conflict with the sense of external control imposed by performance metrics.

Mannion et al. (2006) suggested that performance targets could go beyond unintended consequence to being dysfunctional provoking a rigidity in managerial focus, bullying of staff to achieve these targets and a sapping of confidence for staff and the public. Smith (2005) argues that performance targets have, for a large part, been aimed at senior managers in the NHS and have been directed at supporting government priorities. A great weakness, then, of the traditional performance management philosophy has been its failure to engage the health professionals. Perhaps this is captured most starkly by Behn (2014), who suggests that choosing particular targets to measure must be linked to having leadership strategies to achieve them. In his view, it is the leadership team that is critical. It is their behaviour and influence (leadership) that can make the difference to performance, not mechanistic performance levers.

This is a really important link in elaborating the argument as to how medical leadership and engagement can link to organisational performance. The rest of this chapter will explore these concepts and illustrate how since the first edition of this text the evidence has grown markedly stronger.

6.3 LEADERSHIP AND PERFORMANCE

Previous chapters have articulated the importance attached to effective leadership in the health sector. In some instances, this material relates to leaders of any professional background and, at others, to medical leadership specifically. However, in both cases, it is much more difficult to ascertain just how the process of leadership operates. This in turn adds to the problems of demonstrating the link between medical leadership and organisational performance.

Chapman et al. (2014) describe several leadership styles adopted by senior medical leaders and suggest that organisational culture, context and individual propensity all interact in the choice of approach. Similarly, Lega and Sartivana (2015), looking at medical leadership in various different countries, outline a variety of historic and system influences that mean that the role of medical leader is enacted in a variety of ways. Various studies have sought to get inside the term leadership to understand how the process operates and thereby affects performance. Hardacre et al. (2010) took a competency-based approach and identified aspects such as (a) *interacting authentically,* (b) *acting effectively* and (c) *conceptualising* issues as key behaviours in supporting service improvement.

West et al. (2002) focused particularly on people management and what might be called human resource management. An index of good human resource management practices was found to relate significantly to patient mortality in a sample of acute hospitals. The conduct of good appraisal and training systems was identified as being of particular importance. The paper makes a persuasive argument for the role of appraisal describing the process as 'directing employee performance towards achieving organisational goals and to improve individual performance' (p. 1308).

The data are consistent with findings in the private sector. The establishment of good appraisal systems with good levels of coverage and follow-up action may well be part of a well-run organisation (see Chapter 8 for discussion of appraisal and revalidation). It is a little less clear how the link between appraisal of medical staff, which was relatively new to this staff group (and hence variable in coverage and focus), and specific clinical outcome measures like death after emergency surgery might be operating in an attributional model. It could be that the emergence of better performance data to inform the appraisal process is a key aspect. Nonetheless, the study has stimulated many attempts to explore the causal linkage more specifically and, in particular, how leadership may relate to performance.

The difficulty of obtaining clear evidence of attribution between leadership and organisational performance is well illustrated by Sutherland and Dodd (2008) in a description of their study evaluating the impact of a major leadership development initiative on clinical practice. In many ways, it was an exemplary qualitative study, reporting many statements of perceived benefits from participants such as greater self-awareness, self-confidence and a more positive perspective on problem solving. However, it failed to identify any particular organisational benefits or specific changes to clinical practice. They conclude that this supports the assertion (Edmonstone and Western, 2002) that there is no established consensus on what organisational benefits might be anticipated from leadership development programmes.

A report by Spurgeon and Flanagan (2012) sought to respond to the challenge of whether NHS expenditure on leadership could be justified. In terms of evaluation of models currently in use, they concluded that if 'personal mastery' (self-report of perceived benefits and reaction) is used, then the evaluation is very positive. However, more direct evidence of the linkage between leadership development and patient care or organisational performance was much more scarce. They write, 'it is important not to confuse the question of does leadership development have an impact upon organisational performance with does leadership influence organisational performance. The latter is concerned with the impact of certain styles of leadership or critical mass of trained leaders upon the organisation. In this respect there is a growing body of literature supporting the motion that leadership is important for organisational success (Csoka 1997, Anderson et al. 2003 and Doran et al. 2004) although it is often found to be via quite indirect routes such as improved teamwork, lower staff turnover and higher staff satisfaction'. Such studies would suggest then that building up organisational capability in terms of leadership may well have a positive impact on organisational performance, including potentially patient care (see discussion of leadership in Chapter 9). However, this is a different question from can we identify the impact of an individual's participation in a leadership development programme upon patient care. It is almost certainly the wrong question if located at an individual level'. Ovretveit (2005) is also of this view, suggesting that there is a need to move away from the idea of individual leaders to the notion of system leaders.

Keroack et al. (2007) took a different approach in attempting to determine what features of leadership might relate to high-performing academic medical centres. They identified key factors such as leaders with an authentic, hands-on style able to relate day-to-day events to the overall goal and a strong alliance between executive leadership and the clinical department chairs: Shipton et al. (2008) set out to examine the mechanisms by which leadership influences performance. It should be noted that the nature and level of leadership was assessed through staff perceptions of leadership. The findings suggest significant relationships between perceived leadership effectiveness and Commission for Health Improvement Star Ratings and with patient complaints. As the authors acknowledge, attribution of causality is not certain. Regardless, the paper concludes that 'effective leaders shape organisational outcomes through creating a vision and building the allegiance of individuals and teams' (p. 443).

Angood and Shannon (2014) argue that physicians (an American perspective) are uniquely qualified to provide leadership, citing their status, understanding of front-line practice and acceptability to other clinicians as key attributes. However, the combination of leadership implicit in this description is of a leader who influences to beneficial effect. There is of course value in individual leaders, but the health system is then vulnerable, or at least dependent, on these outstanding leaders being found in every health service delivery environment. It is a notion that retains as its basis the heroic leader who brings about change. In no way would one want to decry any such efforts, but to improve on a comprehensive scale, health systems may need to incorporate a more extended concept of how leadership may improve organisations.

A recent paper (Spurgeon et al., 2015) has elaborated this proposition by asking whether the key to improved performance in health organisations is more medical leadership or is it really medical engagement that is at the heart of improvement. The proposition here is that increasing the number of medical leaders per se—as many advocate—is not enough. We have seen that the enactment of the process of medical leadership varies. Virtually all NHS organisations have a designated group of medical leaders and yet the performance of these organisations varies significantly. Therefore, just having medical leaders does not ensure success. Self-evidently, it is effective medical leaders that are needed. Bohmer (2012) has a similar insight, suggesting that doctor excellence is not enough, rather they need to be capable of influencing the wider construct of medical leadership. We believe this is the concept of medical engagement, as this incorporates the more extended notion of engaging the whole medical workforce in offering leadership across all services in the organisation. It is after all the whole medical workforce that provides the service (alongside other healthcare professionals) upon which quality assessments are made, rather than a small group of medical leaders. We will now explore the concept of medical engagement and how it operates to improve organisational performance.

6.4 MEDICAL ENGAGEMENT: EXPLORING THE CONCEPT

Engagement has become a popular, much used term supplanting more traditional concepts such as job satisfaction and motivation. As is often the case with words that acquire a currency of usage, they are often misused, losing specific meaning and acquiring a catch-all status. Politicians often link engagement to an area of conflict, claiming that we must engage the public in a debate about this issue. This presents engagement as a sort of event. It is not clear where, when or how this debate actually takes place, but it is somehow happening, probably in forms of the media. This is probably to use the term engagement more as a form of consultation. This focus on consultation can emphasise the communication aspect of engagement, which, although important, can sometimes feel rather unidirectional; that is, we will communicate until you agree. In the context of medical leadership, this can be interpreted as compliance, which is inappropriate since true engagement would involve participation and exchange from the outset. Equally, some use the term engagement as an action verb—to engage in a task or do something. This is often linked to proposals to seek general practitioner engagement in commissioning, that is, do commissioning. However, if the task changes or even disappears, does it therefore mean that the individual is not engaged? This, in our view, externalises the process of engagement too much, so that it is defined only by the external task. Others use engagement as a solution, a general 'good thing', and that after engagement has happened, there will be progress. In any event, there is rarely any attempt at definition or reference to where the term has come from and what people who use it actually mean by it.

Freeney and Tiernan (2006) provide a helpful overview of the literature on the emergence and development of the concept of engagement. Kahn (1990) argued that 'people can use varying degrees of their selves physically, cognitively and emotionally, in work role performances' (p. 670). Kahn also defined a state of disengagement, and this was akin to Maslach and Jackson's (1986) concept of burnout, where the employee withdraws from the work role. The approach to engagement incorporating the notion of burnout rather emphasises a dimensional concept of burnout at one end and engagement at the other. This is probably an oversimplification, and subsequently, engagement began to be defined as a separate construct in its own right.

Schaufeli and Bakker (2003) describe engagement as 'a persistent, positive affective motivational state of fulfilment in employees that is characterised by vigour, dedication and absorption' (p. 22). It is the differentiation of engagement into sub-components that is critical to attempts to identify relative strengths and weaknesses in terms of levels of engagement and to posit potential interventions that may promote higher levels. The current approach reported later in this chapter builds directly upon this notion.

The essential hypothesis of the engagement model is that higher levels of engagement generate a greater frequency of positive affect, such as satisfaction and commitment, and this in turn flows through to enhanced work performance. It is clearly a multifaceted concept, and some aspects of directionality, that is, which aspects cause what in different circumstances and in different individuals, may be difficult to pin down. However, research has sought to explore the key aspects of what causes higher levels of engagement and what might be the consequences (outcomes) for the organisation of achieving higher levels of engagement.

Harter et al. (2003) report that employee engagement was associated with a range of business outcomes, such as higher levels of performance (0.38), customer satisfaction and loyalty (0.33) and lower levels of staff turnover (−0.30). Although significant, Freeney and Tiernan (2006) suggest the results be treated with caution, as correlations are relatively small. Nonetheless, Salanova et al. (2005) describe improved customer satisfaction in the service sector relating to enhanced engagement, and Bernthal (2003) summarises research conducted by the Center for Applied Behavioral Research within Development Dimensions International that suggests similarly that when engagement scores are high, employees are more satisfied, less likely to leave the organisation and more productive.

In the context of healthcare, Guthrie (2005) argues that physician engagement is one of the key priorities for chief executives and that success in this is one of the markers of better-performing hospitals. He argues that at a structural level (creating appropriate facilitative arrangements) and a personal level (one-to-one communication), it is possible for executives and managers to build up levels of physician engagement. Toto (2005), using Gallup survey data, demonstrates that engaged physicians can have a direct day-to-day impact on the financial bottom-line of hospitals. The relationship between doctors and hospitals in the United States is rather different from that in the United Kingdom and other countries where more direct employment by the healthcare organisation is the norm. In Toto's study, the continued use of and admitting preferences by independent doctors clearly impact upon the hospital's income in a more direct business model arrangement. Engagement of physicians in Toto's study is manifest through aspects such as confidence in the hospital to deliver the services promised, a belief (integrity) that the hospital treats patients fairly and pride and passion about being linked to a high-quality care provider.

Engagement as used by most practitioners involves a form of positive affect or commitment to the organisational goals and values. Dickinson and Ham (2008) talk of staff involvement in decision making and open communication channels. An important development in the evolution of the use of engagement to improve performance is the explicit addition by some authors (Robinson et al., 2004; Spurgeon et al., 2008) to the responsibility of organisations to nurture or promote engagement through mechanisms of management and leadership. Indeed, there has been increasing interest in determining just how the mechanisms of engagement operate especially in respect of its relationship to performance. Attempts to document how engagement operates are hampered by a lack of an agreed definition within the various studies and, similarly a range of different techniques used to measure engagement. Later in this chapter, a particular approach with definition and measure is described that at least allows for the proposition of how engagement may be operating.

An overview report by Macleod and Clarke (2009) provides an excellent account of employee engagement in the United Kingdom and in a range of sectors. In the report, they reiterate, as in this chapter, that the term engagement has acquired a range of meanings and that no universal definition exists. However, despite this, they make some important assertions about the concept:

- That engagement is a two-way process involving organisations working to engage employees and the latter having a degree of choice as to their response
- That engagement is measurable—with some variability in the evidence gained by different measurement tools

- That engagement correlates with performance and with innovation. Whilst recognising that proving direct causal links are important, the report concludes that the consistent nature of the studies of engagement, coupled with individual company case studies, makes for a 'compelling case'
- Engagement levels in the United Kindom are relatively low, and this presents a major challenge given the critical nature of innovation in tackling the recession

Macleod and Clarke (2009) provide many examples of reports and case studies from organisations where levels of engagement or attempts to promote engagement appear to relate to enhanced performance. It should be noted (as Macleod and Clarke acknowledge) that they have not been able to validate all the studies quoted. Many use internal survey instruments with slightly variable ways of assessing engagement, and there is rarely any mention of control or comparison groups, so one cannot be entirely sure that a classic 'Hawthorn' effect is not at play. However, a meta-analysis of a series of Gallup studies by Harter et al. (2006) found consistently that business units in the top half of the engagement scores had 27% higher profitability than those in the bottom half. Similarly, engagement levels seemed to predict sickness absence, with more engaged employees taking 2.7 days per year compared to 6.2 days for disengaged employees.

Alimo-Metcalfe and Bradley (2008), exploring types of leadership in mental health teams in the NHS, report that only 'engaging with others' was a significant predictor of performance. It is not only the organisation that seems to benefit from higher levels of engagement, so too does the individual member of the organisation, with several accounts of a greater sense of well-being, more positive feelings about work and lower levels of mental health problems, for example, anxiety and depression (Waddell and Burton, 2006; Black, 2008).

The evidence then would seem to be very powerful that engagement is a crucially important concept in promoting both individual well-being and organisational success. As Macleod and Clarke (2009) conclude from their review, the role of the leader (or leaders) in developing engagement is vital, but many leaders do not possess, or perhaps do not even value, some of the 'soft' skills that may be necessary. Enhancing engagement is going to demand different and more subtle skills of leadership.

6.5 APPROACHES TO MEASURING AND DEVELOPING ENGAGEMENT FOR ORGANISATIONAL PERFORMANCE

As Ham and Dickenson (2008) comment in their review of medical leadership, engagement and organisational performance, very few measures of engagement are to be found that meet robust psychometric criteria. A major contribution though is that of Reinertsen et al. (2007) from the Institute for Healthcare Improvement (IHI). Given the evidence supporting the importance of engagement, they express surprise at how few hospitals have 'actually articulated a plan to improve the engagement of their physicians' (p. 2). Based upon working with and close observation of high-performing hospitals, they offer a framework for how organisations might go about improving levels of engagement. The basic framework is shown in Figure 6.1.

Each of these areas needs to be placed in the organisation's own context, and inevitably, one or two operate in a US health system more directly than in the United Kingdom, but the principles are sound. An associated checklist presents organisations with the opportunity of rating themselves in terms of key areas of functioning (seven items with a maximum score of seven). Depending upon the score obtained, the Framework then describes some actions organisations can take to improve engagement. The standing of IHI has led to the Framework being quite influential in the area, but as a measure of engagement, it is quite limited even though it works well in stimulating a dialogue and potential action to improve engagement.

It was in this general context—strong support for the concept of medical leadership and engagement as critical to performance, but deficiencies in terms of existing measures of engagement—that the joint Institute for Innovation and Improvement and Academy of Medical Royal Colleges Enhancing Engagement

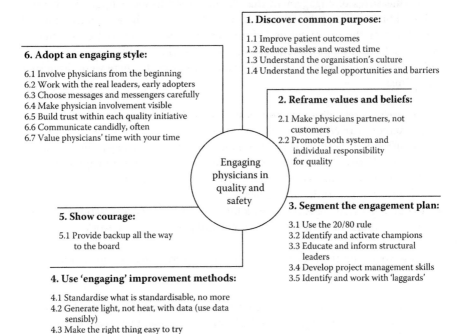

Figure 6.1 Engaging physicians in quality and safety. (From Reinersten, J.L., Gosfield, A.G., Rupp, W. et al., *Engaging Physicians in a Shared Quality Agenda*, Innovation Series (IHI), Cambridge, MA, 2007, 4. Available at: www.IHI.org. Accessed 27 May 2011.)

in Medical Leadership project set out to address the issue of medical engagement and organisational performance.

It is worth noting here that the context of this national project was medical leadership and, hence, medical engagement—a uni-professional orientation to engagement. A very important and potentially confusing issue lurks here within the idea of which groups of health professionals may be the focus of engagement enhancing strategies. Many of the claims about the link between engagement and organisational performance derive from staff engagement metrics (West and Dawson, 2012). This argument seems to assume that all staff groups in an organisation are much the same and the overall level of engagement is some amalgam of them all. The proposition seems somewhat naïve given the complexity of the factors that may influence levels of individual staff engagement. The 'psychological contract' between employees and health organisations may well vary depending upon the particular staff groups, its level of training and education, expectations and working conditions. Therefore, it is likely that each distinct staff group may respond rather differently to approaches to promote engagement. Hence, the focus within this project is to develop a measure of medical engagement for medical professionals.

The measures of engagement that do exist tend to focus upon the feelings of individual staff and do not simultaneously evaluate the associated cultural conditions of the organisation. Moreover, no assessment tool exists that is designed to focus upon medical engagement—the specific context for the Enhancing Engagement in Medical Leadership project. There were three specific aims:

- To develop a reliable and valid measure of medical engagement that will be quick and relatively unobtrusive to complete
- To differentiate within the scale and measure of personal engagement at an individual level (the motivation of the individual to perform in appropriate managerial and leadership roles) from the organisational context (which may foster or constrain engagement)
- To develop a systematic framework for recommending organisational strategies for enhancing medical engagement and performance at work

These goals and the process of development were based on three conceptual premises:

I Medical engagement is critical to implementing many of the radical changes and improvements sought in the NHS, and engagement levels are not universally high.
II Medical engagement cannot be understood from consideration of the individual employee alone. Organisational systems play a crucial role in providing the cultural conditions under which the individual's propensity to engage is either encouraged or inhibited. The measure must therefore simultaneously assess both the individual and cultural components of the engagement

equation, and this is reflected in the operational definition of engagement used in the development process. 'The active and positive contribution of doctors within their normal working roles to maintaining and enhancing the performance of the organisation, which itself recognises this commitment in supporting and encouraging high-quality care' (Spurgeon et al., 2008).

III A distinction is made between competence and performance in the context of work behaviour. Competence may be thought of as what an individual can do, but this is not the same as why they will choose to do. Competence and motivation together equal performance.

6.6 PROCESS OF DEVELOPMENT

Applied Research Ltd. (a relatively small research and consultancy organisation) had previously developed a Professional Engagement Scale, with data on over 23,000 healthcare professionals. In the timescale of the overall project, it was felt that an adaptation of this existing scale to medical engagement was the most effective route. This involved refining the existing scale items to provide a medical engagement focus, piloting the items with an appropriate population and then undertaking relevant psychometric analysis to confirm the reliability and validity of the scales.

The re-analysis of the original data set (23,782 NHS staff) using factor analysis produced a hierarchical scale structure as presented in Table 6.1 (next page).

Here, we can see the overall Index of Medical Engagement made up of a series of sub-scales:

- Meta-scale 1: Working in an open culture
- Meta-scale 2: Having purpose and direction
- Meta-scale 3: Feeling valued and empowered

Each of these meta-scales is then further made up by two sub-scales, one of which relates to individual aspects of engagement (notation I) and another relating to organisational conditions (notation O). This is an important aspect of the Medical Engagement Scale (MES) in that the degree to which the individual or organisational facets are emphasised is part of the diagnostic power of suggesting how improvement may be achieved.

The prototype MES was then piloted with four NHS secondary care trusts. Two of those trusts had been identified and recognised independently for their work on engaging clinicians, another trust was in a state of crisis where a new chief executive suspected that lack of medical engagement was a significant problem and a final volunteer trust was unknown in terms of the likely picture of medical engagement. The MES was then given to a sample of all doctors in these trusts (with a 56% return rate overall) as well as a smaller sample of senior managers (non-medical), who were asked to estimate the level of medical engagement they thought existed in their trust.

Table 6.1 MES scales and definitions

MES scale	Scale definition [The scale is concerned with the extent to which...]
Index: Medical engagement	...doctors adopt a broad organisational perspective with respect to their clinical responsibilities and accountability
Meta-scale 1: Working in an open culture	...doctors have opportunities to authentically discuss issues and problems at work with all staff groups in an open and honest way
Meta-scale 2: Having purpose and direction	...medical staff share a sense of common purpose and agreed direction with others at work particularly with respect to planning, designing and delivering services
Meta-scale 3: Feeling valued and empowered	...doctors feel that their contribution is properly appreciated and valued by the organisation and not taken for granted
Sub-scale 1: [O] Climate for positive learning	....the working climate for doctors is supportive and in which problems are solved by sharing ideas and joint learning
Sub-scale 2: [I] Good interpersonal relationships	...all staff are friendly towards doctors and are sympathetic to their workload and work priorities
Sub-scale 3: [O] Appraisal and rewards effectively aligned	...doctors consider that their work is aligned to the wider organisational goals and mission
Sub-scale 4: [I] Participation in decision making and change	...doctors consider that they are able to make a positive impact through decision making about future developments
Sub-scale 5: [O] Development orientation	...doctors feel that they are encouraged to develop their skills and progress their career
Sub-scale 6: [I] Commitment and work satisfaction	...doctors feel satisfied with their working conditions and feel a real sense of attachment and commitment to the organisation

These resulting data were used to establish a number of key practical and conceptual aspects of the MES, notably that

- The overall and sub-scales were reliable, with Cronbach alpha coefficients from .70 to .93.
- Engagement is part of but distinct from a more general concept of organisational culture.
- The new MES had face validity, being able to differentiate statistically significant differences between the four pilot trust sites and in precisely the predicted order of engagement; that is, they were independently identified as outstanding at the top of the engagement scale, with the crisis trust at the bottom and the unknown in between.

Following this relatively successful pilot stage, the MES was then applied to a further 30 secondary care trusts in the NHS in order

- To establish normative data for patterns of medical engagement and
- To assess the underlying issue relating to medical engagement—does it relate to organisational performance?

An initial set of norms was therefore established based on the 30 secondary care trusts, and this enabled other trusts to be benchmarked and compared. At the time of writing, the MES has now been used with over 100 UK trusts and Health Boards (Wales and Scotland), with over 14,000 individual doctors on the unique database. The issue of medical leadership and medical engagement is an international preoccupation, and as a consequence, MES has also been used in many other countries (Australia, New Zealand, Canada, Denmark, Norway and Malta), with over 5000 doctors in the international database.

The size of this database—expanded significantly since the first edition of this text—has facilitated a large number of studies providing more and more evidence of the key role of engagement in improving organisational performance. Table 6.2 is a simple visual example of this relationship based on the initial 30 NHS Trusts.

Health and social care organisations in England have been subject to performance monitoring and regulation under the auspices of the Care Quality Commission (CQC) as the regulatory body. The Commission represented an overarching framework bringing together previous NHS Performance Frameworks and the activities of Monitor (the regulator for Foundation Trusts within the overall set of NHS Trusts). The cumulative nature of the development has resulted in a very large number of standards across a range of areas. Performance in each area was rated as Achieved, Underachieved or Failed, and the measure is specific to each particular standard. Some standards are generic and others are specific to different types of healthcare providers. Broadly, the many standards can be grouped under the following areas:

Table 6.2 Comparison of the MES index (30 secondary care trusts) to overall Care Quality Commission (CQC) ratings

Trust ID (trust names withheld for confidentiality)	Overall medical engagement scale index (in descending order)	CQC-NHS performance ratings 2008/2009				
		Overall quality score	Financial management score	Core standards score (as a provider of services)	Existing commitment score (as a provider of services)	National priorities score (as a provider of services)
Top 10 trusts						
21	65.8	Good	Excellent	Fully met	Fully met	Good
12	65.2	Good	Good	Fully met	–	Good
15	63.4	Excellent	Good	Fully met	Fully met	Excellent
5	62.0	Excellent	Excellent	Fully met	Fully met	Excellent
24	60.8	Good	Excellent	Fully met	–	Good
1	60.4	Excellent	Excellent	Fully met	Fully met	Excellent
10	59.9	Good	Excellent	Almost met	Fully met	Good
16	59.8	Good	Fair	Fully met	Almost met	Excellent
14	59.7	Excellent	Excellent	Fully met	Fully met	Excellent
11	58.8	Excellent	Excellent	Fully met	Fully met	Excellent

(Continued)

Table 6.2 (Continued) Comparison of the MES index (30 secondary care trusts) to overall Care Quality Commission (CQC) ratings

			CQC-NHS performance ratings 2008/2009			
Trust ID (trust names withheld for confidentiality)	Overall medical engagement scale index (in descending order)	Overall quality score	Financial management score	Core standards score (as a provider of services)	Existing commitment score (as a provider of services)	National priorities score (as a provider of services)
Bottom 10 trusts						
25	56.8	Fair	Fair	Almost met	Fully met	Poor
4	56.7	Fair	Fair	Almost met	Fully met	Fair
22	55.7	Fair	Fair	Partly met	Almost met	Good
23	55.3	Fair	Good	Almost met	Partly met	Excellent
29	54.4	Good	Excellent	Fully met	Fully met	Good
3	54.3	Fair	Excellent	Fully met	Fully met	Poor
26	53.1	Fair	Fair	Almost met	Almost met	Fair
8	52.7	Good	Good	Fully met	Almost met	Good
18	52.1	Fair	Fair	Fully met	Partly met	Good
20	47.0	Poor	Poor	Almost met	Not met	Fair

- Operational standards and targets, for example, cancelled operations, meeting waiting targets
- Finance, for example, utilisation of resources
- User experience, for example, provision of information, treated with respect
- Quality and safety, for example, incidents, infection rates

Ultimately, the performance levels are drawn together into overall trust ratings across the main aspects such that trusts are described as weak, fair, good and excellent in their pattern of service provision.

Table 6.2 (based on 2008–2009 data) provides a simple visual exploration of how the top and bottom scoring trusts on the Medical Engagement Index fare on the main CQC ratings (overall quality, financial management, care standards, existing commitments and national priorities). Although slightly less than perfect, it is quite apparent from visual comparison of, for example, overall quality and financial management, that the top 10 medical engagement index trusts are good or excellent, with one exception. In contrast, the bottom 10 medical engagement index trusts are generally fair or poor (weak), with the odd exception in financial management.

Table 6.3 provides specific examples of how particular standards of the CQC correlate with scores on the MES, both at the Medical Engagement Index level and also in relation to some of the sub-scales of the measure. Virtually all correlations are significant (and positive), with their level of significance indicated in the table. Where fewer than 30 trusts are involved, this is because the particular measure is not applicable to this type of healthcare provider.

A more detailed statistical analysis also reveals a large number of significant relationships between the medical engagement index and other independently collected performance markers. For example, standardised mortality rates correlate significantly at (0.01 level) −0.50 with the overall Engagement Index and −0.50 with Meta-scale 3 (being valued and empowered) and −0.56 with Meta-scale 1 (working in a collaborative culture). Similarly, from the National Patient Safety Agency data, overall Medical Engagement (−0.34) and Meta-scale 2 (−0.46) correlate significantly with incidents resulting in severe harm.

A National Institute of Health Services Research (NIHR) study (Dickinson et al., 2012) sought to establish the relative effectiveness of various models of medical leadership. Eight case study sites participated in the study, and whilst the overall conclusion was that no formal structure was markedly better in terms of predicting performance, the MES was more successful. At both organisational level and within specific clinical directorates, MES was the one metric associated with differential levels of performance. This was in contrast with the NHS Staff Survey data for the eight sites, which showed no systematic linkage to performance. The latter of course includes all staff groups and perhaps reinforces the point about being clear about how individual staff groups (doctors) may have different levels of engagement and may also have more or less impact on performance.

Table 6.3 CQC NHS performance ratings[a]

	Medical engagement index	Meta 1: Working in a collaborative culture	Meta 2: Having purpose and direction	Meta 3: Being valued and empowered	Sub 1: Climate for positive learning	Sub 2: Good interpersonal relationships	Sub 3: Appraisal and rewards effectively aligned	Sub 4: Participation in decision making and change	Sub 5: Development orientation	Sub 6: Work satisfaction	n trusts
The CQC-NHS performance ratings 2008/2009											
Overall quality score	0.68***	0.63***	0.70***	0.65***	0.68***	0.46**	0.73***	0.49**	0.62***	0.62***	30
2008/2009 Financial management score	0.47**	0.48**	0.44**	0.46**	0.50**	0.37*	0.52**	0.24	0.47**	0.41**	30
2008/2009 Core standards score (as a provider of services)	0.34*	0.37*	0.25	0.36*	0.37*	0.31*	0.31*	0.12	0.41*	0.28	30
2008/2009 Existing commitments score (as a provider of services)	0.64***	0.59***	0.67***	0.60***	0.64***	0.45*	0.69***	0.53**	0.61***	0.55**	25
2008/2009 NHS Performance ratings existing commitments and national priorities indicator scores (frequency of 'achieved')	0.69***	0.54**	0.75***	0.70***	0.56**	0.44*	0.76***	0.62***	0.66***	0.68***	25

(Continued)

Table 6.3 (Continued) CQC NHS performance ratings[a]

	Medical engagement index	Meta 1: Working in a collaborative culture	Meta 2: Having purpose and direction	Meta 3: Being valued and empowered	Sub 1: Climate for positive learning	Sub 2: Good interpersonal relationships	Sub 3: Appraisal and rewards effectively aligned	Sub 4: Participation in decision making and change	Sub 5: Development orientation	Sub 6: Work satisfaction	n trusts
The CQC-NHS performance ratings 2008/2009											
Total time in A&E: four hours or less (% level 'achievement')	0.55**	0.55**	0.47*	0.59***	0.52**	0.53**	0.52**	0.33	0.70***	0.46*	24
Inpatients waiting longer than the 26-week standard (% level 'underachievement')	−0.57***	−0.59***	−0.41*	−0.64***	−0.52**	−0.62***	−0.44*	−0.30	−0.72***	−0.52*	25
All cancers: two-month urgent referral to treatment (% level 'achievement')	0.54**	0.52**	0.42*	0.61***	0.49**	0.50**	0.35*	0.46*	0.60***	0.57**	24

[a] Attenuated range of performance ratings.
* $p < .05$; ** $p < .01$. *** $p < .001$.

Table 6.4 Correlations between risk levels identified in acute trusts by CQC (2014) and average MES scores

	Correlation
Overall index of medical engagement	−0.50
Meta-scale 1: Working in a collaborative climate	−0.50
Meta-scale 2: Having purpose and duration	−0.44
Meta-scale 3: Feeling valued and empowered	−0.52

Note: The negative correlation existing because the greater the risk the lower the level of engagement.

As mentioned earlier, the initial database of 30 trusts was linked to CQC data for 2008 to 2009. There is of course always an issue of directionality with correlational data. However, subsequent exploration of the expanding and importantly different set of trusts found a similar set of correlations for CQC data (2014–2015) and specifically found in 2014 very high correlations between medical engagement levels and the risk levels identified by CQC in all acute trusts (see Table 6.4).

Other albeit small-scale studies point to the critical impact of medical engagement upon the willingness of clinicians to change practice. This is in accord with Taitz et al. (2011), who found engagement as the only mechanism to influence variation in practice. Promisingly, too, a study of senior clinicians in a group of hospitals in Canada suggested that, often, a training intervention aimed at improving medical leadership capability of individual clinicians increased their level of engagement.

These powerful and unique data are evidence of a strong association between levels of medical engagement and externally assessed performance parameters in healthcare providers. This is consistent with much of the earlier literature around engagement reported from other sectors. Although the evidence here is correlational, it is difficult to mount the alternative interpretation, that is, that a disaffected, disillusioned and disengaged medical workforce is likely to lead to sustained high levels of organisational performance. The number, strength and the direction and various contexts of the correlation are compelling. It is important that the NHS, just as Macleod and Clarke (2009) recommend, recognise the critical role of engagement and seek to identify better ways to nurture and develop it.

6.7 LEADING FOR ENGAGEMENT

Returning to the premises of the earlier sections of this chapter, the data on engagement and its link to performance reinforce the crucial role of leaders in creating the appropriate cultures for medical engagement to flourish. Armit and Roberts (2009) recognise this too in detailing that the argument that reform and improved performance in health systems is in itself dependent upon fully engaged doctors and that in order for this to happen, the organisational culture, shaped and influenced by its leadership, is going to have to be appropriately supportive and constructive. The acquisition of leadership competence by doctors themselves will form an important element in creating this enhanced engagement.

Building on the evidence of the importance of medical engagement to performance, a follow up enquiry has attempted to explore with the top six trusts on the MES what they have done to create the engagement and how others may go about enhancing their own existing levels. Although preliminary and based on a limited number of case studies, some consistent themes are emerging (Atkinson et al., 2011).

An interesting structural issue that resonates with the work of Ham (2009), when exploring high-performing organisations internationally, is the stability and, hence, continuity of the executive team. If engagement is anything, it must be about relationships, and it takes time to build trust and respect in a relationship. It is something policymakers might wish to give more consideration. Grand gestures involving the sacking of executives for 'failure' may assuage some kind of public demand for blame and accountability, but on the evidence of the importance of stability in organisations, it would seem to be doing little to facilitate sustainable improvement.

More generally, the prescription seems to be that there is a need to build a culture of engagement. As with all cultural change, this may take many forms and be symbolised in the context of a particular situation. However, examples observed in trusts with the highest levels of engagement include the following:

- *Leadership*—Stable, top-level leadership that promotes and fosters relationships, sets expectations and leads by example
- *Selecting and appointing the right doctors to leadership and management roles*—Selecting through open competition, ensuring a choice of candidates and appointing based on ability, attitude, leadership aptitude and potential
- *Promotion of understanding, trust and respect between doctors and managers*—Developing an acknowledgement and acceptance of professional differences, ensuring that managers and doctors share a common goal to deliver high-quality healthcare to patients
- *Clarity of roles and responsibility and empowerment*—Ensuring that doctors and managers work together, are accountable and are empowered to shape and develop the organisation
- *Effective communication*—Building trust and developing relationships through open, honest communication that is persistent, widespread and inclusive
- *Setting expectations, enforcing professional behaviour and firm decision making*—Ensuring that organisation expectations are clearly communicated and that issues relating to unprofessional behaviour and patient safety are dealt with quickly and decisively
- *Providing support, development and leadership opportunities to doctors at all levels*—Investing in training, mentoring and coaching, ensuring formal and

informal leadership opportunities are available, spotting and supporting talent and succession planning
- *Developing a future-focused and outward-looking culture*—Encouraging and engaging in best practice and promoting and contributing at regional and national level

Medical engagement as discussed here and as incorporated into the MES is viewed as an intra-individual concept, involving a motivational state or level of commitment that exists within the individual and can be applied to a range of tasks or settings. It is also seen as critical to the dynamic of medical engagement that the level can be influenced by the way in which the organisation treats that individual. This engagement can be enhanced or inhibited by how the organisation operates. Without this consideration, it is in principle impossible for an organisation to influence the level of engagement of its staff.

Moreover, this interface between individual level of engagement of the organisation is vital to understanding the link between engagement and organisational performance. If an individual's reservoir of engagement (motivation/commitment) can be increased and if this applies to the entire workforce, then it is possible to see how an organisation, by increasing its overall level of engagement, will also have increased its overall 'power' to perform. As a simple analogy, it is rather like a car engine. If the power is increased, the car goes faster. If the level of engagement of a workforce is about 30% (the estimated level for many organisations in the United Kingdom), then increasing this to 40% or 50% obviously increases the potential momentum of the organisation to perform better across all potential metrics.

The authors argue that engagement is a 'process of cultural change' and that four key implementing factors must be present for a successful coherent strategy to embed engagement:

1. An understanding and respect for the differing perspectives of doctors and managers
2. Provision of appropriate (and mandatory) education in management and leadership
3. Evidence that greater levels of medical engagement can produce enhanced organisational performance
4. Organisational strategies, which are focused and persistent, to enhance medical engagement

This approach is captured in the diagram of the Continuum of Medical Engagement, shown in Figure 6.2 (Applied Research Ltd, 2008).

Each organisation will need to make such initiatives meaningful in their own circumstances, but the crucial role of engagement in supporting organisational achievement suggests that the rewards are clear and long-term. The development of such levels of engagement will be crucial to the current coalition government's plans to put clinicians, both primary and secondary, at the forefront of key decision making in the NHS.

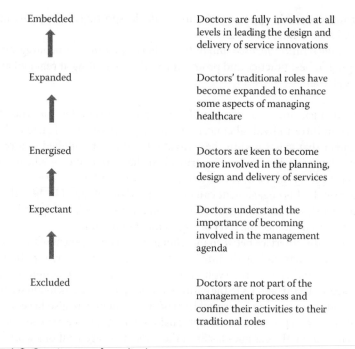

Figure 6.2 Continuum of medical engagement.

REFERENCES

Alimo-Metcalf, B., and Bradley, M. (2008) Cast in a new light. *People Management*, 24: 18–23.

Anderson, R.A., Issel, L.M., and McDaniel Jr., R.R. (2003) Nursing homes as complex adaptive systems: Relationship between management practice and resident outcomes. *Journal of Nursing Research* 52 (1): 12.

Angood, P., and Shannon, D. (2014) Unique benefits of physician leadership—An American perspective. *Leadership in Health Services*, 27(4): 272–282.

Applied Research Ltd (2008) *Continuum of Medical Engagement*. Birmingham, UK: Applied Research Ltd.

Armit, K., and Roberts, H. (2009) Engaging doctors: The NHS needs the very best leaders. *Asia Pacific Journal of Health Management*, 4(2): 47–52.

Atkinson, S., Spurgeon, P., Clark, J. et al. (2011) *Engaging Doctors: What Can We Learn from Trusts with High Levels of Medical Engagement*. University of Warwick campus, Coventry: NHS Institute for Innovation and Improvement and Academy of Royal Colleges.

Behn, R.D. (2014) Performance stat. In *The Oxford Handbook of Public Accountability*, edited by Bovens, M., Goodwin, R.E., Schillemans, T. Oxford, UK: Oxford University Press.

Bernthal, P.R. (2003) *Measuring Employee Engagement* [white paper]. Pittsburgh, PA: Development Dimensions International.

Black, C. (2008) Working for a Healthier Tomorrow: Review of the Health of Britain's Working Age Population. Available at: www.workingforhealth.gov .uk/documents/working-for-a-healthier-tomorrow-tagged.pdf (accessed 23 April 2011).

Bohmer, R. (2012) The instrumental value of medical leadership: Engaging doctors in improving services. Available at: www.kingsfund.org.uk /leadershipreview (accessed November 2016).

Chapman, A.L.N., Johnson, D., and Kilner, K. (2014) Leadership styles used by senior medical leaders. *Leadership in Health Services*, 27(4): 283–298.

Collier, P.M. (2008) Performativity, management and governance. In *Managing to Improve Public Services*, edited by Hartley, J., Donaldson, C., Skelcher, C., Wallace, M. Cambridge, UK: Cambridge University Press.

Csoka, L.S. (1997) Bridging the leadership gap: New York: The Conference Board.

Dickinson, H., and Ham, C. (2008) *Engaging Doctors in Leadership: Review of the Literature*. Birmingham, UK: University of Bingham.

Dickinson, H., Ham, C., Snelling, I., and Spurgeon, P. (2012) *Are We There Yet? Models of Medical Leadership and Their Effectiveness: An Exploratory Study.* Southampton, UK: National Institute for Health Service Research, HMSO.

Doran, D., McCutcheon, A.S., Evans, M.G., MacMillan, K., McGillis Hall, L., Pringle, D., Smith, S., and Valente, A. (2004) Impact of the Manager's Span of Control in Leadership and Performance. Edited by Foundation CHSR.

Edmonstone, J., and Western, J. (2002) Leadership development in healthcare: What do we know? *Journal of Management in Medicine*, 16(1): 34–47.

Freeney, Y., and Tiernan, J. (2006) Employee engagement: An overview of the literature on the proposed antithesis to burnout. *Irish Journal of Psychology*, 27(3–4): 130–141.

Guthrie, M. (2005) Engaging physicians in performance improvement. *American Journal of Medical Quality*, 10(5) 235–238.

Ham, C. (2003) Improving the performance of health services: The role of clinical leadership. *Lancet*, 361(9373): 1978. Available at: http://image.thelancet .com/extras/02art8342web.pdf (accessed 23 April 2011).

Ham, C. (2009) *Health Policy in Britain*, 6th ed. Basingstoke: Macmillan.

Ham, C., and Dickenson, H. (2008) *Engaging Doctors in Leadership: Review of the Literature*. Birmingham, UK: HSMC.

Hardacre, J., Cragg, R., Flanagan, H., Spurgeon, P., and Shapiro, J. (2010) Exploring links between NHS leadership and improvement. *International Journal of Leadership in Public Services*, 6(3): 26–37.

Harter, J.K., Schmidt, F.L., and Keyes, C.L.M. (2003) Well-being in the workplace and its relationship to business outcomes: A review of the Gallup studies. In: *Flourishing: Positive Psychology and the Life Well-Lived*, edited by Keyes, C.L.M., Haidt, J. Washington, DC: American Psychological Association; 205–224.

Harter, J.K., Schmidt, F.L., Kilham, E.A., and Asplund, J.W. (2006) *Q12 Meta-analysis*. Washington DC: Gallup Organisation.

Hood, C. (1991) A public management for all seasons? *Public Administration*, 69: 3–9.

Hood, C., and Margetts, H. (2010) The drive to modernise. A world of surprises? In *Paradoxes of Modernisation: Unintended Consequences of Public Policy Reform*, edited by Margetts, H., Hood, C. Oxford, UK: Oxford University Press.

Kahn, W.A. (1990) Psychological conditions of personal engagement and dis-engagement at work. *Academy of Management Journal*, 33: 692–724.

Keroack, M.A., Youngberg, B.J., Cerese, J.L. et al. (2007) Organisational fac-tors associated with high performance in quality and safety in academic medical centers. *Academic Medicine*, 82(12): 1178–1186.

Klein, R. (2010) *The New Politics of the NHS: From Creation to Reinvention*. Oxford, UK: Oxford Radcliffe.

Lega, F., and Sartirana, M. (2015) An international perspective on medical lead-ership. *Future Hospital Journal*, 2(3): 218–220.

Lewis, J.M. (2016) The paradox of health care performance measurement and management. In *The Oxford Handbook of Health Care Management*, edited by Ferlie, E., Montgomery, K., Pedersen, A.R. Oxford, UK: Oxford University Press.

Macleod, D., and Clarke, N. (2009) Engaging for success: Enhancing per-formance through employee engagement. *Department for Business Innovation & Skills*. Available at: www.bis.gov.uk (accessed 23 April 2011).

Mannion, R., Davies, H., and Marshall, M. (2006) Impact of star performance ratings in English acute hospital trusts. *Journal of Health Services Research & Policy*, 10(1): 18–24.

Maslach, C., and Jackson, S.E. (1986) *Maslach Burnout Inventory*, 2nd ed. Palo Alto, CA: Consulting Psychologists Press.

Ovretveit, J. (2005) *The Leaders Role in Quality and Safety Improvement. A Review of Research Guidance*. Stockholm, Sweden: Karolinska Institute.

Reinertsen, J.L., Gosfield, A.G., Rupp, W. et al. (2007) *Engaging Physicians in a Shared Quality Agenda*. Boston, MA: Innovation Series (IHI).

Robinson, D., Perryman, S., and Hayday, S. (2004) *The Drivers of Employee Engagement*. Report 408. Brighton, UK: Institute of Employment Studies.

Salanova, M., Agut, J., and Piero, J.M. (2005) Linking organisational facilitators and work engagement to employee performance and customer loyalty: The mediation of service climate. *Journal of Applied Psychology*, 90: 1217–1227.

Schaufeli, W.B., and Bakker, A.B. (2003) *Utrecht Work Engagement Scale: Preliminary Manual* [version 1]. Utrecht, the Netherlands: Occupational Health Psychology Unit, Utrecht University.

Shipton, H., Armstrong, C., West, M. et al. (2008). The impact of leadership and quality climate on hospital performance. *International Journal for Quality in Health Care*, 20(6): 439–445.

Smith, P.C. (2005) Performance measurement in health care: History, challenges and prospects. *Public Money & Management*, 25(4): 213–220.

Spurgeon, P., Barwell, F., and Mazelan, P. (2008) Developing a medical engagement scale (MES). *International Journal of Clinical Leadership*, 16: 213–223.

Spurgeon, P., and Flanagan, H. (2012) *Leadership Development: Is the Expenditure Justified by the Outcome?* Stafford, UK: Organisational Research and Consultancy Network International.

Spurgeon, P., Long, P., Clark, J., and Daly, F. (2015) Do we need medical leadership or medical engagement? *Leadership in Health Services*, 28(3): 173–184.

Sutherland, A.M., and Dodd, F. (2008) NHS Lanarkshire's leadership development programme's impact on clinical practice. *International Journal of Health Care Quality Assurance*, 21(6): 509–584.

Taitz, J.M., Lee, T.H., and Sequist, T.D. (2011) A framework for engaging physicians in quality and safety. *BMJ Quality and Safety* 21: 722–728.

Toto, D.A. (2005) *What the Doctor Ordered: The Best Hospitals Create Emotional Bands with Their Physicians*. Available at: http://gmj.gallup.com/content/18361/what-doctor-ordered.aspx (accessed 27 May 2011).

Waddell, G., and Burton, A.K. (2006) *Is Work Good for Your Health and Wellbeing?* London: Stationery Office.

Walshe, K. (2011) Managing performance. In *Healthcare Management*, edited by Walshe, K., Smith, J. Berkshire, UK: Open University Press.

West, M., Borrill, C., Dawson, J. et al. (2002) The link between the management of employees and patient mortality in acute hospitals. *International Journal of Human Resource Management*, 13(8): 1299–1310.

West, M., and Dawson, J.F. (2012) *Employee Engagement and NHS Performance*. London: King's Fund.

7

Medical leadership and primary care

VERONICA WILKIE

7.1 INTRODUCTION

It is probably fair to say that discussions of medical leadership, worldwide, have tended to focus on doctors in secondary care. Indeed, in the first edition of this text, greater weight was given to the hospital sector even though we attempted to describe the principles of medical leadership and engagement in a generic way. Jakeman (2004), a general practitioner (GP) himself, reported that the term 'clinical leadership' is not familiar in general practice and indeed was not found in a search of the index of the *British Journal of General Practice*. This, as he asserts, is not necessarily because of the absence of the requisite skills but more to do with the history of general practice, with its individualistic patient focus, personal autonomy (and often isolation) and a weaker sense of the GP's role in the health economy and collective framework.

Increasingly, general practice and community-based care has become recognised as the cornerstone of the whole health system. In the United Kingdom, in particular, the role of GPs in the commissioning process has begun to significantly shift the balance of power. Alongside commissioning the emergence of much larger groupings of general practices into federations has created a new dynamic that may well serve to stimulate a much greater focus on leadership.

Thus, in this second edition, we have included a chapter to capture the role of doctors in all parts of the system, notably primary care, within the ever-changing landscape of more integrated approaches to health and care.

General practice, often described as the "Jewel in the Crown" of the National Health Service (NHS) in the United Kingdom (Marshall, 2015), has evolved from single handed doctors who could opt into general practice with no additional training, most often working out of their own houses and employing spouses to act as receptionist and manager at the start of the NHS. In the United Kingdom, GPs are the most commonly accessed part of the NHS and mostly the first point of contact in an illness (King's Fund, 2009). In the first part of the twentieth century, practice sizes increased, and in the last 20 years, the workforce has expanded, with most practices employing nurses and increasingly clinical pharmacists, healthcare assistants and administrative staff. GPs have moved from generally reactive care in the 1970s to being the main providers of care for long-term chronic illnesses, and increasingly, population health promotion schemes. GPs currently

- Carry out 90% of all NHS contacts
- Prescribe 98% of all medication and manage the repeat prescribing of most drugs whether or not initiated in primary or secondary care. The cost of primary care prescribing was £8.2 billion in 2009
- Manage chronic diseases
- Act as a first point of call for those acutely unwell
- Treat minor illnesses and many carry out minor surgical procedures
- Run screening programs and carry out national immunisation schemes
- Run health promotion clinics (King's Fund, 2009)

All UK residents are able to be registered with a GP, who acts as the gatekeeper to other NHS services with just over 43,000 GPs on the register held by the General Medical Council in the United Kingdom. Not all of these GPs will work full-time; some GPs will share their working week with NHS management or academic positions. GPs have changed from being nearly all full-time, and all being partners in their practices (in the late 1980s), to a mixture of partners, salaried or increasingly holding a portfolio career—as a GP working across many agencies. There is some evidence that the areas with the greatest number of GPs per population have the greatest life expectancy (King's Fund, 2009). GPs have been described as the public face of the health service (Jackson and Burton, 2003).

The Royal College of General Practitioners describe GPs as 'personal doctors, primarily responsible for the provision of comprehensive and continuing generalist care to every individual seeking medical care irrespective of age, sex and state of health'.

7.2 DEVELOPMENT OF MEDICAL LEADERSHIP IN PRIMARY CARE

Whilst significant, general practice is not the whole of primary care. As the population demographics of the United Kingdom age, the number and complexity of community services have grown, with multiple teams of nurses, adding to the traditional district nurse and health visitor roles. These nurses include enhanced care teams, admission prevention teams, nurses and physiotherapists involved in rehabilitation, and advanced care practitioners involved in the care of those in care homes. The rise and complexity of the community nurse mirror the extension of training of nurses in the United Kingdom, with nurses now being trained to examine, diagnose and prescribe. Primary care also includes dental health practitioners, opticians and mental health practitioners.

A recent report for the Commonwealth Fund, comparing the performance of 11 key first world countries, ranked the United Kingdom best on most indicators (Davis et al., 2014). The report demonstrates that although the United Kingdom lags a little in the timeliness of access to healthcare, its accessibility and coverage of all the population make it outrank countries that spend far more on healthcare to less effect.

In 1950, *The Lancet* published a report by J.S. Collings. The author, a research fellow at Harvard University, who had worked as a GP in New Zealand and Canada, had carried out an ethnographic study of general practice. He sat in at 55 practices for four or five days. He described that working conditions 'are bad enough to require condemnation in the public interest'.

He described rural practice as 'an anachronism', suburban practice a 'casualty clearing service' and inner-city practice as "at best...very unsatisfactory and at worst a positive source of public danger" (Collings, 1950). Although criticised at the time (Petchey, 1995), it shook the establishment and almost certainly had an element of truth. General practices were working outside of the managed hospital system and were not managed or understood. This led to the development of group practices and the first 'GP Charter' in 1960. This was the first time the NHS made provision for GP premises and enabled other healthcare workers, mainly district nurses and health visitors, to be housed under one roof. Although Collings was criticising practice, he was also indirectly criticising the leadership. He was observing a role that had morphed from single practitioners in the community to the early group practices, with no unifying order than the need to process the patients they saw.

Over the next 10 years, the practices started to become more multi-professional and as such started to develop the need for better management. District nurses started to work as practice nurses, and receptionists started to take on quasi-management roles as the groups of clinicians started to expand.

Although GPs had an informal training scheme that emerged in the 1960, it wasn't until 1981, after the vocational training Act of 1977, that all GPs had to do recognised postgraduate training and passing a professional examination of competence was not mandatory until 2007.

As the decades from 1980s passed, general practice became increasingly accountable and the need for its services to be managed developed. In 1989, the white paper 'Working for patients' paved the way for GPs to be formally contracted, enabling them to be more directly accountable for the costs of providing care and introduced targets for key services such as immunisation, cervical cytology and at the time the provision of health promotion clinics. They were also, for the first time, rewarded for attendance at education sessions, the system acknowledging that there was a need for GPs to keep up to date, and some funding was made to recognise the need to take time out. The NHS had designated Family Health Service Authorities (FHSAs) as the accountable body for the provision of care for their population. General practices started to expand their management structures as the need to count and collate their activities was needed in order for them to be paid. Initially, the GP was responsible for the finances, often but not always the senior partner, with a practice manager having a more administrative role. As practices expanded and the complexity of their services changed, practice managers managed more and the GP partners did less of the detail and tended to have a more strategic leadership view. This leadership view was focused around the need for the practice to be financially efficient—as the GPs were not budget-carrying salaried staff but took home a profit share once all the practice expenses (staff salaries, rent, professional fees, costs of vaccine, and information technology [IT] systems) had been deducted.

In the last decade of the twentieth century, the NHS moved with other parts of the public sector to leadership based on aspects of private sector 'business management', described by some as 'New Public Management'. This placed the responsibility for organisational policy, success and efficiency on the managers (Farham and Horton, 1999). GPs were able to hold budgets if their practices were above a certain size (Fundholding Practices) and their practices had to become increasingly business-like. Practice managers became increasingly professionally trained, often working alongside fund managers and business managers with larger numbers of practice administrative staff. As the skills of the managers increased, the leadership skills of the GPs needed to become more focused.

A report by the National Audit office concluded that fundholding had brought about only small improvements in healthcare and that it had led to practices developing services in isolation, often at the expense of services to neighbouring practices (Audit Commission, 1996; Le Grand et al., 1998). Concerns by the public about a two-tier service led the labour government of the time to a change in policy in 1997. The white paper 'The new NHS modern and dependable' sought to deliver healthcare based on partnership driven by performance. Its five key principles were as follows:

- To renew the NHS as a genuinely national service
- To make the delivery of the NHS against these national standards a matter of local responsibility
- To get the NHS to work in partnership and forge stronger links with local authorities
- To shift the focus so that excellence was guaranteed to all patients
- To rebuild public confidence in the NHS

The internal market in healthcare evolved to an orientation towards one of integrated care and described a 10-year evolution rather than a sudden change (Department of Health, 2003). Evidence started to emerge that highly integrated primary care systems that emphasised continuity and coordination of care were associated with better patient experience (Starfield, 1998).

7.3 EMERGING MANAGERIAL AND LEADERSHIP SYSTEMS

In 1999, the management of GPs and their budgets was carried out by Primary Care Groups (PCGs). These 481 bodies across England (Scotland and Northern

Ireland and Wales continued to manage health as one entity rather than separating out primary and secondary care), meaning primary and community health services, were managed within one budget. PCGs, for the first time, had GPs who spent a significant amount of time leading and being responsible for the budget for primary health services. GPs started to take time out, increasingly dropping a full time commitment clinically and within their practices to develop a career in NHS management. Very few had much training, often relying on confidence, communication skills and enthusiasm rather than intimate experience of managing a complex healthcare system. Where PCGs worked well, the managers and clinicians worked together as leaders sharing their relative expertise. As the PCGs demonstrated that they were able to be accountable for their budgets, they became more independent Primary Care Trusts (PCTs). A few GPs previously had advisor roles with FHSAs but were now taking on more significant leadership roles and designing the delivery of healthcare. Primary Care Organisations also started to develop nurse leaders, particularly needed as the community staff were employed and developed according to local need.

We see here clear parallels with the secondary care sector a decade or more previously with some medical staff beginning to undertake managerial tasks, followed by the emergence of formal roles such as lead clinician and clinical director. Often, the development of these roles in both secondary and primary care was not always officially marked but a consequence of changing demands and tasks where clinical staff were best placed to do them.

A research study in 2001 which surveyed PCG chief executives identified that their three greatest achievements were building relationships with primary care professionals, getting the board (which included GPs and primary care nurses) to work as a corporate group and using this to develop the organisation (Wilkin et al., 2001). This survey found evidence that by the second year, GPs were more supportive but that there was more work needed to involve the primary care workforce. All of the PCGs felt that lack of management workforce was an obstacle to a move to PCT status and management of organisational development, the system of rewarding and paying practices was starting to get more and more complex and the business of managing community teams and commissioning healthcare more structured.

At the time this report was being published, there was a drive to increase the size of populations covered by PCGs as they became PCTs, and that the additional management time was spent commissioning and organising hospital provision as well as managing resources.

Looking back over reports at the time, there was already a tension between the need to have some central control (in order to ensure a fair access to high quality services) and the ability to empower local clinicians whilst retaining some autonomy. In 2001, the NHS launched the NHS Modernisation Authority, and the then health Secretary stated that this would give more power to frontline staff (Wise, 2001). PCTs formed from merged PCGs with a continued need for there to be leadership by GPs and primary care staff. As GPs became more accountable for their care and the workload increased, the British Medical Association's then chairman reflected that 'anything that involves taking doctors away from their patients is going to increase the workforce and workload problems that are already there. Local decision making will only work if generous resources are provided locally to allow that process to continue' (Wise, 2001).

Again, the conflict in perspectives and roles as seen in Chapters 3 and 4 is reflected in the evolution of managerial roles in primary care. Management and leadership are viewed as a distraction from professional values and, thereby, patient care. The requirement for these tasks to be done was largely seen as a workload challenge rather than how could high-quality primary care management really contribute to improved care.

The way in which GPs were paid began to diverge from the late 1990s. Some practices had opted to get their budget through a Personal Medical Service (PMS) budget as opposed to a more traditional General Medical Service (GMS) budget. With the former, the need for claiming for defined activity markers was removed, enabling a one-off budget based on audits and previous activities. GPs and their practice managers had become very adept at looking at the economic benefits of each system; the PMS budget enabled GP practices to employ salaried GPs rather than its entire medical workforce being profit share partners in a body that was still an independently contracted organisation. As a result, by 2007, the number of salaried doctors in general practice rose from 846 in 1987 to 6022 (The Information Centre, 2008). The proportion of salaried GPs has continued to rise by over 200% in the decade to 2013 (BMA, 2014). This complexity of how each of the 7000 + practices were paid again led to a shift in how practices and their contracting organisations were working. GP practice managers often met together in joint meetings with the PCTs, a change from a decade before when only the GPs would have attended. PCTs needed to recognise the individuality of practice populations and practices whilst trying to ensure equal access and quality of care. Directors of primary care in the PCTs had teams of managers and clinical advisors working with them. Their mandate had increased and was moving away from a more passive payment of GP services against a very prescribed set of rules to one of managing the workforce and commissioning services reflecting the need of local populations.

In 2004, the contract changed again for general practices. The need for GPs to provide out-of-hours care 24 hours a day 7 days a week was removed and contracted separately by PCTs. Funding for the GP practices changed; all practices (whether GMS or PMS) had to take part in the Quality and Outcomes Framework (QoF). Practices were to be rewarded for providing "good" care across a whole range of activities, mainly the management of long-term conditions, but at the start also for practice organisations. The 2004 contract provided the possibility of each practice getting up to 1050 points in order to regain 40% of the income that had been removed, and the income was calculated according to prevalence of a condition and clinical indicators. Efficient practices actively sought to find the practice population of certain diseases and started to increase the diversity of the workforce. Significant increases in practice nurses were observed, and this drove the general practice workforce to adopt universal coverage of use of computerised patient records. This new contract was for the whole United Kingdom, initially supervised by PCTs in England, Health Boards in Scotland, Regional Boards in Northern Ireland and Local Health Boards in Wales.

Nationally, the NHS started to collect data on chronic diseases and certain related activities, and the data were extracted electronically. PCTs were charged with providing leadership to narrow the gap between the best- and worst-performing practices, and for the first few years, a system to ensure good governance and probity was established.

Since its introduction, the QoF points have been reduced and changed, and alternative methods of payment were devised for services delivered outside of an ill-defined core contract through Local Enhanced Services and Direct Enhanced Services. Practices that were organised and well led were therefore able to make the most of funding. However, practices in areas of great deprivation and therefore greater prevalence of ill health had to work harder.

The aspect of performance management, linked to patient care workers, was essentially externally initiated—government and overall NHS management. Just as in the 1990s, the centralised target setting in secondary care was much resented, so too it seemed an intrusion in primary care. But as we have commented before, this was really a societal change where accountability into professional domains was carried out on behalf of a more demanding public. The demand upon practices to meet targets of course also drove the establishment of better systems of infrastructure to accomplish the task.

7.4 CLINICAL COMMISSIONING GROUPS AND THE RISE OF GPs AS MEDICAL LEADERS

In 2010, the then Health Secretary Andrew Lansley presented a white paper to the House of Commons, 'Equity and Excellence: Liberating the NHS' (Secretary of State for Health, 2010). Its initial aim was to retain the commissioning of care done by the GPs who were closest to the patient and to introduce a focus on clinical outcomes, but also to start to work to merge health and social care, particularly in the community, and to equalise GP practice funding. The first draft stated clearly that 'healthcare will be run from the bottom up, with ownership and decision making in the hands of professionals and patients'. This also continued the progression of market-led forces with hospitals continuing to be funded through a payment by results system. Public health was separated from Health (Public Health England) and co-located in Local Authorities, whereas before they had formed a central role in PCTs.

There was an initial outcry; GPs were thought not to be capable of managing complex budgets and huge concerns over the ability of services to be commissioned by the private sector. The political aim was to continue to increase competition in healthcare provision, and those concerned felt that the disintegration would lead to problems in patient flow and funding and actually decrease efficiency in delivery. After a review and a 'listening exercise' because of the public and professional outcry in 2011, the Health and Social Care Act 2012 came into force. It covers only England (the other three devolved nations continued with a jointly managed system). Clinical Commissioning Groups (CCGs) were to have control over the budgets for most of secondary care and community services; community services had been or were in the process of becoming separately funding and accountable providers of healthcare—commissioners were to be independent of provision of services. Funding of general practice itself and its oversight were to remain with NHS England. In particular, the bill paved the way for the ability of CCGs to put services out to tender outside the NHS usual providers, as 'any qualified providers'.

In addition to CCGs (a change from GP commissioning groups, as other clinicians felt that these would not reflect the diversity of clinicians), the Act established an independent NHS Commissioning Board, established new local authority health and well-being boards and developed Monitor as the economic regulator. All of the British Medical Colleges voiced huge concerns. The Royal College of General Practitioners stated that it felt this bill would significantly destabilise the NHS, and several specialist Medical Royal Colleges felt that there was insufficient specialist input into decision making (Ham, 2012).

The change in the structure of the commissioning bodies to being GP led and the board having a significant number of GPs in its makeup led to many GPs becoming mostly full-time managers and leaders of healthcare—although some retained some clinical work, this was rarely as a GP partner (which was a shift from GP involvement in PCTs). The importance of this should not be underestimated as many more GPs became more engaged in the planning, commissioning and running of primary care just as their secondary care colleagues had in previous decades. It should be noted again that just as this demand and involvement escalated, there was a significant shortfall in training and development of GPs in the skill needed to do these tasks.

A study carried out by the Nuffield Trust and the King's Fund published in 2015 (Holder et al., 2015) found that

- The sustainability of clinical involvement in commissioning was at risk due to waning levels of GP leader engagement in CCGs, potential problems in recruitment and retention of leaders and significant pressures on GPs, time and capacity.
- Initial enthusiasm among GP leaders waned as they perceived they had insufficient support time and resources.
- The researchers observed that the complex external environment of NHS England with tight deadlines and at times inefficient internal governance made engaging the member voice difficult.

In addition, the CCGs faced a 10% budget cut, and in 2016, increased commissioning tasks, including the performance and management of primary care, were added to their responsibilities. They remain as in their outset a membership body—joining a CCG is mandatory for general practices, who are supposed to be represented by the CCG. Holder et al. (2015) identified largely stable levels of GP engagement in their first year, which was higher than any previous NHS organisational models. It still showed a disparity with the CCG view of engagement and the member's sense. CCGs were working hard to commission in a falling economy and needing GPs to take on more of the work as it shifted to the community. GPs were then contracted by an ever distant NHS management system but also managed by the local CCG. GPs and practice managers were spending more and more time chasing and organising payments as well as trying to keep up with the rising demand for access.

Although measurement of activity in other parts of the NHS has become increasingly sophisticated, the NHS stopped counting GP activity in 2009. Management of the whole system as changes were made to shift care from the acute sector to the community sector has been incompletely assessed, with the impact on general practice workload a missing factor. As a result, GPs and their teams have found a significant increase in workload that has, until 2015/2016, gone unrecorded and unmeasured as the drive to manage more people in the community increased. Managers in commissioning bodies were assessed according to key performance indicators and the activity of the primary care staff against referral numbers, attendances at emergency departments (A&E), quality of chronic disease management without any means of understanding the impact on general practice or influence to support the practices (Baird, 2016; Wilkie and Ralphs, 2016).

Holder et al. surveyed the extent of leadership training for CCG leaders. Only 35% of governing board GP members and practice representatives felt that they had received the training and development needs to fulfil their role—46% felt they had the support necessary to make robust decisions. A number of challenges were identified between wearing 'practice hat' and 'corporate hat':

> I think one of the things I hadn't taken account of is how much this was to do with people and politics with a small p... So I think what I hadn't realised was just how much it would be about making sure that you have healthy, balanced relationships, not colluding, and the whole healthy challenge thing is quite tricky, and all of those things have been new. (GP governing body member) (Holder et al., 2015)

7.5 CHANGING LEADERSHIP ROLE OF THE GP IN THE PRACTICE

In 2007, the Royal College of General Practitioners published a paper on the future direction of general practice (Royal College of General Practitioners, 2007). It offered a vision of the future GP role to design and coordinate pathways spanning healthcare providers and teams of clinicians, echoing the white paper that led to the Health and Social Care Act, 2012. The historical role of the GP working with individual patients on a personal basis and based on good continuity of care was replaced by new roles for GPs, who have to translate this working with interdisciplinary health teams (community and specialist care) and increasingly with local authorities and other providers of healthcare, financial directors and regulatory bodies. The Care Quality Commission (CQC), which started to examine practices in 2015 (in England only), has established that the vast majority of practices it inspected were good or outstanding (the biggest proportion of any health sector), providing a crude indication that GP practices as small organisations are able, at least according to the CQC standards, to provide good or outstanding care to their patients.

Giordano (2015), in a paper exploring the leadership roles of the future GP, suggests that these should include the following:

- Change management at the practice level
- Strategic management and planning (particularly for the development of consortia and federations)
- Building leadership capacity among GPs to support lagging GP practices
- Knowing how to interact with news media
- Influencing local and national politicians
- Influencing policy
- Serving on and chairing boards at both the consortia and secondary care levels
- Knowing how to work effectively with management and knowing when/how to use managerial support
- Having excellent financial management skills
- Building teams within and across organisational and functional boundaries

Giordano recognises that GPs must work in organisations that need to have the following:

- An organisational ability to self-organise quickly
- An organisational ability to learn and adapt
- A willingness to engender leadership behaviours in everyone at all levels and function of the organisation
- A culture of innovation
- The ability, among all parties, to understand at once the local context—from a unit as small as the office visit to the big picture (national policy)—and their place in it

Giordano's paper nicely captures the transition of general practice and primary care to a managed system from an individualised provision focus. The tasks outlined are likely to be found in different contexts in many organisations. The managerial and leadership overlay on these tasks is obvious and serves to emphasise that GPs with the requisite leadership skills will be crucial to determining future success (or not) in primary care provision. The challenge for general practice is to recognise this position and equip its members appropriately.

In 2014, NHS England published a *Five Year Forward View of the NHS*. It recognised that the silo funding of providers is struggling to provide care for a population that spans primary, secondary and tertiary care and that greater integration is needed between health and social care, between family doctors and specialists and between physical and mental health. The strategy points to a direction of integrated healthcare horizontally (primary care and community health trusts) or vertically (primary care and secondary care trusts) and sets out the direction for commissioners to commission services according to place (or geographic population) rather than from an organisation. It makes a commitment for 'far more care to be delivered locally' (NHS, 2014) and sets out plans for GPs to combine with nurses and hospital specialists to become a Multi-Specialty Community Provider and a Primary and Acute Care System (integrated hospital and primary care system).

Rising workload (increase in clinical workload of 16% from 2007, 99.6% increase in telephone consultations; Hobbs et al., 2016) and the distance of NHS England as a manager and commissioner of GP services have led to a reduction in GP funding from 11% to 8.4%. Increasing numbers of GPs were retiring, and for several years, GP training posts had remained unfilled. The NHS chief executive, Simon Stevens, acknowledges the problems in primary care and has published a new deal or a five-year forward view for general practice in 2016. This strategy recognises the need to increase recruitment of new GPs, increase retention of those who are thinking of leaving by streamlining work demands, changing the regulation and providing support for burnout and stress. He also stresses that GP practices need to continue to work hard to develop larger organisations either as collectives of many practices through federations or 'super partnerships'. Hospitals are no longer able to pass on administrative duties to GPs, nor is the action required to cut demand on GP practices the sole responsibility of the primary care sector.

The document also sets the challenge that GPs must work collaboratively with an emerging set of health professionals, nurses, physician associates, paramedics and clinical pharmacists to make sure that the right person is seeing the right patient at the right time. For the first time, the problem of working and staffing rural general practice is recognised.

This means that GPs in practices will no longer be able to look to their own tasks but will have to develop skills of leadership and of followership in larger organisations.

The fund also recognises the need to develop other healthcare staff members to take some of the workload from GPs, which will need skills in organisation learning, safety culture and greater team working, alongside the need to integrate IT and newer systems of care to streamline processes.

General practice and medical leadership in primary care have never been more necessary as the shape of healthcare services start to change to larger, integrated teams and away from the partnership model of general practice. Emerging leaders will need to harness skills in adaptability, distributive or shared leadership in order to continue to provide a safe healthcare system where those who have the greatest need can still have continuity in their care. The healthcare system can manage rising demand and the demographic time bomb in a digital age.

REFERENCES

Audit Commission (1996) *What the Doctor Ordered. A Study of GP Fundholders in England and Wales.* London: HMSO.

Baird, B. (2016) *Pressure in General Practice.* King's Fund. Available at: http://www.kingsfund.org.uk/projects/pressures-in-general-practice (accessed 9 April 2017).

BMA (2014) *General Practice in the UK*. Available at: file:///C:/Users/wilv3/Down loads/PressBriefingGeneralPracticeInTheUK_July2014_v2%20(3).pdf (accessed 9 April 2017).

Collings, J.S. (1950) General practice in England today: A reconnaissance. *The Lancet*, 255(6604): 547–549.

Davis, K., Stremikis, K., Squires, D., and Schoen, C. (2014) *Mirror, Mirror on the Wall. How the Performance of the US Health Care System Compares*. Available at: http://www.commonwealthfund.org/~/media/files/publications /fund-report/2014/jun/1755_davis_mirror_mirror_2014.pdf (accessed 9 April 2017).

Department of Health (2003) *The New NHS: Modern Dependable: Executive Summary*. Available at: http://webarchive.nationalarchives.gov.uk/+/www.dh .gov.uk/en/Publicationsandstatistics/Publications/AnnualReports/Browsable /DH_4916362 (accessed 9 April 2017).

Farham, D., and Horton, S. (1999) Managing public and private organisations. In *Public Management in Britain*, edited by Horton, S., Farham, D. London: Macmillan; 44.

Giordano, R. (2015) *The Leadership Challenge for General Practice in England*. King's Fund. Available at: http://www.kingsfund.org.uk/sites/files/kf /Leadership_challenge_for_general_practice.pdf (accessed 9 April 2017).

Ham, C. (2012) What will the health and social care Bill mean for the NHS in England. *BMJ*, 344: e2159.

Hobbs, R. et al. (2016) Clinical workload in UK primary care; a retrospective analysis of 100 million consultations in England, 2007–14. *The Lancet Online*. Available at: http://dx.doi.org/10.1016/S0140-6736(16)00620-6 (accessed 9 April 2017).

Holder, H., Robertson, R., Ross, S., Bennett, L. et al. (2015) *Risk or Reward? The Changing Role of CCGs in General Practice*. Available at: http:// www.kingsfund.org.uk/sites/files/kf/field/field_publication_file/risk-or -reward-the-changing-role-of-CCGs-in-general-practice.pdf (accessed 9 April 2017).

Jackson, N., and Burton, J. (2003) The practice as a learning organisation. In *Work Based Learning in Primary Care*, edited by Burton, J., Jackson, N. Abingdon, VA: Radcliffe.

Jakeman, P. (2004) Clinician leadership in general practice. *Clinician in Management*, 12: 117–122.

King's Fund (2009) *General Practice: An Overview*. Available at: http://www .kingsfund.org.uk/sites/files/kf/general-practice-in-england-overview -sarah-gregory-kings-fund-september-2009.pdf (accessed 9 April 2017).

Le Grand, J., Mays, N., and Mulligan, J. (1998) *Learning from the NHS Internal Market: A Review of the Evidence*. London: King's Fund.

Marshall, M. (2015) International healthcare systems: A precious jewel—the role of general practice in the English NHS. *New England Journal of Medicine*, 372: 823–897.

NHS (2014) *Five Year Forward Review.* Available at: https://www.england.nhs
.uk/wp-content/uploads/2014/10/5yfv-web.pdf (accessed 9 April 2017).

Petchey, R. (1995) Collings report on general practice in England in 1950;
unrecognised pioneering piece of British Social Research? *British Medical
Journal,* 311:40–42.

Royal College of General Practitioners (2007) *The Future Direction of General
Practice, A Roadmap.* London: RCGP. Available at: http://www.rcgp.org.uk
/policy/rcgp-policy-areas/future-direction-of-general-practice-a-roadmap
.aspx (accessed 9 April 2017).

Secretary of State for Health (2010) *Equity and Excellence: Liberating the
NHS.* Available at: https://www.gov.uk/government/uploads/system/uploads
/attachment_data/file/213823/dh_117794.pdf (accessed 9 April 2017).

Starfield, B. (1998) *Primary Care: Balancing Health Needs, Services and
Technology.* Oxford, UK: Oxford University Press.

The Information Centre (2008) *General and Personal Medical Services England
1997–2007.* Leeds: The Information Centre. Available at: http://www
.hscic.gov.uk/catalogue/PUB00880/nhs-staf-gen-prac-1997-2007-rep1.pdf
(accessed 9 April 2017).

Wilkie, V., and Ralphs, A. (2016) The pressures on general practice. *BMJ,* 11:
353.

Wilkin, D., Gillam, S., and Smith, K. (2001) Tackling organisational change in the
new NHS. *BMJ,* 322(7300): 1464–1467.

Wise, J. (2001) Milburn proposes to decentralise the NHS. *BMJ,* 5(7294): 322.

8

Appraisal and revalidation

8.1 INTRODUCTION

It is evident that those health organisations with effective medical engagement are typified by cultures that adapt good human resource management practices for all staff, not just doctors. In the past, appraisal of doctors has been either non-existent or a low priority. With the advent of revalidation of doctors every five years, it now demands a more rigorous and professional approach. It is setting an example as to how the performance and aspirations of other health staff might be more effectively reviewed. However, it has also added significantly to the workload of medical leaders.

The responsibilities of medical leaders have significantly grown from the early days of a handful of doctors accepting, often reluctantly, to represent their colleagues to management. As we have outlined in earlier chapters, many doctors in both primary and secondary care have assumed greater leadership responsibilities as the governance arrangements for the National Health Service (NHS) have evolved. These responsibilities have increased in line with the greater emphasis on commissioning, regulation and the increased focus on quality and safety. High-profile reviews into poorly performing hospitals have highlighted that, on a few occasions, a very small number of doctors have been allowed to continue delivering unsafe care, without challenge.

Until the early part of this century, doctors were not routinely appraised. There was a general sense of accountability to their patients and to their royal college but not one of accountability to their organisation. Other health staff had been subject to appraisal or performance reviews for many years, although it is fair to say that rigour and frequency were highly variable. At various times, managers had the opportunity to earn performance-related bonuses as part of reward packages. Hospital doctors had historically been considered by their peers for bonuses through a national system of distinction awards ranging from A+ for the most highly regarded clinician through to a C award. This scheme was established at the time of the start of the NHS in 1948 as part of the broader negotiation to gain support from doctors. However, only about 50% consultants were beneficiaries of this system and there were many who were critical of the non-transparent and secretive nature of the process, which tended to reward those consultants working in teaching hospitals and the so-called more glamorous specialties.

A modified system of discretionary points for performance and assuming additional responsibilities was developed before the current system of Clinical Excellence Awards was introduced in 2003. These differ between the home countries, but all the schemes are intended to reward consultants who show commitment to the NHS and are assessed against five domains. One of these is to explicitly recognise leadership and management, which reaffirms the value that the profession has given to the changing role of clinicians. The other domains include assessments around delivering and developing high-quality services, research and innovation and teaching and training.

When the first edition of this book was published in 2011, reference was made to the General Medical Council's (GMC's) plans to introduce revalidation of doctors. There was a sense at that time that the process to get agreement on the process was funereal and many commentators were not convinced that there was sufficient commitment to implementation. Since then, revalidation has been introduced and is now becoming very much part of a doctor's normal role. Perhaps, in the not too distant future, it will not be seen as a leading-edge initiative for the medical profession and the NHS and more as a routine part of being a good doctor and healthcare.

Therefore, we decided to include a new chapter on appraisal and revalidation in this edition as the United Kingdom is the first country to introduce mandatory revalidation of doctors. It is therefore another important step in reinforcing the importance of medical leadership and engagement. The journey from all doctors being autonomous and independent with just a few taking on representative positional leadership roles to having executive responsibility has been taken to a new level. Some medical leaders as Responsible Officers (ROs) now have the responsibility for assessing their peers' competence to continue practising. The importance of this new responsibility should not be underestimated.

8.2 REVALIDATION IMPLEMENTATION

Revalidation is an important element of a wider range of quality improvement initiatives that have been introduced in the NHS over the past decade or so. It applies to all licensed doctors in all parts of the health system. Each employing organisation, including locum medical agencies, has to appoint an RO who is responsible for ensuring that there are effective appraisal and clinical governance systems in place. In most Trusts, this is the responsibility of the medical director, which adds significantly to their leadership workload and responsibility. Whilst many other doctors within the organisation will have been trained to be competent appraisers of their peers, it is the RO who makes the final recommendation every five years, normally to the GMC, around a doctor's 'fitness to practice'. It is anticipated that an individual doctor will undertake between 5 and 20 appraisals a year to maintain an appropriate level of quality and consistency. A doctor should not normally have more than three consecutive appraisals with the same appraiser.

As we have argued elsewhere in the book, doctors are uniquely equipped to assess variations in clinical practice and outcomes. As Professor Bruce Keogh, NHS Medical Director, so aptly stated in the Foreword to the first edition:

> In healthcare provider organisations the quality of clinical leadership always underpins the difference between exceptional or adequate or pedestrian clinical services which in aggregate determine the overall effectiveness, safety and reputation of every healthcare organisation. Similarly, effective clinical leadership in commissioning organisations brings perspectives and challenge which in turn drives up clinical quality for the whole health economy. (Keogh, 2011)

The King's Fund Report (2014) *Medical Revalidation: From Compliance to Commitment* confirms, 'The journey to medical revalidation began in June 2000, when the General Medical Council (GMC) published a consultation document *Revalidating Doctors; Ensuring Standards, Securing the Future* (GMC, 2000)'. Proposals for revalidation were subsequently published in *Trust, Assurance and Safety: The Regulation of Health Professionals in the 21st Century* (Department of Health, 2007). It became a statutory obligation for all employing organisations in December 2012. Whilst the United Kingdom is the first country to introduce mandatory revalidation of doctors, others are looking to try and replicate the process, but from the authors' personal experiences, the reaction from doctors in some other countries suggests that there would be major resistance!

The chief medical officer of Health's report *Good Doctors, Safer Patients* (Department of Health, 2006) was an important stage in the consultation process, and as Thistlewaite and Spencer (2008) suggest (paragraph 44 of the final chapter is worth quoting in full):

> It is important to ensure that the concept of medical regulation is not limited to the identification of poor practice. Arguably, debate and effort have concentrated on designing a system to deliver this objective, and thus the discussion on the future of medical regulation has been more negative and confrontational than it needed to be. Although one of the prime purposes of medical regulation must be to protect the safety of patients, it must also be the true guardian of professionalism. The regulatory system must be able to demonstrate that all practising doctors reach specified standards, which may themselves evolve over time to reflect changes in patterns of work, technology and the expectations of society.

The GMC's *Good Medical Practice* (2013) and updated in 2014 is the key document that outlines the duties of a doctor. The framework consists of four domains that cover the whole spectrum of medical practice:

- Knowledge, skills and performance
- Safety and quality
- Communication, partnership and teamwork
- Maintaining trust

Each domain is described by three attributes that relate to practices or principles of the profession as a whole.

To maintain a licence to practice, doctors have to demonstrate through the revalidation process that they work in line with the principles and values set out in the guidance in *Good Medical Practice*, emphasising that serious or persistent failure to follow this guidance will put registration at risk.

The Department of Health (2011) guide for health leaders preparing for the introduction of medical revalidation states:

> revalidation will be based on a local evaluation of doctors' practice through appraisal, and its purpose is to affirm good practice. By doing so, it will assure patients and public, employers, other healthcare providers, and other health professionals that licensed doctors are practising to the appropriate professional standards, it will also complement other systems that exist within organisations and at other levels for monitoring standards of care and recognising and responding to concerns about doctors' practice.

The GMC lays down some revalidation requirements for doctors, that is, they must

- Be taking part in an annual appraisal process
- Have completed at least one appraisal based on good medical practice
- Have collected and reflected on all six types of supporting information

The six types of supporting information that doctors are required to provide and discuss at their appraisal at least once in each five-year cycle are as follows:

- Continuing professional development
- Quality improvement activity
- Significant events
- Feedback from colleagues
- Feedback from patients
- Review of complaints and compliments

Regular appraisal of doctors has been an integral element of life for postgraduate trainees for many years. Annual appraisals of consultants has been a requirement for consultants since 2001 and for general practitioners since 2002. In Chapter 6, we discussed the relationship between medical engagement and clinical and organisational performance. It is very clear that effective appraisal is one of the important elements of what makes doctors feel valued and engaged and contributes to higher performance.

Whilst being applied to trainee appraisals, the raison d'etre offered by Craven (2015) is particularly relevant to the appraisal of all doctors:

> Appraisals are essential to ensure (trainees) progress through learning and skill acquisition and they are an on-going process looking at mainly education and development needs. An appraisal looks at current performance as well as future personal and training requirements. Appraisals are a two way process benefitting both the individual being appraised and the personal develop in which they work or study.

The Faculty of Medical Leadership and Management (FMLM) undertook a qualitative study of four NHS Trusts in London and South of England in mid-2014 to try and identify the factors that contributed to low appraisal rates and their implications. *Understanding the Drivers of Appraisal Rates within Acute Trusts* (FMLM, 2014) commented that, whilst annual appraisal had been compulsory for over a decade and despite its centrality to medical revalidation, appraisal rates remained variable. Referring to the annual organisational audit, it appeared that completed appraisals was, on average, 80% in 2014 compared with 67% in 2013 amongst acute hospitals. However, the report highlighted that 'averaged figures disguise large variation in appraisal rates between organisations, staff grade, associate specialty doctors and those on short-term contracts had particularly low appraisal rates' (FMLM, 2014, p. 4).

The report offered 10 recommendations for improving rates for appraisals. These are important if appraisal and revalidation are to achieve the desired goals around clinical governance, quality of care and fitness to practice rather than a bureaucratic "tick-box" process to be completed.

1. It is important to have the right people in the right jobs with the right support, that is, time and resources.
2. A supportive and informed board is important to ensure that appraisal receives the resources and priority required.
3. Organisations should learn from best practice of exemplars.
4. Tailored training and support should be given to those doctors who are not engaged and committed to appraisal.
5. Incentives based around resourcing of personal development plans should be made available for those who demonstrate real commitment to using appraisal to improve clinical outcomes and vice versa.
6. Doctors with multiple roles and organisations should, in principle, have only one professional appraisal.
7. Wherever possible, a standard system of appraisal should be adopted within each organisation.

8. Each organisation needs to have a sufficient pool of well-trained appraisers.
9. Specialised information technology (IT) appraisal management systems should be adopted.
10. Whilst the appraisal rate increased from 2013 to 2014 and needed to achieve 100%, the focus should now shift to assuring the quality of appraisal. The FMLM report concluded that

> People, rather than for example IT systems, are considered to be the most important factor in determining appraisal rates. It is clearly important that Trusts put the right people in the right positions. The Board must be supportive, the RO must show leadership, the appraisal lead must be visible and must engage with their peers, the revalidation/appraisal administrator must be organised and must reduce the burden on the other team members. The doctors themselves are not a homogenous group. Some are more easily engaged than others and their reasons for non-engagement are varied. Some need to have their expectations reset while others need to be supported through difficult personal or professional periods. (FMLM, 2014, p. 13)

This study and report came at a very important point in the implementation of revalidation and, as the work by the King's Fund confirms (discussed next), process is important in getting appraisal and revalidation in place in every organisation, but much more needs to be done to make it achieve its purpose of improving clinical outcomes, quality and confirming fitness to practice.

The King's Fund undertook a small research study of the experiences and reflections of ROs in London in 2013. *Making Revalidation Work; What Have We Learnt so Far* was published in October 2013. This formed the basis for a wider qualitative study into the impact to date of medical revalidation on the behaviour of doctors and the culture of organisations within seven case studies across England. These included two primary care area teams, two secondary care trusts, a mental health trust, an independent provider and a locum agency. *Medical Revalidation: From Compliance to Commitment* was published by the King's Fund in March 2014 (King's Fund, 2014).

The study acknowledged that it was early days for revalidation but commented that designated bodies, appraisees and appraisers were focused on implementing the process of revalidation, including new processes, formalised appraisal systems and increased adherence to policies and statutory requirements. This appeared to mean that there was less focus on its potential contribution to quality improvement which 'impacts on patient care and individual professional development' (King's Fund, 2014, p. 1).

The report concluded that 'medical revalidation, with the right conditions, can be a valuable driver of behaviours and cultures that support sustained quality improvement. The time to develop these conditions is now' (King's Fund, 2014, p. 27).

The GMC commissioned a review of revalidation in early 2016. The interim Umbrella Report (GMC, 2016) reports that 90% of respondents had had an appraisal but only about one third believed that revalidation had had a somewhat or very positive impact on the appraisal process.

The study also explored how ROs fulfilled their statutory function of advising the GMC about doctors' fitness to practise and what support they have in this role. ROs appear to reach their revalidation recommendations in a variety of ways. These included a review of the case documentation, such as appraisal summaries, prior to deciding their revalidation recommendation. Other approaches included discussing with someone else or within a formal group or confirming the revalidation recommendation of someone else. What is clear is that revalidation is a significant consumer of time for ROs and other medical leaders. This clearly depends on the size of the organisation and extent of support structures.

Revalidation is therefore a demanding process that it could be argued might only lead to a few doctors having their licence to practice withdrawn. Indeed, it could be argued that employers should not wait for the five-yearly revalidation process to reach that point. But, this would miss the more important point that without validation, regular appraisals around the four domains that cover the spectrum of medical practice would probably continue to be an ad hoc and variable exercise. The medical profession is leading the way in the NHS in taking appraisal seriously. It is time that the same rigour was applied to all other health and care staff.

As we explored in Chapter 6, one of the sub-scales of the Medical Engagement Scale relates to appraisals and rewards being effectively aligned. Clark and Nath (2014) reviewed four Trusts with high levels of medical engagement. It was very evident that each of them had well-developed appraisal and revalidation processes and used them to help identify future medical leaders. These trusts and an increasing number of others see appraisal and revalidation as part of a much broader cultural approach that genuinely values management and leadership. It includes appointing consultants who demonstrate at interview leadership capabilities and then providing development support in the initial months following appointment. They use appraisal to review leadership interests and capabilities and ensure that opportunities are afforded to build their leadership contribution and development. Such Trusts are also typified by offering junior doctors opportunities to build their leadership capabilities particularly around service improvement. Appraisal is therefore an integral part of the organisation's culture and contributes to the identification of those clinicians with the interest and capability to assume leadership roles. Whilst appraisal can be seen as a time-demanding and bureaucratic process, in some organisations, it is evident that when undertaken in a dynamic and ongoing way, it can be a major contributor to the identification and development of clinical leaders from an early stage and help to create a much more distributed leadership culture. Effective medical leadership and engagement are key features of high-performing health organisations and the contribution that appraisal can make to this goal should not be underestimated.

REFERENCES

Clark, J., and Nath, V. (2014) *Medical Engagement: A Journey Not an Event.* London: King's Fund. Available at: www.kingsfund.org.uk/publications /revalidation (accessed 28 March 2017).

Craven, P. (2015) Performance appraisal and assessment. In *Management and Leadership—A Guide for Clinical Professionals,* edited by Patole, S. London: Springer.

Department of Health (2006) *Good Doctors, Safer Patients: Proposals to Strengthen the System to Assure and Improve the Performance of Doctors to Protect the Safety of Patients.* London: Department of Health. Available at: http://webarchive.nationalarchives.gov.uk/20130107105354 (accessed 27 October 2016).

Department of Health (2007) *Trust, Assurance and Safety: The Regulation of Health Professionals in the 21st Century.* London: Stationery Office.

Department of Health, NHS Revalidation Support Team, NHS Employers, GMC (2011) *Preparing for the Introduction of Medical Revalidation: A Guide for NHS Leaders in England.* Available at: http://www.gmc-uk.org /Revalidation-guide-for-NHS-leaders-in-England-updated_November_2011 _pdf_45560731.pdf (accessed 27 October 2016).

Faculty of Medical Leadership and Management (2014) *Understanding the Drivers of Appraisal Rates within Acute Trusts.* London: FMLM.

General Medical Council (2000) *Revalidating Doctors: Ensuring Standards, Securing the Future: Consultation Document.* London: GMC.

General Medical Council (2013) *Good Medical Practice.* Manchester: General Medical Council. Available at: www.gmc-uk.org/guidance/good_medical _practice.asp.

General Medical Council (2016) *UMbRELLA: Shaping the Future of Medical Revalidation, Interim Report.* Available at: www.gmc-uk.org/UMbRELLA _interim-report-FINAL_pdf_65723741pdf (accessed 29 August 2016).

Keogh, B. (2011) Foreword in Medical Leadership: From the dark side to centre stage. London: Radcliffe Publishing.

King's Fund (2014) *Medical Revalidation: From Compliance to Commitment.* London: King's Fund. Available at: www.kingsfund.org.uk/publications /revalidation (accessed 27 October 2016).

Thistlewaite, J., and Spencer, J. (2008) *Professionalism in Medicine.* Oxford, UK: Radcliffe Publishing.

9

Practical examples of initiatives to enhance leadership capacity

9.1 INTRODUCTION

Earlier chapters have outlined the various professional, policy and political drivers to secure greater medical engagement in management, leadership and transformation of services. Chapter 5 described the development of the Medical Leadership Competency Framework (MLCF) (NHS Institute for Innovation and Improvement, Academy of Medical Royal Colleges, 2010) and how it is being embedded into undergraduate and postgraduate curricula and being incorporated into revalidation standards for consultants and general practitioners.

In this chapter, we explore some of the practical initiatives being taken to provide new opportunities for doctors to gain managerial and leadership experiences and competences at earlier stages in their careers. Not all doctors by any means will assume positional leadership roles during their careers. It is our contention based on studies that getting all doctors more engaged in organisational decision making leads to enhanced performance. Thus, there is an imperative to generate opportunities for doctors from an early stage in their training and careers to acquire relevant insights into the nature of management, leadership and service improvement. By so doing, a greater sense of engagement should be realised.

Many of these initiatives in the National Health Service (NHS) are based on the MLCF. Whilst we would advocate this, the implementation case study (later in this chapter) illustrates that the more general and critical feature is that it is important for an organisation to adopt and use a particular model or approach to leadership. The consistent use of a model enables it to become embedded across different professional groups and hence significantly facilitates communication and an understanding of the nature of leadership. This is common practice in most large private sector organisations, thus building a shared and strong leadership culture. For too long, the NHS has accepted a myriad of different leadership approaches, usually driven by the provider, and resulting in a confusing array of conceptualisations which can lead individuals to conclude that the material is irrelevant as it is so diverse and fragmented. Current demands upon the health system suggest that the need for a unified and effective model of leadership has never been greater.

High Quality for All (Darzi, 2008) recognised the need to increase the supply of high-quality leadership within the NHS and identified that there were not enough clinical professionals willing and able to take on leadership roles. Historically, the NHS Graduate Management Training Scheme has been a major pipeline for the current cadre of chief executives and directors. From recruiting about 15 trainees back in 1956, it has now grown to a scheme whereby around 200 are recruited each year across the NHS (United Kingdom). The 'fast-track' programme offers a range of development opportunities including working attachments, action learning, mentoring, postgraduate studies and regular performance review. Hitherto, most of the development, with a few variations, has been undertaken as a uni-disciplinary group within the multi-professional culture of NHS organisations and services. Whilst this programme should continue to be a great source of tomorrows' leaders, the desired distributed leadership approach for NHS organisations and systems requires a much wider population of clinicians contributing to management and leadership.

The NHS Leadership Academy, which became part of Health Education England (HEE), in 2016, has offered a range of national leadership development programs for individuals, many of whom are clinical professionals, including for example, the Elizabeth Garrett Anderson and Nye Bevan programmes. West et al. (2015) concur that leadership is the most influential factor in shaping organisational cultures that ensure the delivery of continuously improving high-quality, safe and compassionate healthcare. Yet, they argue, there is little robust evidence for the effectiveness of specific leadership development programmes. Many individuals returning to their own organisations find themselves isolated and their particular educational processes of little relevance to competing organisational demands and philosophies. We argue that the importance of engaging clinicians in management leadership as part of a more collective or distributed approach confirms the importance of integrating these competencies into undergraduate and postgraduate education and training for all clinical professionals not as something that is made available for some at a later stage in their career.

This reinforces the distinction between individual leader development and leadership development. As West et al. (2015) observe, the former is often provided by external providers. These are often delivered in remote locations, as exemplified by the NHS Leadership Academy's historical suite of programmes. However, the widespread desire for a more distributed approach would suggest that leadership development is better done within an organisation or across a local health community by teams focusing on specific challenges and quality improvement initiatives.

This view is strongly endorsed by West et al.:

The leadership of organisations needs to be consistent in terms of leadership styles and behaviours; in developing shared leadership across the organisation; in embodying the vision and values of the organisation; in ensuring shared and consistent approaches to performance management; in practising compassion as a cultural value in all relationships within the organisation; in encouraging, facilitating and rewarding learning, quality improvement and innovation; and developing team, inter-team and cross-boundary working within and across organisations in health and social care. And leaders must work together and build cultures where the success of patient care overall is every leader's priority, not just the success of their individual areas of responsibility. (2015, p. 4)

Leadership development needs to be part of organisational development. High-performing health organisations fully recognise this and see investment in leadership development as an integral element of their culture. This does not preclude supporting certain individuals participating in external programmes as part of their personal development. However, this is somewhat peripheral to their much stronger focus on internal development.

For junior doctors, this might include a range of introductory management and leadership programmes for foundation year clinicians followed by initiatives for registrars, particularly around service improvement and involving other members of the clinical team. A study by the King's Fund of four NHS organisations that put medical engagement at the core of their culture confirms that investment in leadership development for medical staff is a critical component. The King's Fund Report *Medical Engagement: A Journey Not an Event* (Clark and Nath, 2014) highlights that some high-performing NHS Foundation Trusts, for example, Northumbria and Salford, require all new consultants to participate in uni-professional leadership development programmes within a few months of appointment. These are followed by participation in internal multi-professional senior leadership development programmes. Alas, whilst there are other examples of similar programmes, far too few NHS organisations invest in such development activities.

Junior doctor rotations through different hospitals and specialities offer wide-ranging experiences that enable them to form clear views on best or poor practice. Executives in high-performing hospitals recognise this and positively encourage junior doctors to offer insight and to lead service improvement initiatives. Such engagement at this early stage in their career can only have positive impact on their behaviours and attitudes towards leadership when they move into even more influential positions as consultants and general practitioners. A junior doctor on the national medical director's clinical fellow programme contends that 'medical leadership saves lives, therefore it is imperative that all doctors develop leadership skills' (Jagger, 2015, p. 211). She argues that leadership and management are not only required by senior clinicians or trainees who aspire to potential leadership roles but also are integral components of everyday clinical practice and are essential to the delivery of high-quality, continually improving, compassionate, patient-centred care.

In Sir Robert Francis's report into the failure of care at the Mid Staffordshire NHS Foundation Trust (2013) highlighted the importance of leadership at all levels and called trainees the 'eyes and ears' of the hospital. As Jagger confirms:

> Trainee's leadership capability is currently an undervalued resource in the NHS. No other industry takes their freshest, most enthusiastic and driven employees and uses them solely to deliver a service. (2015, p. 211)

This perspective is shared by Keogh (2013), who confirms the authors' view that trainee doctors are in ideal positions to lead the drive to improve quality, productivity and innovations in the NHS and that they are the clinical leaders not just of tomorrow but also of today.

Micallef and Straw (2014), writing from an Australian perspective, support the view that junior medical staff are in ideal positions to lead service improvement for a number of reasons, including the following:

- Their proximity to patients, family and the multidisciplinary team
- Their role accessing and ordering routine hospital processes and procedures (pathology, pharmacy, patient transfers and referrals etc.)
- Their relatively recent entry to the health system and openness to new approaches without being over invested in existing structures and processes
- Their mobility and ability to experience and share knowledge of the different practices across a range of hospitals and departments in relatively short timeframes

There are also many reasons why junior doctors choose to take part in leadership and improvement initiatives, such as those described by Bagnall (2012):

- To explore their career options
- To take time away from traditional clinical practice
- To achieve greater engagement with doctors' desire to deliver high-quality and cost-effective care
- To develop an understanding of the politics and mechanics of the health system
- To prepare for future leadership roles

In addition to various local and national leadership programmes for junior doctors, a few take the opportunity to undertake a prestigious international programme, for example, the Commonwealth Fund Harkness Fellowship and Institute of Healthcare Improvement Quality Improvement Fellowship.

This chapter offers a sample of some interesting initiatives being taken in different contexts. A number of these are geared to motivating junior doctors to develop leadership competencies around service improvement. Junior doctors are in particularly good positions to identify processes and system of service delivery that frustrate them and impact on optimal care to patients.

9.2 MLCF—EXEMPLAR IMPLEMENTATION: HEALTH EDUCATION ENGLAND (WEST MIDLANDS)

Earlier chapters have described the emergence of the MLCF as a national response as to how the medical profession might prepare individuals for future leadership roles. The endorsement by the General Medical Council (GMC) resulted in the MLCF as a document being incorporated into 'Tomorrow's Doctors' relating to undergraduate medical programmes and into the curriculum of all speciality colleges. However, as with many major projects, the process of implementation is challenging and often protracted. There were several initiatives following the publication of the MLCF, but often, this led to a taught course rather than the intended process—the gradual acquisition of leadership behaviour over the period of the medical career, based on opportunities appropriate to the stage of development of a particular individual and integrated into clinical practice. A major obstacle to this ideal type implementation is that current educational tutors and supervisors have, for the most part, not been trained themselves in the leadership skills within the MLCF. As a consequence, many are not comfortable supporting acquisition of these behaviours preferring to focus on purely clinical training and advising trainees that they can always do a leadership course near the end of their training.

Over the past two years, an initiative by Health Education England (West Midlands) has provided an opportunity for a full ideal type implementation. This has focused upon all trainees in the School of Psychiatry within the region. An initial task in the project was a scoping process to understand what was currently happening with respect to leadership training. Interviews were conducted with trainees, tutors, course organisers and existing consultants. In summary, the picture of current provision that emerged was as follows:

- Neither trainees nor tutors were clear about just what constituted leadership and had no shared language to communicate about it.
- Trainees felt that there were consultants who seemed to exhibit leadership as they understood it, some who lacked it and some who demonstrated a more 'toxic' version of leadership.
- Trainees struggled to identify specific leadership content in their programme, apart from an occasional lecture.
- It was clear that trainers across the region operated in very different ways with no consistency in terms of coverage and content.
- Any leadership input seems to be largely driven by the particular person or institution asked to provide it, thus introducing even further diversity (confusion!) about the nature of leadership to trainees.

As a consequence of these observations, it was recommended that there should be a unified framework, designed to be consistent across the six-year training programme and across different sites. In order to create such a programme, it is essential that a single common model of leadership be adopted. In this instance the MLCF was chosen because of the following:

1. It is the leadership model endorsed by the GMC.
2. It is already included in the college's postgraduate curriculum (at least as a written document).
3. The MLCF uniquely has a full curriculum including knowledge, skills, attitudes and behaviours and more than 60 e-learning units covering the background to leadership theories and models and is freely available.

An absolutely vital further element of the recommendations was that training in the leadership behaviours of the MLCF should be provided to all tutors/ educators across the region. This training, known as level 1, was provided for all and a further more advanced training for a small group of course organisers. The programme for trainees consists of lectures, designated e-learning units to support the lecture, work-based activities and periodic Leadership Development Groups to bring together these experiences every three months. Content for each year of the programme is specified. The programme has been successfully implemented, with an external independent evaluation reporting markedly greater awareness of leadership issues from trainees and greater communication between trainees and trainers using a common language about leadership.

A full account of the programme can be found in Spurgeon and Klaber (2016), but the essential lessons are that a single unified model of leadership must be chosen, that a curriculum and support materials must be developed and that good tutor/educator training is vital. The model is also very attractive in terms of value for money as an approach. After the initial development cost, hundreds of trainees per year can then be given leadership development at no cost—by the fully trained existing tutors, who are also best placed to integrate leadership skills with clinical practice. It is clear too that sending some junior doctors on individually based programmes will never address the issue of getting the entire profession geared up to undertake leadership roles.

9.3 DEVELOPING JUNIOR DOCTORS AS LEADERS OF SERVICE IMPROVEMENT IN WESTERN AUSTRALIA

In 2012, the Western Australia Department of Health initiated a project to develop the leadership capacity of its junior medical staff. Micallef and Straw (2014) describe the impetus for the project being a groundswell of interest from junior medical staff wanting greater involvement in the way services are designed and delivered.

The Western Australia Medical Service Improvement Programme was designed to address both structural and attitudinal barriers to engaging junior doctors in improvement. This has been achieved by offering a paid supernumerary rotation away from the time pressures of clinical work and by recruiting junior doctors who have a clear passion for patient-centred care and display the attributes of emerging clinical leaders.

The program offers an 11-week programme to design and deliver a service improvement project of their choosing but endorsed by the executive director of the hospital. The dedicated 11-week period is part of a year-long leadership development programme that also includes three days training in service improvement techniques. This training provides the participants with Clinical Service Redesign and general project management concepts and skills. In addition, the junior doctors on the programme are offered other leadership development opportunities, including the following:

- Leadership masterclasses
- Presentational skills
- Assessment and development of leadership style
- Mindfulness
- Shadowing hospital executives
- Industry visits to see improvement initiatives in non-health contexts

The participants have successfully completed a range of service improvement projects that have led to measurable improvements in quality and fiscal performance. As Micallef and Straw (2014) conclude, at an organisational level, the participating hospitals (and therefore patients) have benefitted from the outcomes of the improvement projects undertaken. From an engagement perspective, the programme has contributed to greater involvement of junior doctors and the development of a 'critical mass' of clinical professionals interested in improvement at each participating site.

The impact of this type of initiative should not be underestimated. In Western Australia, the enthusiasm of those involved has infected an increasing number of junior doctors to apply for similar opportunities. Despite fiscal pressures, executives continue to commit resources to not only sustain but also expand the programme, recognising not only the short-term benefits but also the longer-term cultural change opportunities of greater medical engagement.

9.4 THE UNIVERSITY OF WARWICK MEDICAL SCHOOL: IN-TRUST POSTGRADUATE LEADERSHIP FOR HEALTHCARE CERTIFICATE

The authors have been actively involved in leading postgraduate leadership programmes for clinicians at the University of Warwick Medical School for a number of years. A more recent initiative has been to deliver a Leadership for Healthcare Post Graduate Certificate programme for groups of clinical professionals (mostly doctors) in leadership roles, or identified as potential heads of department, within specific NHS Trusts or across a health economy. This approach combines all the benefits of an accredited university approach, with the advantage of local delivery, the development of case studies based on local challenges and a tailored mode of delivery. It provides opportunities for executives to contribute to the programme as well as for participants to share some of their challenges, aspirations and frustrations.

There are three core modules delivered over five days divided into two blocks. These modules are as follows:

- Induction to leadership
- Improving safety and quality in healthcare
- Finance and productivity in healthcare

Assessment is by 4000 words (or equivalent) written assignment for each module, designed to integrate the theoretical knowledge gained during the module with local application. This can include, for example, applying the learning from the evidence of studies into high-performing organisations for their own service, organisation or local system. Other assignments might include the design and implementation of a service improvement initiative or the development of a business case for a change in clinical service.

This type of programme meets the view of West et al. (2015) in that it brings together groups of influential clinical leaders within the same organisation or system to learn together. It also puts into practice an organisation's philosophy around distributed leadership. The experience from the Trusts who have undertaken this programme is that participants put considerable energy into their studies and seek to apply the learning to effect changes in behaviour, attitudes and practice. It does require a similar commitment from the executive in not only contributing to the programme but also being prepared to take on board ideas emanating from the programme.

9.5 NATIONAL MEDICAL DIRECTOR'S CLINICAL FELLOW SCHEME

The Faculty of Medical Leadership and Management (FMLM) lead the National Medical Director's Clinical Fellow Scheme, which is sponsored by Professor Sir Bruce Keogh, NHS Medical Director (England).

The scheme was established to fast track and support those doctors in training who demonstrate potential to develop as future medical leaders. Full details are available at https://www.fmlm.ac.uk/professional-development.

The initiative started in 2005 as the Clinical Advisor Scheme by the chief medical officer for England with just one place. In 2011, the scheme was revamped and changed to its current title with management of the programme being assumed by the FMLM. A total of 31 junior doctors were appointed to the programme in 2015/2016. Over 100 doctors have participated in the scheme, which provides doctors in training with opportunities to spend 12 months in an affiliated national healthcare organisation outside of clinical practice to develop their skills in leadership, project management and health policy. Similar schemes operate in Wales, Scotland and Northern Ireland, offering six places in each country as well as other regional programmes.

Whilst the bulk of the Fellow's time is spent within an organisation, the scheme is an integrated personal leadership development experience. The programme includes a range of wider development interventions. These include visits to both the House of Commons and House of Lords, observing the parliamentary process as well as a range of health bodies. Fellows are also encouraged to arrange workshops on agreed topics, including inviting national and international speakers from both health and non-healthcare organisations and producing webinars for others to access. This scheme has grown considerably over the past decade and is highly competitive. There are other not dissimilar programmes, for example, the Darzi Clinical Fellowship Scheme in London, and highlights that there is a thirst amongst many junior doctors to take leadership seriously.

These types of national programmes need to be part of a broader strategy that includes relevant leadership development for all doctors (and indeed all clinical professionals). This should be the responsibility of all medical royal colleges, deaneries and NHS organisations. National programmes inevitably involve only a few, and critics might argue that they are just the tip of the iceberg. However, they have an important role in not only developing a group of emerging doctors with potential to progress to senior medical leaders but perhaps more importantly contribute to the strategic movement of more effective medical leadership and engagement. The few junior doctors on these prestigious national programmes can help infect their peers, professional and educational bodies and health organisations to incorporate management leadership, particularly around service improvement, into the training and development of all trainees.

9.6 CASE STUDY: HOW THE MEDICAL ENGAGEMENT SCALE CATALYSED CHANGE IN BUCKINGHAMSHIRE HEALTHCARE NHS TRUST

Apart from supporting the development of individual doctors, it is vital that organisations provide the culture to facilitate use of any leadership skills required—this can be described as medical engagement (see Chapter 6). The diagnostic around medical engagement afforded by use of Medical Engagement Survey (MES) allows organisations a focused pathway to enhancing levels of engagement and hence improve performance. The following case study is an example of this in practice.

9.6.1 Background

Buckinghamshire Healthcare NHS Trust (BHT) is an integrated acute and community trust comprised of the original hospitals of High Wycombe, Stoke Mandeville and Amersham together with a number of community hospitals. Between 2005 and 2012, these hospitals were merged and a number of services moved sites through the Better Healthcare in Bucks initiative. To understand the engagement of the medical staff, BHT undertook the MES in 2012. With some variation, the results were generally at the lower end of the medium range. SAS (Staff, Associate Specialist and Specialty) doctors were least engaged (see

Figure 1). Perhaps the most striking finding was the disparity between the views of managers and those of doctors; 93% of managers thought that medical staff were well informed about wider organisational initiatives; however, only 36% of doctors agreed.

Following receipt of the results, a workshop with a large number of both consultant and SAS medical staff was held to identify the issues and solutions. The themes that emerged from that workshop and directly reflected components of the MES were as follows:

1. Issues
   a. Trust vision and goals not clear or aligned to the clinical vision
   b. Lack of alignment between board and clinical staff priorities
   c. A feeling of negativity and a failure to communicate successes
   d. Lack of cohesion between operational leadership and medical leadership
   e. A feeling of not being listened to as a profession and a loss of control
   f. A feeling of focusing on financial targets rather than improving patient care
2. Actions to address the findings
   The group considered that the solutions to addressing the findings were for the trust to
   a. Create institutional loyalty, brand identity, a shared vision and a sense of team spirit
   b. Engender respect between the clinicians and the trust board
   c. Establish values, trust and responsibility with doctors and managers
   d. Set behavioural standards, intercept quickly and enforce when necessary
   e. Promote a stronger sense of involvement from doctors
   f. Create more influential Service Development Unit (SDU) lead roles (a medical leadership role within the trust—SDU leads—equivalent to clinical directors)
   g. Provide leadership and financial training for SDU leads

Although there were a number of leadership roles, they had not been provided with the development to enable them to fulfil those roles to their fullest potential. As a result, a leadership development programme was developed, initially for SDU leads, and continues to be extended on a multi-disciplinary basis.

Twice-yearly full-day workshops are held for SAS doctors, which are very well attended.

Trust values have been refreshed and developed further, involving large numbers of staff and patients in this process and have taken a robust approach to behaviour which is not in keeping with our values.

A number of initiatives have been taken that see non-executive directors and executives 'walking the floor' to increase that all important board visibility and have established the BHT Way. This is a quarterly series of meetings between executives and the top 500 leaders across the trust, including all consultants and SAS doctors.

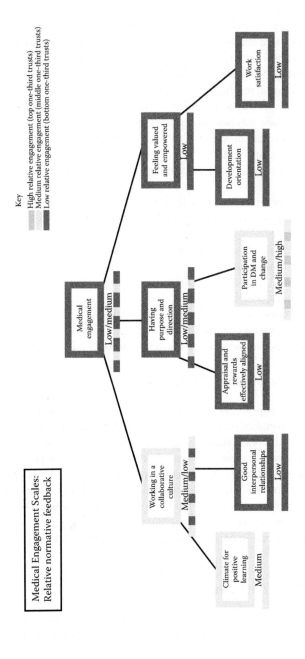

Figure 9.1 2012 MES results. Graph of the 2012 MES results.

The communication department has been instrumental in increasing the quality, quality and variety of our communications across the organisation especially about the clinical strategy.

The medical director meets each new consultant, and in 2015, all but one doctor was appraised and 96% had an agreed job plan.

The impact of these changes can be seen in the MES data of 2016 (Figure 9.2).

This was a significant change from the 2012 results, with each one of the domains improving. This indicated that the trust was going in the right direction with its approach to increasing medical engagement.

A further multi-professional workshop, which included a number of consultant and SAS doctors, was held to discuss the results.

The aim of the workshop was to agree what actions were now needed to further improve medical engagement.

The actions proposed at this workshop were for the trust to

- Improve the selection process for leaders
- Link clinical engagement, decision making and funding flows—empower to make a difference
- See engagement more as a team approach and focus on continuous engagement and communication
- Review SDUs and the communication within the divisional structures
- Develop staff relationships
- Promote team away days
- Positive reinforcement of achievement
- Manage workload through prioritisation, planning and focused contracting

9.6.2 Summary of case study

Reflecting on the proposed actions from 2012, it is clear that a number of the proposals sought to embed basic organisational factors that drive high-performing organisations and increase staff engagement. The proposals also sought to create a framework, expectations and standards and draw doctors more into the organisation itself, reducing the perceived gap between the board and services. The proposals from 2016 suggest less transactional and more transformational themes. These themes relate to a multi-professional team working, recognising outcomes from teams and placing doctors in a position to be more 'part of the solution', reflecting perhaps more complex thinking to engagement and empowerment.

9.6.3 Conclusion of case study

There is no doubt that the MES catalysed the trust to engage with our medical staff, listen to them and act on what we heard. As a result of this, we have improved the care we offer our patients and improved our medical engagement results. Above all, however, we have seen a change in our medical workforce where

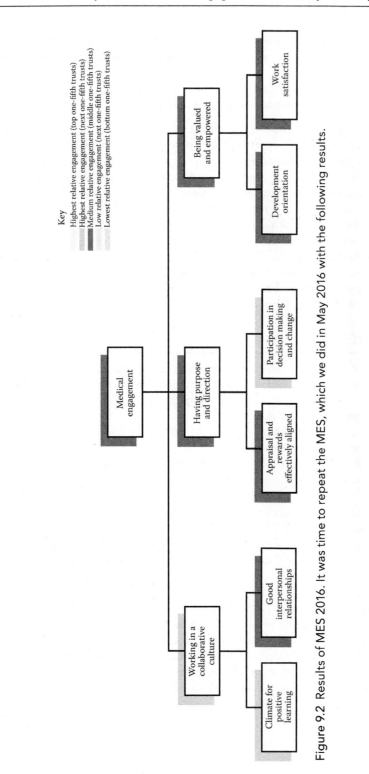

Key
Highest relative engagement (top one-fifth trusts)
Highest relative engagement (next one-fifth trusts)
Medium relative engagement (middle one-fifth trusts)
Low relative engagement (next one-fifth trusts)
Lowest relative engagement (bottom one-fifth trusts)

Figure 9.2 Results of MES 2016. It was time to repeat the MES, which we did in May 2016 with the following results.

some of our medical leaders are now requesting to have increased autonomy in managing their service, recognising that with that comes responsibility for the changes this will bring. It is important to see each of the initiatives as part of a culture change. No one action will solve an issue of medical engagement—it is a process and a different way of organisations relating to its medical workforce.

The examples outlined in this chapter are just a few of the many initiatives being taken in different parts of the system and internationally. As Snell et al. (2014) suggest, the importance of active physician leadership within health organisations is well supported, stressing that it is critical for health organisations to effectively implement leadership development programmes. Whilst it is pleasing to observe more and more initiatives being introduced, it is worrying that, despite the importance of more effective medical engagement and leadership, development initiatives are just that. There is still a tendency for such initiatives to be ad hoc and episodic. The future needs to be that leadership development is an integral part of all doctors', and indeed all clinical professionals', initial and subsequent training and not, as currently, an optional extra offered by just a few enlightened health organisations or medical educationalists.

REFERENCES

Bagnall, P. (2012) *Facilitators and Barriers to Leadership and Quality Improvement*. London: King's Fund Junior Doctor Project, King's Fund.

Clark, J., and Nath, V. (2014) *Medical Engagement: A Journey Not an Event*. London: King's Fund.

Darzi, A. (2008) *High Quality Care for All: NHS Next Stage Review Final Report*. London: Department of Health.

Francis, R. (2013) *Report of the Mid-Staffordshire NHS Foundation Trust Public Inquiry*. London: Stationery Office. Available at: www.midstaffspublicinquiry .com/ (accessed 27 October 2016).

Jagger, O. (2015) Supporting and driving trainee-led leadership. *Future Hospital Journal*, 2(3): 211–217.

Keogh, B. (2013) *Review into the Quality of Care and Treatment Provided by 14 Hospital Trusts in England*. London: NHS England. Available at: www.nhs .uk/NHS England/bruce-Keogh-review/Documents/outcomes/Keoghreview -final-report.pdf (accessed 27 October 2016).

Micallef, J., and Straw, B. (2014) Developing junior doctors as leaders of service improvement. *Leadership in Health Services*, 27(4): 316–329.

NHS Institute for Innovation and Improvement and Academy of Medical Royal Colleges (2010) *Medical Leadership Competency Framework*, 3rd ed. Coventry: NHS Institute for Innovation and Improvement.

Snell, A., Eagle, C., and Van Aerde, J. (2014) Embedding physician leadership development within health organisations. *Leadership in Health Services*, 27(4): 330–342.

Spurgeon, P., and Klaber, R. (2016) *Medical Leadership: A Practical Guide for Tutors and Trainees*. London: BPP Learning Media.

West, M., Armit, K., Lowenthal, L., EcKert, R., West, T., and Lee, A. (2015) *Leadership and Leadership Development in Health Care: The Evidence Base*. London: Faculty of Medical Leadership and Management.

10

Medical leadership and engagement: Towards cultural acceptance and the future

10.1 INTRODUCTION

Previous chapters have given an account of widespread recognition, advocacy and indeed evidence for greater involvement of doctors in the management and leadership tasks that support the achievement of improved healthcare delivery. Each health system has its own history and process of evolution, but there appears to be consensus about the requirement for the powerful profession of medicine to be positively integrated into both strategic and operational aspects of running health services.

Mountford (2010) argues that the time has come for medical leadership to emerge as a significant factor in the way health services are run. He cites issues such as the complexity of policy changes, the safety and quality imperative and the emerging evidence of the impact of medical leadership on organisational performance. Similarly, Bohmer (2010) has called for leadership training, both high-level system leadership and more leadership with an operational focus, to be built into the training and preparation of all doctors.

In many ways, there would seem to be little of a radical or startling nature in advocating such a role for doctors. In many systems, especially in earlier versions of healthcare structures, doctors have always played a prominent role and still do in many current systems (see Chapter 2). However, there are two particular contextual issues that seem to make the notion of enhanced medical leadership quite challenging.

The first concerns the peculiar nature of the personal services provided by doctors. In many other sectors, the key professions have had less difficulty integrating their role within the constraints of a managed system. For example, architects, engineers and others—despite their frustrations—will recognise the interactive dynamic (and constraints) of the system in which they work. Many groups of this type work in a collective system, whereas doctors are largely delivering a highly personalised, individually based service. It can also of course be a highly emotive service where quality of life, as well as life or death, may be involved. Doctors and the public, as patients, have something akin to an implicit contract that the individual transaction around caregiving shall remain the predominant characteristic of health systems. Anything externally imposed that impinges upon this relationship tends to be resented, and this perspective has been how many doctors have viewed managers and management. It is apparent though that since the first edition of this book, there has been considerable progress in overcoming this rather stereotypic and divisive view. The evolution of thinking about medical leadership as outlined in Chapter 2 demonstrates this incremental improvement in attitudes and acceptance of the cultural changes required. The normalising of medical leadership roles is the essence of this cultural transformation. The emphasis in modern healthcare of the necessity of effective teamwork is also acting to fuel this direction of change. A critical cultural challenge for the future is to overcome this quite widely held view and build an approach that recognises the wider system context but without detriment to the crucial patient–doctor relationship.

A second and related issue is that of clinical autonomy. Politicians in many systems have quite legitimate concerns about the escalating cost of healthcare and also more latterly around patient safety. These concerns have frequently manifested themselves as centralised interventions to reduce or control spending or to insist on certain forms of care delivery. Inevitably, many doctors have seen such initiatives as constraining the way they work and thereby affecting their clinical autonomy to practice in accord with their professional values. It is argued that this increasingly centralised approach has created a somewhat alienated medical workforce and that the momentum towards forms of medical leadership is recognition of the need to alter this perspective. The National Health Service (NHS) Next Stage Review as presented by Lord Darzi (2008) was an attempt to be more receptive and consultative towards the medical profession and to refocus attention on quality and patient safety as issues more likely to be embraced by doctors in improving care overall. There is no doubt that this approach has contributed significantly to the impetus to see enhanced engagement in medical leadership. It is disappointing and a little sad that rather than recognising the contributions and commitment of the vast majority of doctors, and encouraging even greater impact through greater engagement in influencing the management of health systems, the present government pursues a punitive attitude based on targeting a very small minority of the profession. It is interesting to contrast the protests from politicians when they are all perceived as involved in the recent expenses scandal, with their delight in castigating the whole profession based on the hostile stereotype of a few rogue practitioners. Initiatives such as seeking to publicise earnings from private practice and the imposition of the junior doctor contract risk alienating the profession, the latter in particular for future generations. As health systems move into the severe constraints of post-recession economies, it is imperative that a positive focus is maintained. Radical change and leading edge innovation in how services are provided will be fundamental to coping with the financial pressures. These will not be achieved without the full and positive engagement of medical staff (and others of course). Medical leadership in this climate is not an optional extra or a nicety but an essential ingredient.

10.2 MISCONCEPTIONS ABOUT MANAGEMENT AND LEADERSHIP

As outlined earlier in this text, there are many models of leadership, many misconceptions about the nature and purpose of management and many unhelpful stereotypes. If medical leadership, as advocated here, is to flourish and become a normal and accepted component of the medical career, then these stereotypes need to be challenged and reframed into a more modern twenty-first century way of thinking.

In advocating that all doctors should acquire competence in management and leadership and that these functions are integral to the professional role, there is no suggestion that doctors should become managers rather than doctors or that each doctor is naturally (by selection into medical school) equipped to be a heroic or charismatic positional leader. Managerial tasks are essential to the effective operation of large organisations. The majority of these will continue to be undertaken by managers, but doctors, by developing a better understanding of the function and purpose of these tasks, can contribute significantly to their functional effectiveness. The management process can no longer be seen as an alien and—as described by some—deliberately undermining to good healthcare delivery. There can of course be poor managers and poor examples of management. Systems can become perseverated and unwieldy, but to regard all management as hostile and deficient is to perpetuate a cultural divide that is not only unhelpful but also unreasonable.

Similarly, to embrace medical leadership in such a way as to suggest that doctors must be the dominant players in an explicitly multi-professional, team-based delivery system is inappropriate and outmoded. The model of shared or distributed leadership as described in Chapter 4 is much more the type of leadership that is needed in the complex health systems of today. Such a model of leadership is essentially flexible, recognising the expertise and contribution of others as and when appropriate, empowering such as to release the skills of others to improve overall performance and consultative in attempting to ensure that the ideas and abilities of others are brought into play. This is a long way from the dominant dictatorial stereotype of the authoritarian leader of the past.

Lee (2010) reinforces this view, suggesting that a new breed of medical leaders is required to meet the challenges of providing twenty-first century healthcare. He particularly emphasises the development of teams as a key leadership strategy for healthcare providers. He cites the experience of Geisinger Health System in

Pennsylvania, where such arrangements have helped the hospital cut re-admission rates by half. Lee suggests that a critical component of this success is 'that physicians be both team leaders and team players' (p. 57). Building teams and inspiring teamwork comprise an important competence for leaders in order to improve performance.

Just as we talk of enhancing engagement in medical leadership, so we need to develop engaging leaders able to relate, empathise and influence others, to build teams that are clear about their roles and motivated to perform them and with the intellectual flexibility to adapt to often fluctuating and contradictory demands.

One of the most significant and important developments since the first edition is the shift in emphasis from medical leadership alone to medical engagement. As discussed in Chapter 6, it is simply not sufficient to advocate medical leadership. Although this position was valuable in promoting the notion of more doctors becoming involved in the running of their organisations, it is both historic and an over-simplification. It fails to recognise the logic that all health organisations have medical leaders in place but their sheer existence fails to eliminate variation in the provision of care and more explicitly that some organisations operate far less effectively than others. Furthermore, it ignores the complexity of just how doctors should be prepared for the roles (the nature and timing of any training, and the model of leadership skills endorsed) and just what do some medical leaders do that make them more effective than others.

The argument linking medical leadership with organisational performance has previously been suggested somewhat vaguely as to do with the culture created within the organisation. The burgeoning evidence presented in Chapter 6 of the relationship between organisational performance and medical engagement provides much clearer definition of what this positive cultural context needs to be. The critical skills of medical leaders must be those that help to foster enhanced medical engagement. Data accumulating from application of the Medical Engagement Scale (now approaching 110 UK-based health organisations) underlines this point in two specific ways:

1. It has become clear that those individuals who have a designated medical leadership role are universally and significantly more engaged than their medical colleagues. The latter is of course much the larger group numerically and crucially the principal medical caregivers in the organisation. It is the promotion of engagement in this group that is key to effective organisations and, hence, effective medical leadership.
2. The medical engagement levels of failing or struggling organisations is similarly low across almost all such organisations. It is perhaps not too much of a claim to suggest that organisations with low levels of medical engagement will have, now or in the future, some type of problem. It is not clear when or exactly how this will manifest, but almost certainly they will. It is hard to argue the opposite perspective—how will an alienated, demotivated, disengaged medical workforce lead to sustained high quality care?

Promoting enhanced medical engagement is then a key task for medical leaders and indeed for all non-medical leaders. The latter group is often rather ignored in the debate about medical leadership. In fact, their role is vital. A threatened or defensive attitude can lead to advocacy of medical leadership but a reluctance in reality to let go of some aspects of control. In contrast, a positive supportive attitude can engender the levels of medical engagement that can bring success for the organisations they lead.

10.3 FUTURE OF MEDICAL LEADERSHIP

On a number of occasions within this text, the nature and picture of medical leadership described have been represented as a significant cultural change. It requires that medical leadership skills are embedded into medical training and medical career development as an important and established element of professionalism. The Medical Leadership Competency Framework (MLCF) (see Chapter 5) is perhaps the most important recent initiative in this respect for decades. Its incorporation into the training of undergraduate medical students will lead to an awareness and understanding of how these skills are relevant to future roles in medicine as well as beginning the process of acquiring competence in them. Further development at the postgraduate level should ensure that doctors are much more competent in the demands of system management, improvement methodologies and leadership; it should also ensure that they emerge with a more positive attitude to the contribution they can make to the management process. It is fair to say that implementation of leadership training at undergraduate and postgraduate level has been uneven and relatively slow. As the case study exemplar in Chapter 9 indicates, it is possible to do it comprehensively and cost-effectively as intended. There exists though a lack of understanding of what is really essential to support widespread implementation. If every postgraduate specialty, irrespective of years of training, is to be covered as a profession, then we have to move away from ad hoc classroom-based leadership programmes where a few attend and the rest don't. We need to adopt a particular model or approach to leadership so that content and coverage can be consistent across sites where trainees are based. Finally, we have to ensure that educators are familiar, competent and confident about the model of leadership the trainees are using. Currently, the MLCF, because of its fully defined postgraduate curriculum and associated set of related online materials and endorsement by the General Medical Council (GMC), is the only leadership model that meets these requirements. As long as providers of leadership training pursue their particular approach in a possibly enthusiastic and well-meaning, but ill-coordinated, way, the necessary training for *all* members of any professional group will not happen.

In the United Kingdom, at least this process of development and acquisition of competence in management and leadership may continue further into the period of continuing practice following specialist certification. The process of revalidation will be overseen by the GMC and will be aimed at assuring patients, the public and employers that doctors are up to date and fit to practice.

Revalidation will be based around the annual appraisal, which will involve evaluation of the doctor's performance against professional standards set by the GMC and the Medical Royal Colleges. Good Medical Practice is the document produced by the GMC, and this defines the standards of care required, and a set of standards framework for appraisal and assessment has been devised. Inclusion or cross-referencing of these standards to the MLCF would therefore ensure that practising doctors continue to refine and develop their leadership skills alongside their clinical work. Chapter 8 discusses the potential contribution of revalidation and appraisal processes in supporting the cultural change we have advocated here. The adoption of the Generic Professional Capabilities (see Chapter 5) with the inclusion of a leadership component based on the MLCF will hopefully consolidate the acquisition of these wider skills within the medical workforce. It should be noted though that the implementation process relating to Generic Professional Capabilities will require just the same support infrastructure (and more) as was involved with the MLCF.

These changes to preparation and the attitude of doctors to management and leadership will not happen overnight, hence the notion of cultural change. But the hostile, unproductive divide between managers and doctors will hopefully be replaced by a more positive recognition and respect for a complementary set of skills. In order for this to happen, the roles taken by doctors (and hence role models) as clinical leads, clinical directors, medical directors and the like must be accepted and valued as a normal component of the medical career. If they are to become valued in this way, it will be important that the reward systems are aligned such that there is no disincentive for doctors to play a full role in the management and leadership of their organisation. Already, junior doctor rotations are beginning to include management and leadership placements that would once have been viewed as unthinkable. The authors interviewed all those NHS chief executives with a medical background in order to identify how those who make this transition may be assisted in the process (Ham et al., 2010). It is not the goal of supporters of medical leadership to see all chief executives as medical in background.

The difficulties that were encountered by doctors moving into chief executive roles (Ham et al., 2010) are very similar to the experiences of those taking on medical leadership roles. If the cultural change sought (in other words, a positive valuing and attraction to these roles) is to be achieved, then a number of key facilitators will need to be put in place. These include the following, for example:

- Clearer career paths that provide opportunities for doctors to experience different leadership roles and to be offered appropriate development (coaching, learning sets) to move into them
- The review of pay and reward systems so that medical leadership roles are properly recognised
- The facilitation of re-training if necessary so that the choice to move towards a leadership role is not seen as final and irrevocable

Francis (2013), in his report into events at Mid Staffordshire NHS Foundation Trust, called for the professionalising of healthcare and praised the coincident relatively recent establishment of the Faculty Medical Leadership. Formed under the auspices of the UK Medical Royal Colleges and Faculties and endorsed by the Academy of Medical Royal Colleges, this provides a focus of professional identity for those individuals moving into these hybrid medical/leadership roles. It will also conduct research and advise as to best practice in developing leadership skills. The publication of *Leadership and Management Standards for Medical Professionals* (FMLM, 2015) coincided with the call for the same by Kirkup (2015) in the Report of the Morecambe Bay Investigation. The 'standards' provide a valuable benchmark for medical leaders, which they can now certify through the recently launched FMLM fellowships. In a portfolio approach, fellowships measure knowledge, behaviours, and experience. Awarded at three levels, the scheme encourages progression and recognises the very large number of doctors in postgraduate training who demonstrate an interest in management and leadership. Perhaps the next step for the Faculty is, as we have argued in this final chapter, to provide training and development in how medical leaders may create the medical engagement levels so crucial to organisational success.

Some work published in Australia by Kippist and Fitzgerald (2009) provides a helpful tailpiece to what may be seen as the underpinning rationale to this text and many of the initiatives described within it. The authors explore the well-documented tensions inherent in the hybrid role of clinician manager, notably the potential conflict between clinical priorities and managerial goals. Apart from the pressures on time and lack of clarity of role, they point to a significant potential inhibitor to the success of such hybrid roles, namely the lack of management expertise held by doctors suddenly thrust into making significant managerially based decisions. They rightly highlight the danger to the organisation of less well-qualified (managerially) individuals making managerial decisions. They cite a number of authors who have also documented aspects of this deficiency, for example lack of awareness of the roles of other staff in the organisation (Ormrod, 1993), poor communication with fellow team members (Lopopolo et al., 2004) and less management training (Fitzgerald, 2002).

These pressures are fully recognised (see Chapter 4), but it is important to also recognise the particular cultural context (Australia) in terms of the place and status of medical leadership within the health system. Moreover, as the authors suggest, a critical missing ingredient in the successful adoption of medical leadership roles is for doctors to have had the necessary training and development in appropriate skills to promote medical engagement. The development and widespread adoption of the MLCF into all levels of training and career development of doctors, as described and advocated here, would go a long way to offsetting the expertise deficiency and acceptability of the medical leadership role. As a final comment to this text, our ambition is to see medical professionalism incorporate the concepts of management and leadership and to see both individuals and the medical profession embrace the potential of doctors to contribute to the wider goals of the organisation as a normal and natural part of the medical role.

REFERENCES

Bohmer, R. (2010) Leadership with a small 'l'. *BMJ*, 340: 265.

Darzi, A. (2008) *High Quality Care for All: NHS Next Stage Review Final Report*. London: Department of Health.

Faculty of Medical Leadership and Management (FMLM) (2015) Leadership and Management Standards for Medical Professionals. Available at: www.fmlm.ac.uk/themes/standards (accessed 28 March 2017).

Fitzgerald, J.A. (2002) *Doctors and Nurses Working Together: A Mixed Methodology in the Construction of Changing Professional Identities*. Sydney, Australia: University of Western Sydney.

Francis, R. (2013) *Report of the Mid-Staffordshire NHS Foundation Trust Public Inquiry, London*. London: Stationery Office. Available at: www.midstaffspublicinquiry.com (accessed 27 October 2016).

Ham, C., Clark, J., Spurgeon, P. et al. (2010) *Medical Chief Executives in the NHS: Facilitators and Barriers to Progress*. Coventry: NHS Institute for Innovation and Improvement, University of Warwick.

Kippist, L., and Fitzgerald, A. (2009) Organisational professional conflict and hybrid clinician managers. *Journal of Health Organization and Management*, 23(6): 642–655.

Kirkup, D. (2015) *The Report of the Morecambe Bay Investigation*. London: Stationery Office.

Lee, T.H. (2010) Turning doctors into leaders. *Harvard Business Review*, 51–58.

Lopopolo, R.B., Schafer, S.D., and Nosse, L.J. (2004) Leadership, administration, management and professionalism (LAMP) in physical therapy: A Delphi study. *Physical Therapy*, 84(2): 137–150.

Mountford, J. (2010) Clinical leadership: Bringing the strands together. In *Clinical Leadership: Bridging the Divide*, edited by Stanton, E., Lemer, C., Mountford, J. London: MA Healthcare.

Ormrod, J. (1993) Decision making in health service managers. *Management Decision*, 31(7): 8–14.

Index

Page numbers followed by f and t indicate figures and tables, respectively.

MASTERWORKS OF PROSE

MASTERWORKS
OF PROSE

Edited by

Thomas Parkinson

UNIVERSITY OF CALIFORNIA

BERKELEY

THE **BOBBS-MERRILL** COMPANY, INC.
A SUBSIDIARY OF HOWARD W. SAMS & CO., INC.
Publishers • INDIANAPOLIS • NEW YORK

PREFACE

This book grew out of my dozen years of teaching freshman English at the University of California at Berkeley. The aim of that course is to teach students how to read difficult expository prose and how to write clearly and responsibly. Each instructor uses one book-length expository text written by a single man—e.g., Thoreau's *Walden*—and usually this is supplemented by an anthology of readings. The theory behind this course is that freshman English should be at once a general service to the university and an introduction to the study of the masterpieces of the English language. The first semester—for which this book is appropriate—emphasizes expository reading and writing; the second semester deals with imaginative reading and continues the discipline in expository writing. In both semesters, the stress is on the reading of works that are comparable to those read in our courses in literary periods, genres, and major authors. In making selections for the present anthology, I have used this criterion: is this a work of literature of such high quality that one would use it in a course in Elizabethan literature or the literature of the Enlightenment or a course in Shakespeare or Dickens? And further, does it communicate urgently across the barriers of time and cultural differences?

I have tried, then, to select works that have at their center important ideas eloquently expressed. Two extremes plague courses in freshman composition, and in this anthology I am suggesting a third way that embraces the virtues of the "humanities" course on the one hand and the "communications" course on the other. The English language provides a vast store of expository writing that treats basic human problems in a manner at once exact and stirring, and the problems that concern freshman students do not have to be phrased in a spirit of narrow topicality. The communications course generally operates at what it (often insultingly) takes to be the student's level. The humanities course is constantly threatened by discussion of ideas at a lofty level where questions of exactness of expression and style can be conveniently ignored or—since so much of the material is in translation—shunted to the irrelevant. No literature provides greater works than the *Areopagitica* or the King James Bible, and in studying such works the student's mind is stretched to accommodate modes of expression that are so varied that his capacity for understanding other cultures and men is necessarily enlarged. And the issues posed by the Sermon on the Mount, Thoreau's essay on "Civil Disobedience," and Jefferson's *Declaration of Independence* are at least as lively as those of yesterday's newspaper.

The book is unapologetically Anglo-American. Whitman, thinking of the language required for a masterwork, was satisfied with English:

... it is brawny enough and limber and full enough. On the tough stock of a race who through all change of circumstances was never without the idea of political liberty, which is the animus of all liberty, it has attracted the terms of daintier and gayer and subtler and more elegant tongues. It is the powerful language of resistance ... it is the dialect of common sense. It is the speech of the proud and melancholy races and of all who aspire. It is the chosen tongue to express growth faith self-esteem freedom justice equality friendliness amplitude prudence decision and courage. It is the medium that shall well nigh express the inexpressible.

The intensive study of masterworks in such a language seems to me the prime mode of learning its possibilities, both to increase one's apprehension of human experience and to sharpen one's facility in handling the language. We should be happy with the accident that makes our heritage double, so that we as Americans are by birth committed to literacy in two cultures.

The masterworks in this book can be used in the study of composition in various ways. When our students enter our beginning course in English at Berkeley, they are free of grosser illiteracies, thanks largely to the examination in high-school competence that is given on entrance. They are intelligent, alert, and ready to learn, but they have read neither widely nor intensively. The reasons for this empty-headedness come from major stresses in American culture that may be lamentable but must be recognized as conditioning facts. The point, then, is to fill the student's minds and to give them the skills for further independent work. But their minds should not be filled with the mud of sloppy generalizing but with clearly distinguished articulations. The student generally has read nothing in English before 1900 or, at best, 1850, with the exception of a play or two by Shakespeare. He has no sense of the richness or flexibility of the language, and he is time-bound to the simpler works of the twentieth century. A student who finds George Orwell or Carl Becker impenetrably obscure should not be given essays from the latest edition of a monthly magazine. He should be forced to paraphrase the *Areopagitica,* and after several exercises in stretching his mind and vocabulary to cover Milton's sentences, he will return with a sense of triumphant relief not only to Orwell or Becker but also to Emerson and Hume. He knows, from that experience, that a sentence has a claim upon him, requires his *active* understanding, that he as a reader is responsible for making this understanding active. His sense of style can then move past the norm of the short sentence and the simple word to the norm of the clearest expression of the most significant idea and judgment. He may then find, in the ideals suggested by the style of Swift or Hazlitt, a stylistic ambition of high order.

He will find in the works presented here subjects about which he can write, as well as directions for further study. If a student has read the second chapter of Mill's *Essay on Liberty*, he might for a term paper be assigned the reading of the complete essay, along with Mill's *Autobiography* and one or two useful secondary sources. If he has read Hume on miracles, he might make his term paper a study of Hume's *Enquiry* or as a contrast, he might study Newman on miracles. There is a natural organic movement from this anthology toward directed independent study. From Chesterton to Dickens, from Johnson to Shakespeare, from Wordsworth's "Preface" to his poetry, from Jefferson's *Declaration* and Locke to a study of the place of Locke's ideas in the history of thought—the selections fan out to the widest possibilities, just as they narrow to the most minute linguistic scrutinies.

And they are not boring. The constant search for textbooks appropriate to the teaching of freshman composition is a restless attempt to keep students from being bored by the course. English professors are compelled to pick up the educational spilled beans of the entire university system by teaching "writing" (a subject that is not a subject), and the tendency is to search out gimmicks that will "work," and, when one fails, to search out yet another one. Why shouldn't we let our own subject—great literature in English—provide the base? The sense of glory that we associate with great writing is not confined to poetry and fiction but exists with equal force and beauty in the monuments of expository writing.

This collection should be supplemented by a book of expository writing in contemporary idiom. At Berkeley, the department insists that each section of freshman English read one major text that is preferably a single argument but always the product of a single mind. Each instructor is given considerable freedom of choice, and characteristic authors used are Edmund Wilson, Aldous Huxley, George Orwell, Bertrand Russell, and Carl Becker. Some instructors, however, prefer to use such classics as *Walden* or *Culture and Anarchy*. My own predilection is for a contemporary work, to suggest the liveliness and currency of the traditions of English exposition.

The choice of an additional book of exposition would compensate for the omission of any author later than Chesterton in this text.

The notes in this text gloss words and names not glossed by a standard college dictionary. One function of a freshman English course is to send students flying to the dictionary, and a text that usurps the dictionary's function defeats one purpose of the course. No "apparatus" is included with the text because of my belief that most teachers of English find apparatus disconcerting and, from their point of view, misleading to students.

The book grows from three simple convictions:

1. Freshman students deserve the best literature as a subject for study.

2. Teachers of composition should teach writing in relation to their own subject, that is, great writing in English.

3. The issues raised by masterworks of English exposition are immediately important as well as having permanent and historical interest.

I am indebted to my colleagues at the University of California at Berkeley for their readiness to argue approaches to freshman composition and discuss the present text. And, once again, I am indebted to Miss Bess Lowry and her associates in the Humanities Reference Service of the University Library.

THOMAS PARKINSON

Berkeley, California
December 1961

CONTENTS

MASTERWORKS OF PROSE

Sir Walter Raleigh

*SIR WALTER RALEIGH (1552?-1618), although famous
mainly for his feats as soldier and explorer, was also
a fine poet and vivid narrator. The excerpt here
printed, taken from Chapter X of his* History of the
World, *was written during his long incarceration in
the Tower of London and expresses both the characteristic Elizabethan idea of death and Raleigh's
personal condition. Raleigh was educated at Oriel
College, Oxford. Principal works:* A Report of the
Fight about the Isles of the Azores *(1591);* The Discovery of the Empyre of Guiana *(1596);* History of
the World *(1614).*

OF THE FALLS OF EMPIRES

CONCERNING THE INSTABILITY OF KINGLY ESTATES AND
THE CONTINUANCE OF BOUNDLESS AMBITION IN MORTAL
MEN.

* * * * *

Now these great Kings, and conquering Nations, have
bin the subject of those ancient Histories, which have beene
preserved, and yet remaine among us; and withall of so
many tragicall Poets, as in the persons of powerfull Princes,
and other mightie men have complained against Infidelitie,
Time, Destinie, and most of all against the Variable successe
of worldly things, and Instabilitie of Fortune. To these
undertakings, the greatest Lords of the world have beene
stirred up, rather by the desire of *Fame*, which ploweth up
the Aire, and soweth in the Winde; than by the affection of

1

bearing rule, which draweth after it so much vexation, and so many cares. And that this is true, the good advice of *Cineas* to *Pyrrhus* proves.[1] And certainly, as Fame hath often beene dangerous to the living, so is it to the dead of no use at all; because separate from knowledge. Which were it otherwise, and the extreame ill bargaine of buying this lasting discourse, understood by them which are dissolved; they themselves would then rather have wished, to have stolen out of the world without noise; than to be put in minde, that they have purchased the report of their actions in the world, by rapine, oppression, and crueltie, by giving in spoile the innocent and labouring soule to the idle and insolent, and by having emptied the Cities of the world of their ancient Inhabitants, and filled them againe with so many and so variable sorts of sorrowes.

Since the fall of the *Roman* Empire (omitting that of the *Germaines,* which had neither greatnesse nor continuance) there hath beene no State fearefull in the East, but that of the *Turke;* nor in the West any Prince that hath spred his wings farre over his nest, but the *Spaniard;* who since the time that *Ferdinand* expelled the *Moores* out of *Granado,* have made many attempts to make themselves Masters of all *Europe.* And it is true, that by the treasures of both *Indies,* and by the many Kingdomes which they possesse in *Europe,* they are at this day the most powerfull. But as the *Turke* is now counterpoised by the *Persian,* so in stead of so many Millions as have beene spent by the *English, French,* and *Netherlands* in a defensive war, and in diversions against them, it is easie to demonstrate, that with the charge of two hundred thousand pound continued but for two yeares or three at the most, they may not only be perswaded to live in peace, but all their swelling and overflowing streames may be brought backe into their naturall channels and old bankes. These two Nations, I say, are at this day the most eminent, and to be regarded; the one seeking to roote out the Christian Religion altogether,

---

[1] In Plutarch's *Life of Pyrrhus,* Cineas points out the folly of Pyrrhus' imperial ambitions and, in effect, urges him to enjoy his present state.

the other the truth and sincere profession thereof, the one to joyne all *Europe* to *Asia,* the other the rest of all *Europe* to *Spaine.*

For the rest, if we seek a reason of the succession and continuance of this boundlesse ambition in mortall men, we may adde to that which hath been already said; That the Kings and Princes of the world have alwayes laid before them, the actions, but not the ends, of those great Ones which praeceded them. They are alwayes transported with the glorie of the one, but they never minde the miserie of the other, till they finde the experience in themselves. They neglect the advice of GOD, while they enjoy life, or hope it; but they follow the counsell of Death, upon his first approach. It is he that puts into man all the wisdome of the world, without speaking a word; which GOD with all the words of his Law, promises, or threats, doth infuse. *Death* which hateth and destroyeth man, is beleeved; GOD which hath made him and loves him, is alwayes deferred. *I have considered* (saith SALOMON) *all the workes that are under the Sunne, and behold, all is vanitie and vexation of spirit:* [2] but who beleeves it, till Death tells it us? It was Death, which opening the conscience of *Charles* the fift, made him enjoyne his sonne *Philip* to restore *Navarre;* and King *Francis* the first of *France,* to command that justice should be done upon the Murderers of the Protestants in *Merindol* and *Cabrieres,* which till then he neglected. It is therefore Death alone that can suddenly make man to know himselfe. He tells the proud and insolent, that they are but Abjects, and humbles them at the instant; makes them crie, complaine, and repent, yea, even to hate their forepassed happinesse. He takes the account of the rich, and proves him a begger; a naked begger, which hath interest in nothing, but in the gravell that fills his mouth. He holds a Glasse before the eyes of the most beautifull, and makes them see therein, their deformitie and rottennesse; and they acknowledge it.

O eloquent, just and mightie Death! whom none could

2 Ecclesiastes i, 14.

advise, thou hast perswaded; what none hath dared, thou
hast done; and whom all the world hath flattered, thou only
hast cast out of the world and despised: thou hast drawne
together all the farre stretched greatnesse, all the pride,
crueltie, and ambition of man, and covered it all over with
these two narrow words, *Hic iacet.*[3]

Lastly, whereas this Booke, by the title it hath, calles it
selfe, The first part of the *Generall Historie* of the *World,*
implying a *Second* and *Third* Volume; which I also intended,
and have hewen out; besides many other discouragements,
perswading my silence; it hath pleased GOD to take that
glorious *Prince* out of the world, to whom they were directed;
whose unspeakeable and never enough lamented losse, hath
taught mee to say with JOB, *Versa est in Luctum Cithara mea,
& Organum meum in vocem flentium.*[4]

[3] Here lies.

[4] Job xxx, 31. My harp also is turned to mourning, and my organ
into the voice of them that weep.

Francis Bacon

FRANCIS BACON, *first Baron Verulam and Viscount St. Albans (1561-1626), was a courtier and lawyer of great political influence, in addition to being a philosopher. His political career culminated in the office of lord chancellor (1618) and in his conviction on a charge of bribery (1621). His mind was restlessly curious, spacious, and incisive; its capacity for making forceful and useful distinctions is clear in this passage from the* Novum Organum *(1620).* Bacon was educated at Trinity College, Cambridge, and at Gray's Inn. Other principal works:* The Advancement of Learning *(1605);* Essays *(1597, 1625);* The New Atlantis *(1626).*

From THE NOVUM ORGANUM

XXXVIII

The idols and false notions which are now in possession of the human understanding, and have taken deep root therein, not only so beset men's minds that truth can hardly find entrance, but even after entrance is obtained, they will again in the very instauration of the sciences meet and trouble us, unless men being forewarned of the danger fortify themselves as far as may be against their assaults.

* This section, popularly known as the "Idols" section, shows Bacon's mind moving at its most urbane and analytic. The text used here is based on the famous translation (from the Latin) by Spedding, Ellis, and Heath. The entire work is part of Bacon's long struggle against barriers to the accurate observation and understanding of nature. Here, the barriers examined in metaphorical terms are the follies and superstitions of the human mind.

XXXIX

There are four classes of Idols which beset men's minds. To these for distinction's sake I have assigned names, calling the first class *Idols of the Tribe;* the second, *Idols of the Cave;* the third, *Idols of the Market Place;* the fourth, *Idols of the Theater.*

XL

The formation of ideas and axioms by true induction is no doubt the proper remedy to be applied for the keeping off and clearing away of idols. To point them out, however, is of great use; for the doctrine of Idols is to the interpretation of nature what the doctrine of the refutation of sophisms is to common logic.

XLI

The Idols of the Tribe have their foundation in human nature itself, and in the tribe or race of men. For it is a false assertion that the sense of man is the measure of things. On the contrary, all perceptions as well of the sense as of the mind are according to the measure of the individual and not according to the measure of the universe. And the human understanding is like a false mirror, which, receiving rays irregularly, distorts and discolors the nature of things by mingling its own nature with it.

XLII

The Idols of the Cave are the idols of the individual man. For everyone (besides the errors common to human nature in general) has a cave or den of his own, which refracts and discolors the light of nature, owing either to his own proper and peculiar nature; or to his education and conversation with others; or to the reading of books, and the authority of those whom he esteems and admires; or to the differences of impressions, accordingly as they take place in a mind preoccupied and predisposed or in a mind indifferent and settled; or the like. So that the spirit of man (according as it is meted out to different individuals) is in fact a thing variable and full of perturbation, and governed as it were by chance. Whence it was well observed by Heraclitus that men look for sciences in their own lesser worlds, and not in the greater or common world.

XLIII

There are also Idols formed by the intercourse and association of men with each other, which I call Idols of the Market Place, on account of the commerce and consort of men there. For it is by discourse that men associate, and words are imposed according to the apprehension of the vulgar. And therefore the ill and unfit choice of words wonderfully obstructs the understanding. Nor do the definitions or explanations wherewith in some things learned men are wont to guard and defend themselves, by any means set the matter right. But words plainly force and overrule the understanding, and throw all into confusion, and lead men away into numberless empty controversies and Idle fancies.

XLIV

Lastly, there are Idols which have immigrated into men's minds from the various dogmas of philosophies, and also from wrong laws of demonstration. These I call Idols of the Theater, because in my judgment all the received systems are but so many stage plays, representing worlds of their own creation after an unreal and scenic fashion. Nor is it only of the systems now in vogue, or only of the ancient sects and philosophies, that I speak; for many more plays of the same kind may yet be composed and in like artificial manner set forth; seeing that errors the most widely different have nevertheless causes for the most part alike. Neither again do I mean this only of entire systems, but also of many principles and axioms in science, which by tradition, credulity, and negligence have come to be received.

But of these several kinds of Idols I must speak more largely and exactly, that the understanding may be duly cautioned.

XLV

The human understanding is of its own nature prone to suppose the existence of more order and regularity in the world than it finds. And though there be many things in nature which are singular and unmatched, yet it devises for them parallels and conjugates and relatives which do not exist. Hence the fiction that all celestial bodies move in perfect circles, spirals and dragons being (except in name) utterly rejected. Hence too the element of fire with its orb is brought in, to make up the square with the other three which the sense perceives. Hence also the ratio of density of the so-called elements is arbitrarily fixed at ten to one. And so on of other dreams. And these fancies affect not dogmas only, but simple notions also.[1]

XLVI

The human understanding when it has once adopted an opinion (either as being the received opinion or as being agreeable to itself) draws all things else to support and agree with it. And though there be a greater number and weight of instances to be found on the other side, yet these it either neglects and despises, or else by some distinction sets aside and rejects, in order that by this great and pernicious predetermination the authority of its former conclusions may remain inviolate. And therefore it was a good answer that was made by one who, when they showed him hanging in a temple a picture of those who had paid their vows as having escaped shipwreck, and would have him say whether he did not now acknowledge the power of the gods—"Aye," asked he again, "but where are they painted that were drowned after their vows?" And such is the way of all superstition, whether in astrology, dreams, omens, divine judgments, or the like;

---

[1] "Simple notions" here might be rendered as "perceptions."

wherein men, having a delight in such vanities, mark the events where they are fulfilled, but where they fail, though this happen much oftener, neglect and pass them by. But with far more subtlety does this mischief insinuate itself into philosophy and the sciences; in which the first conclusion colors and brings into conformity with itself all that come after, though far sounder and better. Besides, independently of that delight and vanity which I have described, it is the peculiar and perpetual error of the human intellect to be more moved and excited by affirmatives than by negatives; whereas it ought properly to hold itself indifferently disposed toward both alike. Indeed, in the establishment of any true axiom, the negative instance is the more forcible of the two.

XLVII

The human understanding is moved by those things most which strike and enter the mind simultaneously and suddenly, and so fill the imagination; and then it feigns and supposes all other things to be somehow, though it cannot see how, similar to those few things by which it is surrounded. But for that going to and fro to remote and heterogeneous instances by which axioms are tried as in the fire, the intellect is altogether slow and unfit, unless it be forced thereto by severe laws and overruling authority.

XLVIII

The human understanding is unquiet; it cannot stop or rest, and still presses onward, but in vain. Therefore it is that we cannot conceive of any end or limit to the world, but always as of necessity it occurs to us that there is something beyond. Neither, again, can it be conceived how eternity has flowed down to the present day, for that distinction which is commonly received of infinity in time past and in time to come can by no means hold; for it would thence follow that one infinity is greater than another, and that infinity is wasting away and tending to become finite. The like subtlety arises touching the infinite divisibility of lines, from the same inability of thought to stop. But this inability interferes more mischievously in the discovery of causes; for although the most general principles in nature ought to be held merely positive, as they are discovered, and cannot with truth be referred to a cause, nevertheless the human understanding being unable to rest still seeks something prior in the order of nature. And then it is that in struggling toward that which is further off it falls back upon that which is nearer at hand, namely, on final causes, which have relation clearly to the nature of man rather than to the nature of the universe; and from this source have strangely defiled philosophy. But he is no less an unskilled and shallow philosopher who seeks causes of that which is most general, than he who in things subordinate and subaltern omits to do so.

XLIX

The human understanding is no dry light, but receives an infusion from the will and affections; whence proceed sciences which may be called "sciences as one would." For what a man had rather were true he more readily believes. Therefore he rejects difficult things from impatience of research; sober things, because they narrow hope; the deeper things of nature, from superstition; the light of experience, from arrogance and pride, lest his mind should seem to be occupied with things mean and transitory; things not commonly believed, out of deference to the opinion of the vulgar. Numberless, in short, are the ways, and sometimes imperceptible, in which the affections color and infect the understanding.

L

But by far the greatest hindrance and aberration of the human understanding proceeds from the dullness, incompetency, and deception of the senses; in that things which strike the sense outweigh things which do not immediately strike it, though they be more important. Hence it is that speculation commonly ceases where sight ceases; insomuch that of things invisible there is little or no observation. Hence all the working of the spirits enclosed in tangible bodies lies hid and unobserved of men. So also all the more subtle changes of form in the parts of coarser substance (which they commonly call alteration, though it is in truth local motion through exceedingly small spaces) is in like manner unobserved. And yet unless these two things just mentioned be searched out and brought to light, nothing great can be achieved in nature, as far as the production of works is concerned. So again the essential nature of our common air, and of all bodies less dense than air (which are very many), is also unknown. For the sense by itself is a thing infirm and erring; neither can instruments for enlarging or sharpening the senses do much; but all the truer kind of interpretation of nature is effected by instances and experiments fit and apposite; wherein the sense decides touching the experiment only, and the experiment touching the point in nature and the thing itself.

LI

The human understanding is of its own nature prone to abstractions and gives a substance and reality to things which are fleeting. But to resolve nature into abstractions is less to our purpose than to dissect her into parts; as did the school of Democritus, which went further into nature than the rest.[2] Matter rather than forms should be the object of our attention, its configurations and changes of configuration, and simple action, and law of action or motion; for forms are figments of the human mind, unless you will call those laws of action forms.

LII

Such then are the idols which I call *Idols of the Tribe*, and which take their rise either from the homogeneity of the sub-

---

[2] The school of Democritus resolved matter to atomic particles.

stance of the human spirit, or from its preoccupation, or from its narrowness, or from its restless motion, or from an infusion of the affections, or from the incompetency of the senses, or from the mode of impression.

LIII

The *Idols of the Cave* take their rise in the peculiar constitution, mental or bodily, of each individual; and also in education, habit, and accident. Of their kind there is a great number and variety. But I will instance those the pointing out of which contains the most important caution, and which have most effect in disturbing the clearness of the understanding.

LIV

Men become attached to certain particular sciences and speculations, either because they fancy themselves the authors and inventors thereof, or because they have bestowed the greatest pains upon them and become most habituated to them. But men of this kind, if they betake themselves to philosophy and contemplation of a general character, distort and color them in obedience to their former fancies; a thing especially to be noticed in Aristotle, who made his natural philosophy a mere bond servant to his logic, thereby rendering it contentious and well-nigh useless. The race of chemists, again out of a few experiments of the furnace, have built up a fantastic philosophy, framed with reference to a few things; and Gilbert also, after he had employed himself most laboriously in the study and observation of the loadstone, proceeded at once to construct an entire system in accordance with his favorite subject.[3]

---

3 William Gilbert (*ca.* 1540-1603) was famous for his studies of magnetism, and Bacon here argues that Gilbert should have confined his studies to that particular field rather than constructing general theories of small utility.

LV

There is one principal and as it were radical distinction between different minds, in respect of philosophy and the sciences, which is this: that some minds are stronger and apter to mark the differences of things, others to mark their resemblances. The steady and acute mind can fix its contemplations and dwell and fasten on the subtlest distinctions; the lofty and discursive mind recognizes and puts together the finest and most general resemblances. Both kinds, however, easily err in excess, by catching the one at gradations, the other at shadows.

LVI

There are found some minds given to an extreme admiration of antiquity, others to an extreme love and appetite for novelty; but few so duly tempered that they can hold the mean, neither carping at what has been well laid down by the ancients, nor despising what is well introduced by the moderns. This, however, turns to the great injury of the sciences and philosophy, since these affectations of antiquity and novelty are the humors of partisans rather than judgments; and truth is to be sought for not in the felicity of any age, which is an unstable thing, but in the light of nature and experience, which is eternal. These factions therefore must be abjured, and care must be taken that the intellect be not hurried by them into assent.

LVII

Contemplations of nature and of bodies in their simple form break up and distract the understanding, while contemplations of nature and bodies in their composition and configuration overpower and dissolve the understanding, a distinction well seen in the school of Leucippus and Democritus as compared with the other philosophies. For that school is so busied with the particles that it hardly attends to the structure, while the others are so lost in admiration of the structure that they do not penetrate to the simplicity of nature. These kinds of contemplation should therefore be alternated and taken by turns, so that the understanding may be rendered at once penetrating and comprehensive, and the inconveniences above mentioned, with the idols which proceed from them, may be avoided.

LVIII

Let such then be our provision and contemplative prudence for keeping off and dislodging the *Idols of the Cave*, which grow for the most part either out of the predominance of a favorite subject, or out of an excessive tendency to compare or to distinguish, or out of partiality for particular ages, or out of the largeness or minuteness of the objects contemplated. And generally let every student of nature take this as a rule: that whatever his mind seizes and dwells upon with peculiar satisfaction is to be held in suspicion, and that so much the more care is to be taken in dealing with such questions to keep the understanding even and clear.

LIX

But the *Idols of the Market Place* are the most troublesome of all—idols which have crept into the understanding through the alliances of words and names. For men believe that their reason governs words; but it is also true that words react on the understanding; and this it is that has rendered philosophy and the sciences sophistical and inactive. Now words, being commonly framed and applied according to the capacity of the vulgar, follow those lines of division which are most obvious to the vulgar understanding. And whenever an understanding of greater acuteness or a more diligent observation would alter those lines to suit the true divisions of nature, words stand in the way and resist the change. Whence it comes to pass that the high and formal discussions of learned men end oftentimes in disputes about words and names; with which (according to the use and wisdom of the mathematicians) it would be more prudent to begin, and so by means of definitions reduce them to order. Yet even definitions cannot cure this evil in dealing with natural and material things, since the definitions themselves consist of words, and those words beget others. So that it is necessary to recur to individual instances, and those in due series and order, as I shall say presently when I come to the method and scheme for the formation of notions and axioms.

LX

The idols imposed by words on the understanding are of two kinds. They are either names of things which do not exist (for as there are things left unnamed through lack of observation, so likewise are there names which result from fantastic suppositions and to which nothing in reality corresponds), or they are names of things which exist, but yet confused and ill-defined, and hastily and irregularly derived from realities. Of the former kind are Fortune, the Prime Mover, Planetary Orbits, Elements of Fire, and like fictions which owe their origin to false and idle theories. And this class of idols is more easily expelled, because to get rid of them it is only necessary that all theories should be steadily rejected and dismissed as obsolete.

But the other class, which springs out of a faulty and unskillful abstraction, is intricate and deeply rooted. Let us take for example such a word as *humid* and see how far the several things which the word is used to signify agree with each other, and we shall find the word *humid* to be nothing else than a mark loosely and confusedly applied to denote a variety of actions which will not bear to be reduced to any constant meaning. For it both signifies that which easily spreads itself round any other body; and that which in itself is indeterminate and cannot solidize; and that which readily yields in every direction; and that which easily divides and scatters itself; and that which easily unites and collects itself; and that which readily flows and is put in motion; and that which readily clings to another body and wets it; and that which is easily reduced to a liquid, or being solid easily melts. Accordingly, when you come to apply the word, if you take it in one sense, flame is humid; if in another, air is not humid; if in another, fine dust is humid; if in another, glass is humid. So that it is easy to see that the notion is taken by abstraction only from water and common and ordinary liquids, without any due verification.

There are, however, in words certain degrees of distortion and error. One of the least faulty kinds is that of names of substances, especially of lowest species and well-deduced (for the notion of *chalk* and of *mud* is good, of *earth* bad); a more faulty kind is that of actions, as *to generate, to corrupt, to alter;* the most faulty is of qualities (except such as are the immediate objects of the sense) as *heavy, light, rare, dense,* and the like. Yet in all these cases some notions are of necessity a little better than others, in proportion to the greater variety of subjects that fall within the range of the human sense.

LXI

But the *Idols of the Theater* are not innate, nor do they steal into the understanding secretly, but are plainly impressed and received into the mind from the playbooks of philosophical systems and the perverted rules of demonstration. To attempt refutations in this case would be merely inconsistent with what I have already said, for since we agree neither upon principles nor upon demonstrations there is no place for argument. And this is so far well, inasmuch as it leaves the honor of the ancients untouched. For they are no wise disparaged—the question between them and me being only as to the way. For as the saying is, the lame man who keeps the right road outstrips the runner who takes a wrong one. Nay, it is obvious that when a man runs the wrong way, the more active and swift he is, the further he will go astray.

But the course I propose for the discovery of sciences is such as leaves but little to the acuteness and strength of wits, but places all wits and understandings nearly on a level. For as in the drawing of a straight line or a perfect circle, much depends on the steadiness and practice of the hand, if it be done by aim of hand only, but if with the aid of rule or compass, little or nothing; so is it exactly with my plan. But though particular confutations would be of no avail, yet touching the sects and general divisions of such systems I must say something; something also touching the external signs which show that they are unsound; and finally something touching the causes of such great infelicity and of such lasting and general agreement in error; that so the access to truth may be made less difficult, and the human understanding may the more willingly submit to its purgation and dismiss its idols.

LXII

Idols of the Theater, or of Systems, are many, and there can be and perhaps will be yet many more. For were it not that now for many ages men's minds have been busied with religion and theology; and were it not that civil governments, especially monarchies, have been averse to such novelties, even in matters speculative; so that men labor therein to the peril and harming of their fortunes—not only unrewarded, but exposed also to contempt and envy—doubtless there would have arisen many other philosophical sects like those which in great variety flourished once among the Greeks. For as on the phenomena of the heavens many hypotheses may be constructed, so likewise (and more also) many various dogmas may be set up and established on the phenomena of philosophy. And in the plays of this philosophical theater you may observe the same thing which is found in the theater of the poets, that stories invented for the stage are more compact and elegant, and more as one would wish them to be, than true stories out of history.

In general, however, there is taken for the material of philosophy either a great deal out of a few things, or a very little out of many things; so that on both sides philosophy is based on too narrow a foundation of experiment and natural his-

tory, and decides on the authority of too few cases. For the
Rational School of philosophers snatches from experience a
variety of common instances, neither duly ascertained nor
diligently examined and weighed, and leaves all the rest to
meditation and agitation of wit.

There is also another class of philosophers who, having bestowed much diligent and careful labor on a few experiments,
have thence made bold to educe and construct systems, wrest-
ing all other facts in a strange fashion to conformity therewith.

And there is yet a third class, consisting of those who out of
faith and veneration mix their philosophy with theology and
traditions; among whom the vanity of some has gone so far
aside as to seek the origin of sciences among spirits and genii.
So that this parent stock of errors—this false philosophy—is of
three kinds: the Sophistical, the Empirical, and the Superstitious.

LXIII

The most conspicuous example of the first class was Aristotle, who corrupted natural philosophy by his logic: fashion-
ing the world out of categories; assigning to the human soul,
the noblest of substances, a genus from words of the second
intention; doing the business of density and rarity (which is
to make bodies of greater or less dimensions, that is, occupy
greater or less spaces), by the frigid distinction of act and
power; asserting that single bodies have each a single and
proper motion, and that if they participate in any other, then
this results from an external cause; and imposing countless
other arbitrary restrictions on the nature of things; being always more solicitous to provide an answer to the question and
affirm something positive in words, than about the inner truth
of things; a failing best shown when his philosophy is compared with other systems of note among the Greeks. For the
homoeomera of Anaxagoras; [4] the Atoms of Leucippus and
Democritus; the Heaven and Earth of Parmenides; the Strife
and Friendship of Empedocles; Heraclitus' doctrine how

4 Anaxagoras posited an elemental substance (*homoeomera*) from which
all develops.

bodies are resolved into the indifferent nature of fire, and re-
molded into solids, have all of them some taste of the natural
philosopher—some savor of the nature of things, and experience, and bodies; whereas in the physics of Aristotle you hear
hardly anything but the words of logic, which in his metaphysics also, under a more imposing name, and more forsooth
as a realist than a nominalist, he has handled over again. Nor
let any weight be given to the fact that in his books on animals and his problems, and other of his treatises, there is frequent dealing with experiments. For he had come to his conclusion before; he did not consult experience, as he should
have done, for the purpose of framing his decisions and
axioms, but having first determined the question according to
his will, he then resorts to experience, and bending her into
conformity with his placets, leads her about like a captive in a
procession. So that even on this count he is more guilty than
his modern followers, the schoolmen, who have abandoned
experience altogether.

LXIV

But the Empirical school of philosophy gives birth to dogmas more deformed and monstrous than the Sophistical or
Rational school. For it has its foundations not in the light of
common notions (which though it be a faint and superficial
light, is yet in a manner universal, and has reference to many
things), but in the narrowness and darkness of a few experiments. To those therefore who are daily busied with these experiments and have infected their imagination with them,
such a philosophy seems probable and all but certain; to all
men else incredible and vain. Of this there is a notable instance in the alchemists and their dogmas, though it is hardly
to be found elsewhere in these times, except perhaps in the
philosophy of Gilbert. Nevertheless, with regard to philosophies of this kind there is one caution not to be omitted; for
I foresee that if ever men are roused by my admonitions to betake themselves seriously to experiment and bid farewell to
sophistical doctrines, then indeed through the premature

hurry of the understanding to leap or fly to universals and principles of things, great danger may be apprehended from philosophies of this kind, against which evil we ought even now to prepare.

LXV

But the corruption of philosophy by superstition and an admixture of theology is far more widely spread, and does the greatest harm, whether to entire systems or to their parts. For the human understanding is obnoxious to the influence of the imagination no less than to the influence of common notions. For the contentious and sophistical kind of philosophy ensnares the understanding; but this kind, being fanciful and tumid and half poetical, misleads it more by flattery. For there is in man an ambition of the understanding, no less than of the will, especially in high and lofty spirits.

Of this kind we have among the Greeks a striking example in Pythagoras, though he united with it a coarser and more cumbrous superstition; another in Plato and his school, more dangerous and subtle. It shows itself likewise in parts of other philosophies, in the introduction of abstract forms and final causes and first causes, with the omission in most cases of causes indeterminate, and the like. Upon this point the greatest caution should be used. For nothing is so mischievous as the apotheosis of error; and it is a very plague of the understanding for vanity to become the object of veneration. Yet in this vanity some of the moderns have with extreme levity indulged so far as to attempt to found a system of natural philosophy on the first chapter of Genesis, on the book of Job, and other parts of the sacred writings, seeking for the dead among the living; which also makes the inhibition and repression of it the more important, because from this unwholesome mixture of things human and divine there arises not only a fantastic philosophy but also a heretical religion. Very meet it is therefore that we be sober-minded, and give to faith that only which is faith's.

* * * * *

Selections from

THE AUTHORIZED KING JAMES VERSION OF THE BIBLE

THE KING JAMES VERSION OF THE BIBLE *was produced by a committee of scholars at the command of King James I of England. This version is one of the basic masterpieces of literature in English, and, since its first appearance, in 1611, has shaped the idiom and style of English prose with overwhelming force.*

THE OLD TESTAMENT

THE FIRST BOOK OF MOSES, CALLED GENESIS [1]

Chapter 1

In the beginning God created the heaven and the earth. And the earth was without form, and void; and darkness was upon the face of the deep. And the spirit of God moved upon the face of the waters. And God said, "Let there be light": and there was light. And God saw the light, that it was good: and God divided the light from the darkness. And God called the light Day, and the darkness he called Night. And the evening and the morning were the first day.

And God said, "Let there be a firmament in the midst of the waters, and let it divide the waters from the waters." [2] And

---

[1] The first book of the Old Testament, Genesis begins with the story of the Creation.

[2] The sky is here imagined as an inverted bowl, with water beyond it. The earth is imagined to be surrounded by water; the sky prevents the water from inundating the earth.

God made the firmament, and divided the waters which were under the firmament from the waters which were above the firmament: and it was so. And God called the firmament Heaven. And the evening and the morning were the second day.

And God said, "Let the waters under the heaven be gathered together unto one place, and let the dry land appear": and it was so. And God called the dry land Earth; and the gathering together of the waters called he Seas: and God saw that it was good. And God said, "Let the earth bring forth grass, the herb yielding seed, and the fruit tree yielding fruit after his kind, whose seed is in itself, upon the earth"; and it was so. And the earth brought forth grass, and herb yielding seed after his kind, and the tree yielding fruit, whose seed was in itself, after his kind: and God saw that it was good. And the evening and the morning were the third day.

And God said, "Let there be lights in the firmament of the heaven to divide the day from the night; and let them be for signs, and for seasons, and for days, and years: and let them be for lights in the firmament of the heaven to give light upon the earth": and it was so. And God made two great lights; he made the stars also.[3] And God set them in the firmament of the heaven to give light upon the earth, and to rule over the day and over the night, and to divide the light from the darkness: and God saw that it was good. And the evening and the morning were the fourth day.

And God said, "Let the waters bring forth abundantly the moving creature that hath life, and fowl that may fly above the earth in the open firmament of heaven." And God created great whales, and every living creature that moveth, which the waters brought forth abundantly, after their kind, and every winged fowl after his kind: and God saw that it was good. And God blessed them, saying, "Be fruitful, and multiply, and fill the waters in the seas, and let fowl multiply in the earth." And the evening and the morning were the fifth day.

[3] The lights are fixed in the bowl of Heaven as guides and indicators to men.

And God said, "Let the earth bring forth the living creature after his kind, cattle, and creeping thing, and beast of the earth after his kind": and it was so. And God made the beast of the earth after his kind, and cattle after their kind,[4] and every thing that creepeth upon the earth after his kind: and God saw that it was good. And God said, "Let us make man in our image, after our likeness: and let them have dominion over the fish of the sea, and over the fowl of the air, and over the cattle, and over all the earth, and over every creeping thing that creepeth upon the earth." [5] So God created man in his own image, in the image of God created he him; male and female created he them. And God blessed them, and God said unto them, "Be fruitful, and multiply, and replenish the earth, and subdue it: and have dominion over the fish of the sea, and over the fowl of the air, and over every living thing that moveth upon the earth." And God said, "Behold, I have given you every herb bearing seed, which is upon the face of all the earth, and every tree, in the which is the fruit of a tree yielding seed; to you it shall be for meat. And to every beast of the earth, and to every fowl of the air, and to every thing that creepeth upon the earth, wherein there is life, I have given every green herb for meat": and it was so. And God saw every thing that he had made, and, behold, it was very good. And the evening and the morning were the sixth day.

* * * * *

ECCLESIASTES OR, THE PREACHER [1]

Chapter 1

The words of the preacher, the son of David, king in Jerusalem.

---

4 Cattle are domestic animals; beasts of the earth are wild.

5 Man, as God's image and vicar, is given rule over the other creatures, who are less than he because they are not made in God's image.

1 This is a very late (*ca.* 200 B.C.) book of the Old Testament, and, in spite of its haunting unity of tone, its authorship is almost certainly mul-

Vanity of vanities, saith the Preacher, vanity of vanities; all is vanity. What profit hath a man of all his labour which he taketh under the sun? One generation passeth away, and another generation cometh: but the earth abideth for ever. The sun also ariseth, and the sun goeth down, and hasteth to his place where he arose. The wind goeth toward the south, and turneth about unto the north; it whirleth about continually, and the wind returneth again according to his circuits. All the rivers run into the sea; yet the sea is not full; unto the place from whence the rivers come, thither they return again. All things are full of labour; man cannot utter it: the eye is not satisfied with seeing, nor the ear filled with hearing. The thing that hath been, it is that which shall be; and that which is done is that which shall be done: and there is no new thing under the sun. Is there anything whereof it may be said, "See, this is new"? it hath been already of old time, which was before us. There is no remembrance of former things; neither shall there be any remembrance of things that are to come with those that shall come after.

I the Preacher was king over Israel in Jerusalem. And I gave my heart to seek and search out by wisdom concerning all things that are done under heaven: this sore travail hath God given to the sons of man to be exercised therewith. I have seen all the works that are done under the sun; and, behold, all is vanity and vexation of spirit. That which is crooked cannot be made straight: and that which is wanting cannot be numbered. I communed with mine own heart, saying, "Lo, I am come to great estate, and have gotten more wisdom than all they that have been before me in Jerusalem": yea, my heart had great experience of wisdom and knowledge. And I gave my heart to know wisdom, and to know madness and folly: I perceived that this also is vexation of spirit. For in much wisdom is much grief: and he that increaseth knowledge increaseth sorrow.

---

tiple. Obviously, the epilogue (the last three paragraphs of Chapter 12) is by a disciple, and the main text is the product of mixed authorship.

"Ecclesiastes" means "preacher." We are not, however, to take literally the text's identification of the preacher with Solomon.

Chapter 2

I said in mine heart, "Go to now,[2] I will prove thee with mirth, therefore enjoy pleasure": and, behold, this also is vanity. I said of laughter, "It is mad": and of mirth, "What doeth it?" I sought in mine heart to give myself unto wine, yet acquainting mine heart with wisdom; and to lay hold on folly, till I might see what was that good for the sons of men, which they should do under the heaven all the days of their life. I made me great works; I builded me houses; I planted me vineyards: I made me gardens and orchards, and I planted trees in them of all kind of fruits: I made me pools of water, to water therewith the wood that bringeth forth trees: I got me servants and maidens, and had servants born in my house; also I had great possessions of great and small cattle above all that were in Jerusalem before me: I gathered me also silver and gold, and the peculiar treasure of kings and of the provinces: I gat me men singers and women singers, and the delights of the sons of men, as musical instruments, and that of all sorts. So I was great, and increased more than all that were before me in Jerusalem: also my wisdom remained with me. And whatsoever mine eyes desired I kept not from them, I withheld not my heart from any joy; for my heart rejoiced in all my labour: and this was my portion of all my labour. Then I looked on all the works that my hands had wrought, and on the labour that I had laboured to do: and, behold, all was vanity and vexation of spirit, and there was no profit under the sun.

And I turned myself to behold wisdom, and madness, and folly: for what can the man do that cometh after the king? even that which hath been already done. Then I saw that wisdom excelleth folly, as far as light excelleth darkness. The wise man's eyes are in his head; but the fool walketh in darkness: and I myself perceived also that one event happeneth to them all. Then said I in my heart, "As it happeneth to the fool, so it happeneth even to me"; and why was I then more wise?

2 In current idiom, "Go to" would be "Come on."

Then I said in my heart, that this also is vanity. For there is no remembrance of the wise more than of the fool for ever; seeing that which now is in the days to come shall all be forgotten. And how dieth the wise man? as the fool. Therefore I hated life; because the work that is wrought under the sun is grievous unto me: for all is vanity and vexation of spirit.

Yea, I hated all my labour which I had taken under the sun: because I should leave it unto the man that shall be after me. And who knoweth whether he shall be a wise man or a fool? yet shall he have rule over all my labour wherein I have laboured, and wherein I have shewed myself wise under the sun. This is also vanity. Therefore I went about to cause my heart to despair of all the labour which I took under the sun. For there is a man whose labour is in wisdom, and in knowledge, and in equity; yet to a man that hath not laboured therein shall he leave it for his portion. This also is vanity and a great evil. For what hath man of all his labour, and of the vexation of his heart, wherein he hath laboured under the sun? For all his days are sorrows, and his travail grief; yea, his heart taketh not rest in the night. This is also vanity.

There is nothing better for a man, than that he should eat and drink, and that he should make his soul enjoy good in his labour. This also I saw, that it was from the hand of God. For who can eat, or who else can hasten hereunto, more than I? For God giveth to a man that is good in his sight wisdom, and knowledge, and joy: but to the sinner he giveth travail, to gather and to heap up, that he may give to him that is good before God.[3] This also is vanity and vexation of spirit.

Chapter 3

To every thing there is a season, and a time to every purpose under the heaven:
A time to be born, and a time to die;
A time to plant, and a time to pluck up that which is planted;

[3] The good man derives joy, wisdom, and knowledge from his work, but the sinner receives only unrewarding possessions.

A time to kill, and a time to heal;
A time to break down, and a time to build up;
A time to weep, and a time to laugh;
A time to mourn, and a time to dance;
A time to cast away stones, and a time to gather stones together;
A time to embrace, and a time to refrain from embracing;
A time to get, and a time to lose;
A time to keep, and a time to cast away;
A time to rend, and a time to sew;
A time to keep silence, and a time to speak;
A time to love, and a time to hate;
A time of war, and a time of peace.

What profit hath he that worketh in that wherein he laboureth? I have seen the travail, which God hath given to the sons of men to be exercised in it. He hath made every thing beautiful in his time: also he hath set the world in their heart, so that no man can find out the work that God maketh from the beginning to the end. I know that there is no good in them, but for a man to rejoice, and to do good in his life. And also that every man should eat and drink, and enjoy the good of all his labour, it is the gift of God. I know that, whatsoever God doeth, it shall be for ever: nothing can be put to it, nor any thing taken from it: and God doeth it, that men should fear before him. That which hath been is now; and that which is to be hath already been; and God requireth that which is past.

And moreover I saw under the sun the place of judgment, that wickedness was there; and the place of righteousness, that iniquity was there. I said in mine heart, "God shall judge the righteous and the wicked: for there is a time there for every purpose and for every work." I said in mine heart concerning the estate of the sons of men, that God might manifest them, and that they might see that they themselves are beasts. For that which befalleth the sons of men befalleth beasts; even one thing befalleth them: as the one dieth, so dieth the other; yea, they have all one breath; so that a man hath no preeminence above a beast: for all is vanity. All go unto one place; all are of the dust, and all turn to dust again. Who knoweth the spirit of man that goeth upward, and the spirit of the beast that goeth downward to the earth? Wherefore I perceive that there is nothing better, than that a man should rejoice in his own works; for that is his portion: for who shall bring him to see what shall be after him?

Chapter 4

So I returned and considered all the oppressions that are done under the sun: and behold the tears of such as were oppressed, and they had no comforter; and on the side of their oppressors there was power; but they had no comforter. Wherefore I praised the dead which are already dead more than the living which are yet alive. Yea, better is he than both they, which hath not yet been, who hath not seen the evil work that is done under the sun.

Again, I considered all travail, and every right work, that for this a man is envied of his neighbour. This is also vanity and vexation of spirit. The fool foldeth his hands together, and eateth his own flesh.[4] Better is an handful with quietness, than both the hands full with travail and vexation of spirit.

Then I returned, and I saw vanity under the sun. There is one alone, and there is not a second: yea, he hath neither child nor brother: yet is there no end of all his labour; neither is his eye satisfied with riches; neither saith he, "For whom do I labour, and bereave my soul of good?" This is also vanity, yea, it is a sore travail. Two are better than one; because they have a good reward for their labour. For if they fall, the one will lift up his fellow: but woe to him that is alone when he falleth; for he hath not another to help him up. Again, if two lie together, then they have heat: but how can one be warm alone? And if one prevail against him, two

---

[4] The transition to the sentence which follows is abrupt and may indicate a corruption in the text.

shall withstand him; and a threefold cord is not quickly broken.

Better is a poor and a wise child than an old and foolish king, who will no more be admonished. For out of prison he cometh to reign; whereas also he that is born in his kingdom becometh poor. I considered all the living which walk under the sun, with the second child that shall stand up in his stead. There is no end of all the people, even of all that have been before them: they also that come after shall not rejoice in him. Surely this also is vanity and vexation of spirit.

Chapter 5

Keep thy foot when thou goest to the house of God, and be more ready to hear, than to give the sacrifice of fools: for they consider not that they do evil. Be not rash with they mouth, and let not thine heart be hasty to utter any thing before God: for God is in heaven, and thou upon earth: therefore let thy words be few. For a dream cometh through the multitude of business; and a fool's voice is known by multitude of words. When thou vowest a vow unto God, defer not to pay it; for he hath no pleasure in fools: pay that which thou has vowed. Better is it that thou shouldest not vow, than that thou shouldest vow and not pay. Suffer not thy mouth to cause thy flesh to sin; neither say thou before the angel, that it was an error: wherefore should God be angry at thy voice, and destroy the work of thine hands? For in the multitude of dreams and many words there are also divers vanities: but fear thou God.

If thou seest the oppression of the poor, and violent perverting of judgment and justice in a province, marvel not at the matter: for he that is higher than the highest regardeth; and there be higher than they. Moreover the profit of the earth is for all: the king himself is served by the field.

He that loveth silver shall not be satisfied with silver; nor he that loveth abundance with increase: this is also vanity.

When goods increase, they are increased that eat them: and what good is there to the owners thereof, saving the beholding of them with their eyes? The sleep of a labouring man is sweet, whether he eat little or much: but the abundance of the rich will not suffer him to sleep.

There is a sore evil which I have seen under the sun, namely, riches kept for the owners thereof to their hurt. But those riches perish by evil travail: and he begetteth a son, and there is nothing in his hand. As he came forth of his mother's womb, naked shall he return to go as he came, and shall take nothing of his labour, which he may carry away in his hand. And this also is a sore evil, that in all points as he came, so shall he go: and what profit hath he that hath laboured for the wind? All his days also he eateth in darkness, and he hath much sorrow and wrath with his sickness.

Behold that which I have seen: it is good and comely for one to eat and to drink, and to enjoy the good of all his labour that he taketh under the sun all the days of his life, which God giveth him: for it is his portion. Every man also to whom God hath given riches and wealth, and hath given him power to eat thereof, and to take his portion, and to rejoice in his labour; this is the gift of God. For he shall not much remember the days of his life; because God answereth him in the joy of his heart.

Chapter 6

There is an evil which I have seen under the sun, and it is common among men: a man to whom God hath given riches, wealth, and honour, so that he wanteth nothing for his soul of all that he desireth, yet God giveth him not power to eat thereof, but a stranger eateth it: this is vanity, and it is an evil disease. If a man beget an hundred children, and live many years, so that the days of his years be many, and his soul be not filled with good, and also that he have no burial; I say, that an untimely birth is better than he. For he cometh in with vanity, and departeth in darkness, and his name shall be covered with darkness. Moreover he hath not seen the sun, nor known any thing: this hath more rest than the other. Yea, though he live a thousand years twice told, yet hath he seen no good: do not all go to one place? All the labour of man is for his mouth, and yet the appetite is not filled. For what hath the wise more than the fool? what hath the poor, that knoweth to walk before the living? Better is the sight of the eyes than the wandering of desire: this is also vanity and vexation of spirit.

That which hath been is named already, and it is known that it is man: neither may he contend with him that is mightier than he. Seeing there be many things that increase vanity, what is man the better? For who knoweth what is good for man in this life, all the days of his vain life which he spendeth as a shadow? for who can tell a man what shall be after him under the sun?

Chapter 7

A good name is better than precious ointment; and the day of death than the day of one's birth. It is better to go to the house of mourning, than to go to the house of feasting: for that is the end of all men; and the living will lay it to his heart. Sorrow is better than laughter: for by the sadness of the countenance the heart is made better. The heart of the wise is in the house of mourning; but the heart of fools is in the house of mirth. It is better to hear the rebuke of the wise, than for a man to hear the song of fools. For as the crackling of thorns under a pot, so is the laughter of the fool: This also is vanity. Surely oppression maketh a wise man mad; and a gift destroyeth the heart. Better is the end of a thing than the beginning thereof: and the patient in spirit is better than the proud in spirit. Be not hasty in thy spirit to be angry: for anger resteth in the bosom of fools. Say not thou, "What is the cause that the former days wer better than these?" for thou doest not enquire wisely concerning this. Wisdom is good with an inheritance: and by it there is profit to them that see the sun. For wisdom is a defence, and money is a defence: but the excellency of knowledge is, that wisdom giveth life to them that have it. Consider the work of God: for who can make that straight, which he hath made crooked? In the day of prosperity be joyful, but in the day of adversity consider: God also hath set the one over against the other, to the end that man should find nothing after him.

All things have I seen in the days of my vanity: there is a a just man that perisheth in his righteousness, and there is a wicked man that prolongeth his life in his wickedness. Be not righteous over much; neither make thyself over wise: why shouldest thou destroy thyself? Be not over much wicked, neither be thou foolish: why shouldest thou die before thy time? It is good that thou shouldest take hold of this; yea, also from this withdraw not thine hand: for he that feareth God shall come forth of them all.

Wisdom strengtheneth the wise more than ten mighty men which are in the city. For there is not a just man upon earth, that doeth good, and sinneth not. Also take no heed unto all words that are spoken; lest thou hear they servant curse thee: for oftentimes also thine own heart knoweth that thou thyself likewise hast cursed others.

All this have I proved by wisdom: I said, "I will be wise"; but it was far from me. That which is far off, and exceeding deep, who can find it out? I applied mine heart to know, and to search, and to seek out wisdom, and the reason of things, and to know the wickedness of folly, even of foolishness and madness: and I find more bitter than death the woman, whose heart is snares and nets, and her hands as bands: whoso pleaseth God shall escape from her; but the sinner shall be taken by her. "Behold, this have I found," saith the Preacher, "counting one by one, to find out the account: which yet my soul seeketh, but I find not: one man among a thousand have I found; but a woman among all those have I not found. Lo, this only have I found, that God hath made man upright; but they have sought out many inventions."

Chapter 8

Who is as the wise man? and who knoweth the interpretation of a thing? a man's wisdom maketh his face to shine, and the boldness of his face shall be changed. I counsel thee to keep the king's commandment, and that in regard of the oath of God. Be not hasty to go out of his sight: stand not in an evil thing; for he doeth whatsoever pleaseth him. Where the word of a king is, there is power: and who may say unto him, "What doest thou"? Whoso keepeth the commandment shall feel no evil thing: and a wise man's heart discerneth both time and judgment. Because to every purpose there is time and judgment, therefore the misery of man is great upon him. For he knoweth not that which shall be: for who can tell him when it shall be? There is no man that hath power over the spirit to retain the spirit; neither hath he power in the day of death: and there is no discharge in that war; neither shall wickedness deliver those that are given to it. All this have I seen, and applied my heart unto every work that is done under the sun: there is a time wherein one man ruleth over another to his own hurt.

And so I saw the wicked buried, who had come and gone from the place of the holy, and they were forgotten in the city where they had so done: this is also vanity. Because sentence against an evil work is not executed speedily, therefore the heart of the sons of men is fully set in them to do evil. Though a sinner do evil an hundred times, and his days be prolonged, yet surely I know that it shall be well with them that fear God, which fear before him: but it shall not be well with the wicked, neither shall he prolong his days, which are as a shadow; because he feareth not before God. There is a vanity which is done upon the earth; that there be just men, unto whom it happeneth according to the work of the wicked; again, there be wicked men, to whom it happeneth according to the work of the righteous: I said that this also is vanity. Then I commended mirth, because a man hath no better thing under the sun, than to eat, and to drink, and to be merry: for that shall abide with him of his labour the days of his life, which God giveth him under the sun.

When I applied mine heart to know wisdom, and to see the business that is done upon the earth: (for also there is that neither day nor night seeth sleep with his eyes:) then I beheld all the work of God, that a man cannot find out the work that is done under the sun: because though a man labour to seek it out, yet he shall not find it; yea further; though a wise man think to know it, yet shall he not be able to find it.

Chapter 9

For all this I considered in my heart even to declare all this, that the righteous, and the wise, and their works, are in the hand of God: no man knoweth either love or hatred by all that is before them. All things come alike to all: there is one event to the righteous, and to the wicked; to the good and to the clean, and to the unclean; to him that sacrificeth, and to him that sacrificeth not: as is the good, so is the sinner; and he that sweareth, as he that feareth an oath. This is an evil among all things that are done under the sun, that there is one event unto all: yea, also the heart of the sons of men is full of evil, and madness is in their heart while they live, and after that they go to the dead. For to him that is joined to all the living there is hope: for a living dog is better than a dead lion. For the living know that they shall die: but the dead know not anything, neither have they any more a reward; for the memory of them is forgotten. Also their love, and their hatred, and their envy, is now perished; neither have they any more a portion forever in any thing that is done under the sun.

Go thy way, eat thy bread with joy, and drink thy wine with a merry heart; for God now accepteth thy works. Let thy garments be always white; and let thy head lack no ointment. Live joyfully with the wife whom thou lovest all the days of life of thy vanity, which he hath given thee under the sun, all the days of thy vanity: for that is thy portion in this life, and in thy labour which thou takest under the sun. Whatsoever thy hand findeth to do, do it with thy might; for there is no work, nor device, nor knowledge, nor wisdom, in the grave, whither thou goest.

I returned, and saw under the sun, that the race is not to the swift, nor the battle to the strong, neither yet bread to the wise, nor yet riches to men of understanding, nor yet favour to men of skill; but time and chance happeneth to them all. For man also knoweth not his time: as the fishes that are taken in an evil net, and as the birds that are caught in the snare; so are the sons of men snared in an evil time, when it falleth suddenly upon them.

This wisdom have I seen also under the sun, and it seemed great unto me: there was a little city, and few men within it; and there came a great king against it, and besieged it, and built great bulwarks against it: now there was found in it a poor wise man, and he by his wisdom delivered the city; yet no man remembered that same poor man. Then said I, "Wisdom is better than strength: nevertheless the poor man's wisdom is despised, and his words are not heard."

The words of wise men are heard in quiet more than the cry of him that ruleth among fools. Wisdom is better than weapons of war: but one sinner destroyeth much good.

Chapter 10

Dead flies cause the ointment of the apothecary to send forth a stinking savour: so doth a little folly him that is in reputation for wisdom and honour. A wise man's heart is at his right hand; but a fool's heart at his left. Yea also, when he that is a fool walketh by the way, his wisdom faileth him, and he saith to every one that he is a fool. If the spirit of the ruler rise up against thee, leave not thy place; for yielding pacifieth great offences. There is an evil which I have seen under the sun, as an error which proceedeth from the ruler: folly is set in great dignity, and the rich sit in low place. I have seen servants upon horses, and princes walking as servants upon the earth. He that diggeth a pit shall fall into it; and whoso breaketh an hedge, a serpent shall bite him. Whoso removeth stones shall be hurt therewith; and he that cleaveth wood shall be endangered thereby. If the iron be blunt, and he do not whet the edge, then must he put to more strength: but wisdom is profitable to direct. Surely the serpent will bite without enchantment; and a babbler is no better. The words of a wise man's mouth are gracious; but the lips of a fool will swallow up himself. The beginning of the words of his mouth is foolishness: and the end of his talk is mischievous madness. A fool also is full of words: a man cannot tell what shall be; and what shall be after him, who can tell him? The labour of the foolish wearieth every one of them, because he knoweth not how to go to the city. Woe to thee, O land, when thy king is a child, and thy princes eat in the morning! Blessed art thou, O land, when thy king is the son of nobles, and thy princes eat in due season, for strength, and not for drunkenness! By much slothfulness the building decayeth; and through idleness of the hands the house droppeth through. A feast is made for laughter, and wine maketh merry: but money answereth all things. Curse not the king, no not in thy thought; and curse not the rich in thy bed-chamber: for a bird of the air shall carry the voice, and that which hath wings shall tell the matter.

Chapter 11

Cast thy bread upon the waters: for thou shalt find it after many days. Give a portion to seven, and also to eight; for thou knowest not what evil shall be upon the earth. If the clouds be full of rain, they empty themselves upon the earth: and if the tree fall toward the south, or toward the north, in the place where the tree falleth, there it shall be. He that observeth the wind shall not sow; and he that regardeth the clouds shall not reap. As thou knowest not what is the way of the spirit, nor how the bones do grow in the womb of her that is with child: even so thou knowest not the works of God who maketh all. In the morning sow thy seed, and in the evening withold not thine hand: for thou knowest not whether shall prosper, either this or that, or whether they both shall be alike good. Truly the light is sweet, and a pleasant thing it is for the eyes to behold the sun: but if a man live many years, and rejoice in them all; yet let him remember the days of darkness; for they shall be many. All that cometh is vanity.

Rejoice, O young man, in thy youth; and let thy heart cheer thee in the days of thy youth, and walk in the ways of thine heart, and in the sight of thine eyes: but know thou, that for all these things God will bring thee into judgment. Therefore remove sorrow from thy heart, and put away evil from thy flesh: for childhood and youth are vanity.

Chapter 12

Remember now thy Creator in the days of thy youth, while the evil days come not, nor the years draw nigh, when thou shalt say, "I have no pleasure in them"; while the sun, or the light, or the moon, or the stars, be not darkened, nor the clouds return after the rain: in the day when the keepers of the house shall tremble, and the strong men shall bow themselves, and the grinders cease because they are few, and those that look out of the windows be darkened, and the doors shall be shut in the streets, when the sound of the grinding is low, and he shall rise up at the voice of the bird, and all the daughters of musick shall be brought low; also when they shall be afraid of that which is high, and fears shall be in the way, and the almond tree shall flourish, and the grasshopper shall be a burden, and desire shall fail: because man goeth to his long home, and the mourners go about the streets: or ever the silver cord be loosed, or the golden bowl be broken, or the pitcher be broken at the fountain, or the wheel broken at the cistern. Then shall the dust return to the earth as it was: and the spirit shall return unto God who gave it. Vanity of vanities, saith the Preacher; all is vanity.

And moreover, because the Preacher was wise, he still taught the people knowledge; yea, he gave good heed, and sought out, and set in order many proverbs. The Preacher sought to find out acceptable words: and that which was written was upright, even words of truth.

The words of the wise are as goads, and as nails fastened by the masters of assemblies, which are given from one shepherd.[5] And further, by these, my son, be admonished: of making many books there is no end; and much study is a weariness of the flesh.

Let us hear the conclusion of the whole matter: Fear God, and keep his commandments: for this is the whole duty of man. For God shall bring every work into judgment, with every secret thing, whether it be good, or whether it be evil.

THE NEW TESTAMENT

THE GOSPEL ACCORDING TO ST. MATTHEW [1]

Chapter 4

Then was Jesus led up of the Spirit [2] into the wilderness to be tempted of the devil. And when he had fasted forty days and forty nights, he was afterward an hungred. And when the tempter came to him, he said, "If thou be the Son of God, command that these stones be made bread." But he answered and said, "It is written, 'Man shall not live by bread alone, but by every word that proceedeth out of the mouth of God.'"

[5] The words of the wise are as instigations to proper conduct; or, they are nails—that is, they support a firm structure.

[1] This selection includes the Sermon on the Mount, which is the great center of Christian doctrine.

[2] The Holy Spirit.

Then the devil taketh him up into the holy city, [3] and setteth him on a pinnacle of the temple, and saith unto him, "If thou be the Son of God, cast thyself down: for it is written,

'He shall give his angels charge concerning thee:
And in their hands they shall bear thee up,
Lest at any time thou dash thy foot against a stone.' "

Jesus said unto him, "It is written again, 'Thou shalt not tempt the Lord thy God.' " Again, the devil taketh him up into an exceeding high mountain, and sheweth him all the kingdoms of the world, and the glory of them; and saith unto him, "All these things will I give thee, if thou wilt fall down and worship me." Then saith Jesus unto him, "Get thee hence, Satan: for it is written, 'Thou shalt worship the Lord thy God, and him only shalt thou serve.' " Then the devil leaveth him, and, behold, angels came and ministered unto him.

Now when Jesus had heard that John was cast into prison, he departed into Galilee; and leaving Nazareth, he came and dwelt in Capernaum, which is upon the sea coast, in the borders of Zabulon and Nephthalim: that it might be fulfilled which was spoken by Esaias the prophet, [4] saying,

"The land of Zabulon, and the land of Nephthalim,
By the way of the sea, beyond Jordan,
Galilee of the Gentiles; [5]
The people which sat in darkness
Saw great light;
And to them which sat in the region and shadow of death
Light is sprung up."

From that time Jesus began to preach, and to say, "Repent: for the kingdom of heaven is at hand."

And Jesus, walking by the sea of Galilee, saw two brethren, Simon called Peter, and Andrew his brother, casting a net into the sea: for they were fishers. And he saith unto them, "Follow me, and I will make you fishers of men." And they

[3] Jerusalem.
[4] Isaiah ix:1-2.
[5] "Galilee of the Gentiles" refers to the region of non-Jews or pagans.

straightway left their nets, and followed him. And going on from thence, he saw other two brethren, James the son of Zebedee, and John his brother, in a ship with Zebedee their father, mending their nets; and he called them. And they immediately left the ship and their father, and followed him.

And Jesus went about all Galilee, teaching in their synagogues, and preaching the gospel of the kingdom, and healing all manner of sickness and all manner of disease among the people. And his fame went throughout all Syria: and they brought unto him all sick people that were taken with divers diseases and torments, and those which were possessed with devils, and those which were lunatick, and those that had the palsy; and he healed them. And there followed him great multitudes of people from Galilee, and from Decapolis, and from Jerusalem, and from Judea, and from beyond Jordan.[6]

Chapter 5

And seeing the multitudes, he went up into a mountain: and when he was set, his disciples came unto him: and he opened his mouth, and taught them, saying,

"Blessed are the poor in spirit: for theirs is the kingdom of heaven.

"Blessed are they that mourn: for they shall be comforted.

"Blessed are the meek: for they shall inherit the earth.

"Blessed are they which do hunger and thirst after righteousness: for they shall be filled.

"Blessed are the merciful: for they shall obtain mercy.

"Blessed are the pure in heart: for they shall see God.

"Blessed are the peacemakers: for thy shall be called the children of God.

"Blessed are they which are persecuted for righteousness' sake: for theirs is the kingdom of heaven. Blessed are ye, when men shall revile you, and persecute you, and shall say all manner of evil against you falsely, for my sake. Rejoice, and

[6] Jesus drew his followers from a large area, much of which was pagan.

be exceeding glad: for great is your reward in heaven: for so persecuted they the prophets which were before you.

"Ye are the salt of the earth: but if the salt have lost his savour, wherewith shall it be salted? it is thenceforth good for nothing, but to be cast out, and to be trodden under foot of men. Ye are the light of the world. A city that is set on an hill cannot be hid. Neither do men light a candle, and put it under a bushel, but on a candlestick; and it giveth light unto all that are in the house. Let your light so shine before men, that they may see your good works, and glorify your Father which is in heaven.

"Think not that I am come to destroy the law, or the prophets: I am not come to destroy, but to fulfil. For verily I say unto you, Till heaven and earth pass, one jot or one tittle shall in no wise pass from the law, till all be fulfilled. Whosoever therefore shall break one of these least commandments, and shall teach men so, he shall be called the least in the kingdom of heaven: but whosoever shall do and teach them, the same shall be called great in the kingdom of heaven. For I say unto you, that except your righteousness shall exceed the righteousness of the scribes and Pharisees, [7] ye shall in no case enter into the kingdom of heaven.

"Ye have heard that it was said by them of old time, 'Thou shalt not kill; and whosoever shall kill shall be in danger of the judgment': but I say unto you, that whosoever is angry with his brother without a cause shall be in danger of the judgment: and whosoever shall say to his brother, 'Raca,' [8] shall be in danger of the council: but whosoever shall say, 'Thou fool,' shall be in danger of hell fire. Therefore if thou bring thy gift to the altar, and there rememberest that thy brother hath aught against thee; leave there thy gift before the altar, and go thy way; first be reconciled to thy brother, and then come and offer thy gift. Agree with thine adversary

[7] The scribes and Pharisees are placed (some commentators say unfairly so) in the category of those who mechanically follow set laws or expediency.
[8] Good-for-nothing or wretch.

quickly, whiles thou art in the way with him; lest at any time the adversary deliver thee to the judge, and the judge deliver thee to the officer, and thou be cast into prison. Verily I say unto thee, Thou shalt by no means come out thence, till thou hast paid the uttermost farthing.

"Ye have heard that it was said by them of old time, 'Thou shalt not commit adultery': but I say unto you, that whosoever looketh on a woman to lust after her hath committed adultery with her already in his heart. And if thy right eye offend thee, pluck it out, and cast it from thee: for it is profitable for thee that one of thy members should perish, and not that thy whole body should be cast into hell. And if thy right hand offend thee, cut it off, and cast it from thee: for it is profitable for thee that one of thy members should perish, and not that thy whole body should be cast into hell. It hath been said, 'Whosoever shall put away his wife, let him give her a writing of divorcement': but I say unto you, that whosoever shall put away his wife, saving for the cause of fornication, causeth her to commit adultery: and whosoever shall marry her that is divorced committeth adultery.

"Again, ye have heard that it hath been said by them of old time, 'Thou shalt not forswear thyself, but shalt perform unto the Lord thine oaths': but I say unto you, Swear not at all; neither by heaven; for it is God's throne: nor by the earth; for it is his footstool: neither by Jerusalem; for it is the city of the great King. Neither shalt thou swear by thy head, because thou canst not make one hair white or black. But let your communication be, 'Yea, yea'; 'Nay, nay': for whatsoever is more than these cometh of evil.

"Ye have heard that it hath been said, 'An eye for an eye, and a tooth for a tooth': but I say unto you, that ye resist not evil: but whosoever shall smite thee on thy right cheek, turn to him the other also. And if any man will sue thee at the law, and take away thy coat, let him have thy cloke also. And whosoever shall compel thee to go a mile, go with him twain. Give to him that asketh thee, and from him that would borrow of thee turn not thou away.

"Ye have heard that it hath been said, 'Thou shalt love thy neighbour, and hate thine enemy.' But I say unto you, Love your enemies, bless them that curse you, do good to them that hate you, and pray for them which despitefully use you, and persecute you; that ye may be the children of your Father which is in heaven: for he maketh his sun to rise on the evil and on the good, and sendeth rain on the just and on the unjust. For if ye love them which love you, what reward have ye? do not even the publicans [9] the same? And if ye salute your brethren only, what do ye more than others? do not even the publicans so? Be ye therefore perfect, even as your Father which is in heaven is perfect."

Chapter 6

"Take heed that ye do not your alms before men, to be seen of them: otherwise ye have no reward of your Father which is in heaven.

"Therefore when thou doest thine alms, do not sound a trumpet before thee, as the hypocrites do in the synagogues and in the streets, that they may have glory of men. Verily I say unto you, They have their reward. But when thou doest alms, let not thy left hand know what thy right hand doeth: that thine alms may be in secret: and thy Father which seeth in secret himself shall reward thee openly.

"And when thou prayest, thou shalt not be as the hypocrites are: for they love to pray standing in the synagogues and in the corners of the streets, that they may be seen of men. Verily I say unto you, They have their reward. But thou, when thou prayest, enter into thy closet, and when thou hast shut thy door, pray to thy Father which is in secret; and thy Father which seeth in secret shall reward thee openly. But when ye pray, use not vain repetitions, as the heathen do: for they think that they shall be heard for their much speaking. Be not ye therefore like unto them: for your Father knoweth

[9] Roman tax-gatherers, held in contempt as representatives of an oppressive government and as pagans.

what things ye have need of, before ye ask him. After this manner therefore pray ye: 'Our Father which art in heaven, Hallowed be thy name. Thy kingdom come. Thy will be done in earth, as it is in heaven. Give us this day our daily bread. And forgive us our debts, as we forgive our debtors. And lead us not into temptation, but deliver us from evil: For thine is the kingdom, and the power, and the glory, for ever. Amen.' For if ye forgive men their trespasses, your heavenly Father will also forgive you: but if ye forgive not men their trespasses, neither will your Father forgive your trespasses.

"Moreover when ye fast, be not, as the hypocrites, of a sad countenance: for they disfigure their faces, that they may appear unto men to fast. Verily I say unto you, They have their reward. But thou, when thou fastest, anoint thine head, and wash thy face; that thou appear not unto men to fast, but unto thy Father which is in secret: and thy Father, which seeth in secret, shall reward thee openly.

"Lay not up for yourselves treasures upon earth, where moth and rust doth corrupt, and where thieves break through and steal: but lay up for yourselves treasures in heaven, where neither moth nor dust doth corrupt, and where thieves do not break through nor steal: for where your treasure is, there will your heart be also. The light of the body is the eye: if therefore thine eye be single, thy whole body shall be full of light. But if thine eye be evil, thy whole body shall be full of darkness. If therefore the light that is in thee be darkness, how great is that darkness! No man can serve two masters: for either he will hate the one, and love the other; or else he will hold to the one, and despise the other. Ye cannot serve God and mammon.[10] Therefore I say unto you, Take no thought for your life, what ye shall eat, or what ye shall drink; nor yet for your body, what ye shall put on. Is not the life more than meat, and the body than raiment? Behold the fowls of the air: for they sow not, neither do they reap, nor gather into

10 Property, material wealth.

barns; yet your heavenly Father feedeth them. Are ye not much better than they? Which of you by taking thought can add one cubit unto his stature? And why take ye thought for raiment? Consider the lilies of the field, how they grow; they toil not, neither do they spin: and yet I say unto you, that even Solomon in all his glory was not arrayed like one of these. Wherefore, if God so clothe the grass of the field, which to day is, and to morrow is cast into the oven, shall he not much more clothe you, O ye of little faith? Therefore take no thought, saying, 'What shall we eat?' or, 'What shall we drink?' or, 'Wherewithal shall we be clothed?' (for after all these things do the Gentiles [11] seek:) for your heavenly Father knoweth that ye have need of all these things. But seek ye first the kingdom of God, and his righteousness; and all these things shall be added unto you. Take therefore no thought for the morrow: for the morrow shall take thought for the things of itself. Sufficient unto the day is the evil thereof."

Chapter 7

"Judge not, that ye be not judged. For with what judgment ye judge, ye shall be judged: and with what measure ye mete, it shall be measured to you again. And why beholdest thou the mote that is in thy brother's eye, but considerest not the beam that is in thine own eye? Or how wilt thou say to thy brother, 'Let me pull out the mote out of thine eye'; and, behold, a beam is in thine own eye? Thou hypocrite, first cast out the beam out of thine own eye; and then shalt thou see clearly to cast out the mote out of thy brother's eye.

"Give not that which is holy unto the dogs, neither cast ye your pearls before swine, lest they trample them under their feet, and turn again and rend you.

"Ask, and it shall be given you; seek, and ye shall find; knock, and it shall be opened unto you: for every one that

[11] Heathens.

asketh receiveth; and he that seeketh findeth; and to him that knocketh it shall be opened. Or what man is there of you, whom if his son ask bread, will he give him a stone? Or if he ask a fish, will he give him a serpent? If ye then, being evil, know how to give good gifts unto your children, how much more shall your Father which is in heaven give good things to them that ask him? Therefore all things whatsoever ye would that men should do to you, do ye even so to them: for this is the law and the prophets.

"Enter ye in at the strait gate: for wide is the gate, and broad is the way, that leadeth to destruction, and many there be which go in thereat: because strait is the gate, and narrow is the way, which leadeth unto life, and few there be that find it.

"Beware of false prophets, which come to you in sheep's clothing, but inwardly they are ravening wolves. Ye shall know them by their fruits. Do men gather grapes of thorns, or figs of thistles? Even so every good tree bringeth forth good fruit; but a corrupt tree bringeth forth evil fruit. A good tree cannot bring forth evil fruit, neither can a corrupt tree bring forth good fruit. Every tree that bringeth not forth good fruit is hewn down, and cast into the fire. Wherefore by their fruits ye shall know them. Not every one that saith unto me, 'Lord, Lord' shall enter into the kingdom of heaven; but he that doeth the will of my Father which is in heaven. Many will say to me in that day, 'Lord, Lord, have we not prophesied in thy name? and in thy name have cast out devils? and in thy name done many wonderful works?' And then will I profess unto them, I never knew you: depart from me, ye that work iniquity. Therefore whosoever heareth these sayings of mine, and doeth them, I will liken him unto a wise man, which built his house upon a rock: and the rain descended, and the floods came, and the winds blew, and beat upon that house; and it fell not: for it was founded upon a rock. And every one that heareth these sayings of mine, and doeth them not, shall be likened unto a foolish man, which built his house upon the sand: and the rain descended, and the floods came, and the winds blew, and beat upon that house; and it fell: and great was the fall of it."

And it came to pass, when Jesus had ended these sayings, the people were astonished at his doctrine: for he taught them as one having authority, and not as the scribes.[12]

* * * * *

THE FIRST EPISTLE OF PAUL THE APOSTLE
TO THE CORINTHIANS

Chapter 13 [1]

Though I speak with the tongues of men and of angels, and have not charity,[2] I am become as sounding brass, or a tinkling cymbal. And though I have the gift of prophecy, and understand all mysteries, and all knowledge; and though I have all faith, so that I could remove mountains, and have not charity, I am nothing. And though I bestow all my goods to feed the poor, and though I give my body to be burned, and have not charity, it profiteth me nothing. Charity suffereth long, and is kind; charity envieth not; charity vaunteth not itself, is not puffed up, doth not behave itself unseemly, seeketh not her own, is not easily provoked, thinketh no evil; rejoiceth not in iniquity, but rejoiceth in the truth; beareth all things, believeth all things, hopeth all things, endureth all things. Charity never faileth: but whether there be prophecies, they shall fail; whether there be tongues, they shall cease; whether there be knowledge, it shall vanish away. For we know in part, and we prophesy in part. But when that which is perfect

12 He speaks as one who is bringing a new law, rather than as one who is merely interpreting an old one.

1 This famous passage is from Paul's letter to the Corinthian Church. Corinth was a center of culture and moral depravity. Chapter 13 is part of a section of the letter devoted to answering questions raised by the congregation in a letter to Paul.

2 The alternative rendering of "charity" is "love."

is come, then that which is in part shall be done away. When I was a child, I spake as a child, I understood as a child, I thought as a child: but when I became a man, I put away childish things. For now we see through a glass, darkly; but then face to face: now I know in part; but then shall I know even as also I am known. And now abideth faith, hope, charity, these three; but the greatest of these is charity.

* * * * *

Thomas Hobbes

THOMAS HOBBES *(1588-1679), philosopher and writer, during his long life came to know most of the chief scientific and literary figures of both England and the Continent, including Bacon and Galileo, as well as Ben Jonson and Abraham Cowley. He traveled widely on the Continent and spent much of the Commonwealth period in Paris. His basic ideas are conservative, and his style is at times cryptic and a little crabbed. Nevertheless, he met great issues directly and wrote of them economically, so that he remains one of the most important of English thinkers on subjects ranging from semantics to politics. Hobbes was educated at Magdalen Hall, Oxford. Principal works:* Human Nature *(1650);* Leviathan *(1651);* Behemoth, or the Long Parliament *(1680).*

OF THE NATURAL CONDITION OF MANKIND AS CONCERNING THEIR FELICITY, AND MISERY [1]

Men by nature equal

Nature hath made men so equal, in the faculties of the body, and mind; as that though there be found one man sometimes manifestly stronger in body, or of quicker mind than another; yet when all is reckoned together, the difference between man, and man, is not so considerable, as that one man can there-

[1] This selection comprises Chapter XIII of *Leviathan.*

upon claim to himself any benefit, to which another may not pretend, as well as he. For as to the strength of body, the weakest has strength enough to kill the strongest, either by secret machination, or by confederacy with others, that are in the same danger with himself.

And as to the faculties of the mind, setting aside the arts grounded upon words, and especially that skill of proceeding upon general, and infallible rules, called science; which very few have, and but in few things; as being not a native faculty, born with us; nor attained, as prudence, while we look after somewhat else, I find yet a greater equality amongst men, than that of strength. For prudence, is but experience; which equal time, equally bestows on all men, in those things they equally apply themselves unto. That which may perhaps make such equality incredible, is but a vain conceit of one's own wisdom, which almost all men think they have in a greater degree, than the vulgar; that is, than all men but themselves, and a few others, whom by fame, or for concurring with themselves, they approve. For such is the nature of men, that howsoever they may acknowledge many others to be more witty, or more eloquent, or more learned; yet they will hardly believe there be many so wise as themselves; for they see their own wit at hand, and other men's at a distance. But this proveth rather that men are in that point equal, than unequal. For there is not ordinarily a greater sign of the equal distribution of any thing, than that every man is contented with his share.

From equality proceeds diffidence

From this equality of ability, ariseth equality of hope in the attaining of our ends. And therefore if any two men desire the same thing, which nevertheless they cannot both enjoy, they become enemies; and in the way to their end, which is principally their own conservation, and sometimes their delectation only, endeavour to destroy, or subdue one another. And from hence it comes to pass, that where an invader hath no more to fear, than another man's single power; if one plant, sow, build, or possess a convenient seat, others may probably be expected to come prepared with forces united, to dispossess, and deprive him, not only of the fruit of his labour, but also of his life, or liberty. And the invader again is in the like danger of another.

From diffidence war

And from this diffidence of one another, there is no way for any man to secure himself, so reasonable, as anticipation; that is, by force, or wiles, to master the persons of all men he can, so long, till he see no other power great enough to endanger him: and this is no more than his own conservation requireth, and is generally allowed. Also because there be some, that taking pleasure in contemplating their own power in the acts of conquest, which they pursue farther than their security requires; if others, that otherwise would be glad to be at ease within modest bounds, should not by invasion increase their power, they would not be able, long time, by standing only on their defence, to subsist. And by consequence, such augmentation of dominion over men being necessary to a man's conservation, it ought to be allowed him.

Again, men have no pleasure, but on the contrary a great deal of grief, in keeping company, where there is no power able to over-awe them all. For every man looketh that his companion should value him, at the same rate he sets upon himself: and upon all signs of contempt, or undervaluing, naturally endeavours, as far as he dares, (which amongst them that have no common power to keep them in quiet, is far enough to make them destroy each other), to extort a greater value from his contemners, by damage; and from others, by the example.

So that in the nature of man, we find three principal causes of quarrel. First, competition; secondly, diffidence; thirdly, glory.

The first, maketh men invade for gain; the second, for

safety; and the third, for reputation. The first use violence, to make themselves masters of other men's persons, wives, children, and cattle; the second, to defend them; the third, for trifles, as a word, a smile, a different opinion, and any other sign of undervalue, either direct in their persons, or by reflection in their kindred, their friends, their nation, their profession, or their name.

Out of civil states, there is always war of every one against every one

Hereby it is manifest, that during the time men live without a common power to keep them all in awe, they are in that condition which is called war; and such a war, as is of every man, against every man. For WAR, consisteth not in battle only, or in the act of fighting; but in a tract of time, wherein the will to contend by battle is sufficiently known: and therefore the notion of *time,* is to be considered in the nature of war; as it is in the nature of weather. For as the nature of foul weather, lieth not in a shower or two of rain; but in an inclination thereto of many days together: so the nature of war, consisteth not in actual fighting; but in the known disposition thereto, during all the time there is no assurance to the contrary. All other time is PEACE.

The incommodities of such a war.

Whatsoever therefore is consequent to a time of war, where every man is enemy to every man; the same is consequent to the time, wherein men live without other security, than what their own strength, and their own invention shall furnish them withal. In such condition, there is no place for industry; because the fruit thereof is uncertain: and consequently no culture of the earth; no navigation, nor use of the commodities that may be imported by sea; no commodious building; no instruments of moving, and removing, such things as require much force; no knowledge of the face of the earth;

no account of time; no arts; no letters; no society; and which is worst of all, continual fear, and danger of violent death; and the life of man, solitary, poor, nasty, brutish, and short.

It may seem strange to some man, that has not well weighed these things; that nature should thus dissociate, and render men apt to invade, and destroy one another: and he may therefore, not trusting to this inference, made from the passions, desire perhaps to have the same confirmed by experience. Let him therefore consider with himself, when taking a journey, he arms himself, and seeks to go well accompanied; when going to sleep, he locks his doors; when even in his house he locks his chests; and this when he knows there be laws, and public officers, armed, to revenge all injuries shall be done him; what opinion he has of his fellow-subjects, when he rides armed; of his fellow citizens, when he locks his doors; and of his children, and servants, when he locks his chests. Does he not there as much accuse mankind by his actions, as I do by my words? But neither of us accuse man's nature in it. The desires, and other passions of man, are in themselves no sin. No more are the actions, that proceed from those passions, till they know a law that forbids them: which till laws be made they cannot know: nor can any law be made, till they have agreed upon the person that shall make it.

It may peradventure be thought, there was never such a time, nor condition of war as this; and I believe it was never generally so, over all the world: but there are many places, where they live so now. For the savage people in many places of America, except the government of small families, the concord whereof dependeth on natural lust, have no government at all; and live at this day in that brutish manner, as I said before. Howsoever, it may be perceived what manner of life there would be, where there were no common power to fear, by the manner of life, which men that have formerly lived under a peaceful government, use to degenerate into, in a civil war.

But though there had never been any time, wherein particular men were in a condition of war one against another;

yet in all times, kings, and persons of sovereign authority, because of their independency, are in continual jealousies, and in the state and posture of gladiators; having their weapons pointing, and their eyes fixed on one another; that is, their forts, garrisons, and guns upon the frontiers of their kingdoms; and continual spies upon their neighbours; which is a posture of war. But because they uphold thereby, the industry of their subjects; there does not follow from it, that misery, which accompanies the liberty of particular men.

In such a war nothing is unjust

To this war of every man, against every man, this also is consequent; that nothing can be unjust. The notions of right and wrong, justice and injustice have there no place. Where there is no common power, there is no law: where no law, no injustice. Force, and fraud, are in war the two cardinal virtues. Justice, and injustice are none of the faculties neither of the body, nor mind. If they were, they might be in a man that were alone in the world, as well as his senses, and passions. They are qualities, that relate to men in society, not in solitude. It is consequent also to the same condition, that there be no propriety, no dominion, no *mine* and *thine* distinct; but only that to be every man's, that he can get: and for so long, as he can keep it. And thus much for the ill condition, which man by mere nature is actually placed in; though with a possibility to come out of it, consisting partly in the passions, partly in his reason.

The passions that incline men to peace

The passions that incline men to peace, are fear of death; desire of such things as are necessary to commodious living; and a hope by their industry to obtain them. And reason suggesteth convenient articles of peace, upon which men may be drawn to agreement. These articles, are they, which otherwise are called the Laws of Nature . . .

John Milton

*JOHN MILTON (1608-1674) was a poet whose verse ranks
as one of the incomparable achievements of English
literature and also a prolific writer of prose on religious and political questions. After an early appren-
ticeship as a poet, Milton devoted his energies to the
service of the Puritan Commonwealth. In 1649 he was
appointed Latin Secretary to the Council of State and
despite increasing blindness held this post until 1660.
In the* Areopagitica, *first published in 1644 as a protest against Parliament's 1643 ordinance for licensing
the press, he uses classical oratorical forms to communicate his basic ideals of religious, political, and
personal freedom. The result is one of the central
documents of the English-speaking world, not only on
the freedom of the press but on the basic dignity of
the individual will and reason. Although couched as
an oration addressed to Parliament, it was not delivered, and the* Areopagitica *was printed (as a pamphlet) only once in Milton's lifetime. Milton was educated at Christ's College, Cambridge. Other principal
works:* "Lycidas" (1637); Paradise Lost (1667); Paradise Regained (1671); Samson Agonistes (1671).

AREOPAGITICA Abridged [1]

* * * * *

I deny not but that it is of greatest concernment in the
church and commonwealth, to have a vigilant eye how books
demean themselves as well as men; and thereafter to confine,

[1] The title is taken from the Areopagus, the court that traditionally
sat on the hill of Ares (Mars) in Athens. Milton's oration emulates a
speech of the same name by Isocrates (436-338 B.C.), and its effect is to
urge Parliament to act in the spirit of freedom that motivated the
Areopagus.

imprison, and do sharpest justice on them as malefactors: for books are not absolutely dead things, but do contain a potency of life in them to be as active as that soul was whose progeny they are; nay, they do preserve as in a vial the purest efficacy and extraction of that living intellect that bred them. I know they are as lively, and as vigorously productive, as those fabulous dragon's teeth; [2] and being sown up and down, may chance to spring up armed men. And yet, on the other hand, unless wariness be used, as good almost kill a man as kill a good book: who kills a man kills a reasonable creature, God's image; but he who destroys a good book, kills reason itself, kills the image of God, as it were, in the eye. Many a man lives a burden to the earth; but a good book is the precious life-blood of a master-spirit, embalmed and treasured up on purpose to a life beyond life. 'Tis true, no age can restore a life, whereof, perhaps, there is no great loss; and revolutions of ages do not oft recover the loss of a rejected truth, for the want of which whole nations fare the worse. We should be wary therefore what persecution we raise against the living labors of public men, how we spill that seasoned life of man, preserved and stored up in books; since we see a kind of homicide may be thus committed, sometimes a martyrdom; and if it extent to the whole impression, a kind of massacre, whereof the execution ends not in the slaying of an elemental life, but strikes at that ethereal and fifth essence, [3] the breath of reason itself; slays an immortality rather than a life. But lest I should be condemned of introducing license while I oppose licensing, I refuse not the pains to be so much historical as will serve to show what hath been done by ancient and famous commonwealths against this disorder, till the very time that this project of licensing crept out of the Inquisition, [4] was catched up by our prelates, and hath caught some of our presbyters.

[2] Ovid, *Metamorphoses*, III, 95-126. The fabulous teeth which, when sown, produced a crop of armed men who destroyed each other.

[3] The ethereal quintessence, or fifth element, an imperishable substance identified with the spirit.

In Athens, where books and wits were ever busier than in any other part of Greece, I find but only two sorts of writings which the magistrate cared to take notice of: those either blasphemous and atheistical, or libellous. Thus the books of Protagoras were by the judges of Areopagus commanded to be burnt, and himself banished the territory, for a discourse begun with his confessing not to know "whether there were gods or whether not." And against defaming, it was decreed that none should be traduced by name, as was the manner of Vetus Comoedia, [5] whereby we may guess how they censured libelling; and this course was quick [6] enough, as Cicero writes, to quell both the desperate wits of other atheists and the open way of defaming, as the event showed. Of other sects and opinions, though tending to voluptuousness and the denying of divine Providence, they took no heed. Therefore we do not read that either Epicurus, or that libertine school of Cyrene, [7] or what the Cynic impudence [8] uttered, was ever questioned by the laws. Neither is it recorded that the writings of those old comedians were suppressed, though the acting of them were forbid; and that Plato commended the reading of Aristophanes, the loosest of them all, to his royal scholar Dionysius, is commonly known, and may be excused, if holy Chrysostom, [9] as is reported, nightly studied so much the same author, and had the art to cleanse a scurrilous vehemence into the style of a rousing sermon.

---

[4] Suppression of heresy, beginning in the thirteenth century, especially effective in Spain. The Council of Trent (1546) ordered indices compiled of books and authors whose reading was prohibited in whole or in part.

[5] The Old Comedy of Athens, which was curtailed by law during only a three-year period.

[6] Lively, vigorous.

[7] Both the Epicureans and the Cyrenaics were committed to the concept that pleasure was the end of life.

[8] The most famous Cynic was Diogenes, who looked with a lamp in broad daylight for an honest man. The members of the Cynic school were sardonic and "impudent."

[9] St. John Chrysostom (A.D. 347-407) opposed the adulation of inferior shows and plays, but he was so fond of Aristophanes that he kept a copy of that writer's plays under his pillow at night.

That other leading city of Greece, Lacedaemon, considering that Lycurgus [10] their lawgiver was so addicted to elegant learning as to have been the first that brought out of Ionia the scattered works of Homer, and sent the poet Thales from Crete to prepare and mollify the Spartan surliness with his smooth songs and odes, the better to plant among them law and civility, it is to be wondered how museless and unbookish they were, minding nought but the feats of war. There needed no licensing of books among them, for they disliked all but their own laconic apothegms, and took a slight occasion to chase Archilochus out of their city, perhaps for composing in a higher strain that their own soldierly ballads and roundels could reach to; or if it were for his broad verses, they were not therein so cautious but they were as dissolute in their promiscuous conversing, whence Euripides affirms, in *Andromache,* that their women were all unchaste. Thus much may give us light after what sort [11] books were prohibited among the Greeks.

The Romans also, for many ages trained up only to a military roughness, resembling most the Lacedaemonian guise, knew of learning little but what their Twelve Tables [12] and the Pontific College with their augurs and flamens taught them in religion and law; so unacquainted with other learning that when Carneades and Critolaus, with the Stoic Diogenes, [13] coming ambassadors to Rome, took thereby occasion to give the city a taste of their philosophy, they were suspected for seducers by no less a man than Cato the Censor, who moved it in the Senate to dismiss them speedily, and to banish all such Attic babblers out of Italy. But Scipio and others of the noblest senators withstood him and his old Sabine austerity; honored and admired the men; and the censor himself at last, in his old age, fell to the study of that whereof

---

10 A legendary figure, the subject of one of Plutarch's *Lives.*
11 In what manner.
12 The earliest statement of Roman law, dating from *ca.* 450 B.C.
13 Carneades, Critolaus, and Diogenes were respectively a skeptic, Aristotelian, and a Stoic sent from Athens to Rome in 155 B.C. to protest a fine assessed against the Athenians.

before he was so scrupulous. And yet at the same time Naevius and Plautus, [14] the first Latin comedians, had filled the city with all the borrowed scenes of Menander and Philemon. [15] Then began to be considered there also what was to be done to libellous books and authors; for Naevius was quickly cast into prison for his unbridled pen, and released by the tribunes upon his recantation: we read also that libels were burnt, and the makers punished, by Augustus.

The like severity, no doubt, was used if aught were impiously written against their esteemed gods. Except in these two points, how the world went in books the magistrate kept no reckoning. And therefore Lucretius, without impeachment, versifies his Epicurism to Memmius, [16] and had the honor to be set forth the second time by Cicero, so great a father of the commonwealth; although himself disputes against that opinion in his own writings. Nor was the satirical sharpness or naked plainness of Lucilius, [17] or Catullus, [18] or Flaccus, [19] by any order prohibited. And for matters of state, the story of Titus Livius,[20] though it extolled that part which Pompey held, was not therefore suppressed by Octavius Caesar of the other faction. But that Naso [21] was by him banished in his old age, for the wanton poems of his youth, was but a mere covert of state over some secret cause; and besides, the books were neither banished nor called in. From hence we shall meet with little else but tyranny in the Roman empire, that we may not marvel if not so often bad as good books were silenced. I shall therefore deem to have been large enough

[14] Roman writers of dramatic comedies.

[15] Greek writers of dramatic comedy, on whom the Roman writers modeled their work.

[16] Lucretius' great poem *De Rerum Naturae* was dedicated to his patron Memmius and, according to tradition, was edited by Cicero.

[17] Lucilius (148-103 B.C.) was the founder of Roman satire.

[18] Catullus (87-47 B.C.), the greatest Latin lyric poet, was exiled for his satiric attacks on Caesar.

[19] Quintus Horatius Flaccus (Horace).

[20] Livy's *History of Rome*.

[21] Ovid (Publius Ovidius Naso), the great Roman poet, was banished, as Catullus had been before him.

in producing what among the ancients was punishable to write, save only which all other arguments were free to treat on.

(4) By this time the emperors were become Christians, whose discipline in this point I do not find to have been more severe than what was formerly in practice. The books of those whom they took to be grand heretics were examined, refuted, and condemned in the general councils; and not till then were prohibited, or burnt, by authority of the emperor. As for the writings of heathen authors, unless they were plain invectives against Christianity, as those of Porphyrius and Proclus,[22] they met with no interdict that can be cited, till about the year 400 in a Carthaginian Council, wherein bishops themselves were forbid to read the books of Gentiles,[23] but heresies they might read; while others long before them, on the contrary, scrupled more the books of heretics than Gentiles. And that the primitive councils and bishops were wont only to declare what books were not commendable, passing no further but leaving it to each one's conscience to read or to lay by, till after the year 800, is observed already by Padre Paolo, [24] the great unmasker of the Trentine Council. After which time the Popes of Rome, engrossing what they pleased of political rule into their own hands, extended their dominion over men's eyes, as they had before over their judgments, burning and prohibiting to be read what they fancied not; yet sparing in their censures, and the books not many which they dealt with; till Martin V, [25] by his bull, not only prohibited, but was the first that excommunicated the reading of heretical books; for about that time Wyclif and Huss growing terrible, were they who first drove the Papal Court to a

22 Neoplatonists and firm enemies of the Christian religion.
23 The question was whether there was more danger in reading heathen (Gentile) works or in reading heretical Christians.
24 Paolo Sarpi (1552-1623), author of a *Historie of the Council of Trent*, translated into English in 1620 and used by Milton for much of his information on the Council of Trent.
25 Pope from 1417 to 1431. His bull of 1418 specifically excommunicated contumacious heretics.

stricter policy of prohibiting. Which course Leo X and his successors followed, until the Council of Trent and the Spanish Inquisition, engendering together, brought forth or perfected those catalogues and expurging indexes [26] that rake through the entrails of many an old good author with a violation worse than any could be offered to his tomb.

Nor did they stay in matters heretical, but any subject that was not to their palate they either condemned in a prohibition, or had it straight into the new purgatory of an index. To fill up the measure of encroachment, their last invention was to ordain that no book, pamphlet, or paper should be printed (as if St. Peter had bequeathed them the keys of the press also out of Paradise) unless it were approved and licensed under the hands of two or three glutton friars. For example:

Let the Chancellor Cini be pleased to see if in this present work be contained aught that may withstand the printing.
                    Vincent Rabatta, Vicar of Florence.
I have seen this present work, and find nothing athwart the Catholic faith and good manners: in witness whereof I have given, &c.
                    Nicolo Cini, Chancellor of Florence.
Attending the precedent relation, it is allowed that this present work of Davanzati may be printed.
                    Vincent Rabatta, &c.
It may be printed, July 15.
                    Friar Simon Mompei d'Amelia,
                    Chancellor of the Holy Office in Florence.

Sure they have a conceit, if he of the bottomless pit had not long since broke prison, that this quadruple exorcism would bar him down. I fear their next design will be to get into their custody the licensing of that which they say Claudius [27] intended but went not through with. Vouchsafe to see another of their forms, the Roman stamp:

[26] The first index of forbidden reading was issued in 1559.
[27] Milton's note: *Quo veniam daret flatum crepitumque ventris in convivio emittendi. Sueton. in Claudio.*

Imprimatur, [28] If it seem good to the reverend Master of
the Holy Palace,

Belcastro, Vicegerent.

Imprimatur,

Friar Nicolo Rodolphi,
Master of the Holy Palace.

Sometimes five imprimaturs are seen together, dialoguewise,
in the piazza of one title-page, complimenting and ducking
each to other with their shaven reverences, whether the author,
who stands by in perplexity at the foot of his epistle, shall to
the press or to the sponge. These are the pretty responsories,
these are the dear antiphonies, that so bewitched of late our
prelates and their chaplains, with the goodly echo they made,
and besotted us to the gay imitation of a lordly imprimatur,
one from Lambeth House,[29] another from the west end of
Paul's;[30] so apishly Romanising that the word of command
still was set down in Latin, as if the learned grammatical pen
that wrote it would cast no ink without Latin; or perhaps, as
they thought, because no vulgar tongue was worthy to express
the pure conceit of an imprimatur; but rather, as I hope, for
that our English, the language of men ever famous and fore-
most in the achievements of liberty, will not easily find servile
letters enow to spell such a dictatory presumption English.

And thus ye have the inventors and the original of book-
licensing ripped up and drawn as lineally as any pedigree.
We have it not, that can be heard of, from any ancient state,
or polity, or church, nor by any statute left us by our ancestors elder or later; nor from the modern custom of any reformed city or church abroad; but from the most anti-christian
council and the most tyrannous inquisition that ever inquired.
Till then books were ever as freely admitted into the world as
any other birth; the issue of the brain was no more stifled than
the issue of the womb: no envious Juno [31] sat cross-legged over

28 It may be printed.
29 One from the residence of the Archbishop of Canterbury.
30 One from the Bishop of London.
31 Ovid, *Metamorphoses* IX, 285-319. Juno placed the goddess of child-

the nativity of any man's intellectual offspring; but if it proved
a monster, who denies but that it was justly burnt or sunk into
the sea? But that a book, in worse condition than a peccant
soul, should be to stand before a jury ere it be born to the
world, and undergo yet in darkness the judgment of Rada-
manth and his colleagues, ere it can pass the ferry backward
into light, was never heard before, till that mysterious iniquity,
provoked and troubled at the first entrance of reformation,
sought out new limboes and new hells wherein they might
include our books also within the number of their damned.
And this was the rare morsel so officiously snatched up, and
so ill-favoredly imitated by our inquisiturient [32] bishops and
the attendant minorites their chaplains. That ye like not now
these most certain authors of this licensing order, and that all
sinister intention was far distant from your thoughts when ye
were importuned the passing it, all men who know the integrity of your actions, and how ye honor truth, will clear ye
readily.

But some will say, what though the inventors were bad, the
thing for all that may be good. It may so; yet if that thing
be no such deep invention, but obvious and easy for any man
to light on, and yet best and wisest commonwealths through
all ages and occasions have forborne to use it, and falsest
seducers and oppressors of men were the first who took it up,
and to no other purpose but to obstruct and hinder the first
approach of reformation, I am of those who believe it will be
a harder alchemy than Lullius [33] ever knew, to sublimate any
good use out of such an invention. Yet this only is what I
request to gain from this reason, that it may be held a dangerous and suspicious fruit, as certainly it deserves, for the tree
that bore it, until I can dissect one by one the properties it
has. But I have first to finish, as was propounded, what is to

---

birth cross-legged beside Alcmena, muttering charms to prevent the birth
of Hercules. Juno's efforts failed: Alcmena's maid tricked the goddess into
rising.

32 Eager to play the inquisitor.

33 Raymond Lullius (*ca.* 1235-1315), logician and student of Arabic,
reputed to have been an alchemist.

be thought in general of reading books, whatever sort they be, and whether be more the benefit or the harm that thence proceeds.

Not to insist upon the examples of Moses, Daniel, and Paul, who were skilful in all the learning of the Egyptians, Chaldeans, and Greeks, which could not probably be without reading their books of all sorts, in Paul especially, who thought it no defilement to insert into Holy Scripture the sentences of three Greek poets, and one of them a tragedian; the question was notwithstanding sometimes controverted among the primitive doctors, but with great odds on that side which affirmed it both lawful and profitable, as was then evidently perceived when Julian, the Apostate,[34] and subtlest enemy to our faith, made a decree forbidding Christians the study of heathen learning; for, said he, they wound us with our own weapons, and with our own arts and sciences they overcome us. And indeed the Christians were put so to their shifts by this crafty means, and so much in danger to decline into all ignorance, that the two Apollinarii [35] were fain, as a man may say, to coin all the seven liberal sciences out of the Bible, reducing it into divers forms of orations, poems, dialogues, even to the calculating of a new Christian grammar. But, saith the historian Socrates,[36] the providence of God provided better than the industry of Apollinarius and his son, by taking away that illiterate law with the life of him who devised it.

So great an injury they then held it to be deprived of Hellenic learning; and thought it a persecution more undermining, and secretly decaying the church, than the open cruelty of Decius or Diocletian.[37] And perhaps it was [with] the same politic drift that the devil whipped St. Jerome in a Lenten

34 Emperor (A.D. 361-363) who excluded the Christians from the schools and attempted to revive, in rationalized form, the classical gods.

35 When Julian forbade the Christians to participate in classical learning, the two Apollinariuses (father and son) reshaped the Bible so that it could serve the purposes of classical learning.

36 Church historian of the fifth century.

37 Persecution of the Christians was especially vigorous during the reign of Decius (A.D. 249-251) and that of Diocletian (A.D. 284-305).

dream for reading Cicero; or else it was a phantasm bred by
the fever which had then seized him. For had an angel been
his discipliner, unless it were for dwelling too much upon
Ciceronianisms, and had chastised the reading, not the vanity,
it had been plainly partial, first, to correct him for grave
Cicero and not for scurril Plautus, whom he confesses to have
been reading not long before; next, to correct him only, and
let so many more ancient fathers wax old in those pleasant
and florid studies, without the lash of such a tutoring appari-
tion; insomuch that Basil teaches how some good use may be
made of Margites,[38] a sportful poem, not now extant, writ by
Homer; and why not then of Morgante,[39] an Italian romance
much to the same purpose?

But if it be agreed we shall be tried by visions, there is a
vision recorded by Eusebius,[40] far ancienter than this tale of
Jerome to the nun Eustochium, and besides, has nothing of a
fever in it. Dionysius Alexandrinus was, about the year 240,
a person of great name in the church for piety and learning,
who was wont to avail himself much against heretics by being
conversant in their books; until a certain presbyter laid it
scrupulously to his conscience, how he durst venture himself
among those defiling volumes. The worthy man, loath to give
offence, fell into a new debate with himself what was to be
thought; when suddenly a vision sent from God (it was his
own epistle that so avers it) confirmed him in these words:
"Read any books whatever come to thy hands, for thou art
sufficient both to judge aright and to examine each matter."
To this revelation he assented the sooner, as he confesses,
because it was answerable to that of the Apostle to the Thessalonians: "Prove all things, hold fast that which is good."[41]

And he might have added another remarkable saying of

---

[38] Basil the Great, Bishop of Cappodocia from A.D. 370 to A.D. 379, was
the author of *The Right to Use Greek Literature*, and he argued for the
study of Homer's (now lost) comic epic.

[39] A mock-heroic romance by Luigi Pulci (1431-1487).

[40] Milton is referring to Eusebius' *Ecclesiastical History*, in which the
letter from Dionysius to Philemon appears.

[41] I Thessalonians v, 21.

the same author: "To the pure all things are pure;" [42] not only meats and drinks, but all kind of knowledge whether of good or evil; the knowledge cannot defile, nor consequently the books, if the will and conscience be not defiled. For books are as meats and viands are, some of good, some of evil substance; and yet God in that unapocryphal vision said without exception, "Rise, Peter, kill and eat," [43] leaving the choice to each man's discretion. Wholesome meats to a vitiated stomach differ little or nothing from unwholesome; and best books to a naughty mind are not unappliable to occasions of evil. Bad meats will scarce breed good nourishment in the healthiest concoction; [44] but herein the difference is of bad books, that they to a discreet and judicious reader serve in many respects to discover, to confute, to forewarn, and to illustrate. Whereof what better witness can ye expect I should produce than one of your own now sitting in Parliament, the chief of learned men reputed in this land, Mr. Selden,[45] whose volume of natural and national laws proves, not only by great authorities brought together, but by exquisite reasons and theorems almost mathematically demonstrative, that all opinions, yea, errors, known, read, and collated, are of main service and assistance toward the speedy attainment of what is truest.

I conceive therefore that when God did enlarge the universal diet of man's body (saving ever the rules of temperance), he then also, as before, left arbitrary the dieting and repasting of our minds; as wherein every mature man might have to exercise his own leading capacity. How great a virtue is temperance, how much of moment through the whole life of man! Yet God commits the managing of so great a trust, without particular law or prescription, wholly to the demeanor of every grown man. And therefore, when he himself tabled the Jews from heaven, that omer, which was every man's daily portion of manna, is computed to have been more

[42] Titus i, 15.
[43] Acts xi, 5-10.
[44] Digestions.
[45] John Selden (1584-1654), English scholar, author of *De jure naturali et gentium justa disciplinam Ebraeorum* (1640).

than might have well sufficed the heartiest feeder thrice as
many meals. For those actions which enter into a man, rather
than issue out of him, and therefore defile not, God uses not
to captivate under a perpetual childhood of prescription, but
trusts him with the gift of reason to be his own chooser; there
were but little work left for preaching, if law and compulsion
should grow so fast upon those things which heretofore were
governed only by exhortation. Solomon informs us that much
reading is a weariness to the flesh; but neither he nor other
inspired author tells us that such or such reading is unlawful:
yet certainly had God thought good to limit us herein, it
had been much more expedient to have told us what was
unlawful than what was wearisome.

As for the burning of those Ephesian books by St. Paul's
converts, 'tis replied the books were magic, the Syriac so
renders them. It was a private act, a voluntary act, and leaves
us to a voluntary imitation: the men in remorse burnt those
books which were their own; the magistrate by this example
is not appointed; these men practised the books, another
might perhaps have read them in some sort usefully.[46]

Good and evil we know in the field of this world grow up
together almost inseparably; and the knowledge of good is
so involved and interwoven with the knowledge of evil, and
in so many cunning resemblances hardly to be discerned,
that those confused seeds which were imposed upon Psyche [47]
as an incessant labor to cull out and sort asunder, were not
more intermixed. It was from out the rind of one apple tasted
that the knowledge of good and evil, as two twins cleaving
together, leaped forth into the world. And perhaps this is that
doom which Adam fell into of knowing good and evil, that is
to say, of knowing good by evil.

As therefore the state of man now is, what wisdom can there
be to choose, what continence to forbear, without the knowl-

[46] Acts xix, 19.
[47] Venus, jealous of Cupid's love for Psyche, gave her the impossible
task of separating various seeds, but the sympathetic ants did the task
for her. See Apuleius' book *The Golden Ass*, V-VI.

The man who's been tempted with evil and has chosen good is truly better than [handwritten note]

edge of evil? He that can apprehend and consider vice with all her baits and seeming pleasures, and yet abstain, and yet distinguish, and yet prefer that which is truly better, he is the true wayfaring [48] Christian. I cannot praise a fugitive and cloistered virtue, unexercised and unbreathed, that never sallies out and sees her adversary, but slinks out of the race, where that immortal garland is to be run for, not without dust and heat. Assuredly we bring not innocence into the world, we bring impurity much rather: that which purifies us is trial, and trial is by what is contrary. That virtue therefore which is but a youngling in the contemplation of evil, and knows not the utmost that vice promises to her followers, and rejects it, is but a blank virtue, not a pure; her whiteness is but an excremental whiteness; which was the reason why our sage and serious poet Spenser [49] (whom I dare be known to think a better teacher than Scotus or Aquinas [50]), describing true temperance under the person of Guion, brings him in with his palmer through the cave of Mammon and the bower of earthly bliss, that he might see and know, and yet abstain.

[handwritten margin note: original sin]

Since therefore the knowledge and survey of vice is in this world so necessary to the constituting of human virtue, and the scanning of error to the confirmation of truth, how can we more safely and with less danger scout into the regions of sin and falsity than by reading all manner of tractates, and hearing all manner of reason? And this is the benefit which may be had of books promiscuously read.

But of the harm that may result hence three kinds are usually reckoned. First, is feared the infection that may spread; but then, all human learning and controversy in religious points must remove out of the world, yea, the Bible itself; for that ofttimes relates blasphemy not nicely; [51] it describes the carnal sense of wicked men not unelegantly, it brings in holiest men passionately murmuring against Providence

[48] Possibly warfaring.

[49] See Spenser's *Faerie Queene*, II, viii.

[50] John Duns Scotus (1265-1308) and Thomas Aquinas (1225-1274), two great Scholastic philosophers. *Catholic theologians* [handwritten]

[51] Delicately or squeamishly.

through all the arguments of Epicurus: in other great disputes
it answers dubiously and darkly to the common reader: and
ask a Talmudist what ails the modesty of his marginal Keri,
that Moses and all the prophets cannot persuade him to pronounce the textual Chetiv.[52] For these causes we all know the
Bible itself put by the papist into the first rank of prohibited
books. The ancientest fathers must be next removed, as
Clement of Alexandria, and that Eusebian book of evangelic
preparation transmitting our ears through a hoard of heathen-
ish obscenities to receive the Gospel. Who finds not that
Irenaeus,[53] Epiphanius,[54] Jerome,[55] and others discover [56] more
heresies than they well confute, and that oft for heresy which
is the truer opinion?

Nor boots it to say for these, and all the heathen writers
of greatest infection, if it must be thought so, with whom
is bound up the life of human learning, that they writ in an
unknown tongue, so long as we are sure those languages are
known as well to the worst of men, who are both most able
and most diligent to instil the poison they suck, first into the
courts of princes, acquainting them with the choicest delights and criticism [57] of sin. As perhaps did that Petronius,
whom Nero called his Arbiter, the master of his revels; and
that notorious ribald of Arezzo,[58] dreaded and yet dear to
the Italian courtiers. I name not him, for posterity's sake,
whom Harry VIII named in merriment his vicar of hell.[59]
By which compendious way all the contagion that foreign
books can infuse will find a passage to the people far easier

52 The Keri was a gloss put in the margin to be read in place of the
text (Chetiv) when the latter was judged too coarse for speech.

53 Irenaeus (A.D. 140?-202?) wrote *Against Heresies* to confute Gnosticism.

54 Epiphanius (A.D. 315-403) wrote a tract against heretics.

55 St. Jerome (*ca.* A.D. 340-420) was a famous controversialist in matters
of church doctrine.

56 Bring to light, i.e., make more current.

57 Refinements.

58 Pietro Aretino (1492-1557), a celebrated libertine. His association with
Petronius, the author of the *Satyricon*, comes from their common interest
in elaborating and indulging refined vices.

59 Sir Francis Brian. Milton apparently did not want to identify him,
in order to protect his descendants from calumny.

and shorter than an Indian voyage, though it could be sailed either by the north of Cathay eastward, or of Canada westward, while our Spanish licensing gags the English press never so severely.

But on the other side, that infection which is from books of controversy in religion is more doubtful and dangerous to the learned than to the ignorant; and yet those books must be permitted untouched by the licenser. It will be hard to instance where any ignorant man hath been ever seduced by papistical book in English, unless it were commended and expounded to him by some of that clergy; and indeed all such tractates, whether false or true, are as the prophecy of Isaiah was to the eunuch, not to be "understood without a guide." But of our priests and doctors how many have been corrupted by studying the comments of Jesuits and Sorbonists,[60] and how fast they could transfuse that corruption into the people, our experience is both late and sad. It is not forgot, since the acute and distinct Arminius [61] was perverted merely by the perusing of a nameless discourse written at Delft, which at first he took in hand to confute.

Seeing therefore that those books, and those in great abundance, which are likeliest to taint both life and doctrine, cannot be suppressed without the fall of learning and of all ability in disputation, and that these books of either sort are most and soonest catching to the learned (from whom to the common people whatever is heretical or dissolute may quickly be conveyed), and that evil manners are as perfectly learned without books a thousand other ways which cannot be stopped, and evil doctrine not with books can propagate except a teacher guide, which he might also do without writing and so beyond prohibiting, I am not able to unfold how this

[60] Catholic theologians. The school for poor students founded by Robert de Sorbon in 1252 at the University of Paris soon gave its name to the entire institution.

[61] Arminius (1560-1609) was persuaded against Calvin's view of predestination by reading an anonymous tract. "Nameless" can mean obscure or anonymous.

cautelous [62] enterprise of licensing can be exempted from the
number of vain and impossible attempts. And he who were
pleasantly disposed could not well avoid to liken it to the
exploit of that gallant man who thought to pound up the
crows by shutting his park gate.

Besides another inconvenience, if learned men be the first
receivers out of books and dispreaders both of vice and
error, how shall the licensers themselves be confided in, unless we can confer upon them, or they assume to themselves
above all others in the land, the grace of infallibility and
uncorruptedness? And again, if it be true that a wise man
like a good refiner can gather gold out of the drossiest volume, and that a fool will be a fool with the best book, yea,
or without book, there is no reason that we should deprive
a wise man of any advantage to his wisdom, while we seek
to restrain from a fool that which being restrained will be
no hindrance to his folly. For if there should be so much
exactness always used to keep that from him which is unfit
for his reading, we should in the judgment of Aristotle not
only, but of Solomon and of our Saviour, not vouchsafe him
good precepts, and by consequence not willingly admit him
to good books; as being certain that a wise man will make
better use of an idle pamphlet than a fool will do of sacred
Scripture.

'Tis next alleged we must not expose ourselves to temptations without necessity, and next to that, not employ our
time in vain things. To both these objections one answer
will serve, out of the grounds already laid, that to all men
such books are not temptations nor vanities, but useful drugs
and materials wherewith to temper and compose effective
and strong medicines, which man's life cannot want.[63] The
rest, as children and childish men, who have not the art to
qualify and prepare these working minerals, well may be
exhorted to forbear, but hindered forcibly they cannot be by

[62] Uncertain, tricky.
[63] Be without.

all the licensing that sainted Inquisition could ever yet contrive; which is what I promised to deliver next: that this order of licensing conduces nothing to the end for which it was framed; and hath almost prevented [64] me by being clear already while thus much hath been explaining. See the ingenuity [65] of Truth, who, when she gets a free and willing hand, opens herself faster than the pace of method and discourse can overtake her.

It was the task which I began with to show that no nation or well instituted state, if they valued books at all, did ever use this way of licensing; and it might be answered that this is a piece of prudence lately discovered. To which I return, that as it was a thing slight and obvious to think on, so if it had been difficult to find out, there wanted not among them long since who suggested such a course; which they not following, leave us a pattern of their judgment that it was not the not knowing, but the not approving, which was the cause of their not using it.

Plato, a man of high authority indeed, but least of all for his commonwealth, in the book of his laws, which no city ever yet received, fed his fancy with making many edicts to his airy burgomasters, which they who otherwise admire him wish had been rather buried and excused in the genial cups of an Academic night sitting. By which laws [66] he seems to tolerate no kind of learning but by unalterable decree, consisting most of practical traditions, to the attainment whereof a library of smaller bulk than his own dialogues would be abundant. And there also enacts that no poet should so much as read to any private man what he had written, until the judges and law-keepers had seen it and allowed it; but that Plato meant this law peculiarly to that commonwealth which he had imagined, and to no other, is evident. Why was he not else a lawgiver to himself, but a transgressor, and to be

[64] Anticipate or outrun another person in thought or action.
[65] Ingenuousness, liberality, candor.
[66] Plato, *Laws*, Book VIII, and *The Republic*, Book III.

expelled by his own magistrates, both for the wanton epigrams and dialogues which he made, and his perpetual reading of Sophron Mimus [67] and Aristophanes, books of grossest infamy; and also for commending the latter of them, though he were the malicious libeler of his chief friends, to be read by the tyrant Dionysius, who had little need of such trash to spend his time on?—but that he knew this licensing of poems had reference and dependence to many other provisoes there set down in his fancied republic, which in this world could have no place; and so neither he himself, nor any magistrate or city, ever imitated that course, which, taken apart from those other collateral injunctions, must needs be vain and fruitless.

For if they fell upon one kind of strictness, unless their care were equal to regulate all other things of like aptness to corrupt the mind, that single endeavor they knew would be but a fond labor: to shut and fortify one gate against corruption, and be necessitated to leave others round about wide open. If we think to regulate printing, thereby to rectify manners, we must regulate all recreations and pastimes, all that is delightful to man. No music must be heard, no song be set or sung, but what is grave and Doric. There must be licensing dancers, that no gesture, motion, or deportment be taught our youth, but what by their allowance shall be thought honest; for such Plato was provided of. It will ask more than the work of twenty licensers to examine all the lutes, violins, and the guitars in every house; they must not be suffered to prattle as they do, but must be licensed what they may say. And who shall silence all the airs and madrigals that whisper softness in chambers? The windows also and the balconies, must be thought on; there are shrewd [68] books, with dangerous frontispieces, set to sale: who shall prohibit them, shall twenty licensers? The villages also must have their visitors to inquire what lectures the bagpipe and the rebec

[67] Sophron the Mimer, author of comedies intended primarily for study.
[68] Malicious, wicked.

reads, even to the balladry and the gamut of every municipal fiddler, for these are the countryman's Arcadias [69] and his Monte Mayors.[70]

Next, what more national corruption, for which England hears ill [71] abroad, than household gluttony? Who shall be the rectors of our daily rioting? And what shall be done to inhibit the multitudes that frequent those houses where drunkenness is sold and harbored? Our garments also should be referred to the licensing of some more sober workmasters, to see them cut into a less-wanton garb. Who shall regulate all the mixed conversation [72] of our youth, male and female together, as is the fashion of this country? Who shall still appoint what shall be discoursed, what presumed, and no further? Lastly, who shall forbid and separate all idle resort, all evil company? These things will be, and must be; but how they shall be least hurtful, how least enticing, herein consists the grave and governing wisdom of a state.

To sequester out of the world into Atlantic and Utopian polities,[73] which never can be drawn into use, will not mend our condition; but to ordain wisely as in this world of evil, in the midst whereof God hath placed as unavoidably. Nor is it Plato's licensing of books will do this, which necessarily pulls along with it so many other kinds of licensing as will make us all both ridiculous and weary, and yet frustrate; but those unwritten or at least unconstraining laws of virtuous education, religious and civil nurture, which Plato there mentions as the bonds and ligaments of the commonwealth, the pillars and the sustainers of every written statute; these they be which will bear chief sway in such matters as these, when all licensing will be easily eluded. Impunity and remissness, for certain, are the bane of a commonwealth; but here the great art lies, to discern in what the law is to

[69] Sir Philip Sidney's *Arcadia.*
[70] Jorge de Montemayor's *Diana Enamorada.*
[71] Hears ill spoken of herself.
[72] Association or social intercourse.
[73] Imaginary societies such as those described in Bacon's *New Atlantis* and Sir Thomas More's *Utopia.*

bid restraint and punishment, and in what things persuasion
only is to work. If every action which is good or evil in man
at ripe years were to be under pittance,[74] and prescription,
and compulsion, what were virtue but a name, what praise
could be then due to well-doing, what gramercy [75] to be sober,
just, or continent?

Many there be that complain of divine Providence for
suffering Adam to transgress. Foolish tongues! When God
gave him reason, he gave him freedom to choose, for reason
is but choosing; he had been else a mere artificial Adam,
such an Adam as he is in the motions.[76] We ourselves esteem
not of that obedience, or love, or gift, which is of force:
God therefore left him free, set before him a provoking object
ever almost in his eyes; herein consisted his merit, herein the
right of his reward, the praise of his abstinence. Wherefore
did he create passions within us, pleasures round about us,
but that these rightly tempered are the very ingredients of
virtue? They are not skilful considerers of human things,
who imagine to remove sin by removing the matter of sin;
for, besides that it is a huge heap increasing under the very
act of diminishing, though some part of it may for a time
be withdrawn from some persons, it cannot from all, in such
a universal thing as books are; and when this is done, yet the
sin remains entire. Though ye take from a covetous man all
his treasure, he has yet one jewel left: ye cannot bereave him
of his covetousness. Banish all objects of lust, shut up all
youth into the severest discipline that can be exercised in any
hermitage, ye cannot make them chaste that came not thither
so: such great care and wisdom is required to the right managing of this point.

Suppose we could expel sin by this means; look how much
we thus expel of sin, so much we expel of virtue: for the
matter of them both is the same; remove that, and ye remove
them both alike. This justifies the high providence of God,

74 Ration, allowance.
75 Thanks.
76 Puppet shows.

who, though he command us temperance, justice, continence,
yet pours out before us even to a profuseness all desirable
things, and gives us minds that can wander beyond all limit
and satiety. Why should we then affect a rigor contrary to
the manner of God and of nature, by abridging or scanting
those means, which books freely permitted are, both to the
trial of virtue and the exercise of truth?

It would be better done to learn that the law must needs
be frivolous which goes to restrain things uncertainly and
yet equally working to good and to evil. And were I the
chooser, a dram of well-doing should be preferred before
many times as much the forcible hindrance of evil-doing. For
God sure esteems the growth and completing of one virtuous
person more than the restraint of ten vicious. And albeit
whatever thing we hear or see, sitting, walking, travelling, or
conversing, may be fitly called our book, and it is of the same
effect that writings are, yet grant the thing to be prohibited
were only books, it appears that this order hitherto is far
insufficient to the end which it intends. Do we not see, not
once or oftener but weekly, that continued court-libel[77] against
the Parliament and City, printed, as the wet sheets can witness, and dispersed among us, for all that licensing can do?
Yet this is the prime service, a man would think, wherein
this Order should give proof of itself. If it were executed,
you'll say. But certain, if execution be remiss or blindfold now,
and in this particular, what will it be hereafter, and in other
books?

If then the Order shall not be vain and frustrate, behold
a new labor, Lords and Commons: ye must repeal and pro-
scribe all scandalous and unlicensed books already printed
and divulged; after ye have drawn them up into a list,
that all may know which are condemned and which not;
and ordain that no foreign books be delivered out of custody, till they have been read over. This office will require
the whole time of not a few overseers, and those no vulgar
men. There be also books which are partly useful and excel-

---

[77] A Royalist journal, *Mercurius Aulicus* (published 1642-1645).

lent, partly culpable and pernicious; this work will ask as
many more officials to make expurgations and expunctions,
that the commonwealth of learning be not damnified. In
fine, when the multitude of books increase upon their hands,
ye must be fain to catalogue all those printers who are
found frequently offending, and forbid the importation of
their whole suspected typography. In a word, that this your
Order may be exact and not deficient, ye must reform it
perfectly according to the model of Trent and Seville,[78]
which I know ye abhor to do.

Yet though ye should condescend to this, which God forbid,
the Order still would be but fruitless and defective to that
end whereto ye meant it. If to prevent sects and schisms, who
is so unread or so uncatechized in story, that hath not heard
of many sects refusing books as a hindrance, and preserving
their doctrine unmixed for many ages, only by unwritten traditions? The Christian faith (for that was once a schism) is
not unknown to have spread all over Asia, ere any Gospel or
Epistle was seen in writing. If the amendment of manners be
aimed at, look into Italy and Spain, whether those places be
one scruple the better, the honester, the wiser, the chaster,
since all the inquisitional rigor that hath been executed upon
books.

Another reason, whereby to make it plain that this Order
will miss the end it seeks, consider by the quality which
ought to be in every licenser. It cannot be denied but that
he who is made judge to sit upon the birth or death of books,
whether they may be wafted into this world or not, had need
to be a man above the common measure, both studious,
learned, and judicious; there may be else no mean mistakes
in the censure [79] of what is passable or not, which is also
no mean injury. If he be of such worth as behooves him, there
cannot be a more tedious and unpleasing journey-work,[80]

[78] Further reference to the Council of Trent and to the Inquisition,
which was notoriously oppressive in Seville.
[79] Judge, with no implication of "condemn."
[80] Day labor.

a greater loss of time levied upon his head, than to be made
the perpetual reader of unchosen books and pamphlets, ofttimes huge volumes. There is no book that is acceptable
unless at certain seasons; but to be enjoined the reading of
that at all times, and in a hand scarce legible, whereof three
pages would not down at any time in the fairest print, is an
imposition which I cannot believe how he that values time,
and his own studies, or is but of a sensible [81] nostril, should
be able to endure.

In this one thing I crave leave of the present licensers to
be pardoned for so thinking: who doubtless took this office
up, looking on it through their obedience to the Parliament,
whose command perhaps made all things seem easy and un-
laborious to them; but that this short trial hath wearied
them out already, their own expressions and excuses to them
who make so many journeys to solicit their license are testimony enough. Seeing therefore those who now possess the
employment by all evident signs wish themselves well rid
of it, and that no man of worth, none that is not a plain
unthrift of his own hours, is ever likely to succeed them,
except he mean to put himself to the salary of a press cor-
rector, we may easily forsee what kind of licensers we are to
expect hereafter, either ignorant, imperious, and remiss, or
basely pecuniary.

This is what I had to show wherein this Order cannot
conduce to that end whereof it bears the intention.

I lastly proceed from the no good it can do, to the manifest hurt it causes, in being first the greatest discouragement
and affront that can be offered to learning and to learned
men. It was the complaint and lamentation of prelates, upon
every least breath of a motion to remove pluralities [82] and
distribute more equally church revenues, that then all learning would be for ever dashed and discouraged. But as for

[81] Sensitive.

[82] The concurrent holding of two or more livings in the church by
one person.

that opinion, I never found cause to think that the tenth
part of learning stood or fell with the clergy: nor could I
ever but hold it for a sordid and unworthy speech of any
churchman who had a competency left him. If therefore ye
be loath to dishearten utterly and discontent, not the mercenary crew of false pretenders to learning, but the free and
ingenuous sort of such as evidently were born to study and
love learning for itself, not for lucre or any other end but
the service of God and of truth, and perhaps that lasting
fame and perpetuity of praise which God and good men
have consented shall be the reward of those whose published
labors advance the good of mankind: then know, that so
far to distrust the judgment and the honesty of one who
hath but a common repute in learning and never yet offended,
as not to count him fit to print his mind without a tutor
and examiner, lest he should drop a schism or something of
corruption, is the greatest displeasure and indignity to a free
and knowing spirit that can be put upon him.

What advantage is it to be a man, over it is to be a boy
at school, if we have only escaped the ferula to come under
the fescue of an imprimatur? [83]—if serious and elaborate writings, as if they were no more than the theme of a grammar-
lad under his pedagogue, must not be uttered without the
cursory eyes of a temporizing and extemporizing licenser?
He who is not trusted with his own actions, his drift not being
known to be evil, and standing to the hazard of law and penalty, has no greater argument to think himself reputed in
the commonwealth wherein he was born for other than a fool
or a foreigner. When a man writes to the world, he summons
up all his reason and deliberation to assist him; he searches,
meditates, is industrious, and likely consults and confers with
his judicious friends; after all which done he takes himself
to be informed in what he writes as well as any that writ

[83] What does a man gain if he matures to the point where he is not
subject to a teacher's cane (ferula) only to find himself subject to the
pointer (fescue) of a censor.

No new ideas can be set forth

before him; if in this, the most consummate act of his fidelity and ripeness, no years, no industry, no former proof of his abilities, can bring him to that state of maturity as not to be still mistrusted and suspected, unless he carry all his considerate diligence, all his midnight watchings, and expense of Palladian [84] oil, to the hasty view of an unleisured licenser, perhaps much his younger, perhaps far his inferior in judgment, perhaps one who never knew the labor of book-writing; and if he be not repulsed, or slighted, must appear in print like a puny [85] with his guardian, and his censor's hand on the back of his title to be his bail and surety that he is no idiot or seducer, it cannot be but a dishonor and derogation to the author, to the book, to the privilege and dignity of learning.

And what if the author shall be one so copious of fancy as to have many things well worth the adding come into his mind after licensing, while the book is yet under the press, which not seldom happens to the best and diligentest writers; and that perhaps a dozen times in one book? The printer dares not go beyond his licensed copy; so often then must the author trudge to his leave-giver, that those his new insertions may be viewed; and many a jaunt will be made, ere that licenser, for it must be the same man, can either be found or found at leisure; meanwhile either the press must stand still, which is no small damage, or the author lose his accuratest thoughts, and send the book forth worse than he had made it, which to a diligent writer is the greatest melancholy and vexation that can befall.

And how can a man teach with authority which is the life of teaching, how can he be a doctor [86] in his book as he ought to be, or else had better be silent, whenas all he teaches, all he delivers, is but under the tuition, under the correction of his patriarchal licenser, to blot or alter what precisely accords not with the hide-bound humor which he calls his judgment?—

[84] The oil used in a scholar's lamp, associated with the oil of Pallas Athena's olive tree.
[85] A child or any other person not legally responsible for himself.
[86] Teacher.

when every acute reader, upon the first sight of a pedantic
license, will be ready with these like words to ding [87] the
book a quoit's distance from him: "I hate a pupil teacher;
I endure not an instructor that comes to me under the ward-
ship of an overseeing fist. I know nothing of the licenser, but
that I have his own hand here for his arrogance; who shall
warrant me his judgment?" "The State, sir," replies the
stationer,[88] but has a quick return: "The State shall be my
governors, but not my critics; they may be mistaken in the
choice of a licenser, as easily as this licenser may be mistaken
in an author; this is some common stuff." And he might
add from Sir Francis Bacon, that "Such authorized books are
but the language of the times." [89] For though a licenser should
happen to be judicious more than ordinary, which will be a
great jeopardy of the next succession, yet his very office and
his commission enjoins him to let pass nothing but what is
vulgarly received already.

Nay, which is more lamentable, if the work of any deceased
author, though never so famous in his lifetime and even
to this day, come to their hands for license to be printed or
reprinted, if there be found in his book one sentence of a
venturous edge, uttered in the height of zeal (and who knows
whether it might not be the dictate of a divine spirit), yet not
suiting with every low, decrepit humor of their own, though
it were Knox [90] himself, the reformer of a kingdom, that spake
it, they will not pardon him their dash: [91] the sense of that
great man shall to all posterity be lost for the fearfulness or
the presumptuous rashness of a perfunctory licenser. And to
what an author this violence hath been lately done, and in
what book of greatest consequence to be faithfully published,
I could now instance, but shall forbear till a more convenient

87 Throw.
88 Publisher.
89 Bacon, *An Advertisement Touching the Controversies of the Church
of England.*
90 John Knox (1505-1572), Scottish reformer.
91 Stroke deleting a passage. Knox's *History of the Reformation* **suffered**
some mutilation in its edition of 1644.

season. Yet if these things be not resented seriously and timely by them who have the remedy in their power, but that such iron-moulds [92] as these shall have authority to gnaw out the choicest periods of exquisitest books, and to commit such a treacherous fraud against the orphan remainders of worthiest men after death, the more sorrow will belong to that hapless race of men, whose misfortune it is to have understanding. Henceforth let no man care to learn, or care to be more than worldly wise; for certainly in higher matters to be ignorant and slothful, to be a common steadfast [93] dunce, will be the only pleasant life and only in request.

And as it is a particular disesteem of every knowing person alive, and most injurious to the written labors and monuments of the dead, so to me it seems an undervaluing and vilifying of the whole nation. I cannot set so light by all the invention, the art, the wit, the grave and solid judgment which is in England, as that it can be comprehended in any twenty capacities, how good soever; much less that it should not pass except their superintendence be over it, except it be sifted and strained with their strainers, that it should be uncurrent without their manual stamp. Truth and understanding are not such wares as to be monopolised and traded in by tickets, and statutes, and standards.[94] We must not think to make a staple commodity of all the knowledge in the land, to mark and license it like our broadcloth and our woolpacks. What is it but a servitude like that imposed by the Philistines, not to be allowed the sharpening of our own axes and coulters, but we must repair from all quarters to twenty licensing forges?

* * * * *

92 Rust spots.
93 Fixed in stupidity.
94 Commercial measures and devices.

John Locke

JOHN LOCKE *(1632-1704), developed a political philosophy and theories of psychology which are as important and influential in the history of ideas as
Newton's physics. Locke's political theories underlie
many of the major documents of the American
Revolution, and his psychological theories permeate
literary theory of the eighteenth and nineteenth
centuries. Locke was educated at Westminster and
at Christ Church, Oxford. Principal works:* Essay
Concerning Human Understanding *(1690);* two
Treatises of Government *(1690);* The Reasonable-
ness of Christianity *(1695).*

OF THE STATE OF NATURE[1]

* * * * *

4. To understand political power right, and derive it from
its original, we must consider what state all men are naturally
in, and that is a state of perfect freedom to order their actions
and dispose of their possessions and persons as they think fit,
within the bounds of the law of nature, without asking leave
or depending upon the will of any other man.

A state also of equality, wherein all the power and jurisdiction is reciprocal, no one having more than another; there
being nothing more evident than that creatures of the same
species and rank, promiscuously born to all the same advantages of nature and the use of the same faculties, should also
be equal one amongst another without subordination or sub-

[1] Chapter II of *The Second Treatise of Civil Government* (1690).

jection; unless the lord and master of them all should, by any manifest declaration of his will, set one above another, and confer on him by an evident and clear appointment an undoubted right to dominion and sovereignty.

5. This equality of men by nature the judicious Hooker [2] looks upon as so evident in itself and beyond all question that he makes it the foundation of that obligation to mutual love amongst men on which he builds the duties we owe one another, and from whence he derives the great maxims of justice and charity. His words are:

The like natural inducement hath brought men to know that it is no less their duty to love others than themselves; for seeing those things which are equal must needs all have one measure; if I cannot but wish to receive good, even as much at every man's hands as any man can wish unto his own soul, how should I look to have any part of my desire herein satisfied unless myself be careful to satisfy the like desire, which is undoubtedly in other men, being of one and the same nature? To have anything offered them repugnant to this desire must needs in all respects grieve them as much as me; so that, if I do harm, I must look to suffer, there being no reason that others should show greater measure of love to me than they have by me showed unto them; my desire therefore to be loved of my equals in nature, as much as possibly may be, imposeth upon me a natural duty of bearing to them-ward fully the like affection; from which relation of equality between ourselves and them that are as ourselves, what several rules and canons natural reason hath drawn, for direction of life, no man is ignorant. (*Eccl. Pol.* lib. i.).

6. But though this be a state of liberty, yet it is not a state of license; though man in that state have an uncontrollable liberty to dispose of his person or possessions, yet he has not liberty to destroy himself, or so much as any creature in his possession, but where some nobler use than its bare preservation calls for it. The state of nature has a law of nature to govern it which obliges every one; and reason, which is that law, teaches all mankind who will but consult it that, being

2 Richard Hooker (1554?-1600), author of *The Laws of Ecclesiastical Polity*, which Locke subsequently quotes at length.

all equal and independent, no one ought to harm another in his life, health, liberty, or possessions; for men being all the workmanship of one omnipotent and infinitely wise Maker—all the servants of one sovereign master, sent into the world by his order, and about his business—they are his property whose workmanship they are, made to last during his, not one another's, pleasure; and being furnished with like faculties, sharing all in one community of nature, there cannot be supposed any such subordination among us that may authorize us to destroy another, as if we were made for one another's uses as the inferior ranks of creatures are for ours. Every one, as he is bound to preserve himself and not to quit his station wilfully, so by the like reason, when his own preservation comes not in competition, ought he, as much as he can, to preserve the rest of mankind, and may not, unless it be to do justice to an offender, take away or impair the life, or what tends to the preservation of life: the liberty, health, limb, or goods of another.

7. And that all men may be restrained from invading others' rights and from doing hurt to one another, and the law of nature be observed which willeth the peace and preservation of all mankind, the execution of the law of nature is, in that state, put into every man's hands, whereby everyone has a right to punish the transgressors of that law to such a degree as may hinder its violation; for the law of nature would, as all other laws that concern men in this world, be in vain, if there were nobody that in the state of nature had a power to execute that law and thereby preserve the innocent and restrain offenders. And if any one in the state of nature may punish another for any evil he has done, every one may do so; for in that state of perfect equality where naturally there is no superiority or jurisdiction of one over another, what any may do in persecution of that law, every one must needs have a right to do.

8. And thus in the state of nature one man comes by a power over another; but yet no absolute or arbitrary power to use a criminal, when he has got him in his hands, according

to the passionate heats or boundless extravagancy of his own will; but only to retribute to him, so far as calm reason and conscience dictate, what is proportionate to his transgression, which is so much as may serve for reparation and restraint; for these two are the only reasons why one man may lawfully do harm to another, which is that we call punishment. In transgressing the law of nature, the offender declares himself to live by another rule than that of reason and common equity, which is that measure God has set to the actions of men for their mutual security; and so he becomes dangerous to mankind, the tie which is to secure them from injury and violence being slighted and broken by him. Which being a trespass against the whole species and the peace and safety of it provided for by the law of nature, every man upon this score, by the right he hath to preserve mankind in general, may restrain, or, where it is necessary, destroy things noxious to them, and so may bring such evil on any one who hath transgressed that law, as may make him repent the doing of it and thereby deter him, and by his example others, from doing the like mischief. And in this case, and upon this ground, *every man hath a right to punish the offender and be executioner of the law of nature.*

9. I doubt not but this will seem a very strange doctrine to some men; but before they condemn it, I desire them to resolve me by what right any prince or state can put to death or punish any alien for any crime he commits in their country. It is certain their laws, by virtue of any sanction they receive from the promulgated will of the legislative, reach not a stranger; they speak not to him, nor, if they did, is he bound to hearken to them. The legislative authority, by which they are in force over the subjects of that commonwealth, hath no power over him. Those who have the supreme power of making laws in England, France, or Holland, are to an Indian but like the rest of the world, men without authority; and therefore, if by the law of nature every man hath not a power to punish offences against it as he soberly judges the case to require, I see not how the magistrates of

any community can punish an alien of another country, since, in reference to him, they can have no more power than what every man naturally may have over another.

10. Besides the crime which consists in violating the law and varying from the right rule of reason, whereby a man so far becomes degenerate and declares himself to quit the principles of human nature and to be a noxious creature, there is commonly injury done to some person or other, and some other man receives damage by his transgression; in which case he who hath received any damage has, besides the right of punishment common to him with other men, a particular right to seek reparation from him that has done it; and any other person, who finds it just, may also join with him that is injured and assist him in recovering from the offender so much as may make satisfaction for the harm he has suffered.

11. From these two distinct rights—the one of punishing the crime for restraint and preventing the like offence, which right of punishing is in everybody; the other of taking reparation, which belongs only to the injured party—comes it to pass that the magistrate, who by being magistrate hath the common right of punishing put into his hands, can often, where the public good demands not the execution of the law, remit the punishment of criminal offences by his own authority, but yet cannot remit the satisfaction due to any private man for the damage he has received. That he who has suffered the damage has a right to demand in his own name, and he alone can remit; the damnified person has this power of appropriating to himself the goods or service of the offender by right of self-preservation, as every man has a power to punish the crime to prevent its being committed again, by the right he has of preserving all mankind, and doing all reasonable things he can in order to that end; and thus it is that every man, in the state of nature, has a power to kill a murderer, both to deter others from doing the like injury, which no reparation can compensate, by the example of the punishment that attends it from everybody, and also to secure men from the attempts of a criminal who, having renounced reason—the

common rule and measure God hath given to mankind—hath, by the unjust violence and slaughter he hath committed upon one, declared war against all mankind; and therefore may be destroyed as a lion or a tiger, one of those wild savage beasts with whom men can have no society nor security. And upon this is grounded that great law of nature, "Whoso sheddeth man's blood, by man shall his blood be shed." And Cain was so fully convinced that every one had a right to destroy such a criminal that, after the murder of his brother, he cries out, "Every one that findeth me, shall slay me"; so plain was it writ in the hearts of mankind.

12. By the same reason may a man in the state of nature punish the lesser breaches of that law. It will perhaps be demanded: with death? I answer: Each transgression may be punished to that degree and with so much severity as will suffice to make it an ill bargain to the offender, give him cause to repent, and terrify others from doing the like. Every offence that can be committed in the state of nature may in the state of nature be also punished equally, and as far forth as it may in a commonwealth; for though it would be beside my present purpose to enter here into the particulars of the law of nature, or its measures of punishment, yet it is certain there is such a law, and that, too, as intelligible and plain to a rational creature and a studier of that law as the positive laws of commonwealth, nay, possibly plainer, as much as reason is easier to be understood than the fancies and intricate contrivances of men, following contrary and hidden interests put into words; for so truly are a great part of the municipal laws of countries, which are only so far right as they are founded on the law of nature, by which they are to be regulated and interpreted.

13. To this strange doctrine—viz., that in the state of nature every one has the executive power of the law of nature—I doubt not but it will be objected that it is unreasonable for men to be judges in their own cases, that self-love will make men partial to themselves and their friends, and, on the other side, that ill-nature, passion, and revenge will carry them too

far in punishing others, and hence nothing but confusion and
disorder will follow; and that therefore God hath certainly
appointed government to restrain the partiality and violence
of men. I easily grant that civil government is the proper remedy for the inconveniences of the state of nature, which must
certainly be great where men may be judges in their own case;
since it is easy to be imagined that he who was so unjust
as to do his brother an injury will scarce be so just as to
condemn himself for it; but I shall desire those who make
this objection to remember that absolute monarchs are but
men, and if government is to be the remedy of those evils
which necessarily follow from men's being judges in their own
cases, and the state of nature is therefore not to be endured,
I desire to know what kind of government that is, and how
much better it is than the state of nature, where one man com-
manding a multitude has the liberty to be judge in his own
case, and may do to all his subjects whatever he pleases, without the least liberty to any one to question or control those
who execute his pleasure, and in whatsoever he doth, whether
led by reason, mistake, or passion, must be submitted to? Much
better it is in the state of nature, wherein men are not bound
to submit to the unjust will of another; and if he that judges,
judges amiss in his own or any other case, he is answerable for
it to the rest of mankind.

14. It is often asked as a mighty objection, "Where are or
ever were there any men in such a state of nature?" To which
it may suffice as an answer at present that, since all princes
and rulers of independent governments all through the world
are in a state of nature, it is plain the world never was, nor
ever will be, without numbers of men in that state. I have
named all governors of independent communities, whether
they are, or are not, in league with others; for it is not every
compact that puts an end to the state of nature between men,
but only this one of agreeing together mutually to enter into
one community and make one body politic; other promises
and compacts men may make one with another and yet still
be in the state of nature. The promises and bargains for truck,

etc., between the two men in the desert island, mentioned by Garcilasso de la Vega, in his *History of Peru*, or between a Swiss and an Indian, in the woods of America, are binding to them, though they are perfectly in a state of nature in reference to one another; for truth and keeping of faith belongs to men, and not as members of society.

15. To those that say there were never any men in the state of nature, I will not only oppose the authority of the judicious Hooker, *Eccl. Pol.*, lib. i, sect. 10, where he says,

The laws which have been hitherto mentioned (*i.e.*, the laws of nature) do bind men absolutely, even as they are men, although they have never any settled fellowship, never any solemn agreement amongst themselves what to do, or not to do; but forasmuch as we are not by ourselves sufficient to furnish ourselves with competent store of things needful for such a life as our nature doth desire, a life fit for the dignity of man; therefore to supply those defects and imperfections which are in us, as living singly and solely by ourselves, we are naturally induced to seek communion and fellowship with others. This was the cause of men's uniting themselves at first in politic societies.

But I, moreover, affirm that all men are naturally in that state and remain so till by their own consents they make themselves members of some politic society; and I doubt not in the sequel of this discourse to make it very clear.

Jonathan Swift

JONATHAN SWIFT *(1667-1745) was a clergyman who served as dean of St. Patrick's Cathedral (Dublin) from 1713 to his death. He was both active and effective in the politics of his era, especially in relation to the troubles of Ireland. He is the finest satirist of a great period of satire, and the vivid violence of his style gives his work great metaphorical force as well as clarity. Swift was educated at Trinity College, Dublin. Principal works:* A Tale of a Tub *(1704);* The Battle of the Books *(1704);* Drapier's Letters *(1724);* Gulliver's Travels *(1726);* A Modest Proposal *(1729).*

A MODEST PROPOSAL FOR PREVENTING THE CHILDREN OF POOR PEOPLE FROM BEING A BURTHEN TO THEIR PARENTS OR COUNTRY, AND FOR MAKING THEM BENEFICIAL TO THE PUBLIC[1]

It is a melancholly Object to those, who walk through this great Town or travel in the Country, when they see the Streets, the Roads and Cabbin-doors crowded with Beggers of the Female Sex, followed by three, four, or six Children, all in

[1] *A Modest Proposal* (1729) is the most famous of Swift's pamphlets relating to Ireland.

Rags, and importuning every Passenger for an Alms. These Mothers instead of being able to work for their honest lively-hood, are forced to employ all their time in Stroling to beg Sustenance for their helpless Infants, who, as they grow up, either turn Thieves for want of Work, or leave their dear Native Country,[2] to fight for the Pretender in Spain, or sell themselves to the Barbadoes.

I think it is agreed by all Parties, that this prodigious num-ber of Children in the Arms, or on the Backs, or at the Heels of their Mothers, and frequently of their Fathers, is in the present deplorable state of the Kingdom, a very great addi-tional grievance; and therefore whoever could find out a fair, cheap and easy method of making these Children sound and useful Members of the Common-wealth, would deserve so well of the publick, as to have his Statue set up for a Preserver of the Nation.

But my Intention is very far from being confined to provide only for the Children of professed Beggers, it is of a much greater Extent, and shall take in the whole Number of Infants at a certain Age, who are born of Parents in effect as little able to support them, as those who demand our Charity in the Streets.

As to my own part, having turned my Thoughts, for many Years, upon this important Subject, and maturely weighed the several Schemes of other Projectors, I have always found them grossly mistaken in their computation. It is true, a Child just dropt from its Dam, may be supported by her Milk, for a Solar Year with little other Nourishment, at most not above the Value of two Shillings, which the Mother may certainly get, or the Value in Scraps, by her lawful Occupation of Beg-ging; and it is exactly at one Year Old that I propose to pro-vide for them in such a manner, as, instead of being a Charge upon their Parents, or the Parish, or wanting Food and Rai-ment for the rest of their Lives, they shall, on the Contrary, contribute to the Feeding and partly to the Cloathing of many Thousands.

2 Ireland.

There is likewise another great Advantage in my Scheme, that it will prevent those voluntary Abortions, and that horrid practice of Women murdering their Bastard Children, alas! too frequent among us, Sacrificing the poor innocent Babes, I doubt, more to avoid the Expence than the Shame, which would move Tears and Pity in the most Savage and inhuman breast.

The number of Souls in this Kingdom being usually reckoned one Million and a half, Of these I calculate there may be about two hundred thousand Couple whose Wives are Breeders; from which number I substract thirty Thousand Couples, who are able to maintain their own Children, although I apprehend there cannot be so many, under the present Distresses of the Kingdom; but this being granted, there will remain an hundred and seventy thousand Breeders. I again Substract fifty Thousand, for those Women who miscarry, or whose Children die by accident, or disease within the Year. There only remain an hundred and twenty thousand Children of poor Parents annually born: The question therefore is, How this number shall be reared, and provided for? which, as I have already said, under the present Situation of Affairs, is utterly impossible by all the Methods hitherto proposed; for we can neither employ them in Handicraft or Agriculture; we neither build House, (I mean in the Country) nor cultivate Land: They can very seldom pick up a Livelihood by Stealing till they arrive at six years Old; except where they are of towardly parts; [3] although, I confess, they learn the Rudiments much earlier; during which time they can however be properly looked upon only as Probationers; as I have been informed by a principal Gentleman in the County of Cavan, who protested to me, that he never knew above one or two Instances under the Age of six, even in a part of the Kingdom so renowned for the quickest proficiency in that Art.

I am assured by our Merchants, that a Boy or a Girl before twelve years Old, is no saleable Commodity, and even when they come to this Age, they will not yield above three Pounds,

[3] Of precocious intelligence.

or three Pounds and half a Crown at most, on the Exchange; which cannot turn to Account either to the parents or Kingdom, the Charge of Nutriment and Rags having been at least four times that Value.

I shall now therefore humbly propose my own Thoughts, which I hope will not be liable to the least Objection.

I have been assured by a very knowing American of my acquaintance in London, that a young healthy Child well Nursed is at a year Old a most delicious nourishing and wholesome Food, whether Stewed, Roasted, Baked, or Boiled; and I make no doubt that it will equally serve in a Fricasie, or a Ragoust.

I do therefore humbly offer it to publick consideration, that of the Hundred and twenty thousand Children, already computed, twenty thousand may be reserved for Breed, whereof only one fourth part to be Males; which is more than we allow to Sheep, black Cattle, or Swine, and my Reason is, that these Children are seldom the Fruits of Marriage, a Circumstance not much regarded by our Savages, therefore one Male will be sufficient to serve four Females. That the remaining Hundred thousand may at a year Old be offered in Sale to the Persons of Quality and Fortune, through the Kingdom, always advising the Mother to let them Suck plentifully in the last Month, so as to render them Plump, and Fat for a good Table. A Child will make two dishes at an Entertainment for Friends, and when the Family dines alone, the fore or hind Quarter will make a reasonable Dish, and seasoned with a little Pepper or Salt will be very good Boiled on the Fourth Day, especially in Winter.

I have reckoned upon a Medium, that a Child just born will weigh 12 pounds, and in a solar Year, if tolerably nursed, encreaseth to 28 Pounds.

I grant this food will be somewhat dear, and therefore very proper for Landlords, who, as they have already devoured most of the Parents seem to have the best Title to the Children.

Infant's flesh will be in Season throughout the Year, but

more plentiful in March, and a little before and after; for we are told by a grave Author an eminent French Physician, that Fish being a prolifick Dyet, there are more Children born in Roman Catholick Countries about nine Months after Lent, than at any other Season; therefore reckoning a Year after Lent, the Markets will be more glutted than usual, because the Number of Popish Infants, is at least three to one in this Kingdom, and therefore it will have one other Collateral advantage, by lessening the Number of Papists among us.

I have already computed the Charge of nursing a Begger's Child (in which List I reckon all Cottagers, Labourers, and four fifths of the Farmers) to be about two Shillings per Annum, Rags included; and I believe no Gentleman would repine to give Ten Shillings for the Carcass of a good fat Child, which, as I have said will make four Dishes of excellent Nutritive Meat, when he hath only some particular Friend, or his own Family to dine with him. Thus the Squire will learn to be a good Landlord, and grow popular among his Tenants, the Mother will have Eight Shillings neat Profit, and be fit for Work till she produces another Child.

Those who are more thrifty (as I must confess the Times require) may flay the Carcass; the Skin of which, Artificially dressed, will make admirable Gloves for Ladies, and Summer Boots for fine Gentlemen.

As to our City of Dublin, Shambles may be appointed for this purpose, in the most convenient parts of it, and Butchers we may be assured will not be wanting; although I rather recommend buying the Children alive, and dressing them hot from the Knife, as we do roasting Pigs.

A very worthy Person, a true Lover of his Country, and whose Virtues I highly esteem, was lately pleased, in discoursing on this matter, to offer a refinement upon my Scheme. He said, that many Gentlemen of this Kingdom, having of late destroyed their Deer, he conceived that the Want of Venison might be well supply'd by the Bodies of young Lads and Maidens, not exceeding fourteen Years of Age, nor under twelve; so great a Number of both Sexes in every Country being now ready to Starve, for want of Work and Service: And these to be disposed of by their Parents if alive, or otherwise by their nearest Relations. But with due deference to so excellent a Friend, and so deserving a Patriot, I cannot be altogether in his Sentiments; for as to the Males, my American acquaintance assured me from frequent Experience, that their Flesh was generally Tough and Lean, like that of our Schoolboys, by continual exercise, and their Taste disagreeable, and to fatten them would not answer the Charge.[4] Then as to the Females, it would, I think with humble Submission, be a Loss to the Publick, because they soon would become Breeders themselves: And besides it is not improbable that some scrupulous People might be apt to Censure such a Practice, (although indeed very unjustly) as a little bordering upon Cruelty, which, I confess, hath always been with me the strongest Objection against any Project, how well soever intended.

But in order to justify my Friend, he confessed, that this expedient, was put into his Head by the famous Sallmanaazor, a Native of the Island Formosa, who came from thence to London, above twenty Years ago, and in Conversation told my Friend, that in his Country when any young Person happened to be put to Death, the Executioner sold the Carcass to Persons of Quality, as a prime Dainty, and that, in his Time, the Body of a plump Girl of fifteen, who was crucified for an attempt to poison the Emperor, was sold to his Imperial Majesty's prime Minister of State, and other great Mandarins of the Court, in Joints from the Gibbet, at four hundred Crowns. Neither indeed can I deny, that if the same Use were made of several plump young Girls in this Town, who, without one single Groat to their Fortunes, cannot stir abroad without a Chair, and appear at a Play-house, and Assemblies in Foreign fineries, which they never will pay for; the Kingdom would not be the worse.

Some Persons of a desponding Spirit are in great concern about that vast Number of poor People, who are Aged, Diseased, or Maimed, and I have been desired to imploy my

---

4 Would not be worth the expense.

Thoughts what Course may be taken, to ease the Nation of so grievous an Incumbrance. But I am not in the least Pain upon that matter, because it is very well known, that they are every Day dying, and rotting, by cold and famine, and filth, and vermin, as fast as can be reasonably expected. And as to the younger Labourers, they are now in almost as hopeful a Condition. They cannot get Work, and consequently pine away for want of Nourishment, to a degree, that if at any Time they are accidentally hired to common Labour, they have not Strength to perform it, and thus the Country and themselves are happily delivered from the Evils to come.

I have too long digressed, and therefore shall return to my Subject. I think the Advantages by the Proposal which I have made are obvious and many, as well as of the highest Importance.

For *First*, as I have already observed, it would greatly lessen the Number of Papists, with whom we are Yearly over-run, being the principal Breeders of the Nation, as well as our most dangerous Enemies, and who stay at home on purpose with a Design to deliver the Kingdom to the Pretender, hoping to take their Advantage by the Absence of so many good Protestants, who have chosen rather to leave their Country, than stay at home, and pay Tithes against their Conscience, to an Episcopal Curate.

Secondly, The poorer Tenants will have something valuable of their own which by Law may be made lyable to Distress, and help to pay their Landlord's Rent, their Corn and Cattle being already seized, and Money a Thing unknown.

Thirdly, Whereas the Maintenance of an hundred thousand Children, from two Years old, and upwards, cannot be computed at less than Ten Shillings a Piece per Annum, the Nation's Stock will be thereby increased fifty thousand Pounds per Annum, besides the Profit of a new Dish, introduced to the Tables of all Gentlemen of Fortune in the Kingdom, who have any Refinement in Taste, and the Money will circulate among our Selves, the Goods being entirely of our own Growth and Manufacture.

Fourthly, The constant Breeders, besides the gain of eight Shillings Sterling per Annum, by the Sale of their Children, will be rid of the Charge of maintaining them after the first Year.

Fifthly, This Food would likewise bring great Custom to Taverns, where the Vintners will certainly be so prudent as to procure the best Receipts for dressing it to Perfection; and consequently have their Houses frequented by all the fine Gentlemen, who justly value themselves upon their Knowledge in good Eating; and a skilful Cook, who understands how to oblige his Guests, will contrive to make it as expensive as they please.

Sixthly, This would be a great Inducement to Marriage, which all wise Nations have either encouraged by Rewards, or enforced by Laws and Penalties. It would encrease the Care and Tenderness of Mothers towards their Children, when they were sure of a Settlement for Life, to the poor Babes, provided in some Sort by the Publick, to their annual Profit instead of Expence; we should soon see an honest Emulation among the married Women, which of them could bring the fattest Child to the Market. Men would become as fond of their Wives, during the Time of their Pregnancy, as they are now of their Mares in Foal, their Cows in Calf, or Sows when they are ready to farrow, nor offer to beat or kick them (as is too frequent a Practice) for fear of a Miscarriage.

Many other Advantages might be enumerated. For Instance, the Addition of some thousand Carcasses in our Exportation of Barrel'd Beef: The Propagation of Swine's Flesh, and Improvement in the Art of making good Bacon, so much wanted among us by the great Destruction of Pigs, too frequent at our Tables, which are no way comparable in Taste, or Magnificence to a well grown, fat yearling Child, which roasted whole will make a considerable Figure at a Lord Mayor's Feast, or any other Publick Entertainment. But this, and many others, I omit, being studious of Brevity.

Supposing that one thousand Families in this City, would be constant Customers for Infant's Flesh, besides others who might have it at merry Meetings, particularly at Weddings and Christenings, I compute that Dublin would take off Annually about twenty thousand Carcasses, and the rest of the Kingdom (where probably they will be sold somewhat cheaper) the remaining eighty Thousand.

I can think of no one Objection, that will possibly be raised against this Proposal, unless it should be urged, that the Number of People will be thereby much lessened in the Kingdom. This I freely own, and 'twas indeed one principal Design in offering it to the World. I desire the Reader will observe, that I calculate my Remedy for this one individual Kingdom of Ireland, and for no Other that ever was, is, or, I think, ever can be upon Earth. Therefore let no man talk to me of other Expedients: Of taxing our Absentees at five Shillings a Pound: Of using neither Cloaths, nor Household Furniture, except what is of our Growth and Manufacture: Of utterly rejecting the Materials and Instruments that promote Foreign Luxury: Of curing the Expensiveness of Pride, Vanity, Idleness, and Gaming in our Women: Of introducing a Vein of Parcimony, Prudence and Temperance: Of learning to love our Country, wherein we differ even from Laplanders, and the Inhabitants of Topinamboo: Of quitting our Animosities, and Factions, nor act any longer like the Jews, who were murdering one another at the very Moment their City was taken: Of being a little cautious not to sell our Country and Consciences for nothing: Of teaching Landlords to have at least one Degree of Mercy towards their Tenants. Lastly, Of putting a Spirit of Honesty, Industry, and Skill into our Shop-keepers, who, if a Resolution could now be taken to buy only our Native Goods, would immediately unite to cheat and exact upon us in the Price, the Measure, and the Goodness, nor could ever yet be brought to make one fair Proposal of just Dealing, thought often and earnestly invited to it.

Therefore I repeat, let no Man talk to me of these and the

like Expedients, till he hath at least some Glimpse of Hope, that there will ever be some hearty and sincere Attempt to put them in Practice.

But as to my self, having been wearied out for many Years with offering vain, idle, visionary Thoughts, and at length utterly despairing of Success, I fortunately fell upon this Proposal, which as it is wholly new, so it hath something Solid and Real, of no Expence and little Trouble, full in our own Power, and whereby we can incur no Danger in disobliging England. For this kind of Commodity will not bear Exportation, the Flesh being of too tender a Consistence, to admit a long Continuance in Salt, although perhaps I cou'd name a Country,[5] which wou'd be glad to eat up our whole Nation without it.

After all, I am not so violently bent upon my own Opinion, as to reject any Offer, proposed by wise Men, which shall be found equally Innocent, Cheap, Easy, and Effectual. But before something of that Kind shall be advanced in Contradiction to my Scheme, and offering a better, I desire the Author or Authors, will be pleased maturely to consider two Points. *First*, As Things now stand, how they will be able to find Food and Raiment for a hundred Thousand useless Mouths and Backs. And *Secondly*, There being a round Million of Creatures in Human Figure, throughout this Kingdom, whose whole Subsistence put into a common Stock, would leave them in Debt (two Millions of Pounds Sterling, adding those, who are Beggers by Profession, to the Bulk of Farmers, Cottagers and Labourers, with their Wives and Children, who are Beggers in Effect; I desire those Politicians, who dislike my Overture, and may perhaps be so bold to attempt an Answer, that they will first ask the Parents of these Mortals, Whether they would not at this Day think it a great Happiness to have been sold for Food at a Year Old, in the manner I prescribe, and thereby have avoided such a perpetual Scene of Misfortunes, as they have since gone through, by the Oppression of Landlords, the Impossibility of paying Rent with-

[5] England.

out Money or Trade, the Want of common Sustenance, with neither House nor Cloaths to cover them from the Inclemencies of the Weather, and the most inevitable Prospect of intailing the like, or greater Miseries, upon their Breed for ever.

I profess in the Sincerity of my Heart, that I have not the least Personal Interest in endeavouring to promote this necessary Work, having no other motive than the Publick Good of my Country, by advancing our Trade, providing for Infants, relieving the Poor, and giving some Pleasure to the Rich. I have no Children, by which I can propose to get a single Penny; the youngest being nine Years Old, and my Wife past Child-bearing.

app apose public interest
in the terrible conditions of Ireland
amount to what the landlords have done already
eating children, but eating
children seems so much worse because
it strikes at the seat of human
emotions

Malthus - "Essay on Population"
1798
checks on population - war, famine, disease
David Ricardo - "Treatise on Economics"
justifies slave wages

Samuel Johnson

SAMUEL JOHNSON *(1709-84) was one of the most comprehensive men of letters in the history of English.
Lexicographer, biographer, poet, essayist, editor, he
wrote in practically every major form. He is the subject of Boswell's great biography and dominated the
literary life of his age by the force of his person and
the cogency of his work. Johnson was educated at
Pembroke College, Oxford. Principal works:* Dictionary *(1755); essays in the* Rambler *(1750-2) and
the* Idler *(1758-60);* Rasselas *(1759);* The Plays of
Shakespeare *(1765);* Lives of the Poets *(1779-81).*

PREFACE TO SHAKESPEARE [1]

That praises are without reason lavished on the dead, and
that the honours due only to excellence are paid to antiquity,
is a complaint likely to be always continued by those, who,
being able to add nothing to truth, hope for eminence from
the heresies of paradox; or those, who, being forced by disappointment upon consolatory expedients, are willing to hope
from posterity what the present age refuses, and flatter themselves that the regard which is yet denied by envy, will be at
last bestowed by time.

Antiquity, like every other quality that attracts the notice
of mankind, has undoubtedly votaries that reverence it, not
from reason, but from prejudice. Some seem to admire indis-

[1] This selection comprises a portion of the preface to Johnson's edition
of Shakespeare (1765). The remainder of Johnson's essay is principally
devoted to reviewing various previous editions of Shakespeare's plays; it
is omitted from this text in the interest of brevity.

102

criminately whatever has been long preserved, without considering that time has sometimes co-operated with chance; all perhaps are more willing to honour past than present excellence; and the mind contemplates genius through the shades of age, as the eye surveys the sun through artificial opacity. The great contention of criticism is to find the faults of the moderns, and the beauties of the ancients. While an authour is yet living we estimate his powers by his worst performance, and when he is dead we rate them by his best.

To works, however, of which the excellence is not absolute and definite, but gradual and comparative; to works not raised upon principles demonstrative and scientifick, but appealing wholly to observation and experience, no other test can be applied than length of duration and continuance of esteem. What mankind have long possessed they have often examined and compared, and if they persist to value the possession, it is because frequent comparisons have confirmed opinion in its favour. As among the works of nature no man can properly call a river deep or a mountain high, without the knowledge of many mountains and many rivers; so in the productions of genius, nothing can be stiled excellent till it has been compared with other works of the same kind. Demonstration immediately displays its power, and has nothing to hope or fear from the flux of years; but works tentative and experimental must be estimated by their proportion to the general and collective ability of man, as it is discovered in a long succession of endeavours. Of the first building that was raised, it might be with certainty determined that it was round or square, but whether it was spacious or lofty must have been referred to time. The Pythagorean scale of numbers was at once discovered to be perfect; but the poems of *Homer* we yet know not to transcend the common limits of human intelligence, but by remarking, that nation after nation, and century after century, has been able to do little more than transpose his incidents, new name his characteres, and paraphrase his sentiments.

The reverence due to writings that have long subsisted

arises therefore not from any credulous confidence in the superior wisdom of past ages, or gloomy persuasion of the degeneracy of mankind, but is the consequence of acknowledged and indubitable positions, that what has been longest known has been most considered, and what is most considered is best understood.

The Poet, of whose works I have undertaken the revision, may now begin to assume the dignity of an ancient, and claim the privilege of established fame and prescriptive veneration. He has long outlived his century, the term commonly fixed as the test of literary merit. Whatever advantages he might once derive from personal allusions, local customs, or temporary opinions, have for many years been lost; and every topick of merriment or motive of sorrow, which the modes of artificial life afforded him, now only obscure the scenes which they once illuminated. The effects of favour and competition are at an end; the tradition of his friendships and his enmities has perished; his works support no opinion with arguments, nor supply any faction with inventives; they can neither indulge vanity nor gratify malignity, but are read without any other reason than the desire of pleasure, and are therefore praised only as pleasure is obtained; yet, thus unassisted by interest or passion, they have past through variations of taste and changes of manners, and, as they devolved from one generation to another, have received new honours at every transmission.

But because human judgment, though it be gradually gaining upon certainty, never becomes infallible; and approbation, though long continued, may yet be only the approbation of prejudice or fashion; it is proper to inquire, by what peculiarities of excellence *Shakespeare* has gained and kept the favour of his countrymen.

Nothing can please many, and please long, but just representations of general nature. Particular manners can be known to few, and therefore few only can judge how nearly they are copied. The irregular combinations of fanciful invention may delight a-while, by that novelty of which the common satiety of life sends us all in quest: but the pleasures of sudden wonder are soon exhausted, and the mind can only repose on the stability of truth.

Shakespeare is above all writers, at least above all modern writers, the poet of nature; the poet that holds up to his readers a faithful mirrour of manners and of life. His characters are not modified by the customs of particular places, unpractised by the rest of the world; by the peculiarities of studies or professions, which can operate but upon small numbers; or by the accidents of transient fashions or temporary opinions: they are the genuine progeny of common humanity, such as the world will always supply, and observation will always find. His persons act and speak by the influence of those general passions and principles by which all minds are agitated, and the whole system of life is continued in motion. In the writings of other poets a character is too often an individual; in those of *Shakespeare* it is commonly a species.

It is from this wide extension of design that so much instruction is derived. It is this which fills the plays of *Shakespeare* with practical axioms and domestick wisdom. It was said of *Euripides,* that every verse was a precept; and it may be said of *Shakespeare,* that from his works may be collected a system of civil and economical prudence. Yet his real power is not shown in the splendour of particular passages, but by the progress of his fable, and the tenour of his dialogue; and he that tries to recommend him by select quotations, will succeed like the pedant in *Hierocles,*[2] who, when he offered his house to sale, carried a brick in his pocket as a specimen.

It will not easily be imagined how much *Shakespeare* excells in accommodating his sentiments to real life, but by comparing him with other authours. It was observed of the ancient schools of declamation, that the more diligently they were frequented, the more was the student disqualified for the world, because he found nothing there which he should

2 *Hieroclis Commentarius in Aurea Carmina,* ed. Needham, 1709.

ever meet in any other place. The same remark may be applied to every stage but that of *Shakespeare*. The theatre, when it is under any other direction, is peopled by such characters as were never seen, conversing in a language which was never heard, upon topicks which will never arise in the commerce of mankind. But the dialogue of this authour is often so evidently determined by the incident which produces it, and is pursued with so much ease and simplicity, that it seems scarcely to claim the merit of fiction, but to have been gleaned by diligent selection out of common conversation, and common occurrences.

Upon every other stage the universal agent is love, by whose power all good and evil is distributed, and every action quickened or retarded. To bring a lover, a lady and a rival into the fable; to entangle them in contradictory obligations, perplex them with oppositions of interest, and harass them with violence of desires inconsistent with each other; to make them meet in rapture and part in agony; to fill their mouths with hyperbolical joy and outrageous sorrow; to distress them as nothing human ever was distressed; to deliver them as nothing human ever was delivered, is the business of a modern dramatist. For this probability is violated, life is misrepresented, and language is depraved. But love is only one of many passions, and as it has no great influence upon the sum of life, it has little operation in the dramas of a poet, who caught his ideas from the living world, and exhibited only what he saw before him. He knew, that any other passion, as it was regular or exorbitant, was a cause of happiness or calamity.

Characters thus ample and general were not easily discriminated and preserved, yet perhaps no poet ever kept his personages more distinct from each other. I will not say with *Pope*,[3] that every speech may be assigned to the proper speaker, because many speeches there are which have nothing characteristical; but, perhaps, though some may be equally adapted to every person, it will be difficult to find, any that

[3] See Pope's preface to his edition of Shakespeare, paragraph four.

can be properly transferred from the present possessor to another claimant. The choice is right, when there is reason for choice.

Other dramatists can only gain attention by hyperbolical or aggravated characters, by fabulous and unexampled excellence or depravity, as the writers of barbarous romances invigorated the reader by a giant and a dwarf; and he that should form his expectations of human affairs from the play, or from the tale, would be equally deceived. *Shakespeare* has no heroes; his scenes are occupied only by men, who act and speak as the reader thinks that he should himself have spoken or acted on the same occasion: Even where the agency is supernatural the dialogue is level with life. Other writers disguise the most natural passions and most frequent incidents; so that he who contemplates them in the book will not know them in the world: *Shakespeare* approximates the remote, and familiarizes the wonderful; the event which he represents will not happen, but if it were possible, its effects would be probably such as he has assigned; and it may be said, that he has not only shewn human nature as it acts in real exigences, but as it would be found in trials, to which it cannot be exposed.

This therefore is the praise of *Shakespeare,* that this drama is the mirrour of life; that he who has mazed his imagination, in following the phantoms which other writers raise up before him, may here be cured of his delirious extasies, by reading human sentiments in human language; by scenes from which a hermit may estimate the transactions of the world, and a confessor predict the progress of the passions.

His adherence to general nature has exposed him to the censure of criticks, who form their judgments upon narrower principles. *Dennis* and *Rhymer* think his *Romans* not sufficiently Roman; and *Voltaire* censures his kings as not completely royal. *Dennis* is offended, that *Menenius,* a senator of *Rome,*[4] should play the buffoon; and *Voltaire* perhaps thinks decency violated when the *Danish* Usurper is represented as a

4 In *Coriolanus.*

drunkard. But *Shakespeare* always makes nature predominate over accident; and if he preserves the essential character, is not very careful of distinctions superinduced and adventitious. His story requires Romans or kings, but he thinks only on men. He knew that *Rome,* like every other city, had men of all dispositions; and wanting a buffoon, he went into the senate-house for that which the senate-house would certainly have afforded him. He was inclined to shew an usurper and a murderer not only odious but despicable, he therefore added drunkenness to his other qualities, knowing that kings love wine like other men, and that wine exerts its natural power upon kings. These are the petty cavils of petty minds; a poet overlooks the casual distinction of country and condition, as a painter, satisfied with the figure, neglects the drapery.

The censure which he has incurred by mixing comick and tragick scenes, as it extends to all his works, deserves more consideration. Let the fact be first stated, and then examined.

Shakespeare's plays are not in the rigorous and critical sense either tragedies or comedies, but compositions of a distinct kind; exhibiting the real state of sublunary nature, which partakes of good and evil, joy and sorrow, mingled with endless variety of proportion and innumerable modes of combination; and expressing the course of the world, in which the loss of one is the gain of another; in which, at the same time, the reveller is hasting to his wine, and the mourner burying his friend; in which the malignity of one is sometimes defeated by the frolick of another; and many mischiefs and many benefits are done and hindered without design.

Out of this chaos of mingled purposes and casualties the ancient poets, according to the laws which custom had prescribed, selected some the crimes of men, and some their absurdities; some the momentous vicissitudes of life, and some the lighter occurrences; some the terrours of distress, and some the gayeties of prosperity. Thus rose the two modes of imitation, known by the names of *tragedy* and *comedy,* compositions intended to promote different ends by contrary means, and considered as so little allied, that I do not recollect among the *Greeks* or *Romans* a single writer who attempted both.

Shakespeare has united the powers of exciting laughter and sorrow not only in one mind, but in one composition. Almost all his plays are divided between serious and ludicrous characters, and, in the successive evolutions of the design, sometimes produce seriousness and sorrow, and sometimes levity and laughter.

That this is a practice contrary to the rules of criticism will be readily allowed; but there is always an appeal open from criticism to nature. The end of writing is to instruct; the end of poetry is to instruct by pleasing. That the mingled drama may convey all the instructions of tragedy or comedy cannot be denied, because it includes both in its alternations of exhibition, and approaches nearer than either to the appearance of life, by shewing how great machinations and slender designs may promote or obviate one another, and the high and the low co-operate in the general system by unavoidable concatenation.

It is objected, that by this change of scenes the passions are interrupted in their progression, and that the principal event, being not advanced by a due gradation of preparatory incidents, wants at last the power to move, which constitutes the perfection of dramatick poetry. This reasoning is so specious, that it is received as true even by those who in daily experience feel it to be false. The interchanges of mingled scenes seldom fail to produce the intended vicissitudes of passion. Fiction cannot move so much, but that the attention may be easily transferred; and though it must be allowed that pleasing melancholy be sometimes interrupted by unwelcome levity, yet let it be considered likewise, that melancholy is often not pleasing, and that the disturbance of one man may be the relief of another; that different auditors have different habitudes; and that, upon the whole, all pleasure consists in variety.

The players' who in their edition [5] divided our authour's

5 The first folio (1623).

works into comedies, histories, and tragedies, seem not to have distinguished the three kinds, by any very exact or definite ideas.

An action which ended happily to the principal persons, however serious or distressful through its intermediate incidents, in their opinion constituted a comedy. This idea of a comedy continued long amongst us, and plays were written, which, by changing the catastrophe, were tragedies to-day and comedies to-morrow.

Tragedy was not in those times a poem of more general dignity or elevation than comedy; it required only a calamitous conclusion, with which the common criticism of that age was satisfied, whatever lighter pleasure it afforded in its progress.

History was a series of actions, with no other than chronological succession, independent of each other, and without any tendency to introduce or regulate the conclusion. It is not always very nicely distinguished from tragedy. There is not much nearer approach to unity of action in the tragedy of *Antony and Cleopatra,* than in the history of *Richard the Second.* But a history might be continued through many plays; as it had no plan, it had no limits.

Through all these denominations of the drama, *Shakespeare's* mode of composition is the same; an interchange of seriousness and merriment, by which the mind is softened at one time, and exhilarated at another. But whatever be his purpose, whether to gladden or depress, or to conduct the story, without vehemence or emotion, through tracts of easy and familiar dialogue, he never fails to attain his purpose; as he commands us, we laugh or mourn, or sit silent with quiet expectation, in tranquillity without indifference.

When *Shakespeare's* plan is understood, most of the criticisms of *Rhymer* and *Voltaire* vanish away. The play of *Hamlet* is opened, without impropriety, by two sentinels; *Iago* bellows at *Brabantio's* window, without injury to the scheme of the play, though in terms which a modern audience would not easily endure; the character of *Polonius* is seasonable and useful; and the Grave-diggers themselves may be heard with applause.

Shakespeare engaged in dramatick poetry with the world open before him; the rules of the ancients were yet known to few; the publick judgment was unformed; he had no example of such fame as might force him upon imitation, nor criticks of such authority as might restrain his extravagance: He therefore indulged his natural disposition, and his disposition, as *Rhymer* has remarked, led him to comedy. In tragedy he often writes with great appearance of toil and study, what is written at last with little felicity; but in his comick scenes, he seems to produce without labour, what no labour can improve. In tragedy he is always struggling after some occasion to be comick, but in comedy he seems to repose, or to luxuriate, as in a mode of thinking congenial to his nature. In his tragick scenes there is always something wanting, but his comedy often surpasses expectation or desire. His comedy pleases by the thoughts and the language, and his tragedy for the greater part by incident and action. His tragedy seems to be skill, his comedy to be instinct.

The force of his comick scenes has suffered little diminution from the changes made by a century and a half, in manners or in words. As his personages act upon principles arising from genuine passion, very little modified by particular forms, their pleasures and vexations are communicable to all times and to all places; they are natural, and therefore durable; the adventitious peculiarities of personal habits, are only superficial dies, bright and pleasing for a little while, yet soon fading to a dim tinct, without any remains of former lustre; but the discriminations of true passion are the colours of nature; they pervade the whole mass, and can only perish with the body that exhibits them. The accidental compositions of heterogeneous modes are dissolved by the chance which combined them; but the uniform simplicity of primitive qualities neither admits increase, nor suffers decay. The sand heaped by one flood is scattered by another, but the rock always continues in its place. The stream of time, which is continually washing the dissoluble fabricks of other poets, passes without injury by the adamant of *Shakespeare*.

If there be, what I believe there is, in every nation, a stile which never becomes obsolete, a certain mode of phraseology so consonant and congenial to the analogy and principles of its respective language as to remain settled and unaltered; this stile is probably to be sought in the common intercourse of life, among those who speak only to be understood, without ambition of elegance. The polite are always catching modish innovations, and the learned depart from established forms of speech, in hope of finding or making better; those who wish for distinction forsake the vulgar, when the vulgar is right; but there is a conversation above grossness and below refinement, where propriety resides, and where this poet seems to have gathered his comick dialogue. He is therefore more agreeable to the ears of the present age than any other authour equally remote, and among his other excellencies deserves to be studied as one of the original masters of our language.

These observations are to be considered not as unexceptionably constant, but as containing general and predominant truth. *Shakespeare's* familiar dialogue is affirmed to be smooth and clear, yet not wholly without ruggedness or difficulty; as a country may be eminently fruitful, though it has spots unfit for cultivation: His characters are praised as natural, though their sentiments are sometimes forced, and their actions improbable; as the earth upon the whole is spherical, though its surface is varied with protuberances and cavities.

Shakespeare with his excellencies has likewise faults, and faults sufficient to obscure and overwhelm any other merit. I shall shew them in the proportion in which they appear to me, without envious malignity or superstitious veneration. No question can be more innocently discussed than a dead poet's pretensions to renown; and little regard is due to that bigotry which sets candour higher than truth.

His first defect is that to which may be imputed most of the evil in books or in men. He sacrifices virtue to convenience, and is so much more careful to please than to instruct, that he seems to write without any moral purpose. From his writings indeed a system of social duty may be selected, for he that thinks reasonably must think morally; but his precepts and axioms drop casually from him; he makes no just distribution of good or evil, nor is always careful to shew in the virtuous a disapprobation of the wicked; he carries his persons indifferently through right and wrong, and at the close dismisses them without further care, and leaves their examples to operate by chance. This fault the barbarity of his age cannot extenuate; for it is always a writer's duty to make the world better, and justice is a virtue independant on time or place.

The plots are often so loosely formed, that a very slight consideration may improve them, and so carelessly pursued, that he seems not always fully to comprehend his own design. He omits opportunities of instructing or delighting which the train of his story seems to force upon him, and apparently rejects those exhibitions which would be more affecting, for the sake of those which are more easy.

It may be observed, that in many of his plays the latter part is evidently neglected. When he found himself near the end of his work, and, in view of his reward, he shortened the labour, to snatch the profit. He therefore remits his efforts where he should most vigorously exert them, and his catastrophe is improbably produced or imperfectly represented.

He had no regard to distinction of time or place, but gives to one age or nation, without scruple, the customs, institutions, and opinions of another, at the expence not only of likelihood, but of possibility. These faults *Pope* has endeavoured, with more zeal than judgment, to transfer to his imagined interpolators. We need not wonder to find *Hector* quoting *Aristotle*, when we see the loves of *Theseus* and *Hippolyta* combined with the *Gothick* mythology of fairies. *Shakespeare*, indeed, was not the only violator of chronology, for in the same age *Sidney*, who wanted not the advantages of learning, has, in his *Arcadia*, confounded the pastoral with the feudal times, the days of innocence, quiet and security, with those of turbulence, violence and adventure.

In his comick scenes he is seldom very successful, when he

engages his characters in reciprocations of smartness and contest of sarcasm; their jests are commonly gross, and their pleasantry licentious; neither his gentlemen nor his ladies have much delicacy, nor are sufficient distinguished from his clowns by any appearance of refined manners. Whether he represented the real conversation of his time is not easy to determine; the reign of *Elizabeth* is commonly supposed to have been a time of stateliness, formality and reserve, yet perhaps the relaxations of that severity were not very elegant. There must, however, have been always some modes of gayety preferable to others, and a writer ought to chuse the best.

In tragedy his performance seems constantly to be worse, as his labour is more. The effusions of passion which exigence forces out are for the most part striking and energetick; but whenever he solicits his invention, or strains his faculties, the offspring of his throes is tumour, meanness, tediousness, and obscurity.

In narration he affects a disproportionate pomp of diction and a wearisome train of circumlocution, and tells the incident imperfectly in many words, which might have been more plainly delivered in few. Narration in dramatick poetry is naturally tedious, as it is unanimated and inactive, and obstructs the progress of the action; it should therefore always be rapid, and enlivened by frequent interruption. *Shakespeare* found it an encumbrance, and instead of lightening it by brevity, endeavoured to recommend it by dignity and splendour.

His declamations or set speeches are commonly cold and weak, for his power was the power of nature; when he endeavoured, like other tragick writers, to catch opportunities of amplification, and instead of inquiring what the occasion demanded, to show how much his stores of knowledge could supply, he seldom escapes without the pity or resentment of his reader.

It is incident to him to be now and then entangled with an unwieldy sentiment, which he cannot well express, and will not reject; he struggles with it a while, and if it continues stubborn, comprises it in words such as occur, and leaves it to be disentangled and evolved by those who have more leisure to bestow upon it.

Not that always where the language is intricate the thought is subtle, or the image always great where the line is bulky; the equality of words to things is very often neglected, and trivial sentiments and vulgar ideas disappoint the attention, to which they are recommended by sonorous epithets and swelling figures.

But the admirers of this great poet have never less reason to indulge their hopes of supreme excellence, than when he seems fully resolved to sink them in dejection, and mollify them with tender emotions by the fall of greatness, the danger of innocence, or the crosses of love. He is not long soft and pathetick without some idle conceit, or contemptible equivocation. He no sooner begins to move, than he counteracts himself; and terrour and pity, as they are rising in the mind, are checked and blasted by sudden frigidity.

A quibble is to *Shakespeare,* what luminous vapours are to the traveller; he follows it at all adventures, it is sure to lead him out of his way, and sure to engulf him in the mire. It has some malignant power over his mind, and its fascinations are irresistible. Whatever be the dignity or profoundity of his disquisition, whether he be enlarging knowledge or exalting affection, whether he be amusing attention with incidents, or enchaining it in suspense, let but a quibble spring up before him, and he leaves his work unfinished. A quibble is the golden apple for which he will always turn aside from his career, or stoop from his elevation. A quibble poor and barren as it is, gave him such delight, that he was content to purchase it, by the sacrifice of reason, propriety and truth. A quibble was to him the fatal *Cleopatra* for which he lost the world, and was content to lose it.

It will be thought strange, that, in enumerating the defects of this writer, I have not yet mentioned his neglect of the unities; his violation of those laws which have been instituted and established by the joint authority of poets and of criticks.

For his other deviations from the art of writing, I resign him to critical justice, without making any other demand in his favour, than that which must be indulged to all human excellence; that his virtues be rated with his failings: But, from the censure which this irregularity may bring upon him, I shall, with due reverence to that learning which I must oppose, adventure to try how I can defend him.

His histories, being neither tragedies nor comedies, are not subject to any of their laws; nothing more is necessary to all the praise which they expect, than that the changes of action be so prepared as to be understood, that the incidents be various and affecting, and the characters consistent, natural and distinct. No other unity is intended, and therefore none is to be sought.

In his other works he has well enough preserved the unity of action. He has not, indeed, an intrigue regularly perplexed and regularly unravelled; he does not endeavour to hide his design only to discover it, for this is seldom the order of real events, and *Shakespeare* is the poet of nature: But his plan has commonly what *Aristotle* requires, a beginning, a middle, and an end; one event is concatenated with another, and the conclusion follows by easy consequence. There are perhaps some incidents that might be spared, as in other poets there is much talk that only fills up time upon the stage; but the general system makes gradual advances, and the end of the play is the end of expectation.

To the unities of time and place he has shewn no regard, and perhaps a nearer view of the principles on which they stand will diminish their value, and withdraw from them the veneration which, from the time of *Corneille,* they have very generally received by discovering that they have given more trouble to the poet, than pleasure to the auditor.

The necessity of observing the unities of time and place arises from the supposed necessity of making the drama credible. The criticks hold it impossible, that an action of months or years can be possibly believed to pass in three hours; or that the spectator can suppose himself to sit in the theatre, while ambassadors go and return between distant kings, while armies are levied and towns besieged, while an exile wanders and returns, or till he whom they saw courting his mistress, shall lament the untimely fall of his son. The mind revolts from evident falsehood, and fiction loses its force when it departs from the resemblance of reality.

From the narrow limitation of time necessarily arises the contraction of space. The spectator, who knows that he saw the first act at *Alexandria*, cannot suppose that he sees the next at *Rome*, at a distance to which not the dragons of *Medea* could, in so short a time, have transported him; he knows with certainty that he has not changed his place; and he knows that place cannot change itself; that what was a house cannot become a plain; that what was *Thebes* can never be *Persepolis*.

Such is the triumphant language with which a critick exults over the misery of an irregular poet, and exults commonly without resistance or reply. It is time therefore to tell him, by the authority of *Shakespeare*, that he assumes, as an unquestionable principle, a position, which, while his breath is forming it into words, his understanding pronounces to be false. It is false, that any representation is mistaken for reality; that any dramatick fable in its materiality was ever credible, or, for a single moment, was ever credited.

The objection arising from the impossibility of passing the first hour at *Alexandria*, and the next at *Rome*, supposes, that when the play opens the spectator really imagines himself at *Alexandria*, and believes that his walk to the theatre has been a voyage to *Egypt*, and that he lives in the days of *Antony* and *Cleopatra*. Surely he that imagines this, may imagine more. He that can take the stage at one time for the palace of the *Ptolemies*, may take it in half an hour for the promontory of *Actium*. Delusion, if delusion be admitted, has no certain limitation; if the spectator can be once persuaded, that his old acquaintances are *Alexander* and *Caesar*, that a room illuminated with candles is the plain of *Pharsalia*, or the bank of *Granicus*, he is in a state of elevation above the reach of reason, or of truth, and from the heights of empyrean poetry, may despise the circumscriptions of terrestrial nature. There is no reason why a mind thus wandering in extasy should count the clock, or why an hour should not be a century in that calenture of the brains that can make the stage a field.

The truth is, that the spectators are always in their senses, and know, from the first act to the last, that the stage is only a stage, and that the players are only players. They come to hear a certain number of lines recited with just gesture and elegant modulation. The lines relate to some action, and an action must be in some place; but the different actions that compleat a story may be in places very remote from each other; and where is the absurdity of allowing that space to represent first *Athens*, and then *Sicily*, which was always known to be neither *Sicily* nor *Athens*, but a modern theatre?

By supposition, as place is introduced, time may be extended; the time required by the fable elapses for the most part between the acts; for, of so much of the action as is represented, the real and poetical duration is the same. If, in the first act, preparations for war again *Mithridates* [6] are represented to be made in *Rome*, the event of the war may, without absurdity, be represented, in the catastrophe, as happening in *Pontus;* we know that there is neither war, nor preparation for war; we know that we are neither in *Rome* nor *Pontus;* that neither *Mithridates* nor *Lucullus* are before us. The drama exhibits successive imitations of successive actions, and why may not the second imitation represent an action that happened years after the first; if it be so connected with it, that nothing but time can be supposed to intervene? Time is, of all modes of existence, most obsequious to the imagination; a lapse of years is as easily conceived as a passage of hours. In contemplation we easily contract the time of real actions, and therefore willingly permit it to be contracted when we only see their imitation.

It will be asked, how the drama moves, if it is not credited.

6 Mithridates was the king of Pontus, and Lucullus was his Roman antagonist in the Mithridatic Wars, which extended from 88 B.C. to 63 B.C.

It is credited with all the credit due to a drama. It is credited, whenever it moves, as a just picture of a real original; as representing to the auditor what he would himself feel, if he were to do or suffer what is there feigned to be suffered or to be done. The reflection that strikes the heart is not, that the evils before us are real evils, but that they are evils to which we ourselves may be exposed. If there be any fallacy, it is not that we fancy the players, but that we fancy ourselves unhappy for a moment; but we rather lament the possibility than suppose the presence of misery, as a mother weeps over her babe, when she remembers that death may take it from her. The delight of tragedy proceeds from our consciousness of fiction; if we thought murders and treasons real, they would please no more.

Imitations produce pain or pleasure, not because they are mistaken for realities, but because they bring realities to mind. When the imagination is recreated by a painted landscape, the trees are not supposed capable to give us shade, or the fountains coolness; but we consider, how we should be pleased with such fountains playing beside us, and such woods waving over us. We are agitated in reading the history of *Henry* the Fifth, yet no man takes his book for the field of *Agencourt*. A dramatick exhibition is a book recited with concomitants that encrease or diminish its effect. Familiar comedy is often more powerful on the theatre, than in the page; imperial tragedy is always less. The humour of *Petruchio* may be heightened by grimace; but what voice or what gesture can hope to add dignity or force to the soliloquy of *Cato*.[7]

A play read, affects the mind like a play acted. It is therefore evident, that the action is not supposed to be real, and it follows that between the acts a longer or shorter time may be allowed to pass, and that no more account of space or duration is to be taken by the auditor of a drama, than by the reader of a narrative, before whom may pass in an hour the life of a hero, or the revolutions of an empire.

7 In Addison's *Cato*, Act V, Sc. i. Cato is an "imperial tragedy," here used as an antithesis to the comedy *The Taming of the Shrew*.

Whether *Shakespeare* knew the unities, and rejected them
by design, or deviated from them by happy ignorance, it is,
I think, impossible to decide, and useless to inquire. We may
reasonably suppose, that, when he rose to notice, he did not
want [8] the counsels and admonitions of scholars and criticks,
and that he at last deliberately persisted in a practice, which
he might have begun by chance. As nothing is essential to
the fable, but unity of action, and as the unities of time and
place arise evidently from false assumptions, and, by circum-
scribing the extent of the drama, lessen its variety, I cannot
think it much to be lamented, that they were not known by
him, or not observed: Nor, if such another poet could arise,
should I very vehemently reproach him, that his first act passed
at *Venice*, and his next in *Cyprus*. Such violations of rules
merely positive, become the comprehensive genius of *Shakespeare*, and such censures are suitable to the minute and
slender criticism of *Voltaire*:

> *Non usque adeo permiscuit imis*
> *Longus summa dies, ut non, si voce Metelli*
> *Serventur leges, malint a Caesare tolli.*[9]

Yet when I speak thus slightly of dramatick rules, I cannot
but recollect how much wit and learning may be produced
against me; before such authorities I am afraid to stand, not
that I think the present question one of those that are to be
decided by mere authority, but because it is to be suspected,
that these precepts have not been so easily received but for
better reasons than I have yet been able to find. The result of
my enquiries, in which it would be ludicrous to boast of im-
partiality, is, that the unities of time and place are not essential to a just drama, that though they may sometimes conduce
to pleasure, they are always to be sacrificed to the nobler beauties of variety and instruction; and that a play, written with

---

8 He did not lack, i.e., he was not aware of.

9 Lucan, *Pharsalia*, III, 138-140. "The course of time has not wrought
such confusion that the laws would not rather be trampled by Caesar
than saved by Metellus."

nice observation of critical rules, is to be contemplated as an elaborate curiosity, as the product of superfluous and ostentatious art, by which is shewn, rather what is possible, than what is necessary.

He that, without diminution of any other excellence, shall preserve all the unities unbroken, deserves the like applause with the architect, who shall display all the orders of architecture in a citadel, without any deduction from its strength; but the principal beauty of a citadel is to exclude the enemy; and the greatest graces of a play, are to copy nature and instruct life.

Perhaps, what I have here not dogmatically but deliberately written, may recal the principles of the drama to a new examination.[10] I am almost frighted at my own temerity; and when I estimate the fame and the strength of those that maintain the contrary opinion, am ready to sink down in reverential silence; as *Aeneas* withdrew from the defence of *Troy,* when he saw *Neptune* shaking the wall, and *Juno* heading the besiegers.

Those whom my arguments cannot persuade to give their approbation to the judgment of *Shakespeare,* will easily, if they consider the condition of his life, make some allowance for his ignorance.

Every man's performances, to be rightly estimated, must be compared with the state of the age in which he lived, and with his own particular opportunities; and though to the reader a book be not worse or better for the circumstances of the authour, yet as there is always a silent reference of human works to human abilities, and as the enquiry, how far man may extend his designs, or how high he may rate his native force, is of far greater dignity than in what rank we shall place any particular performance, curiosity is always busy to discover the instruments, as well as to survey the workmanship, to know how much is to be ascribed to original powers, and how much to casual and adventitious help. The palaces of *Peru* or

10 Johnson is offering his observations not as the delivery of axioms but as the presentation of his deliberations on the subject.

Mexico were certainly mean and incommodious habitations, if compared to the houses of *European* monarchs; yet who could forbear to view them with astonishment, who remembered that they were built without the use of iron?

The *English* nation, in the time of *Shakespeare*, was yet struggling to emerge from barbarity. The philology of *Italy* had been transplanted hither in the reign of *Henry* the Eighth; and the learned languages had been successfully cultivated by *Lilly, Linacer,* and *More*; by *Pole, Cheke, and Gardiner;* and afterwards by *Smith, Clerk, Haddon,* and *Ascham.*[11] Greek was now taught to boys in the principal schools; and those who united elegance with learning, read, with great diligence, the *Italian* and *Spanish* poets. But literature was yet confined to professed scholars, or to men and women of high rank. The publick was gross and dark; and to be able to read and write, was an accomplishment still valued for its rarity.

Nations, like individuals, have their infancy. A people newly awakened to literary curiosity, being yet unacquainted with the true state of things, knows not how to judge of that which is proposed as its resemblance. Whatever is remote from common appearances is always welcome to vulgar, as to childish credulity; and of a country unenlightened by learning, the whole people is the vulgar. The study of those who then aspired to plebeian learning was laid out upon adventures, giants, dragons, and enchantments. *The Death of Arthur* [12] was the favourite volume.

The mind, which has feasted on the luxurious wonders of fiction, has no taste of the insipidity of truth. A play which imitated only the common occurrences of the world, would, upon the admirers of *Palmerin* and *Guy of Warwick,*[13] have made little impression; he that wrote for such an audience was under the necessity of looking round for strange events and

11 The various people listed here are all Renaissance humanists who were engaged in the pursuit of classical studies. The most famous of them are Thomas More and Roger Ascham.

12 Malory's *Morte d'Arthur* (1485).

13 *Palmerin* and *Guy of Warwick* were two medieval romances notable for their fabulous transactions and strange events.

fabulous transactions, and that incredibility, by which maturer knowledge is offended, was the chief recommendation of writings, to unskilful curiosity.

Our authour's plots are generally borrowed from novels, and it is reasonable to suppose, that he chose the most popular, such as were read by many, and related by more; for his audience could not have followed him through the intricacies of the drama, had they not held the thread of the story in their hands.

The stories, which we now find only in remoter authours, were in his time accessible and familliar. The fable of *As you like it*, which is supposed to be copied from *Chaucer's* Gamelyn,[14] was a little pamphlet of those times; and old Mr. *Cibber*[15] remembered the tale of *Hamlet* in plain *English* prose, which the criticks have now to seek in *Saxo Grammaticus*.

His *English* histories he took from *English* chronicles and *English* ballads; and as the ancient writers were made known to his countrymen by versions, they supplied him with new subjects; he dilated some of *Plutarch's* lives into plays, when they had been translated by *North*.

His plots, whether historical or fabulous, are always crouded with incidents, by which the attention of a rude people was more easily caught than by sentiment or argumentation; and such is the power of the marvellous even over those who despise it, that every man finds his mind more strongly seized by the tragedies of *Shakespeare* than of any other writer; others please us by particular speeches, but he always makes us anxious for the event, and has perhaps excelled all but *Homer* in securing the first purpose of a writer, by exciting restless and unquenchable curiosity, and compelling him that reads his work to read it through.

The shows and bustle with which his plays abound have the same original. As knowledge advances, pleasure passes from

---

[14] The tale of *Gamelyn*, no longer regarded as Chaucer's work, was the ancestor of Thomas Lodge's *Rosalynde* (1590), which in turn supplied Shakespeare with a plot.

[15] Colley Cibber, eighteenth-century actor and playwright.

the eye to the ear, but returns, as it declines, from the ear to the eye. Those to whom our authour's labours were exhibited had more skill in pomps or processions than in poetical language, and perhaps wanted some visible and discriminated events, as comments on the dialogue. He knew how he should most please; and whether his practice is more agreeable to nature, or whether his example has prejudiced the nation, we still find that on our stage something must be done as well as said, and inactive declamation is very coldly heard, however musical or elegant, passionate or sublime.

Voltaire expresses his wonder,[16] that our authour's extravagancies are endured by a nation, which has seen the tragedy of *Cato*. Let him be answered, that *Addison* speaks the language of poets, and *Shakespeare*, of men. We find in *Cato* innumerable beauties which enamour us of its authour, but we see nothing that acquaints us with human sentiments or human actions; we place it with the fairest and the noblest progeny which judgment propagates by conjunction with learning, but *Othello* is the vigorous and vivacious offspring of observation impregnated by genius. *Cato* affords a splendid exhibition of artificial and fictitious manners, and delivers just and noble sentiments, in diction easy, elevated and harmonious, but its hopes and fears communicate no vibration to the heart; the composition refers us only to the writer; we pronounce the name of *Cato*, but we think on *Addison*.

The work of a correct and regular writer is a garden accurately formed and diligently planted, varied with shades, and scented with flowers; the composition of *Shakespeare* is a forest, in which oaks extend their branches, and pines tower in the air, interspersed sometimes with weeds and brambles, and sometimes giving shelter to myrtles and to roses; filling the eye with awful pomp, and gratifying the mind with endless diversity. Other poets display cabinets of precious rarities, minutely finished, wrought into shape, and polished unto brightness. *Shakespeare* opens a mine which contains gold and diamonds

16 Voltaire repeatedly expressed his impatience with Shakespeare's violation of the unities.

in unexhaustible plenty, though clouded by incrustations, debased by impurities, and mingled with a mass of meaner minerals.

It has been much disputed, whether *Shakespeare* owed his excellence to his own native force, or whether he had the common helps of scholastick education, the precepts of critical science, and the examples of ancient authours.

There has always prevailed a tradition, that *Shakespeare* wanted learning, that he had no regular education, nor much skill in the dead languages. *Jonson*,[17] his friend, affirms, that *he had small Latin, and no Greek;* who, besides that he had no imaginable temptation to falsehood, wrote at a time when the character and acquisitions of *Shakespeare* were known to multitudes. His evidence ought therefore to decide the controversy, unless some testimony of equal force could be opposed.

Some have imagined, that they have discovered deep learning in many imitations of old writers; but the examples which I have known urged, were drawn from books translated in his time; or were such easy coincidencies of thought, as will happen to all who consider the same subjects; or such remarks on life or axioms of morality as float in conversation, and are transmitted through the world in proverbial sentences.

I have found it remarked, that, in this important sentence, *Go before, I'll follow,* we read a translation of, *I prae, sequar.*[18] I have been told, that when *Caliban*, after a pleasing dream, says, *I cry'd to sleep again*, the authour imitates *Anacreon*, who had, like every other man, the same wish on the same occasion.

There are a few passages which may pass for imitations, but so few, that the exception only confirms the rule; he obtained them from accidental quotations, or by oral communication, and as he used what he had, would have used more if he had obtained it.

17 Ben Jonson, in his verses to the memory of Shakespeare, said that Shakespeare had "small Latin, and *less* Greek."

18 Zachary Grey, an eighteenth-century critic, had suggested that the line in *Richard III* was a paraphrase of Terence. Johnson is here ridiculing the suggestion.

The *Comedy of Errors* is confessedly taken from the *Menaechmi* of *Plautus;* from the only play of *Plautus* which was then in *English*. What can be more probable, than that he who copied that, would have copied more; but that those which were not translated were inaccessible?

Whether he knew the modern languages is uncertain. That his plays have some *French* scenes proves but little; he might easily procure them to be written, and probably, even though he had known the language in the common degree, he could not have written it without assistance. In the story of *Romeo* and *Juliet* he is observed to have followed the *English* translation, where it deviates from the *Italian;* but this on the other part proves nothing against his knowledge of the original. He was to copy, not what he knew himself, but what was known to his audience.

It is most likely that he had learned *Latin* sufficiently to make him acquainted with construction, but that he never advanced to an easy perusal of the *Roman* authours. Concerning his skill in modern languages, I can find no sufficient ground of determination; but as no imitations of *French* or *Italian* authours have been discovered, though the *Italian* poetry was then high in esteem, I am inclined to believe, that he read little more than *English*, and chose for his fables only such tales as he found translated.

That much knowledge is scattered over his works is very justly observed by *Pope*, but it is often such knowledge as books did not supply. He that will understand *Shakespeare*, must not be content to study him in the closet, he must look for his meaning sometimes among the sports of the field, and sometimes among the manufactures of the shop.

There is however proof enough that he was a very diligent reader, nor was our language then so indigent of books, but that he might very liberally indulge his curiosity without excursion into foreign literature. Many of the *Roman* authours were translated, and some of the *Greek;* the reformation had filled the kingdom with theological learning; most of the topicks of human disquisition had found *English* writers; and poetry had been cultivated, not only with diligence, but success. This was a stock of knowledge sufficient for a mind so capable of appropriating and improving it.

But the greater part of his excellence was the product of his own genius. He found the *English* stage in a state of the utmost rudeness; no essays either in tragedy or comedy had appeared, from which it could be discovered to what degree of delight either one or other might be carried. Neither character nor dialogue were yet understood. *Shakespeare* may be truly said to have introduced them both amongst us, and in some of his happier scenes to have carried them both to the utmost height.

By what gradations of improvement he proceeded, is not easily known; for the chronology of his works is yet unsettled. *Rowe* is of opinion, that *perhaps we are not to look for his beginning, like those of other writers, in his least perfect works; art had so little, and nature so large a share in what he did, that for ought I know,* says he, *the performances of his youth, as they were the most vigorous, were the best.*[19] But the power of nature is only the power of using to any certain purpose the materials which diligence procures, or opportunity supplies. Nature gives no man knowledge, and when images are collected by study and experience, can only assist in combining or applying them. *Shakespeare,* however favoured by nature, could impart only what he had learned; and as he must increase his ideas, like other mortals, by gradual acquisition, he, like them, grew wiser as he grew older, could display life better, as he knew it more, and instruct with more efficacy, as he was himself more amply instructed.

There is a vigilance of observation and accuracy of distinction which books and precepts cannot confer; from this almost all original and native excellence proceeds. *Shakespeare* must have looked upon mankind with perspicacity, in the highest degree curious and attentive. Other writers borrow their characters from preceding writers, and diversify them only by the accidental appendages of present manners; the dress is a little

[19] From Rowe's "Life of Shakespeare," prefixed to his edition, 1789.

varied, but the body is the same. Our authour had both matter and form to provide; for except the characters of *Chaucer,* to whom I think he is not much indebted, there were no writers in *English,* and perhaps not many in other modern languages, which shewed life in its native colours.

The contest about the original benevolence or malignity of man had not yet commenced. Speculation had not yet attempted to analyse the mind, to trace the passions to their sources, to unfold the seminal principles of vice and virtue, or sound the depths of the heart for the motives of action. All those enquiries, which from that time that human nature became the fashionable study, have been made sometimes with nice discernment, but often with idle subtilty, were yet unattempted. The tales, with which the infancy of learning was satisfied, exhibited only the superficial appearances of action, related the events but omitted the causes, and were formed for such as delighted in wonders rather than in truth. Mankind was not then to be studied in the closet; he that would know the world, was under the necessity of gleaning his own remarks, by mingling as he could in its business and amusements.

Boyle congratulated himself upon his high birth, because it favoured his curiosity, by facilitating his access. *Shakespeare* had no such advantage; he came to *London* a needy adventurer, and lived for a time by very mean employments. Many works of genius and learning have been performed in states of life, that appear very little favourable to thought or to enquiry; so many, that he who considers them is inclined to think that he sees enterprise and perseverance predominating over all external agency, and bidding help and hindrance vanish before them. The genius of *Shakespeare* was not to be depressed by the weight of poverty, nor limited by the narrow conversation to which men in want are inevitably condemned; the incumbrances of his fortune were shaken from his mind, *as dewdrops from a lion's mane.*[20]

Though he had so many difficulties to encounter, and so little assistance to surmount them, he has been able to obtain

[20] *Troilus and Cressida,* Act III, Sc. iii, l. 225.

an exact knowledge of many modes of life, and many casts of native dispositions; to vary them with great multiplicity; to mark them by nice distinctions; and to shew them in full view by proper combinations. In this part of his performances he had none to imitate, but has himself been imitated by all succeeding writers; and it may be doubted, whether from all his successors more maxims of theoretical knowledge, or more rules of practical prudence, can be collected, than he alone has given to his country.

Nor was his attention confined to the actions of men; he was an exact surveyor of the inanimate world; his descriptions have always some peculiarities, gathered by contemplating things as they really exist. It may be observed, that the oldest poets of many nations preserve their reputation, and that the following generations of wit, after a short celebrity, sink into oblivion. The first, whoever they be, must take their sentiments and descriptions immediately from knowledge; the resemblance is therefore just, their descriptions are verified by every eye, and their sentiments acknowledged by every breast. Those whom their fame invites to the same studies, copy partly them, and partly nature, till the books of one age gain such authority, as to stand in the place of nature to another, and imitation, always deviating a little, becomes at last capricious and casual. *Shakespeare,* whether life or nature be his subject, shews plainly, that he has seen with his own eyes; he gives the image which he receives, not weakened or distorted by the intervention of any other mind; the ignorant feel his representations to be just, and the learned see that they are compleat.

Perhaps it would not be easy to find any authour, except *Homer,* who invented so much as *Shakespeare,* who so much advanced the studies which he cultivated, or effused so much novelty upon his age or country. The form, the characters, the language, and the shows of the *English* drama are his. *He seems,* says *Dennis, to have been the very original of our* English *tragical harmony, that is, the harmony of blank verse, diversified often by dissyllable and trissyllable terminations. For the diversity distinguishes it from heroick harmony, and by*

*bringing it nearer to common use makes it more proper to
gain attention, and more fit for action and dialogue. Such verse
we make when we are writing prose; we make such verse in
common conversation.*[21]

I know not whether this praise is rigorously just. The dissyllable termination, which the critick rightly appropriates to
the drama, is to be found, though, I think, not in *Gorboduc*
which is confessedly before our authour; yet in *Hieronnymo*,[22]
of which the date is not certain, but which there is reason to
believe at least as old as his earliest plays. This however is certain, that he is the first who taught either tragedy or comedy
to please, there being no theatrical piece of any older writer,
of which the name is known, except to antiquaries and col-
lectors of books, which are sought because they are scarce, and
would not have been scarce, had they been much esteemed.

To him we must ascribe the praise, unless *Spenser* may divide it with him, of having first discovered to how much
smoothness and harmony the *English* language could be softened. He has speeches, perhaps sometimes scenes, which have
all the delicacy of *Rowe*,[23] without his effeminacy. He endeavours indeed commonly to strike by the force and vigour of his
dialogue, but he never executes his purpose better, than when
he tries to sooth by softness.

Yet it must be at last confessed, that as we owe every thing
to him, he owes something to us; that, if much of his praise is
paid by perception and judgement, much is likewise given by
custom and veneration. We fix our eyes upon his graces, and
turn them from his deformities, and endure in him what we
should in another loath or despise. If we endured without
praising, respect for the father of our drama might excuse us;
but I have seen, in the book of some modern critick, a collection of anomalies which shew that he has corrupted language

21 *An Essay on the Genius and Writings of Shakespear*, 1712.

22 Either the play of that title, printed in 1605, or Thomas Kyd's *The
Spanish Tragedy*, printed in 1594.

23 Eighteenth-century playwright, author of *The Fair Penitent* and *Jane
Shore*, tragedies of sentiment that adapt Elizabethan subjects and plots to
eighteenth-century taste.

by every mode of depravation, but which his admirer has accumulated as a monument of honour.

He has scenes of undoubted and perpetual excellence, but perhaps not one play, which, if it were now exhibited as the work of a contemporary writer, would be heard to the conclusion. I am indeed far from thinking, that his works were wrought to his own ideas of perfection; when they were such as would satisfy the audience, they satisfied the writer. It is seldom that authours, though more studious of fame than *Shakespeare*, rise much above the standard of their own age; to add a little of what is best will always be sufficient for present praise, and those who find themselves exalted into fame, are willing to credit their encomiasts, and to spare the labour of contending with themselves.

It does not appear, that *Shakespeare* thought his works worthy of posterity, that he levied any ideal tribute upon future times, or had any further prospect, than of present popularity and present profit. When his plays had been acted, his hope was at an end; he solicited no addition of honour from the reader. He therefore made no scruple to repeat the same jests in many dialogues, or to entangle different plots by the same knot of perplexity, which may be at least forgiven him, by those who recollect, that of *Congreve's* four comedies, two are concluded by a marriage in a mask, by a deception, which perhaps never happened, and which, whether likely or not, he did not invent.

So careless was this great poet of future fame, that, though he retired to ease and plenty, while he was yet little *declined into the vale of years*,[24] before he could be disgusted with fatigue, or disabled by infirmity, he made no collection of his works, nor desired to rescue those that had been already published from the depravations that obscured them, or secure to the rest a better destiny, by giving them to the world in their genuine state.

* * * * *

24 *Othello*, Act III, Sc. iii, l. 265.

David Hume

DAVID HUME *(1711-1776) was not only a great inno-*
vative philosopher but also a distinguished historian.
All his works are marked by his great lucidity and the
clear play of enlightened intellect on the basic prob-
lems of human knowing. His mind and style are of
the same substance, skeptical, incisive, broad. Born
in Edinburgh, Scotland, Hume was largely self-edu-
cated. He lived for a long period at the Jesuit college
at La Flèche, France, and traveled widely on the Con-
tinent. Principal works: Treatise of Human Nature
(1739-40); Enquiry Concerning Human Understanding *(1748);* Political Discourses *(1752);* History of
Great Britain *(1754-61);* Autobiography *(1777).*

OF MIRACLES [1]

PART I

There is, in Dr. Tillotson's writings,[2] an argument against
the *real presence*,[3] which is as concise, and elegant, and strong
as any argument can possibly be supposed against a doctrine,
so little worthy of a serious refutation. It is acknowledged on
all hands, says that learned prelate, that the authority, either
of the scripture or of tradition, is founded merely in the testimony of the apostles, who were eye-witnesses to those mira-

1 Section X of *An Enquiry Concerning Human Understanding* (1748).
2 John Tillotson (1630-1694), English theologian.
3 Tillotson argued against the idea that the body and blood of Christ
become present in substance with the bread and wine of the Holy Eucha-
rist. In so arguing, he was expressing the attitude taken by numerous
Christians that the bread and wine are symbolic of the presence of Christ.

cles of our Saviour, by which he proved his divine mission. Our evidence, then, for the truth of the *Christian* religion is less than the evidence for the truth of our senses; because, even in the first authors of our religion, it was no greater; and it is evident it must diminish in passing from them to their disciples; nor can any one rest such confidence in their testimony, as in the immediate object of his senses. But a weaker evidence can never destroy a stronger; and therefore, were the doctrine of the real presence ever so clearly revealed in scripture, it were directly contrary to the rules of just reasoning to give our assent to it. It contradicts sense, though both the scripture and tradition, on which it is supposed to be built, carry not such evidence with them as sense; when they are considered merely as external evidences, and are not brought home to every one's breast, by the immediate operation of the Holy Spirit.

Nothing is so convenient as a decisive argument of this kind, which must at least *silence* the most arrogant bigotry and superstition, and free us from their impertinent solicitations. I flatter myself, that I have discovered an argument of a like nature, which, if just, will, with the wise and learned, be an everlasting check to all kinds of superstitious delusion, and consequently, will be useful as long as the world endures. For so long, I presume, will the accounts of miracles and prodigies be found in all history, sacred and profane.

Though experience be our only guide in reasoning concerning matters of fact; it must be acknowledged, that this guide is not altogether infallible, but in some cases is apt to lead us into errors. One, who in our climate, should expect better weather in any week of June than in one of December, would reason justly, and conformably to experience; but it is certain, that he may happen, in the event, to find himself mistaken. However, we may observe, that, in such a case, he would have no cause to complain of experience; because it commonly informs us beforehand of the uncertainty, by that contrariety of events, which we may learn from a diligent observation. All effects follow not with like certainty from their supposed causes. Some events are found, in all countries and all ages, to have been constantly conjoined together: Others are found to have been more variable, and sometimes to disappoint our expectations; so that, in our reasonings concerning matter of fact, there are all imaginable degrees of assurance, from the highest certainty to the lowest species of moral evidence.

A wise man, therefore, proportions his belief to the evidence. In such conclusions as are founded on an infallible experience, he expects the event with the last degree of assurance, and regards his past experience as a full *proof* of the future existence of that event. In other cases, he proceeds with more caution: He weighs the opposite experiments: He considers which side is supported by the greater number of experiments: to that side he inclines, with doubt and hesitation; and when at last he fixed his judgement, the evidence exceeds not what we properly call *probability*. All probability, then, supposes an opposition of experiments and observations, where the one side is found to overbalance the other, and to produce a degree of evidence, proportioned to the superiority. A hundred instances or experiments on one side, and fifty on another, afford a doubtful expectation of any event; though a hundred uniform experiments, with only one that is contradictory, reasonably begets a pretty strong degree of assurance. In all cases, we must balance the opposite experiments, where they are opposite, and deduct the smaller number from the greater, in order to know the exact force of the superior evidence.

To apply these principles to a particular instance; we may observe, that there is no species of reasoning more common, more useful, and even necessary to human life, than that which is derived from the testimony of men, and the reports of eye-witnesses and spectators. This species of reasoning, perhaps, one may deny to be founded on the relation of cause and effect. I shall not dispute about a word. It will be sufficient to observe that our assurance in any argument of this kind is derived from no other principle than our observation of the veracity of human testimony, and of the usual conformity of facts to the reports of witnesses. It being a general maxim, that no objects have any discoverable connexion together, and that all the inferences, which we can draw from one to another, are founded merely on our experience of their constant and regular conjunction; it is evident, that we ought not to make an exception to this maxim in favour of human testimony, whose connexion with any event seems, in itself, as little necessary as any other. Were not the memory tenacious to a certain degree; had not men commonly an inclination to truth and a principle of probity, were they not sensible to shame, when detected in a falsehood: Were not these, I say, discovered by *experience* to be qualities, inherent in human nature, we should never repose the least confidence in human testimony. A man delirious, or noted for falsehood and villany, has no manner of authority with us.

And as the evidence, derived from witnesses and human testimony, is founded on past experience, so it varies with the experience, and is regarded either as *proof* or a *probability*, according as the conjunction between any particular kind of report and any kind of object has been found to be constant or variable. There are a number of circumstances to be taken into consideration in all judgements of this kind; and the ultimate standard, by which we determine all disputes, that may arise concerning them, is always derived from experience and observation. Where this experience is not entirely uniform on any side, it is attended with an unavoidable contrariety in our judgements, and with the same opposition and mutual destruction of argument as in every other kind of evidence. We frequently hesitate concerning the reports of others. We balance the opposite circumstances, which cause any doubt or uncertainty; and when we discover a superiority on one side, we incline to it; but still with a diminution of assurance, in proportion to the force of its antagonist.

This contrariety of evidence, in the present case, may be derived from several different causes; from the opposition of contrary testimony; from the character or number of the witnesses; from the manner of their delivering their testimony; or from the union of all these circumstances. We entertain a suspicion concerning any matter of fact, when the witnesses contradict each other; when they are but few, or of a doubtful character; when they have an interest in what they affirm; when they deliver their testimony with hesitation, or, on the contrary, with too violent asseverations. There are many other particulars of the same kind, which may diminish or destroy the force of any argument, derived from human testimony.

Suppose, for instance, that the fact, which the testimony endeavours to establish, partakes of the extraordinary and the marvellous; in that case, the evidence, resulting from the testimony, admits of a diminution, greater or less, in proportion as the fact is more or less unusual. The reason why we place any credit in witnesses and historians, is not derived from any *connexion*, which we perceive *a priori*, between testimony and reality, but because we are accustomed to find a conformity between them. But when the fact attested is such a one as has seldom fallen under our observation, here is a contest of two opposite experiences; of which the one destroys the other, as far as its force goes, and the superior can only operate on the mind by the force which remains. The very same principle of experience, which gives us a certain degree of assurance in the testimony of witnesses, gives us also, in this case, another degree of assurance against the fact, which they endeavour to establish; from which contradiction there necessarily arises a counterpoize, and mutual destruction of belief and authority.

I should not believe such a story were it told me by Cato, was a proverbial saying in Rome, even during the lifetime of that philosophical patriot.[4] The incredibility of a fact, it was allowed, might invalidate so great an authority.

The Indian prince, who refused to believe the first relations concerning the effects of frost, reasoned justly; and it naturally required very strong testimony to engage his assent to facts, that arose from a state of nature, with which he was unacquainted, and which bore so little analogy to those events, of which he had had constant and uniform experience.

4 Hume's note: Plutarch in the *Life of Cato*.

Though they were not contrary to his experience, they were not conformable to it.[5]

But in order to encrease the probability against the testimony of witnesses, let us suppose, that the fact, which they affirm, instead of being only marvelous, is really miraculous; and suppose also, that the testimony considered apart and in itself, amounts to an entire proof; in that case, there is proof against proof, of which the strongest must prevail, but still with a diminution of its force, in proportion to that of its antagonist.

A miracle is a violation of the laws of nature; and as a firm and unalterable experience has established these laws, the proof against a miracle, from the very nature of the fact, is as entire as any argument from experience can possibly be imagined. Why is it more than probable, that all men must die; that lead cannot, of itself, remain suspended in the air; that fire consumes wood, and is extinguished by water; unless it be, that these events are found agreeable to the laws of nature, and there is required a violation of these laws, or in other words, a miracle to prevent them? Nothing is esteemed a miracle, if it ever happen in the common course of nature. It is no miracle that a man, seemingly in good health, should

5 Hume's note: No Indian, it is evident, could have experience that water did not freeze in cold climates. This is placing nature in a situation quite unknown to him; and it is impossible for him to tell *a priori* what will result from it. It is making a new experiment, the consequence of which is always uncertain. One may sometimes conjecture from analogy what will follow; but still this is but conjecture. And it must be confessed, that, in the present case of freezing, the event follows contrary to the rules of analogy, and is such as a rational Indian would not look for. The operations of cold upon water are not gradual, according to the degrees of cold; but whenever it comes to the freezing point, the water passes in a moment, from the utmost liquidity to perfect hardness. Such an event, therefore, may be denominated *extraordinary*, and requires a pretty strong testimony, to render it credible to people in warm climate: But still it is not miraculous, nor contrary to uniform experience of the course of nature in cases where all the circumstances are the same. The inhabitants of Sumatra have always seen water fluid in their own climate, and the freezing of their rivers ought to be deemed a prodigy; But they never saw water in Muscovy during the winter; and therefore they cannot reasonably be positive what would there be the consequence.

die on a sudden: because such a kind of death, though more unusual than any other, has yet been frequently observed to happen. But it is a miracle, that a dead man should come to life; because that has never been observed in any age or country. There must, therefore, be a uniform experience against every miraculous event, otherwise the event would not merit that appellation. And as a uniform experience amounts to a proof, there is here a direct and full *proof*, from the nature of the fact, against the existence of any miracle; nor can such a proof be destroyed, or the miracle rendered credible, but by an opposite proof, which is superior.[6]

The plain consequence is (and it is a general maxim worthy of our attention), "That no testimony is sufficient to establish a miracle, unless the testimony be of such a kind, that its falsehood would be more miraculous, than the fact, which it endeavours to establish; and even in that case there is a mutual destruction of arguments, and the superior only gives us an assurance suitable to that degree of force, which remains, after deducting the inferior.' When anyone tells me, that he saw a dead man restored to life, I immediately consider with myself, whether it be more probable, that this person should

6 Hume's note: Sometimes an event may not, *in itself, seem* to be contrary to the laws of nature, and yet, if it were real, it might, by reason of some circumstances, be denominated a miracle because, *in fact*, it is contrary to these laws. Thus if a person, claiming a divine authority, should command a sick person to be well, a healthful man to fall down dead, the clouds to pour rain, the winds to blow, in short, should order many natural events, which immediately follow upon his command; these might justly be esteemed miracles, because they are really, in this case, contrary to the laws of nature. For if any suspicion remain, that the event and command concurred by accident, there is no miracle and no transgression of the laws of nature. If this suspicion be removed, there is evidently a miracle, and a transgression of these laws; because nothing can be more contrary to nature than that the voice or command of a man should have such an influence. A miracle may be accurately defined, *a transgression of a law of nature by a particular volition of the Deity, or by the interposition of some invisible agent.* A miracle may be either discoverable by men or not. This alters not its nature and essence. The raising of a house or ship into the air is a visible miracle. The raising of a feather, when the wind wants ever so little of a force requisite for that purpose, is as real a miracle, though not so sensible with regard to us.

either deceive or be deceived, or that the fact, which he relates, should really have happened. I weigh the one miracle against the other; and according to the superiority, which I discover, I pronounce my decision, and always reject the greater miracle. If the falsehood of his testimony would be more miraculous, than the event which he relates; then, and not till then, can he pretend to command my belief or opinion.

PART II

In the foregoing reasoning we have supposed, that the testimony, upon which a miracle is founded, may possibly amount to an entire proof, and that the falsehood of that testimony would be a real prodigy: But it is easy to shew, that we have been a great deal too liberal in our concession, and that there never was a miraculous event established on so full an evidence.

For *first*, there is not to be found, in all history, any miracle attested by a sufficient number of men, of such unquestioned good-sense, education, and learning, as to secure us against all delusion in themselves; of such undoubted integrity, as to place them beyond all suspicion of any design to deceive others; of such credit and reputation in the eyes of mankind, as to have a great deal to lose in case of their being detected in any falsehood; and at the same time, attesting facts performed in such a public manner and in so celebrated a part of the world, as to render the detection unavoidable: All which circumstances are requisite to give us a full assurance in the testimony of men.

Secondly. We may observe in human nature a principle which, if strictly examined, will be found to diminish extremely the assurance, which we might, from human testimony, have, in any kind of prodigy. The maxim, by which we commonly conduct ourselves in our reasonings, is, that the objects, of which we have no experience, resemble those, of which we have; that what we have found to be most usual is always most probable; and that where there is an opposition of arguments, we ought to give the preference to such as are founded on the greatest number of past observations. But though, in proceeding by this rule, we readily reject any fact which is unusual and incredible in an ordinary degree; yet in advancing further, the mind observes not always the same rule; but when anything is affirmed utterly absurd and miraculous, it rather the more readily admits of such a fact, upon account of that very circumstance, which ought to destroy all its authority. The passion of *surprise* and *wonder*, arising from miracles, being an agreeable emotion, gives a sensible tendency towards the belief of those events, from which it is derived. And this goes so far, that even those who cannot enjoy this pleasure immediately, nor can believe those miraculous events, of which they are informed, yet love to partake of the satisfaction at second-hand or by rebound, and place a pride and delight in exciting the admiration of others.

With what greediness are the miraculous accounts of travellers received, their descriptions of sea and land monsters, their relations of wonderful adventures, strange men, and uncouth manners? But if the spirit of religion join itself to the love of wonder, there is an end of common sense; and human testimony, in these circumstances, loses all pretensions to authority. A religionist may be an enthusiast, and imagine he sees what has no reality: he may know his narrative to be false, and yet persevere in it, with the best intentions in the world, for the sake of promoting so holy a cause: or even where this delusion has not place, vanity, excited by so strong a temptation, operates on him more powerfully than on the rest of mankind in any other circumstances; and self-interest with equal force. His auditors may not have, and commonly have not, sufficient judgement to canvass his evidence: what judgement they have, they renounce by principle, in these sublime and mysterious subjects: or if they were ever so willing to employ it, passion and a heated imagination disturb the regularity of its operations. Their credulity increases his impudence: and his impudence overpowers their credulity.

Eloquence, when at its highest pitch, leaves little room

for reason or reflection; but addressing itself entirely to the fancy or the affections, captivates the willing hearers, and subdues their understanding. Happily, this pitch seldom attains. But what a Tully or a Demosthenes [7] could scarcely effect over a Roman or Athenian audience, every *Capuchin,* every itinerant or stationary teacher can perform over the generality of mankind, and in a higher degree, by touching such gross and vulgar passions.

The many instances of forged miracles, and prophecies, and supernatural events, which, in all ages, have either been detected by contrary evidence, or which detect themselves by their absurdity, prove sufficiently the strong propensity of mankind to the extraordinary and the marvellous, and ought reasonably to beget a suspicion against all relations of this kind. This is our natural way of thinking, even with regard to the most common and most credible events. For instance: There is no kind of report which rises so easily, and spreads so quickly, especially in country places and provincial towns, as those concerning marriages; insomuch that two young persons of equal condition never see each other twice, but the whole neighbourhood immediately join them together. The pleasure of telling a piece of news so interesting, of propagating it, and of being the first reporters of it, spreads the intelligence. And this is so well known, that no man of sense gives attention to these reports, till he find them confirmed by some greater evidence. Do not the same passions, and others still stronger, incline the generality of mankind to believe and report, with the greatest vehemence and assurance, all religious miracles?

Thirdly. It forms a strong presumption against all supernatural and miraculous relations, that they are observed chiefly to abound among ignorant and barbarous nations; or if a civilized people has ever given admission to any of them, that people will be found to have received them from

[7] In this sentence, Hume argues that the great classical orators appealed to reason, whereas the religious enthusiast works on "gross and vulgar passions."

ignorant and barbarous ancestors, who transmitted them with that inviolable sanction and authority, which always attend received opinions. When we peruse the first histories of all nations, we are apt to imagine ourselves transported into some new world; where the whole frame of nature is disjointed, and every element performs its operations in a different manner, from what it does at present. Battles, revolutions, pestilence, famine and death, are never the effect of those natural causes, which we experience. Prodigies, omens, oracles, judgements, quite obscure the few natural events, that are intermingled with them. But as the former grow thinner every page, in proportion as we advance nearer the enlightened ages, we soon learn, that there is nothing mysterious or supernatural in the case, but that all proceeds from the usual propensity of mankind towards the marvellous, and that, though this inclination may at intervals receive a check from sense and learning, it can never be thoroughly extirpated from human nature.

It is strange, a judicious reader is apt to say, upon the perusal of these wonderful historians, *that such prodigious events never happen in our days.* But it is nothing strange, I hope, that men should lie in all ages. You must surely have seen instances enough of that frailty. You have yourself heard many such marvellous relations started, which, being treated with scorn by all the wise and judicious, have at last been abandoned even by the vulgar. Be assured, that those renowned lies, which have spread and flourished to such a monstrous height, arose from like beginnings; but being sown in a more proper soil, shot up at last into prodigies almost equal to those which they relate.

It was a wise policy in that false prophet, Alexander,[8] who though now forgotten, was once so famous, to lay the first scene of his impostures in Paphlagonia, where as Lucian

8 Alexander of Abonuteichos, who claimed to have a new manifestation of Asclepius in the form of a serpent. He gave oracles and conducted mysteries, gaining a large following in the Rome of Marcus Aurelius.

tells us, the people were extremely ignorant and stupid, and ready to swallow even the grossest delusion. People at a distance, who are weak enough to think the matter at all worth enquiry, have no opportunity of receiving better information. The stories come magnified to them by a hundred circumstances. Fools are industrious in propagating the imposture; while the wise and learned are contented, in general, to deride its absurdity, without informing themselves of the particular facts, by which it may be distinctly refuted. And thus the impostor above mentioned was enabled to proceed, from his ignorant Paphlagonians, to the enlisting of votaries, even among the Grecian philosophers, and men of the most eminent rank and distinction in Rome: nay, could engage the attention of that sage emperor Marcus Aurelius; so far as to make him trust the success of a military expedition to his delusive prophecies.

The advantages are so great, of starting an imposture among an ignorant people, that, even though the delusion should be too gross to impose on the generality of them *(which, though seldom, is sometimes the case)* it has a much better chance for succeeding in remote countries, than if the first scene had been laid in a city renowned for arts and knowledge. The most ignorant and barbarous of these barbarians carry the report abroad. None of their countrymen have a large correspondence, or sufficient credit and authority to contradict and beat down the delusion. Men's inclination to the marvellous has full opportunity to display itself. And thus a story, which is universally exploded in the place where it was first started, shall pass for certain at a thousand miles distance. But had Alexander fixed his residence at Athens, the philosophers of that renowned mart of learning had immediately spread, throughout the whole Roman empire, their sense of the matter; which, being supported by so great authority, and displayed by all the force of reason and eloquence, had entirely opened the eyes of mankind. It is true; Lucian, passing by chance through Paphlagonia, had an opportunity of performing this good office. But, though much to be wished, it does not always happen, that every Alexander meets with Lucian, ready to expose and detect his impostures.

I may add as a *fourth* reason, which diminishes the authority of prodigies, that there is no testimony for any, even those which have not been expressly detected, that is not opposed by an infinite number of witnesses; so that not only the miracle destroys the credit of testimony, but the testimony destroys itself. To make this the better understood, let us consider, that, in matters of religion, whatever is different is contrary; and that it is impossible the religions of ancient Rome, of Turkey, of Siam, and of China should, all of them, be established on any solid foundation. Every miracle, therefore, pretended to have been wrought in any of these religions (and all of them abound in miracles), as its direct scope is to establish the particular system to which it is attributed; so has it the same force, though more indirectly, to overthrow every other system. In destroying a rival system, it likewise destroys the credit of those miracles, on which that system was established; so that all the prodigies of different religions are to be regarded as contrary facts, and the evidences of these prodigies, whether weak or strong, as opposite to each other. According to this method of reasoning, when we believe any miracle of Mahomet or his successors, we have for our warrant the testimony of a few barbarous Arabians: And on the other hand, we are to regard the authority of Titus Livius, Plutarch, Tacitus,[9] and, in short, of all the authors and witnesses, Grecian, Chinese, and Roman Catholic, who have related any miracle in their particular religion; I say, we are to regard their testimony in the same light as if they had mentioned that Mahometan miracle, and had in express terms contradicted it, with the same certainty as they have for the miracle they relate. This argument may appear over subtile and refined; but is not in reality different from the reasoning of a judge, who supposes, that the credit of two

---

[9] Titus Livius, Plutarch, and Tacitus were historians of great prestige.

witnesses, maintaining a crime against any one, is destroyed by the testimony of two others, who affirm him to have been two hundred leagues distant, at the same instant when the crime is said to have been committed.

One of the best attested miracles in all profane history, is that which Tacitus reports of Vespasian,[10] who cured a blind man in Alexandria, by means of his spittle, and a lame man by the mere touch of his foot; in obedience to a vision of the god Serapis, who had enjoined them to have recourse to the Emperor, for these miraculous cures. The story may be seen in that fine historian; where every circumstance seems to add weight to the testimony, and might be displayed at large with all the force of argument and eloquence, if any one were now concerned to enforce the evidence of that exploded and idolatrous superstition. The gravity, solidity, age, and probity of so great an emperor, who, through the whole course of his life, conversed in a familiar manner with his friends and courtiers, and never affected those extraordinary airs of divinity assumed by Alexander and Demetrius. The historian, a contemporary writer, noted for candour and veracity, and withal, the greatest and most penetrating genius, perhaps, of all antiquity; and so free from any tendency to credulity, that he even lies under the contrary imputation, of atheism and profaneness: The persons, from whose authority he related the miracle, or established character for judgement and veracity, as we may well presume; eye-witnesses of the fact, and confirming their testimony, after the Flavian family was despoiled of the empire, and could no longer give any reward, as the price of a lie. *Utrumque, qui interfuere, nunc quoque memorant, postquam nullum mendacio pretium.*[11] To which if we add the public nature of the facts, as related, it will appear, that no evidence can well be supposed stronger for so gross and so palpable a falsehood.

---

10 Hume's note: *Historiae*, Book IV, Chapter 8. Suetonius gives nearly the same account in the *Life of Vespasian*.

11 Both facts are attested at this day, when falsehood can bring no reward, by those who were present on the occasion.

There is also a memorable story related by Cardinal de Retz, which may well deserve our consideration. When that intriguing politician fled into Spain, to avoid the persecution of his enemies, he passed through Saragossa, the capital of Arragon, where he was shewn, in the cathedral, a man, who had served seven years as a doorkeeper, and was well known to everybody in town, that had ever paid his devotions at that church. He had been seen, for so long a time, wanting a leg; but recovered that limb by the rubbing of holy oil upon the stump; and the cardinal assures us that he saw him with two legs. This miracle was vouched by all the canons of the church; and the whole company in town were appealed to for a confirmation of the fact: whom the cardinal found, by their zealous devotion, to be thorough believers of the miracle. Here the relater was also contemporary to the supposed prodigy, of an incredulous and libertine character, as well as of great genius; the miracle of so *singular* a nature as could scarcely admit of a counterfeit, and the witnesses very numerous, and all of them, in a manner, spectators of the fact, to which they gave their testimony. And what adds mightily to the force of the evidence, and may double our surprise on this occasion, is, that the cardinal himself, who relates the story, seems not to give any credit to it, and consequently cannot be suspected of any concurrence in the holy fraud. He considered justly, that it was not requisite, in order to reject a fact of this nature, to be able accurately to disprove the testimony, and to trace its falsehood, through all the circumstances of knavery and credulity which produced it. He knew, that, as this was commonly altogether impossible at any small distance of time and place; so was it extremely difficult, even where one was immediately present, by reason of the bigotry, ignorance, cunning, and roguery of a great part of mankind. He therefore concluded, like a just reasoner, that such an evidence carried falsehood upon the very face of it, and that a miracle, supported by any human testimony, was more properly a subject of derision than of argument.

There surely never was a greater number of miracles

ascribed to one person, than those, which were lately said to have been wrought in France upon the tomb of Abbé Paris, the famous Jansenist, with whose sanctity the people were so long deluded. The curing of the sick, giving hearing to the deaf, and sight to the blind, were every where talked of as the usual effects of that holy sepulchre. But what is more extraordinary; many of the miracles were immediately proved upon the spot, before judges of unquestioned integrity, attested by witnesses of credit and distinction, in a learned age, and on the most eminent theatre that is now in the world. Nor is this all: a relation of them was published and dispersed everywhere; nor were the *Jesuits,* though a learned body, supported by the civil magistrate, and determined enemies to those opinions, in whose favour the miracles were said to have been wrought, ever able distinctly to refute or detect them. Where shall we find such a number of circumstances, agreeing to the corroboration of one fact? And what have we to oppose to such a cloud of witnesses, but the absolute impossibility or miraculous nature of the events, which they relate? And this surely, in the eyes of all reasonable people, will alone be regarded as a sufficient refutation.

Is the consequence just, because some human testimony has the utmost force and authority in some cases, when it relates the battle of Philippi or Pharsalia for instance; that therefore all kinds of testimony must, in all cases, have equal force and authority? Suppose that the Caesarean and Pompeian factions had, each of them, claimed the victory in these battles, and that the historians of each party had uniformly ascribed the advantage to their own side; how could mankind at this distance, have been able to determine between them? The contrariety is equally strong between the miracles related by Herodotus or Plutarch, and those delivered by Mariana, Bede, or any monkish historian.

The wise lend a very academic faith to every report which favours the passion of the reporter; whether it magnifies his country, his family, or himself, or in any other way strikes in with his natural inclinations and propensities. But what greater temptation than to appear a missionary, a prophet, an ambassador from heaven? Who would not encounter many dangers and difficulties, in order to attain so sublime a character? Or if, by the help of vanity and a heated imagination, a man has first made a convert of himself, and entered seriously into the delusion; who ever scruples to make use of pious frauds, in support of so holy and meritorious a cause?

The smallest spark may here kindle into the greatest flame; because the materials are always prepared for it. The *avidum genus auricularum*,[12] the gazing populace, receive greedily, without examination, whatever soothes superstition, and promotes wonder.

How many stories of this nature have, in all ages, been detected and exploded in their infancy? How many more have been celebrated for a time, and have afterwards sunk into neglect and oblivion? Where such reports, therefore, fly about, the solution of the phenomenon is obvious; and we judge in conformity to regular experience and observation, when we account for it by the known and natural principles of credulity and delusion. And shall we, rather than have a recourse to so natural a solution, allow a miraculous violation of the most established laws of nature?

I need not mention the difficulty of detecting a falsehood in any private or even public history, at the place, where it is said to happen; much more when the scene is removed to ever so small a distance. Even a court of judicature, with all the authority, accuracy, and judgement, which they can employ, find themselves often at a loss to distinguish between truth and falsehood in the most recent actions. But the matter never comes to any issue, if trusted to the common method of altercations and debate and flying rumours; especially when men's passions have taken part on either side.

In the infancy of new religions, the wise and learned commonly esteem the matter too inconsiderable to deserve their

12 The human race has itching ears. *Lucretius* IV, 594.

attention or regard. And when afterwards they would willingly detect the cheat, in order to undeceive the deluded
multitude, the season is now past, and the records and witnesses, which might clear up the matter, have perished beyond recovery.

No means of detection remain, but those which must be
drawn from the very testimony itself of the reporters: and
these, though always sufficient with the judicious and knowing, are commonly too fine to fall under the comprehension
of the vulgar.

Upon the whole, then, it appears, that no testimony for
any kind of miracle has ever amounted to a probability,
much less to a proof; and that, even supposing it amounted
to a proof, it would be opposed by another proof; derived
from the very nature of the fact, which it would endeavour to
establish. It is experience only, which gives authority to human testimony; and it is the same experience, which assures
us of the laws of nature. When, therefore, these two kinds
of experience are contrary, we have nothing to do but substract the one from the other, and embrace an opinion, either
on one side or the other, with that assurance which arises
from the remainder. But according to the principle here
explained, this substraction, with regard to all popular religions, amounts to an entire annihilation; and therefore we
may establish it as a maxim, that no human testimony can
have such force as to prove a miracle, and make it a just
foundation for any such system of religion.

I beg the limitations here made may be remarked, when
I say, that a miracle can never be proved, so as to be the
foundation of a system of religion. For I own, that otherwise,
there may possibly be miracles, or violations of the usual
course of nature, of such a kind as to admit of proof from
human testimony, though, perhaps, it will be impossible to
find any such in all the records of history. Thus, suppose, all
authors, in all languages, agree, that, from the first of January 1600, there was a total darkness over the whole earth
for eight days: suppose that the tradition of this extraordi-

nary event is still strong and lively among the people: that all travellers, who return from foreign countries, bring us accounts of the same tradition, without the least variation or contradition: it is evident, that our present philosophers, instead of doubting the fact, ought to receive it as certain, and ought to search for the causes whence it might be derived. The decay, corruption, and dissolution of nature, is an event rendered probable by so many analogies, that any phenomenon, which seems to have a tendency towards that catastrophe, comes within the reach of human testimony, if that testimony be very extensive and uniform.

But suppose, that all the historians who treat of England, should agree, that, on the first of January 1600, Queen Elizabeth died; that both before and after her death she was seen by her physicians and the whole court, as is usual with persons of her rank; that her successor was acknowledged and proclaimed by the parliament; and that, after being interred a month, she again appeared, resumed the throne, and governed England for three years: I must confess that I should be surprised at the concurrence of so many odd circumstances, but should not have the least inclination to believe so miraculous an event. I should not doubt of her pretended death, and of those other public circumstances that followed it: I should only assert it to have been pretended, and it neither was, nor possibly could be real. You would in vain object to me the difficulty, and almost impossibility of deceiving the world in an affair of such consequence; the wisdom and solid judgement of that renowned queen; with the little or no advantage which she could reap from so poor an artifice: All this might astonish me; but I would still reply, that the knavery and folly of men are such common phenomena, that I should rather believe the most extraordinary events to arise from their concurrence, than admit of so signal a violation of the laws of nature.

But should this miracle be ascribed to any new system of religion; men, in all ages, have been so much imposed on by ridiculous stories of that kind, that this very circumstance would be a full proof of a cheat, and sufficient, with all men of sense, not only to make them reject the fact, but even reject it without further examination. Though the Being to whom the miracle is ascribed, be, in this case, Almighty, it does not, upon that account, become a whit more probable; since it is impossible for us to know the attributes or actions of such a Being, otherwise than from the experience which we have of his productions, in the usual course of nature. This still reduces us to past observation, and obliges us to compare the instances of the violation of truth in the testimony of men, with those of the violation of the laws of nature by miracles, in order to judge which of them is most likely and probable. As the violations of truth are more common in the testimony concerning religious miracles, than in that concerning any other matter of fact; this must diminish very much the authority of the former testimony, and make us form a general resolution, never to lend any attention to it, with whatever specious pretence it may be covered.

Lord Bacon seems to have embraced the same principles of reasoning. 'We ought,' says he, 'to make a collection or particular history of all monsters and prodigious births or productions, and in a word of every thing new, rare, and extraordinary in nature. But this must be done with the most severe scrutiny, lest we depart from truth. Above all, every relation must be considered as suspicious, which depends in any degree upon religion, as the prodigies of Livy: And no less so, every thing that is to be found in the writers of natural magic or alchimy, or such authors, who seem, all of them, to have an unconquerable appetite for falsehood and fable.' [13]

I am the better pleased with the method of reasoning here delivered, as I think it may serve to confound those dangerous friends or disguised enemies to the *Christian Religion,* who have undertaken to defend it by the principles of human reason. Our most holy religion is founded on *Faith,* not on reason; and it is a sure method of exposing it to put

[13] *Novum Organum,* Book II, Aphorism 29.

it to such a trial as it is, by no means, fitted to endure. To make this more evident, let us examine those miracles, related in scripture; and not to lose ourselves in too wide a field, let us confine ourselves to such as we find in the *Pentateuch*, which we shall examine, according to the principles of these pretended Christians, not as the word or testimony of God himself, but as the production of a mere human writer and historian. Here then we are first to consider a book, presented to us by a barbarous and ignorant people, written in an age when they were still more barbarous, and in all probability long after the facts which it relates, corroborated by no concurring testimony, and resembling those fabulous accounts, which every nation gives of its origin. Upon reading this book, we find it full of prodigies and miracles. It gives an account of a state of the world and of human nature entirely different from the present: Of our fall from that state: Of the age of man, extended to near a thousand years: Of the destruction of the world by a deluge: Of the arbitrary choice of one people, as the favourites of heaven; and that people the countrymen of the author: Of their deliverance from bondage by prodigies the most astonishing imaginable: I desire any one to lay his hand upon his heart, and after a serious consideration declare, whether he thinks that the falsehood of such a book, supported by such a testimony, would be more extraordinary and miraculous than all the miracles it relates; which is, however, necessary to make it be received, according to the measures of probability above established.

What we have said of miracles may be applied, without any variation, to prophecies; and indeed, all prophecies are real miracles, and as such only, can be admitted as proofs of any revelation. If it did not exceed the capacity of human nature to foretell future events, it would be absurd to employ any prophecy as an argument for a divine mission or authority from heaven. So that, upon the whole, we may conclude, that the *Christian Religion* not only was at first attended with miracles, but even at this day cannot be believed by any reasonable person without one. Mere reason is insufficient to convince us of its veracity: And whoever is moved by *Faith* to assent to it, is conscious of a continued miracle in his own person, which subverts all the principles of his understanding, and gives him a determination to believe what is most contrary to custom and experience.

Thomas Jefferson

THOMAS JEFFERSON *(1743-1826), third President of the United States, practiced law from 1767 to 1774, but from 1769 on devoted his energies to political activity. He was chosen to write "The Declaration of Independence" because of the felicity of his style. Despite the rewriting of the document by Congress, Jefferson thought the* Declaration *his highest accomplishment. In his own epitaph, he gave it a position of great prominence: "Here was buried Thomas Jefferson, Author of the Declaration of American Independence, of the Statute of Virginia for Religious Freedom, and Father of the University of Virginia." Jefferson was educated at William and Mary College. Principal works:* Autobiography *(1829);* Notes on Virginia *(1784); various public papers.*

Two Versions of
THE DECLARATION
OF INDEPENDENCE [1]

* * * * *

It appearing in the course of these debates, [2] that the colonies of New York, New Jersey, Pennsylvania, Delaware, Maryland, and South Carolina were not yet matured for falling from the parent stem, but that they were fast ad-

[1] Taken from *The Autobiography of Thomas Jefferson* (1829).
[2] Jefferson has just been describing the arguments made for and against the immediate issuing of a Declaration of Independence.

vancing to that state, it was thought most prudent to wait
a while for them, and to postpone the final decision to July
1st; but, that this might occasion as little delay as possible, a
committee was appointed to prepare a Declaration of Independence. The committee were John Adams, Dr. Franklin,
Roger Sherman, Robert R. Livingston, and myself. Committees were also appointed, at the same time, to prepare a plan
of confederation for the colonies, and to state the terms
proper to be proposed for foreign alliance. The committee for
drawing the Declaration of Independence, desired me to do
it. It was accordingly done, and being approved by them,
I reported it to the House on Friday, the 28th of June, when
it was read, and ordered to lie on the table. On Monday, the
1st of July, the House resolved itself into a committee of the
whole, and resumed the consideration of the original motion
made by the delegates of Virginia, which, being again debated
through the day, was carried in the affirmative by the votes of
New Hampshire, Connecticut, Massachusetts, Rhode Island,
New Jersey, Maryland, Virginia, North Carolina and Georgia.
South Carolina and Pennsylvania voted against it. Delaware
had but two members present, and they were divided. The
delegates from New York declared they were for it themselves,
and were assured their constituents were for it; but that their
instructions having been drawn near a twelvemonth before,
when reconciliation was still the general object, they were enjoined by them to do nothing which should impede that object. They, therefore, thought themselves not justifiable in
voting on either side, and asked leave to withdraw from the
question; which was given them. The committee rose and reported their resolution to the House. Mr. Edward Rutledge,
of South Carolina, then requested the determination might be
put off to the next day, as he believed his colleagues, though
they disapproved of the resolution, would then join in it
for the sake of unanimity. The ultimate question, whether
the House would agree to the resolution of the committee,
was accordingly postponed to the next day, when it was again
moved, and South Carolina concurred in voting for it. In the

mean time, a third member had come post from the Delaware counties, and turned the vote of that colony in favor of the resolution. Members of a different sentiment attending that morning from Pennsylvania also, her vote was changed, so that the whole twelve colonies who were authorized to vote at all, give their voices for it; and, within a few days, the convention of New York approved of it, and thus supplied the void occasioned by the withdrawing of her delegates from the vote.

Congress proceeded the same day to consider the Declaration of Independence, which had been reported and lain on the table the Friday preceding, and on Monday referred to a committee of the whole. The pusillanimous idea that we had friends in England worth keeping terms with, still haunted the minds of many. For this reason, those passages which conveyed censures on the people of England were struck out, lest they should give them offence. The clause too, reprobating the enslaving the inhabitants of Africa, was struck out in complaisance to South Carolina and Georgia, who had never attemped to restrain the importation of slaves, and who, on the contrary, still wished to continue it. Our northern brethren also, I believe, felt a little tender under those censures; for though their people had very few slaves themselves, yet they had been pretty considerable carriers of them to others. The debates, having taken up the greater parts of the 2d, 3d, and 4th days of July, were, on the evening of the last, closed; the Declaration was reported by the committee, agreed to by the House, and signed by every member present, except Mr. Dickinson. As the sentiments of men are known not only by what they receive, but what they reject also, I will state the form of the Declaration as originally reported. The parts struck out by Congress shall be distinguished by a black line drawn under them; and those inserted by them shall be placed in the margin, or in a concurrent column.[3]

3 In this edition, those parts of the *Declaration* which remained unchanged from the original version are printed in roman; those cut out by Congress, in italics; those later substituted, in small capitals.

A DECLARATION BY THE REPRESENTA-
TIVES OF THE UNITED STATES OF AMER-
ICA, IN *GENERAL* CONGRESS ASSEMBLED

When, in the course of human events, it becomes necessary for one people to dissolve the political bands which have
connected them with another, and to assume among the
powers of the earth the separate and equal station to which
the laws of nature and of nature's God entitle them, a decent
respect to the opinions of mankind requires that they should
declare the causes which impel them to the separation.

We hold these truths to be self evident: that all men are
created equal; that they are endowed by their Creator with
CERTAIN [*inherent and*] inalienable rights; that among these
are life, liberty, and the pursuit of happiness; that to secure
these rights, governments are instituted among men, deriving
their just powers from the consent of the governed; that
whenever any form of government becomes destructive of
these ends, it is the right of the people to alter or to abolish
it, and to institute new government, laying its foundation on
such principles, and organizing its powers in such form, as
to them shall seem most likely to effect their safety and happiness. Prudence, indeed, will dictate that governments long
established should not be changed for light and transient
causes; and accordingly all experience hath shown that mankind are more disposed to suffer while evils are sufferable,
than to right themselves by abolishing the forms to which
they are accustomed. But when a long train of abuses and
usurpations, [*begun at a distinguished period and*] pursuing
invariably the same object, evinces a design to reduce them
under absolute despotism, it is their right, it is their duty to
throw off such government, and to provide new guards for
their future security. Such has been the patient sufferance of
these colonies; and such is now the necessity which constrains
them to ALTER [*expunge*] their former systems of government. The history of the present king of Great Britain is a
history of REPEATED [*unremitting*] injuries and usurpations,

ALL HAVING [*among which appears no solitary fact to contradict the uniform tenor of the rest, but all have*] in direct object the establishment of an absolute tyranny over these states.
To prove this, let facts be submitted to a candid world [*for
the truth of which we pledge a faith yet unsullied by falsehood.*]

He has refused his assent to laws the most wholesome and
necessary for the public good.

He has forbidden his governors to pass laws of immediate
and pressing importance, unless suspended in their operation
till his assent should be obtained; and, when so suspended,
he has utterly neglected to attend to them.

He has refused to pass other laws for the accommodation
of large districts of people, unless those people would re-
linquish the right of representation in the legislature, a right
inestimable to them, and formidable to tyrants only.

He has called together legislative bodies at places unusual,
uncomfortable, and distant from the depository of their public
records, for the sole purpose of fatiguing them into compliance with his measures.

He has dissolved representative houses repeatedly [*and
continually*] for opposing with manly firmness his invasions
on the rights of the people.

He has refused for a long time after such dissolutions to
cause others to be elected, whereby the legislative powers, incapable of annihilation, have returned to the people at large
for their exercise, the state remaining, in the meantime, exposed to all the dangers of invasion from without and con-
vulsions within.

He has endeavored to prevent the population of these
states, for that purpose obstructing the laws for naturaliza-
tion of foreigners, refusing to pass others to encourage their
migrations hither, and raising the conditions of new appropri-
ations of lands.

He has OBSTRUCTED [*suffered*] the administration of justice
BY [*totally to cease in some of these states*] refusing his assent
to laws for establishing judiciary powers.

He has made [*our*] judges dependent on his will alone for the tenure of their offices, and the amount and payment of their salaries.

He has erected a multitude of new offices, [*by a self-assumed power*] and sent hither swarms of new officers to harass our people and eat out their substance.

He has kept among us in times of peace standing armies [*and ships of war*] without the consent of our legislatures.

He has affected to render the military independent of, and superior to, the civil power.

He has combined with others to subject us to a jurisdiction foreign to our constitutions and unacknowledged by our laws, giving his assent to their acts of pretended legislation for quartering large bodies of armed troops among us; for protecting them by a mock trial from punishment for any murders which they should commit on the inhabitants of these states; for cutting off our trade with all parts of the world; for imposing taxes on us without our consent; for depriving US IN MANY CASES of the benefits of trial by jury; for transporting us beyond seas to be tried for pretended offences; for abolishing the free system of English laws in a neighboring province, establishing therein an arbitrary government, and enlarging its boundaries, so as to render it at once an example and fit instrument for introducing the same absolute rule into these COLONIES [*states*]; for taking away our charters, abolishing our most valuable laws, and altering fundamentally the forms of our governments; for suspending our own legislatures, and declaring themselves invested with power to legislate for us in all cases whatsoever.

He has abdicated government here BY DECLARING US OUT OF HIS PROTECTION, AND WAGING WAR AGAINST US [*withdrawing his governors, and declaring us out of his allegiance and protection*].

He has plundered our seas, ravaged our coasts, burnt our towns, and destroyed the lives of our people.

He is at this time transporting large armies of foreign mercenaries to complete the works of death, desolation and tyranny already begun with circumstances of cruelty and perfidy SCARCELY PARALLELED IN THE MOST BARBAROUS AGES, AND TOTALLY unworthy the head of a civilized nation.

He has constrained our fellow citizens taken captive on the high seas, to bear arms against their country, to become the executioners of their friends and brethren, or to fall themselves by their hands.

He has EXCITED DOMESTIC INSURRECTION AMONG US, AND HAS endeavored to bring on the inhabitants of our frontiers, the merciless Indian savages, whose known rule of warfare is an undistinguished destruction of all ages, sexes and conditions [*of existence*].

[*He has incited treasonable insurrections of our fellow citizens, with the allurements of forfeiture and confiscation of our property.*

He has waged cruel war against human nature itself, violating its most sacred rights of life and liberty in the persons of a distant people who never offended him, captivating and carrying them into slavery in another hemisphere, or to incur miserable death in their transportation hither. This piratical warfare, the opprobrium of INFIDEL powers, is the warfare of the CHRISTIAN king of Great Britain. Determined to keep open a market where MEN should be bought and sold, he has prostituted his negative for suppressing every legislative attempt to prohibit or to restrain this execrable commerce. And that this assemblage of horrors might want no fact of distinguished die, he is now exciting those very people to rise in arms among us, and to purchase that liberty of which he has deprived them, by murdering the people on whom he also obtruded them: thus paying off former crimes committed against the LIBERTIES of one people, with crimes which he urges them to commit against the LIVES of another.]

In every stage of these oppressions we have petitioned for redress in the most humble terms: our repeated petitions have been answered only by repeated injuries.

A prince whose character is thus marked by every act which may define a tyrant is unfit to be the ruler of a FREE people

[*who mean to be free. Future ages will scarcely believe that
the hardiness of one man adventured, within the short compass of twelve years only, to lay a foundation so broad and so
undisguised for tyranny over a people fostered and fixed in
principles of freedom.*]

Nor have we been wanting in attentions to our British
brethren. We have warned them from time to time of attempts
by their legislature to extend AN UNWARRANTABLE [*a*] jurisdiction over US [*these our states*]. We have reminded them of the
circumstances of our emigration and settlement here, [*no one
of which could warrant so strange a pretension: that these
were effected at the expense of our own blood and treasure,
unassisted by the wealth or the strength of Great Britain: that
in constituting indeed our several forms of government, we
had adopted one common king, thereby laying a foundation
for perpetual league and amity with them: but that submission
to their parliament was no part of our constitution, nor ever
in idea, if history may be credited: and*] WE HAVE appealed to
their native justice and magnanimity AND WE HAVE CONJURED
THEM BY [*as well as to*] the ties of our common kindred to dis-
avow these usurpations which WOULD INEVITABLY [*were likely
to*] interrupt our connection and correspondence. They too
have been deaf to the voice of justice and of consanguinity.
WE MUST THEREFORE [*and when occasions have been given
them, by the regular course of their laws, of removing from
their councils the disturbers of our harmony, they have, by
their free election, re-establish them in power. At this very
time too, they are permitting their chief magistrate to send
over not only soldiers of our common blood, but Scotch and
foreign mercenaries to invade and destroy us. These facts have
given the last stab to agonizing affection, and manly spirit
bids us to renounce forever these unfeeling brethren. We must
endeavor to forget our former love for them, and hold them
as we hold the rest of mankind, enemies in war, in peace
friends. We might have a free and a great people together; but
a communication of grandeur and of freedom, it seems, is below their dignity. Be it so, since they will have it. The road to*

happiness and to glory is open to us, too. We will tread it apart from them, and] acquiesce in the necessity which denounces our *[eternal]* separation AND HOLD THEM AS WE HOLD THE REST OF MANKIND, ENEMIES IN WAR, IN PEACE FRIENDS!

We, therefore, the representatives of the United States of America in General Congress assembled, appealing to the supreme judge of the world for the rectitude of our intentions, do in the name, and by the authority of the good people of these COLONIES, SOLEMNLY PUBLISH AND DECLARE, THAT THESE UNITED COLONIES ARE, AND OF RIGHT OUGHT TO BE FREE AND INDEPENDENT STATES; THAT THEY ARE ABSOLVED FROM ALL ALLEGIANCE TO THE BRITISH CROWN, AND THAT ALL POLITICAL CONNECTION BETWEEN THEM AND THE STATE OF GREAT BRITAIN IS, AND OUGHT TO BE, TOTALLY DISSOLVED; *[states reject and renounce all allegiance and subjection to the kings of Great Britain and all others who may hereafter claim by, through or under them; we utterly dissolve all political connection which may heretofore have subsisted between us and the people or parliament of Great Britain: and finally we do assert and declare these colonies to be free and independent states,]* and that as free and independent states, they have full power to levy war, conclude peace, contract alliances, establish commerce, and to do all other acts and things which independent states may of right do.

And for the support of this declaration, with a firm reliance on the protection of divine providence, we mutually pledge to each other our lives, our fortunes, and our sacred honor.

The Declaration thus signed on the 4th, on paper, was engrossed on parchment, and signed again on the 2d of August.

* * * * *

William Wordsworth

WILLIAM WORDSWORTH *(1770-1850) spent most of his life in the Lake District of England where many of his greatest poems were set, although he traveled widely. Poet laureate from 1843 until his death, he is generally considered not only the greatest English poet of the nineteenth century but one of the greatest of all English poets. Wordsworth was educated at St. John's College, Cambridge. Principal works:* Lyrical Ballads *(1798);* The Prelude *(1805, 1850); and numerous lyrics ("Ode on the Intimations of Immortality," "Lucy Poems," etc.). His "Preface" to the* Lyrical Ballads *is one of the noblest expressions of a poet's dedication to his art.*

PREFACE TO LYRICAL BALLADS [1]

The first volume of these poems has already been submitted to general perusal.[2] It was published as an experiment, which I hoped might be of some use to ascertain how far, by fitting to metrical arrangement a selection of the real language of men in a state of vivid sensation, that sort of pleasure and that quantity of pleasure may be imparted, which a poet may rationally endeavor to impart.

1 From *Lyrical Ballads* (1800).

2 The first edition of *Lyrical Ballads*, including poems by Wordsworth and by Samuel Taylor Coleridge, appeared in 1798. The famous "Preface" of 1800 attempted to justify the poems against the critics of the first edition.

I had formed no very inaccurate estimate of the probable effect of those poems: I flattered myself that they who should be pleased with them would read them with more than common pleasure: and, on the other hand, I was well aware that by those who should dislike them they would be read with more than common dislike. The result has differed from my expectation in this only, that a greater number have been pleased than I ventured to hope I should please.

Several of my friends are anxious for the success of these poems, from a belief that, if the views with which they were composed were indeed realized, a class of poetry would be produced, well adapted to interest mankind permanently, and not unimportant in the quality and in the multiplicity of its moral relations: and on this account they have advised me to prefix a systematic defence of the theory upon which the poems were written. But I was unwilling to undertake the task, knowing that on this occasion the reader would look coldly upon my arguments, since I might be suspected of having been principally influenced by the selfish and foolish hope of *reasoning* him into an approbation of these particular poems; and I was still more unwilling to undertake the task, because adequately to display the opinions, and fully to enforce the arguments, would require a space wholly disproportionate to a preface. For to treat the subject with the clearness and coherence of which it is susceptible, it would be necessary to give a full account of the present state of the public taste in this country, and to determine how far this taste is healthy or depraved; which, again, could not be determined, without pointing out in what manner language and the human mind act and re-act on each other, and without retracing the revolutions, not of literature alone, but likewise of society itself. I have therefore altogether declined to enter regularly upon this defence; yet I am sensible that there would be something like impropriety in abruptly obtruding upon the public, without a few words of introduction, poems so materially different from those upon which general approbation is at present bestowed.

It is supposed that by the act of writing in verse an author makes a formal engagement that he will gratify certain known habits of association; that he not only thus apprises the reader that certain classes of ideas and expressions will be found in his book, but that others will be carefully excluded. This exponent or symbol held forth by metrical language must in different eras of literature have excited very different expectations: for example, in the age of Catullus, Terence, and Lucretius, and that of Statius or Claudian; and in our own country, in the age of Shakespeare and Beaumont and Fletcher, and that of Donne and Cowley, or Dryden, or Pope.[3] I will not take upon me to determine the exact import of the promise which, by the act of writing in verse, an author in the present day makes to his reader; but it will undoubtedly appear to many persons that I have not fulfilled the terms of an engagement thus voluntarily contracted. They who have been accustomed to the gaudiness and inane phraseology of many modern writers, if they persist in reading this book to its conclusion, will, no doubt, frequently have to struggle with feelings of strangeness and awkwardness: they will look round for poetry, and will be induced to inquire by what species of courtesy these attempts can be permitted to assume that title. I hope, therefore, the reader will not censure me for attempting to state what I have proposed to myself to perform; and also (as far as the limits of a preface will permit) to explain some of the chief reasons which have determined me in the choice of my purpose: that at least he may be spared any unpleasant feeling of disappointment, and that I myself may be protected from one of the most dishonorable accusations which can be brought against an author; namely, that of an indolence which prevents him from endeavoring to

3 In making his lists of poets, Wordsworth is at one level pointing out the differences in conventions at different times, the relativity of value. At another level he is suggesting that both Roman and English literature may be seen as in a state of melancholy decline, from the directness of Catullus to the Alexandrianism of Claudian, and from the naturalness of Shakespeare to the artificiality of Pope. His function is to return to the original source of poetry.

ascertain what is his duty, or, when his duty is ascertained, prevents him from performing it.

The principal object, then, proposed in these poems was to choose incidents and situations from common life, and to relate or describe them, throughout, as far as was possible in a selection of language really used by men, and, at the same time, to throw over them a certain coloring of imagination, whereby ordinary things should be presented to the mind in an unusual aspect; and further, and above all, to make these incidents and situations interesting by tracing in them, truly though not ostentatiously, the primary laws of our nature: chiefly, as far as regards the manner in which we associate ideas in a state of excitement. Humble and rustic life was generally chosen, because in that condition the essential passions of the heart find a better soil in which they can attain their maturity, are less under restraint, and speak a plainer and more emphatic language; because in that condition of life our elementary feelings coëxist in a state of greater simplicity, and consequently may be more accurately contemplated and more forcibly communicated; because the manners of rural life germinate from those elementary feelings, and, from the necessary character of rural occupations, are more easily comprehended, and are more durable; and, lastly, because in that condition the passions of men are incorporated with the beautiful and permanent forms of nature. The language, too, of these men has been adopted (purified indeed from what appear to be its real defects, from all lasting and rational causes of dislike or disgust) because such men hourly communicate with the best objects from which the best part of language is originally derived; and because, from their rank in society and the sameness and narrow circle of their intercourse, being less under the influence of social vanity, they convey their feelings and notions in simple and unelaborated expressions. Accordingly, such a language, arising out of repeated experience and regular feelings, is a more permanent and a far more philosophical language than that which is frequently substituted for it by poets, who think that they are conferring honor upon themselves and their art, in proportion as they separate themselves from the sympathies of men, and indulge in arbitrary and capricious habits of expression, in order to furnish food for fickle tastes, and fickle appetites, of their own creation.

I cannot, however, be insensible to the present outcry against the triviality and meanness, both of thought and language, which some of my contemporaries have occasionally introduced into their metrical compositions; and I acknowledge that this defect, where it exists, is more dishonorable to the writer's own character than false refinement or arbitrary innovation, though I should contend at the same time that it is far less pernicious in the sum of its consequences. From such verses the poems in these volumes will be found distinguished at least by one mark of difference, that each of them has a worthy *purpose*. Not that I always began to write with a distinct purpose formally conceived; but habits of meditation have, I trust, so prompted and regulated my feelings, that my descriptions of such objects as strongly excite those feelings will be found to carry along with them a *purpose*. If this opinion be erroneous, I can have little right to the name of a poet. For all good poetry is the spontaneous overflow of powerful feelings: and though this be true, poems to which any value can be attached were never produced on any variety of subjects but by a man who, being possessed of more than usual organic sensibility, had also thought long and deeply. For our continued influxes of feeling are modified and directed by our thoughts, which are indeed the representatives of all our past feelings; and, as by contemplating the relation of these general representatives to each other, we discover what is really important to men, so, by the repetition and continuance of this act, our feelings will be connected with important subjects, till at length, if we be originally possessed of much sensibility, such habits of mind will be produced that, by obeying blindly and mechanically the impulses of those habits, we shall describe objects, and utter sentiments, of such a nature, and in such connection with each other, that the understanding of the reader must necessarily be in some degree enlightened, and his affections strengthened and purified.

It has been said that each of these poems has a purpose. Another circumstance must be mentioned which distinguishes these poems from the popular poetry of the day; it is this, that the feeling therein developed gives importance to the action and situation, and not the action and situation to the feeling.

A sense of false modesty shall not prevent me from asserting that the reader's attention is pointed to this mark of distinction, far less for the sake of these particular poems than from the general importance of the subject. The subject is indeed important! For the human mind is capable of being excited without the application of gross and violent stimulants; and he must have a very faint perception of its beauty and dignity who does not know this, and who does not further know that one being is elevated above another in proportion as he possesses this capability. It has therefore appeared to me that to endeavor to produce or enlarge this capability is one of the best services in which, at any period, a writer can be engaged; but this service, excellent at all times, is especially so at the present day. For a multitude of causes, unknown to former times, are now acting with a combined force to blunt the discriminating powers of the mind, and, unfitting it for all voluntary exertion, to reduce it to a state of almost savage torpor. The most effective of these causes are the great national events which are daily taking place, and the increasing accumulation of men in cities, where the uniformity of their occupations produces a craving for extraordinary incident, which the rapid communication of intelligence hourly gratifies. To this tendency of life and manners the literature and theatrical exhibitions of the country have conformed themselves. The invaluable works of our elder writers, I had almost said the works of Shakespeare and Milton, are driven into neglect by frantic novels, sickly and stupid German tragedies, and deluges of idle and extravagant stories in verse. When I think upon this degrading thirst after outrageous stimulation, I am almost ashamed to have spoken of the feeble endeavor made in these volumes to counteract it; and, reflecting upon the magnitude of the general evil, I should be oppressed with no dishonorable melancholy, had I not a deep impression of certain inherent and indestructible qualities of the human mind, and likewise of certain powers in the great and permanent objects that act upon it, which are equally inherent and indestructible; and were there not added to this impression a belief that the time is approaching when the evil will be systematically opposed, by men of greater powers, and with far more distinguished success.

Having dwelt thus long on the subjects and aim of these poems, I shall request the reader's permission to apprise him of a few circumstances relating to their *style*, in order, among other reasons, that he may not censure me for not having performed what I never attempted. The reader will find that personifications of abstract ideas rarely occur in these volumes, and are utterly rejected, as an ordinary device to elevate the style, and raise it above prose. My purpose was to imitate, and, as far as possible, to adopt the very language of men; and assuredly such personifications do not make any natural or regular part of that language. They are, indeed, a figure of speech occasionally prompted by passion, and I have made use of them as such; but have endeavored utterly to reject them as a mechanical device of style, or as a family language which writers in meter seem to lay claim to by prescription. I have wished to keep the reader in the company of flesh and blood, persuaded that by so doing I shall interest him. Others who pursue a different track will interest him likewise; I do not interfere with their claim, but wish to prefer a claim of my own. There will also be found in these volumes little of what is usually called poetic diction; as much pains has been taken to avoid it as is ordinarily taken to produce it; this has been done for the reason already alleged, to bring my language near to the language of men; and further, because the pleasure which I have proposed to myself to impart is of a kind very different from that which is supposed by many persons to be the proper object of poetry. Without being culpably particular, I do not know how to give my reader a more exact notion of the style in which it was my wish and intention to write, than by informing him that I have at all times endeavored to look steadily at my subject; consequently there is, I hope, in these poems little falsehood of description, and my ideas are expressed in language fitted to their respective importance. Something must have been gained by this practice, as it is friendly to one property of all good poetry, namely, good sense: but it has necessarily cut me off from a large portion of phrases and figures of speech which from father to son have long been regarded as the common inheritance of poets. I have also thought it expedient to restrict myself still further, having abstained from the use of many expressions, in themselves proper and beautiful, but which have been foolishly repeated by bad poets, till such feelings of disgust are connected with them as it is scarcely possible by any art of association to overpower.

If in a poem there should be found a series of lines, or even a single line, in which the language, though naturally arranged, and according to the strict laws of meter, does not differ from that of prose, there is a numerous class of critics, who, when they stumble upon these prosaisms, as they call them, imagine that they have made a notable discovery, and exult over the poet as over a man ignorant of his own profession. Now these men would establish a canon of criticism which the reader will conclude he must utterly reject, if he wishes to be pleased with these volumes. And it would be a most easy task to prove to him that not only the language of a large portion of every good poem, even of the most elevated character, must necessarily, except with reference to the meter, in no respect differ from that of good prose, but likewise that some of the most interesting parts of the best poems will be found to be strictly the language of prose when prose is well written. The truth of this assertion might be demonstrated by innumerable passages from almost all the poetical writings, even of Milton himself. To illustrate the subject in a general manner, I will here adduce a short composition of Gray,[4] who was at the head of those who, by their reasonings, have attempted to widen the space of separation betwixt prose and metrical composition, and was more than any other man curiously elaborate in the structure of his own poetic diction.

> In vain to me the smiling mornings shine,
> And reddening Phoebus lifts his golden fire;
> The birds in vain their amorous descant join,
> Or cheerful fields resume their green attire.
> These ears, alas! for other notes repine;
> *A different object do these eyes require;*
> *My lonely anguish melts no heart but mine;*
> *And in my breast the imperfect joys expire;*
> Yet morning smiles the busy race to cheer,
> And new-born pleasure brings to happier men;
> The fields to all their wonted tribute bear;
> To warm their little loves the birds complain.
> *I fruitless mourn to him that cannot hear,*
> *And weep the more because I weep in vain.*

It will easily be perceived, that the only part of this sonnet which is of any value is the lines printed in italics; it is equally obvious that, except in the rhyme, and in the use of the single word "fruitless" for fruitlessly, which is so far a defect, the language of these lines does in no respect differ from that of prose.

By the foregoing quotation it has been shown that the language of prose may yet be well adapted to poetry; and it was previously asserted that a large portion of the language of every good poem can in no respect differ from that of good prose. We will go further. It may be safely affirmed that there neither is, nor can be, any *essential* difference between the language of prose and metrical composition. We are fond of tracing the resemblance between poetry and painting, and,

[4] Thomas Gray (1716-1771). Although Gray is best known for his "Elegy Composed in a Country Churchyard," he was also extremely representative of the artificial style that Wordsworth so heartily resented and wrote in a famous letter to Thomas Mason that the language of poetry was *always* different from the language of prose.

accordingly, we call them sisters: but where shall we find bonds of connection sufficiently strict to typify the affinity betwixt metrical and prose composition? They both speak by and to the same organs; the bodies in which both of them are clothed may be said to be of the same substance, their affections are kindred, and almost identical, not necessarily differing even in degree; poetry sheds no tears "such as angels weep," but natural and human tears; she can boast of no celestial ichor that distinguishes her vital juices from those of prose; the same human blood circulates through the veins of them both.

If it be affirmed that rhyme and metrical arrangement of themselves constitute a distinction which overturns what has just been said on the strict affinity of metrical language with that of prose, and paves the way for other artificial distinctions which the mind voluntarily admits, I answer that the language of such poetry as is here recommended is, ar far as is possible, a selection of the language really spoken by men; that this selection, wherever it is made with true taste and feeling, will of itself form a distinction far greater than would at first be imagined, and will entirely separate the composition from the vulgarity and meanness of ordinary life; and, if meter be superadded thereto, I believe that a dissimilitude will be produced altogether sufficient for the gratification of a rational mind. What other distinction would we have? Whence is it to come? And where is it to exist? Not, surely, where the poet speaks through the mouths of his characters: it cannot be necessary here, either for elevation of style, or any of its supposed ornaments: for, if the poet's subject be judiciously chosen, it will naturally, and upon fit occasion, lead him to passions the language of which, if selected truly and judiciously, must necessarily be dignified and variegated, and alive with metaphors and figures. I forbear to speak of an incongruity which would shock the intelligent reader, should the poet interweave any foreign splendor of his own with that which the passion naturally suggests: it is sufficient to say that such addition is unnecessary. And surely it is more probable that those passages which with propriety abound with metaphors and figures will have their due effect, if, upon other occasions where the passions are of a milder character, the style also be subdued and temperate.

But as the pleasure which I hope to give by the poems now presented to the reader must depend entirely on just notions upon this subject, and as it is in itself of high importance to our taste and moral feelings, I cannot content myself with these detached remarks. And if, in what I am about to say, it shall appear to some that my labor is unnecessary, and that I am like a man fighting a battle without enemies, such persons may be reminded that, whatever be the language outwardly holden by men, a practical faith in the opinions which I am wishing to establish is almost unknown. If my conclusions are admitted, and carried as far as they must be carried if admitted at all, our judgments concerning the works of the greatest poets both ancient and modern will be far different from what they are at present, both when we praise, and when we censure; and our moral feelings influencing and influenced by these judgments will, I believe, be corrected and purified.

Taking up the subject, then, upon general grounds, let me ask, what is meant by the word Poet? What is a poet? To whom does he address himself? And what language is to be expected from him?—He is a man speaking to men: a man, it is true, endowed with more lively sensibility, more enthusiasm and tenderness, who has a greater knowledge of human nature, and a more comprehensive soul, than are supposed to be common among mankind; a man pleased with his own passions and volitions, and who rejoices more than other men in the spirit of life that is in him; delighting to contemplate similar volitions and passions as manifested in the goings-on of the universe, and habitually impelled to create them where he does not find them. To these qualities he has added a disposition to be affected more than other men by absent things as if they were present; an ability of conjuring up in himself passions which are indeed far from being the same as those produced by real events, yet (especially in those parts of the general sympathy which are pleasing and delightful) do more nearly resemble the passions produced by real events than anything which, from the motions of their own minds merely, other men are accustomed to feel in themselves:—whence, and from practice, he has acquired a greater readiness and power in expressing what he thinks and feels, and especially those thoughts and feelings which, by his own choice, or from the structure of his own mind, arise in him without immediate external excitement.

But whatever portion of this faculty we may suppose even the greatest poet to possess, there cannot be a doubt that the language which it will suggest to him must often, in liveliness and truth, fall short of that which is uttered by men in real life under the actual pressure of those passions, certain shadows of which the poet thus produces, or feels to be produced, in himself.

However exalted a notion we would wish to cherish of the character of a poet, it is obvious that while he describes and imitates passions, his employment is in some degree mechanical, compared with the freedom and power of real and substantial action and suffering. So that it will be the wish of the poet to bring his feelings near to those of the persons whose feelings he describes,—nay, for short spaces of time, perhaps, to let himself slip into an entire delusion, and even confound and identify his own feelings with theirs; modifying only the language which is thus suggested to him by a consideration that he describes for a particular purpose, that of giving pleasure. Here, then, he will apply the principle of selection which has been already insisted upon. He will depend upon this for removing what would otherwise be painful or disgusting in the passion; he will feel that there is no necessity to trick out or to elevate nature: and, the more industriously he applies this principle, the deeper will be his faith that no words which *his* fancy or imagination can suggest will be to be compared with those which are the emanations of reality and truth.

But it may be said by those who do not object to the general spirit of these remarks, that, as it is impossible for the poet to produce upon all occasions language as exquisitely fitted for the passion as that which the real passion itself suggests, it is proper that he should consider himself as in the situation of a translator, who does not scruple to substitute excellencies of another kind for those which are unattainable by him, and endeavors occasionally to surpass his original, in order to make some amends for the general inferiority to which he feels that he must submit. But this would be to encourage idleness and unmanly despair. Further, it is the language of men who speak of what they do not understand; who talk of poetry as of a matter of amusement and idle pleasure; who will converse with us as gravely about a *taste* for poetry, as they express it, as if it were a thing as indifferent as a taste for rope-dancing, or Frontiniac [5] or Sherry. Aristotle, I have been told, has said that poetry is the most philosophic of all writing: it is so: its object is truth, not individual and local, but general, and operative; not standing upon external testimony, but carried alive into the heart by passion; truth which is its own testimony, which gives competence and confidence to the tribunal to which it appeals, and receives them from the same tribunal. Poetry is the image of man and nature. The obstacles which stand in the way of the fidelity of the biographer and historian, and of their consequent utility, are incalculably greater than those which are to be encountered by the poet who comprehends the dignity of his art. The poet writes under one restriction only, namely, the necessity of giving immediate pleasure to a human being possessed of that information which may be expected from him, not as a lawyer, a physician, a mariner, an astronomer, or a natural philosopher, but as a man. Except this one restriction, there is no object standing between the poet and the image of things; between this, and the biographer and historian, there are a thousand.

Nor let this necessity of producing immediate pleasure be considered as a degradation of the poet's art. It is far other-

---

[5] A sweet French wine. There are those who feel that the difference between Frontiniac and sherry is hardly an indifferent matter.

wise. It is an acknowledgment of the beauty of the universe, an acknowledgment the more sincere, because not formal, but indirect; it is a task light and easy to him who looks at the world in the spirit of love: further, it is a homage paid to the native and naked dignity of man, to the grand elementary principle of pleasure, by which he knows, and feels, and lives, and moves. We have no sympathy but what is propagated by pleasure: I would not be misunderstood; but wherever we sympathize with pain, it will be found that the sympathy is produced and carried on by subtle combinations with pleasure. We have no knowledge, that is, no general principles drawn from the contemplation of particular facts, but what has been built up by pleasure, and exists in us by pleasure alone. The man of science, the chemist and mathematician, whatever difficulties and disgusts they may have had to struggle with, know and feel this. However painful may be the objects with which the anatomist's knowledge is connected, he feels that his knowledge is pleasure; and where he has no pleasure he has no knowledge. What then does the poet? He considers man and the objects that surround him as acting and reacting upon each other, so as to produce an infinite complexity of pain and pleasure; he considers man in his own nature and in his ordinary life as contemplating this with a certain quantity of immediate knowledge, with certain convictions, intuitions, and deductions, which from habit acquire the quality of intuitions; he considers him as looking upon this complex scene of ideas and sensations, and finding everywhere objects that immediately excite in him sympathies which, from the necessities of his nature, are accompanied by an over-balance of enjoyment.

To this knowledge which all men carry about with them, and to these sympathies in which, without any other discipline than that of our daily life, we are fitted to take delight, the poet principally directs his attention. He considers man and nature as essentially adapted to each other, and the mind of man as naturally the mirror of the fairest and most interesting properties of nature. And thus the poet, prompted by this feeling of pleasure, which accompanies him through the whole course of his studies, converses with general nature, with affections akin to those which, through labor and length of time, the man of science has raised up in himself, by conversing with those particular parts of nature which are the objects of his studies. The knowledge both of the poet and the man of science is pleasure; but the knowledge of one cleaves to us as a necessary part of our existence, our natural and unalienable inheritance; the other is a personal and individual acquisition, slow to come to us, and by no habitual and direct sympathy connecting us with our fellow-beings. The man of science seeks truth as a remote and unknown benefactor; he cherishes and loves it in his solitude: the poet, singing a song in which all human beings join with him, rejoices in the presence of truth as our visible friend and hourly companion. Poetry is the breath and finer spirit of all knowledge; it is the impassioned expression which is in the countenance of all science. Emphatically may it be said of the poet, as Shakespeare hath said of man, that "he looks before and after." [6] He is the rock of defence for human nature; an upholder and preserver, carrying everywhere with him relationship and love. In spite of difference of soil and climate, of language and manners, of laws and customs; in spite of things silently gone out of mind, and things violently destroyed; the poet binds together by passion and knowledge the vast empire of human society, as it is spread over the whole earth, and over all time. The objects of the poet's thoughts are everywhere; though the eyes and senses of man are, it is true, his favorite guides, yet he will follow wheresoever he can find an atmosphere of sensation in which to move his wings. Poetry is the first and last of all knowledge—it is as immortal as the heart of man. If the labors of men of science should ever create any material revolution, direct or indirect, in our condition, and in the impressions which we habitually receive, the poet will sleep then no more than at present; he

[6] *Hamlet*, Act IV, Sc. 4.

will be ready to follow the steps of the man of science, not only in those general indirect effects, but he will be at his side, carrying sensation into the midst of the objects of the science itself. The remotest discoveries of the chemist, the botanist, or mineralogist, will be as proper objects of the poet's art as any upon which it can be employed, if the time should ever come when these things shall be familiar to us, and the relations under which they are contemplated by the followers of these respective sciences shall be manifestly and palpably material to us as enjoying and suffering beings. If the time should ever come when what is now called science, thus familiarized to men, shall be ready to put on, as it were, a form of flesh and blood, the poet will lend his divine spirit to aid the transfiguration, and will welcome the being thus produced, as a dear and genuine inmate of the household of man.—It is not, then, to be supposed that any one who holds that sublime notion of poetry which I have attempted to convey, will break in upon the sanctity and truth of his pictures by transitory and accidental ornaments, and endeavor to excite admiration of himself by arts the necessity of which must manifestly depend upon the assumed meanness of his subject.

What has been thus far said applies to poetry in general, but especially to those parts of composition where the poet speaks through the mouths of his characters; and upon this point it appears to authorize the conclusion that there are few persons of good sense who would not allow that the dramatic parts of composition are defective, in proportion as they deviate from the real language of nature, and are colored by a diction of the poet's own, either peculiar to him as an individual poet or belonging simply to poets in general,—to a body of men who, from the circumstance of their compositions being in meter, it is expected will employ a particular language.

It is not, then, in the dramatic parts of composition that we look for this distinction of language; but still it may be proper and necessary where the poet speaks to us in his own person and character. To this I answer by referring the reader to the description before given of a poet. Among the qualities there enumerated as principally conducing to form a poet, is implied nothing differing in kind from other men, but only in degree. The sum of what was said is, that the poet is chiefly distinguished from other men by a greater promptness to think and feel without immediate external excitement, and a greater power in expressing such thoughts and feelings as are produced in him in that manner. But these passions and thoughts and feelings are the general passions and thoughts and feelings of men. And with what are they connected? Undoubtedly with our moral sentiments and animal sensations, and with the causes which excite these; with the operations of the elements, and the appearance of the visible universe; with storm and sunshine, with the revolutions of the seasons, with cold and heat, with loss of friends and kindred, with injuries and resentments, gratitude and hope, with fear and sorrow. These, and the like, are the sensations and objects which the poet describes, as they are the sensations of other men, and the objects which interest them. The poet thinks and feels in the spirit of human passions. How, then, can his language differ in any material degree from that of all other men who feel vividly and see clearly? It might be *proved* that it is impossible. But supposing that this were not the case, the poet might then be allowed to use a peculiar language when expressing his feelings for his own gratification, or that of men like himself. But poets do not write for poets alone, but for men. Unless, therefore, we are advocates for that admiration which subsists upon ignorance, and that pleasure which arises from hearing what we do not understand, the poet must descend from this supposed height; and, in order to excite rational sympathy, he must express himself as other men express themselves. To this it may be added that while he is only selecting from the real language of men, or, which amounts to the same thing, composing accurately in the spirit of such selection, he is treading upon safe ground, and we know what we are to expect from him. Our feelings are the same with respect to meter; for, as it may be proper to remind the reader, the distinction of meter is regular and uniform,

and not, like that which is produced by what is usually called
POETIC DICTION, arbitrary, and subject to infinite caprices
upon which no calculation whatever can be made. In the one
case, the reader is utterly at the mercy of the poet, respecting
what imagery or diction he may choose to connect with the
passion; whereas in the other, the meter obeys certain laws,
to which the poet and reader both willingly submit because
they are certain, and because no interference is made by them
with the passion, but such as the concurring testimony of
ages has shown to heighten and improve the pleasure which
co-exists with it.

It will now be proper to answer an obvious question,
namely, Why, professing these opinions, have I written in
verse? To this, in addition to such answer as is included in
what has been already said, I reply, in the first place, Because,
however I may have restricted myself, there is still left open to
me what confessedly constitutes the most valuable object of
all writing, whether in prose or verse—the great and universal
passions of men, the most general and interesting of their
occupations, and the entire world of nature before me—to
supply endless combinations of forms and imagery. Now, supposing for a moment that whatever is interesting in these
objects may be as vividly described in prose, why should I
be condemned for attempting to superadd to such description
the charm which, by the consent of all nations, is acknowledged to exist in metrical language? To this, by such as are
yet unconvinced, it may be answered that a very small part
of the pleasure given by poetry depends upon the meter,
and that it is injudicious to write in meter, unless it be accompanied with the other artificial distinctions of style with which
meter is usually accompanied, and that, by such deviation,
more will be lost from the shock which will thereby be given
to the reader's associations than will be counterbalanced by
any pleasure which he can derive from the general power of
numbers. In answer to those who still contend for the necessity of accompanying meter with certain appropriate colors
of style in order to the accomplishment of its appropriate end,

and who also, in my opinion, greatly underrate the power of meter in itself, it might, perhaps, as far as relates to these volumes, have been almost sufficient to observe that poems are extant, written upon more humble subjects, and in a still more naked and simple style, which have continued to give pleasure from generation to generation. Now if nakedness and simplicity be a defect, the fact here mentioned affords a strong presumption that poems somewhat less naked and simple are capable of affording pleasure at the present day; and what I wished *chiefly* to attempt, at present, was to justify myself for having written under the impression of this belief.

But various causes might be pointed out why, when the style is manly, and the subject of some importance, words metrically arranged will long continue to impart such a pleasure to mankind as he who proves the extent of that pleasure will be desirous to impart. The end of poetry is to produce excitement in co-existence with an overbalance of pleasure; but, by the supposition, excitement is an unusual and irregular state of the mind; ideas and feelings do not, in that state, succeed each other in accustomed order. If the words, however, by which this excitement is produced be in themselves powerful, or the images and feelings have an undue proportion of pain connected with them, there is some danger that the excitement may be carried beyond its proper bounds. Now the co-presence of something regular, something to which the mind has been accustomed in various moods and in a less excited state, cannot but have great efficacy in tempering and restraining the passion by an intertexture of ordinary feeling, and of feeling not strictly and necessarily connected with the passion. This is unquestionably true; and hence, though the opinion will at first appear paradoxical, from the tendency of meter to divest language, in a certain degree, of its reality, and thus to throw a sort of half-consciousness of unsubstantial existence over the whole composition, there can be little doubt but that more pathetic situations and sentiments, that is, those which have a greater proportion of pain connected with them, may be endured in metrical composition, especially in rhyme, than in prose. The meter of the old ballads is very artless, yet they contain many passages which would illustrate this opinion; and, I hope, if the following poems be attentively perused, similar instances will be found in them. This opinion may be further illustrated by appealing to the reader's own experience of the reluctance with which he comes to the reperusal of the distressful parts of *Clarissa Harlowe*,[7] or *The Gamester*,[8] while Shakespeare's writings, in the most pathetic scenes, never act upon us, as pathetic, beyond the bounds of pleasure—an effect which, in a much greater degree than might at first be imagined, is to be ascribed to small but continual and regular impulses of pleasurable surprise from the metrical arrangement.—On the other hand (what it must be allowed will much more frequently happen), if the poet's words should be incommensurate with the passion, and inadequate to raise the reader to a height of desirable excitement, then (unless the poet's choice of his meter has been grossly injudicious) in the feelings of pleasure which the reader has been accustomed to connect with meter in general, and in the feeling, whether cheerful or melancholy, which he has been accustomed to connect with that particular movement of meter, there will be found something which will greatly contribute to impart passion to the words, and to effect the complex end which the poet proposes to himself.

If I had undertaken a SYSTEMATIC defence of the theory here maintained, it would have been my duty to develop the various causes upon which the pleasure received from metrical language depends. Among the chief of these causes is to be reckoned a principle which must be well known to those who have made any of the arts the object of accurate reflection; namely, the pleasure which the mind derives from the perception of similitude in dissimilitude. This principle is the great spring of the activity of our minds, and their chief feeder. From this principle the direction of the sexual appetite, and all the passions connected with it, take their

---

7 Novel by Samuel Richardson.
8 Comic drama by James Shirley.

origin: it is the life of our ordinary conversation; and upon the accuracy with which similitude in dissimilitude, and dissimilitude in similitude are perceived, depend our taste and our moral feelings. It would not be a useless employment to apply this principle to the consideration of meter, and to show that meter is hence enabled to afford much pleasure, and to point out in what manner that pleasure is produced. But my limits will not permit me to enter upon this subject, and I must content myself with a general summary.

I have said that poetry is the spontaneous overflow of powerful feelings; it takes its origin from emotion recollected in tranquillity: the emotion is contemplated till, by a species of reaction, the tranquillity gradually disappears, and an emotion, kindred to that which was before the subject of contemplation, is gradually produced, and does itself actually exist in the mind. In this mood successful composition generally begins, and in a mood similar to this it is carried on; but the emotion, of whatever kind, and in whatever degree, from various causes, is qualified by various pleasures, so that in describing any passions whatsoever, which are voluntarily described, the mind will, upon the whole, be in a state of enjoyment. If Nature be thus cautious to preserve in a state of enjoyment a being so employed, the poet ought to profit by the lesson held forth to him, and ought especially to take care that, whatever passions he communicates to his reader, those passions, if his reader's mind be sound and vigorous, should always be accompanied with an over-balance of pleasure. Now the music of harmonious metrical language, the sense of difficulty overcome, and the blind association of pleasure which has been previously received from works of rhyme or meter of the same or similar construction, an indistinct perception perpetually renewed of language closely resembling that of real life, and yet, in the circumstance of meter, differing from it so widely—all these imperceptibly make up a complex feeling of delight, which is of the most important use in tempering the painful feeling always found intermingled with powerful descriptions of the deeper passions. This effect is always produced in pathetic and impassioned poetry; while in lighter compositions the ease and gracefulness with which the poet manages his numbers are themselves confessedly a principal source of the gratification of the reader. All that it is *necessary* to say, however, upon this subject, may be effected by affirming, what few persons will deny, that of two descriptions, either of passions, manners, or characters each of them equally well executed, the one in prose and the other in verse, the verse will be read a hundred times where the prose is read once.

Having thus explained a few of my reasons for writing in verse, and why I have chosen subjects from common life, and endeavored to bring my language near to the real language of men, if I have been too minute in pleading my own cause, I have at the same time been treating a subject of general interest; and for this reason a few words shall be added with reference solely to these particular poems, and to some defects which will probably be found in them. I am sensible that my associations must have sometimes been particular instead of general, and that, consequently, giving to things a false importance, I may have sometimes written upon unworthy subjects; but I am less apprehensive on this account, than that my language may frequently have suffered from those arbitrary connections of feelings and ideas with particular words and phrases, from which no man can altogether protect himself. Hence I have no doubt that, in some instances, feelings, even of the ludicrous, may be given to my readers by expressions which appeared to me tender and pathetic. Such faulty expressions, were I convinced they were faulty at present, and that they must necessarily continue to be so, I would willingly take all reasonable pains to correct. But it is dangerous to make these alterations on the simple authority of a few individuals, or even of certain classes of men; for where the understanding of an author is not convinced, or his feelings altered, this cannot be done without great injury to himself: for his own feelings are his stay and support; and, if he set them aside in one instance, he may be induced to repeat this act till his mind shall lose all confidence in itself, and become utterly debilitated. To this it may be added that the critic ought never to forget that he is himself exposed to the same errors as the poet, and perhaps in a much greater degree: for there can be no presumption in saying of most readers that it is not probable they will be so well acquainted with the various stages of meaning through which words have passed, or with the fickleness or stability of the relations of particular ideas to each other; and, above all, since they are so much less interested in the subject, they may decide lightly and carelessly.

Long as the reader has been detained, I hope he will permit me to caution him against a mode of false criticism which has been applied to poetry, in which the language closely resembles that of life and nature. Such verses have been triumphed over in parodies, of which Dr. Johnson's stanza is a fair specimen:

> I put my hat upon my head
> And walked into the Strand,
> And there I met another man
> Whose hat was in his hand.

Immediately under these lines let us place one of the most justly admired stanzas of the "Babes in the Woods."

> These pretty babes with hand in hand
> Went wandering up and down;
> But never more they saw the man
> Approaching from the town.

In both these stanzas the words, and the order of the words, in no respect differ from the most unimpassioned conversation. There are words in both, for example, "the Strand," and "the town," connected with none but the most familiar ideas; yet the one stanza we admit as admirable, and the other as a fair example of the superlatively contemptible. Whence arises this difference? Not from the meter, not from the language, not from the order of the words; but the *matter* expressed in Dr. Johnson's stanza is contemptible. The proper method of treating trivial and simple verses to which Dr. Johnson's stanza would be a fair parallelism, is not to say, This is a bad kind of poetry, or This is not poetry; but, This wants sense; it is neither interesting in itself, or can *lead* to anything interesting; the images neither originate in that sane state of feeling which arises out of thought, nor can excite thought or feeling in the reader. This is the only sensible manner of dealing with such verses. Why trouble yourself about the species till you have previously decided upon the genus? Why take pains to prove that an ape is not a Newton, when it is self-evident that he is not a man?

One request I must make of my reader, which is, that in judging these poems he would decide by his own feelings genuinely, and not by reflection upon what will probably be the judgment of others. How common is it to hear a person say, I myself do not object to this style of composition, or this or that expression, but to such and such classes of people it will appear mean or ludicrous! This mode of criticism, so destructive of all sound unadulterated judgment, is almost universal: let the reader then abide, independently, by his own feelings, and, if he finds himself affected, let him not suffer such conjectures to interfere with his pleasure.

If an author, by any single composition, has impressed us with respect for his talents, it is useful to consider this as affording a presumption that on other occasions, where we have been displeased, he nevertheless may not have written ill or absurdly; and further, to give him so much credit for this one composition as may induce us to review what has displeased us with more care than we should otherwise have bestowed upon it. This is not only an act of justice, but, in our decisions upon poetry especially, may conduce in a high degree to the improvement of our own taste; for an *accurate* taste in poetry, and in all the other arts, as Sir Joshua Reynolds has observed, is an *acquired* talent, which can only be produced by thought and a long-continued intercourse with the best models of composition. This is mentioned, not with so ridiculous a purpose as to prevent the most inexperienced reader from judging for himself (I have already said that I wish him to judge for himself), but merely to temper the rashness of decision, and to suggest that, if poetry be a subject on which much time has not been bestowed, the judgment may be erroneous; and that, in many cases, it necessarily will be so.

Nothing would, I know, have so effectually contributed to further the end which I have in view, as to have shown of what kind the pleasure is, and how that pleasure is produced, which is confessedly produced by metrical composition essentially different from that which I have here endeavored to recommend: for the reader will say that he has been pleased by such composition; and what more can be done for him? The power of any art is limited; and he will suspect that, if it be proposed to furnish him with new friends, that can be only upon condition of his abandoning his old friends. Besides, as I have said, the reader is himself conscious of the pleasure which he has received from such composition, composition to which he has peculiarly attached the endearing name of poetry; and all men feel an habitual gratitude, and something of an honorable bigotry, for the objects which have long continued to please them: we not only wish to be pleased, but to be pleased in that particular way in which we have been accustomed to be pleased. There is in these feelings enough to resist a host of arguments; and I should be the less able to combat them successfully, as I am willing to allow that, in order entirely to enjoy the poetry which I am recommending, it would be necessary to give up much of what is ordinarily enjoyed. But, would my limits have permitted me to point out how this pleasure is produced, many obstacles might have been removed, and the reader assisted in perceiving that the powers of language are not so limited as he may suppose; and that it is possible for poetry to give other enjoyments, of a purer, more lasting, and more exquisite nature. This part of the subject has not been altogether neglected, but it has not been so much my present aim to prove that the interest excited by some other kinds of poetry is less vivid, and less worthy of the nobler powers of the mind, as to offer reasons for presuming that, if my purpose were fulfilled, a species of poetry would be produced which is genuine poetry, in its nature well adapted to interest mankind permanently, and likewise important in the multiplicity and quality of its moral relations.

From what has been said, and from a perusal of the poems, the reader will be able clearly to perceive the object which I had in view: he will determine how far it has been attained; and, what is a much more important question, whether it be worth attaining: and upon the decision of these two questions will rest my claim to the approbation of the public.

William Hazlitt

WILLIAM HAZLITT *(1778-1830) was closely associated with Wordsworth, Coleridge, and other English literary figures of his era. From 1812 on, after a brief career as a painter, he became a prolific contributor to various periodicals, writing on political and literary matters in an easy, familiar manner. The son of a Unitarian minister, Hazlitt was educated mainly at home. Principal works:* Characters of Shakespeare's Plays *(1817-8);* Table Talk *(1821-2);* Liber Amoris *(1823);* The Spirit of the Age *(1825).*

CHARACTER OF COBBETT [1]

People have about as substantial an idea of Cobbett as they have of Cribb.[2] His blows are as hard, and he himself is as impenetrable. One has no notion of him as making use of a fine pen, but a great mutton-fist; his style stuns his readers, and he 'fillips the ear of the public with a three-man beetle.' [3] He is too much for any single newspaper antagonist; 'lays

---

[1] From *Table-Talk; or, Original Essays,* Vol. I (1821). Included also in Paris and 2nd English editions of *The Spirit of the Age.* William Cobbett (1763-1835), editor of the *Political Register,* was a vocal political pamphleteer, advocate of Parliamentary reform. He reversed normal human behavior by beginning his career as a Tory and becoming a Radical in his maturity. His best-known work is *Rural Rides* (1830).

[2] Tom Cribb (1781-1848), champion prize fighter.

[3] *Henry IV, Part II,* Act I, Sc. 2, 1. 259. Characteristically, Hazlitt rephrases the quotation to suit his purposes. No mention is made of "the public" in Shakespeare, and the sense of the passage as here cited is that Cobbett bludgeons the public into submission.

waste'[4] a city orator or Member of Parliament, and bears
hard upon the government itself. He is a kind of *fourth
estate* [5] in the politics of the country. He is not only unquestionably the most powerful political writer of the present
day, but one of the best writers in the language. He speaks
and thinks plain, broad, downright English. He might be said
to have the clearness of Swift, the naturalness of Defoe, and
the picturesque satirical description of Mandeville; [6] if all
such comparisons were not impertinent. A really great and
original writer is like nobody but himself. In one sense,
Sterne [7] was not a wit, nor Shakespear a poet. It is easy to
describe second-rate talents, because they fall into a class, and
enlist under a standard; but first-rate powers defy calculation
or comparison, and can be defined only by themselves. They
are *sui generis*, and make the class to which they belong. I have
tried half a dozen times to describe Burke's style [8] without
ever succeeding;—its severe extravagance; its literal boldness;
its matter-of-fact hyperboles; its running away with a subject,
and from it at the same time—but there is no making it out,
for there is no example of the same thing any where else. We
have no common measure to refer to; and his qualities contradict even themselves.

Cobbett is not so difficult. He has been compared to Paine;
and so far it is true there are no two writers who come more
into juxtaposition from the nature of their subjects, from the
internal resources on which they draw, and from the popular
effect of their writings, and their adaptation (though that is a
bad word in the present case) to the capacity of every reader.

---

4 This is so common a phrase that it is hardly necessary to know what
allusion Hazlitt had in mind. One editor suggests "Lay waste thy woods,
destroy thy blissful bower." Dryden, *The Hind and the Panther*, I, 158.
5 The three estates of the realm in England are the Lords Spiritual,
the Lords Temporal, and the Commons. Hazlitt speaks of Cobbett as
having the status of an institution, and the term *fourth estate* has come
to mean the public press.
6 Swift, Defoe, and Mandeville were prose writers of great vigor.
7 English comic novelist of the eighteenth century.
8 Edmund Burke (1729-1797). Anglo-Irish statesman and orator.

But still if we turn to a volume of Paine's [9] (his Common Sense or Rights of Man), we are struck (not to say somewhat refreshed) by the difference. Paine is a much more sententious writer than Cobbett. You cannot open a page in any of his best and earlier works without meeting with some maxim, some antithetical and memorable saying, which is a sort of starting-place for the argument, and the goal to which it returns. There is not a single *bon-mot*, a single sentence in Cobbett that has ever been quoted again. If any thing is ever quoted from him, it is an epithet of abuse or a nickname. He is an excellent hand at invention in that way, and has 'damnable iteration in him.' [10] What could be better than his pestering Erskine [11] year after year with his second title of Baron Clackmannan? He is rather too fond of *the Sons and Daughters of Corruption*. Paine affected to reduce things to first principles, to announce self-evident truths. Cobbett troubles himself about little but the details and local circumstances. The first appeared to have made up his mind beforehand to certain opinions, and to try to find the most compendious and pointed expressions for them: his successor appears to have no clue, no fixed or leading principles, nor ever to have thought on a question till he sits down to write about it; but then there seems no end of his matters of fact and raw materials, which are brought out in all their strength and sharpness from not having been squared of frittered down or vamped up to suit a theory—he goes on with his descriptions and illustrations as if he would never come to a stop; they have all the force of novelty with all the familiarity of old acquaintance; his knowledge grows out of the subject, and his

[9] Thomas Paine (1737-1809). American pamphleteer of the Revolutionary period, at first reviled by Cobbett but later revered by him.

[10] *Henry IV, Part I*, Act I, Sc. 2, l. 101. In Shakespeare, a damnable way of quoting or repeating, especially from Scripture. Hazlitt uses it here only to indicate that Cobbett keeps repeating epithets or nicknames.

[11] Thomas Erskine (1750-1823), Whig politician, Lord Chancellor, one of Cobbett's chief targets. Cobbet played on the odd sound of Clackmannan (county in Scotland), of which Erskine was baron, in order to make him seem ridiculous.

style is that of a man who has an absolute intuition of what
he is talking about, and never thinks of any thing else. He
deals in premises and speaks to evidence—the coming to a
conclusion and summing up (which was Paine's *forte*) lies in a
smaller compass. The one could not compose an elementary
treatise on politics to become a manual for the popular reader;
nor could the other in all probability have kept up a weekly
journal for the same number of years with the same spirit,
interest, and untired perseverance. Paine's writings are a sort
of introduction to political arithmetic on a new plan: Cobbett
keeps a day-book and makes an entry at full of all the occurrences and troublesome questions that start up throughout the
year. Cobbett, with vast industry, vast information, and the
utmost power of making what he says intelligible, never seems
to get at the beginning or come to the end of any question:
Paine, in a few short sentences, seems by his peremptory
manner 'to clear it from all controversy, past, present, and to
come.' [12] Paine takes a bird's-eye view of things. Cobbett sticks
close to them, inspects the component parts, and keeps fast
hold of the smallest advantages they afford him. Or, if I might
here be indulged in a pastoral allusion, Paine tries to enclose
his ideas in a fold for security and repose: Cobbett lets *his*
pour out upon the plain like a flock of sheep to feed and
batten. Cobbett is a pleasanter writer for those to read who do
not agree with him; for he is less dogmatical, goes more
into the common grounds of fact and argument to which all
appeal, is more desultory and various, and appears less to be
driving at a previous conclusion than urged on by the force
of present conviction. He is therefore tolerated by all parties,
though he has made himself by turns obnoxious to all; and
even those he abuses read him. The Reformers read him when
he was a Tory, and the Tories read him now that he is a
Reformer. He must, I think, however, be *cavaire* to the
Whigs.[13]

[12] Not identified, but self-explanatory.
[13] Reformers (Radicals) and Tories take pleasure in him because he
attacks the party in power (the Whigs).

If he is less metaphysical and poetical than his celebrated prototype, he is more picturesque and dramatic. His episodes, which are numerous as they are pertinent, are striking, interesting, full of life and *naïveté*, minute, double measure running over, but never tedious—*nunquam sufflaminandus erat*.[14] He is one of those writers who can never tire us, not even of himself; and the reason is, he is always 'full of matter.'[15] He never runs to lees, never gives us the vapid leavings of himself, is never 'weary, stale, and unprofitable,'[16] but always setting out afresh on his journey, clearing away some old nuisance, and turning up new mold. His egotism is delightful, for there is no affectation in it. He does not talk of himself for lack of something to write about, but because some circumstance that has happened to himself is the best possible illustration of the subject, and he is not the man to shrink from giving the best possible illustration of the subject from a squeamish delicacy. He likes both himself and his subject too well. He does not put himself before it, and say—'admire me first'—but places us in the same situation with himself, and makes us see all that he does. There is no blindman's-buff, no conscious hints, no awkward ventriloquism, no testimonies of applause, no abstract, senseless self-complacency, no smuggled admiration of his own person by proxy: it is all plain and aboveboard. He writes himself plain William Cobbett, strips himself quite as naked as any body would wish—in a word, his egotism is full of individuality, and has room for very little vanity in it. We feel delighted, rub our hands, and draw our chair to the fire, when we come to a passage of this sort: we know it will be something new and good, manly and simple, not the same insipid story of self over again. We sit down at table with the writer, but it is to a course of rich viands, flesh, fish, and wild-fowl, and not to a nominal entertainment, like

---

14 Ben Jonson, *Discoveries*, LXIV. Jonson wrote *sufflaminandus erat* (he ought to have been clogged) ; Hazlitt rephrases the line to mean he ought never to have been clogged.

15 *As You Like It*, Act II, Sc. 1, 1. 68.

16 *Hamlet*, Act I, Sc. 2, 1. 133.

that given by the Barmecide in the Arabian Nights,[17] who put
off his visitors with calling for a number of exquisite things
that never appeared, and with the honour of his company.
Mr. Cobbett is not a *make-believe* writer. His worst enemy
cannot say that of him. Still less is he a vulgar one. He must
be a puny, common-place critic indeed, who thinks him so.
How fine were the graphical descriptions he sent us from
America: what a transatlantic flavour, what a native *gusto*,
what a fine *sauce-piquante* of contempt they were seasoned
with! If he had sat down to look at himself in the glass, instead
of looking about him like Adam in Paradise, he would not
have got up these articles in so capital a style. What a noble
account of his first breakfast after his arrival in America! It
might serve for a month. There is no scene on the stage more
amusing. How well he paints the gold and scarlet plumage of
the American birds, only to lament more pathetically the want
of the wild wood-notes of his native land! The groves of the
Ohio that had just fallen beneath the axe's stroke 'live in his
description,' and the turnips that he transplanted from Botley
'look green' [18] in prose! How well at another time he describes
the poor sheep that had got the tick, and had tumbled down
in the agonies of death! It is a portrait in the manner of
Bewick,[19] with the strength, the simplicity, and feeling of that
great naturalist. What havoc he makes, when he pleases, of
the curls of Dr. Parr's wig [20] and of the Whig consistency of
Mr. ——! [21] His Grammar [22] too is as entertaining as a story-
book. He is too hard upon the style of others, and not enough
(sometimes) on his own.

As a political partisan, no one can stand against him. With
his brandished club, like Giant Despair in the Pilgrim's

[17] The Barber's story of his sixth brother.

[18] *Macbeth*, Act I, Sc. 7, l. 37.

[19] Thomas Bewick (1753-1828), wood-engraver, famed for renderings of
animals.

[20] The reference is to Samuel Parr (1747-1825), Whig controversialist.

[21] Probably Henry Peter Brougham, Baron Brougham, prominent pub-
licist and politician.

[22] *A Grammar of the English Language, in a Series of Letters* (1818).

Progress,[23] he knocks out their brains; and not only no individual, but no corrupt system could hold out against his
powerful and repeated attacks, but with the same weapon,
swung round like a flail, that he levels his antagonists, he lays
his friends low, and puts his own party *hors de combat.* This
is a bad propensity, and a worst principle in political tactics,
though a common one. If his blows were straight forward and
steadily directed to the same object, no unpopular Minister
could live before him; instead of which he lays about right
and left, impartially and remorselessly, makes a clear stage,
has all the ring to himself, and then runs out of it, just when
he should stand his ground. He throws his head into his adversary's stomach, and takes away from him all inclination for
the fight, hits fair or foul, strikes at every thing, and as you
come up to his aid or stand ready to pursue his advantage,
trips up your heels or lays you sprawling, and pummels you
when down as much to his heart's content as ever the
Yanguesian carriers belaboured Rosinante with their pack-
staves.[24] *'He has the back-trick simply the best of any man in
Illyria.'* [25] He pays off both scores of old friendship and new-
acquired enmity in a breath, in one perpetual volley, one
raking fire of 'arrowy sleet' [26] shot from his pen. However his
own reputation or the cause may suffer in consequence, he
cares not one pin about that, so that he disables all who
oppose, or pretend to help him. In fact, he cannot bear success
of any kind, not even of his own views or party; and if any
principle were likely to become popular, would turn round
against it to shew his power in shouldering it on one side. In
short, wherever power is, there is he against it: he naturally
butts at all obstacles, as unicorns are attracted to oak-trees, and
feels his own strength only by resistance to the opinions and

---

[23] *Pilgrim's Progress* by John Bunyan, allegorical tale of redemption in
which the Giant Despair plays an important role.

[24] *Don Quixote,* Book III, Chap. XV.

[25] Paraphrased from *Twelfth Night,* Act I, Sc. 3, l. 133. Hazlitt interprets
the figure as coming from fencing and, therefore, appropriate to the context of struggle and combat.

[26] Probably suggested by *Paradise Regained,* Book III, 323-325.

wishes of the rest of the world. To sail with the stream, to agree with the company, is not his humour. If he could bring about a Reform in Parliament,[27] the odds are that he would instantly fall foul of and try to mar his own handy-work; and he quarrels with his own creatures as soon as he has written them into a little vogue—and a prison. I do not think this is vanity or fickleness so much as a pugnacious disposition, that must have an antagonist power to contend with, and only finds itself at ease in systematic opposition. If it were not for this, the high towers and rotten places of the world would fall before the battering-ram of his hard-headed reasoning: but if he once found them tottering, he would apply his strength to prop them up, and disappoint the expectations of his followers. He cannot agree to any thing established, nor to set up any thing else in its stead. While it is established, he presses hard against it, because it presses upon him, at least in imagination. Let it crumble under his grasp, and the motive to resistance is gone. He then requires some other grievance to set his face against. His principle is repulsion, his nature contradiction: he is made up of mere antipathies, an Ishmaelite [28] indeed without a fellow. He is always playing at *hunt-the-slipper* in politics. He turns round upon whoever is next him. The way to wean him from any opinion, and make him conceive an intolerable hatred against it, would be to place somebody near him who was perpetually dinning it in his ears. When he is in England, he does nothing but abuse the Boroughmongers, and laugh at the whole system: when he is in America, he grows impatient of freedom and a republic. If he had staid there a little longer, he would have become a loyal and a loving subject of his Majesty King George IV. He lampooned the French Revolution when it was hailed as the dawn of liberty by millions: by the time it was brought

27 The struggle for reform in the system of parliamentary representation eventuated in the Reform Bill of 1832, but the system attacked by Cobbett was still in power when Hazlitt wrote this essay. The reference to Boroughmongers below refers to the practice of bribery and corruption that prevailed.

28 A wanderer and outcast.

into almost universal ill-odour by some means or other (partly
no doubt by himself) he had turned, with one or two or three
others, staunch Buonapartist. He is always of the militant,
not of the triumphant party: so far he bears a gallant shew
of magnanimity; but his gallantry is hardly of the right stamp.
It wants principle: [29] for though he is not servile or mercenary,
he is the victim of self-will. He must pull down and pull in
pieces: it is not his disposition to do otherwise. It is a pity;
for with his great talents he might do great things, if he would
go right forward to any useful object, make thorough-stitch [30]
work of any question, or join hand and heart with any principle. He changes his opinions as he does his friends, and
much on the same account. He has no comfort in fixed principles: as soon as any thing is settled in his own mind, he
quarrels with it. He has no satisfaction but in the chase after
truth, runs a question down, worries and kills it, then quits it
like vermin, and starts some new game, to lead him a new
dance, and give him a fresh breathing through bog and brake,
with the rabble yelping at his heels, and the leaders perpetually at fault. This he calls sport-royal. He thinks it as good
as cudgel-playing or single-stick,[31] or any thing else that has
life in it. He likes the cut and thrust, the falls, bruises, and
dry blows of an argument: as to any good or useful results
that may come of the amicable settling of it, any one is welcome to them for him. The amusement is over, when the
matter is once fairly decided.

There is another point of view in which this may be put.
I might say that Mr. Cobbett is a very honest man with a total
want of principle, and I might explain this paradox thus. I
mean that he is, I think, in downright earnest in what he
says, in the part he takes at the time; but in taking that part,
he is led entirely by headstrong obstinacy, caprice, novelty,
pique or personal motive of some sort, and not by a stedfast
regard for truth, or habitual anxiety for what is right upper-

29 It lacks principle.
30 Thorough-going, out and out.
31 A kind of fencing with a stick.

most in his mind. He is not a feed, time-serving, shuffling advocate (no man could write as he does who did not believe himself sincere)—but his understanding is the dupe and slave of his momentary, violent, and irritable humours. He does not adopt an opinion 'deliberately or for money'; [32] yet his conscience is at the mercy of the first provocation he receives, of the first whim he takes in his head; he sees things through the medium of heat and passion, not with reference to any general principles, and his whole system of thinking is deranged by the first object that strikes his fancy or sours his temper.—One cause of this phenomenon is perhaps his want of a regular education. He is a self-taught man, and has the faults as well as excellences of that class of persons in their most striking and glaring excess. It must be acknowledged that the Editor of the Political Register (the *two-penny trash,* as it was called, till a bill passed the House [33] to raise the price to sixpence) is not 'the gentleman and scholar': though he has qualities that, with a little better management, would be worth (to the public) both those titles. For want of knowing what has been discovered before him, he has not certain general landmarks to refer to, or a general standard of thought to apply to individual cases. He relies on his own acuteness and the immediate evidence, without being acquainted with the comparative anatomy or philosophical structure of opinion. He does not view things on a large scale or at the horizon (dim and airy enough perhaps)—but as they affect himself, close, palpable, tangible. Whatever he finds out, is his own, and he only knows what he finds out. He is in the constant hurry and fever of gestation: his brain teems incessantly with some fresh project. Every new light is the birth of a new system, the dawn of a new world to him. He is continually outstripping and overreaching himself. The last opinion is the only true one. He is wiser to-day than he was yesterday. Why should he not be wiser to-morrow than he was today?—Men

[32] Not identified, but self-explanatory.

[33] An attempt by the Whig Government to prevent the wide distribution of Cobbett's *Political Register.*

of a learned education are not so sharp-witted as clever men without it: but they know the balance of the human intellect better; if they are more stupid, they are more steady; and are less liable to be led astray by their own sagacity and the overweening petulance of hard-earned and late-acquired wisdom. They do not fall in love with every meretricious extravagance at first sight, or mistake an old battered hypothesis for a vestal,[34] because they are new to the ways of this old world. They do not seize upon it as a prize, but are safe from gross imposition by being as wise and no wiser than those who went before them.

Paine said on some occasion—'What I have written, I have written'[35]—as rendering any farther declaration of his principles unnecessary. Not so Mr. Cobbett. What he has written is no rule to him what he is to write. He learns something every day, and every week he takes the field to maintain the opinions of the last six days against friend or foe. I doubt whether this outrageous inconsistency, this headstrong fickleness, this understood want of all rule and method, does not enable him to go on with the spirit, vigour, and variety that he does. He is not pledged to repeat himself. Every new Register is a kind of new Prospectus.[36] He blesses himself from all ties and shackles on his understanding; he has no mortgages on his brain; his notions are free and unincumbered. If he was put in trammels, he might become a vile hack like so many more. But he gives himself 'ample scope and verge enough.'[37] He takes both sides of a question, and maintains one as sturdily as the other. If nobody else can argue against him, he is a very good match for himself. He writes better in favour of Reform than any body else;[38] he used to write better against it. Wherever he is, there is the tug of war, the weight of the argument, the strength of abuse. He is not like a man

[34] Look on a cliché as an entirely new (virgin) idea.
[35] Probably taken from oral tradition.
[36] Every issue of his magazine announces a completely new approach.
[37] Thomas Gray, *The Bard*, II, 1.
[38] A reference to the violent change in Cobbett's political position from Tory to Radical.

in danger of being *bed-rid* in his faculties—He tosses and tumbles about his unwieldy bulk, and when he is tried of lying on one side, relieves himself by turning on the other. His shifting his point of view from time to time not merely adds variety and greater compass to his topics (so that the Political Register is an armoury and magazine for all the materials and weapons of political warfare), but it gives a greater zest and liveliness to his manner of treating them. Mr. Cobbett takes nothing for granted as what he has proved before; he does not write a book of reference. We see his ideas in their first concoction, fermenting and overflowing with the ebullitions of a lively conception. We look on at the actual process, and are put in immediate possession of the grounds and materials on which he forms his sanguine, unsettled conclusions. He does not give us samples of reasoning, but the whole solid mass, refuse and all.

> — 'He pours out all as plain
> As downright Shippen or as old Montaigne.' [39]

This is one cause of the clearness and force of his writings. An argument does not stop to stagnate and muddle in his brain, but passes at once to his paper. His ideas are served up, like pancakes, hot and hot. Fresh theories give him fresh courage. He is like a young and lusty bridegroom that divorces a favourite speculation every morning, and marries a new one every night. He is not wedded to his notions, not he. He has not one Mrs. Cobbett among all his opinions. He makes the most of the last thought that has come in his way, seizes fast hold of it, rumples it about in all directions with rough strong hands, has his wicked will of it, takes a surfeit, and throws it away.—Our author's changing his opinions for new ones is not so wonderful: what is more remarkable is his facility in forgetting his old ones. He does not pretend to consistency (like Mr. Coleridge);[40] he frankly disavows all connexion with himself. He feels no personal responsibility in this way, and

39 Alexander Pope, "Imitations of Horace," Satire I, 51-52.
40 Samuel Taylor Coleridge (1772-1834), English poet and critic.

cuts a friend or principle with the same decided indifference
that Antipholis of Ephesus [41] cuts Aegeon of Syracuse. It is a
hollow thing. The only time he ever grew romantic was in
bringing over the relics of Mr. Thomas Paine with him from
America to go a progress with them through the disaffected
districts. Scarce had he landed in Liverpool when he left the
bones of a great man to shift for themselves; and no sooner
did he arrive in London than he made a speech to disclaim
all participation in the political and theological sentiments
of his late idol, and to place the whole stock of his admiration
and enthusiasm towards him to the account of his financial
speculations, and of his having predicted the fate of paper-
money. If he had erected a little gold statue to him, it might
have proved the sincerity of this assertion: but to make a
martyr and a patron-saint of a man, and to dig up 'his can-
onised bones' [42] in order to expose them as objects of devotion
to the rabble's gaze, asks something that has more life and
spirit in it, more mind and vivifying soul, than has to do with
any calculation of pounds, shillings, and pence! The fact is,
he *ratted* from his own project. He found the thing not so
ripe as he had expected. His heart failed him: his enthusiasm
fled, and he made his retractation. His admiration is short-
lived: his contempt only is rooted, and his resentment lasting.
—The above was only one instance of his building too much
on practical *data*. He has an ill habit of prophesying, and goes
on, though still deceived. The art of prophesying does not
suit Mr. Cobbett's style. He has a knack of fixing names and
times and places. According to him, the Reformed Parliament
was to meet in March, 1818—it did not, and we heard no more
of the matter. When his predictions fail, he takes no farther
notice of them, but applies himself to new ones—like the
country-people who turn to see what weather there is in the
almanac for the next week, though it has been out in its
reckoning every day of the last.

Mr. Cobbett is great in attack, not in defence: he cannot

41 *The Comedy of Errors*, Act V, Sc. 1.
42 *Hamlet*, Act I, Sc. 4, l. 47.

fight an up-hill battle. He will not bear the least punishing.
If any one turns upon him (which few people like to do) he
immediately turns tail. Like an overgrown school-boy, he is so
used to have it all his own way, that he cannot submit to any
thing like competition or a struggle for the mastery; he must
lay on all the blows, and take none. He is bullying and
cowardly; a Big Ben in politics,[43] who will fall upon others
and crush them by his weight, but is not prepared for resistance, and is soon staggered by a few smart blows. Whenever
he has been set upon he has slunk out of the controversy. The
Edinburgh Review made (what is called) a dead set at him
some years ago, to which he only retorted by an eulogy on the
superior neatness of an English kitchen-garden to a Scotch
one. I remember going one day into a bookseller's shop in
Fleet-street to ask for the Review; and on my expressing my
opinion to a young Scotchman, who stood behind the counter,
that Mr. Cobbett might hit as hard in his reply, the North
Briton said with some alarm—'But you don't think, Sir, Mr.
Cobbett will be able to injure the Scottish nation?' I said I
could not speak to that point, but I thought he was very well
able to defend himself. He however did not, but has borne
a grudge to the Edinburgh Review ever since, which he hates
worse than the Quarterly. I cannot say I do.[44]

[43] Thomas Moore, "Epistle from Tom Cribb to Big Ben."
What! Ben, my old hero, is this your renown
Is this the new go?—kick a man when he's down?
When the foe has knocked under, to tread on him then—
By the fist of my father, I blush for thee, Ben!

[44] This is an understatement, for the *Quarterly* once referred to Hazlitt's
work as "Loathsome trash." Hazlitt's note: Mr. Cobbett speaks almost as
well as he writes. The only time I ever saw him he seemed to me a very
pleasant man—easy of access, affable, clear-headed, simple and mild in
his manner, deliberate and unruffled in his speech, though some of his
expressions were not very qualified. His figure is tall and portly. He has
a good sensible face—rather full, with little grey eyes, a hard, square
forehead, a ruddy complexion, with hair grey or powered; and had on a
scarlet broadcloth waistcoat with the flaps of the pockets hanging down,
as was the custom for gentlemen-farmers in the last century, or as we
see it in the pictures of Members of Parliament in the reign of George I.
I certainly did not think less favourably of him for seeing him.

William Hazlitt

ON FAMILIAR STYLE [1]

It is not easy to write a familiar style. Many people mistake
a familiar for a vulgar style, and suppose that to write without
affectation is to write at random. On the contrary, there is
nothing that requires more precision, and, if I may so say,
purity of expression, than the style I am speaking of. It utterly
rejects not only all unmeaning pomp, but all low, cant
phrases, and loose, unconnected, *slipshod* allusions. It is not
to take the first word that offers, but the best word in common
use; it is not to throw words together in any combinations we
please, but to follow and avail ourselves of the true idiom of
the language. To write a genuine familiar or truly English
style, is to write as any one would speak in common conversations, who had a thorough command and choice of words, or
who could discourse with ease, force, and perspicuity, setting
aside all pedantic and oratorical flourishes. Or to give another
illustration, to write naturally is the same thing in regard to
common conversation, as to read naturally is in regard to
common speech. It does not follow that it is an easy thing to
give the true accent and inflection to the words you utter,
because you do not attempt to rise above the level of ordinary
life and colloquial speaking. You do not assume indeed the
solemnity of the pulpit, or the tone of stage-declamation:
neither are you at liberty to gabble on at a venture, without
emphasis or discretion, or to resort to vulgar dialect or
clownish pronunciation. You must steer a middle course. You
are tied down to a given and appropriate articulation, which

[1] From *Table-Talk; or, Original Essays*, Vol. II (1822).

is determined by the habitual associations between sense and sound, and which you can only hit by entering into the author's meaning, as you must find the proper words and style to express yourself by fixing your thoughts on the subject you have to write about. Any one may mouth out a passage with a theatrical cadence, or get upon stilts to tell his thoughts: but to write or speak with propriety and simplicity is a more difficult task. Thus it is easy to affect a pompous style, to use a word twice as big as the thing you want to express: it is not so easy to pitch upon the very word that exactly fits it. Out of eight or ten words equally common, equally intelligible, with nearly equal pretensions, it is a matter of some nicety and discrimination to pick out the very one, the preferablesness of which is scarcely perceptible, but decisive. The reason why I object to Dr. Johnson's style [2] is, that there is no discrimination, no selection, no variety in it. He uses none but 'tall, opaque words,' [3] taken from the 'first row of the rubric:' [4]— words with the greatest number of syllables, or Latin phrases with merely English terminations. If a fine style depended on this sort of arbitrary pretension, it would be fair to judge of an author's elegance by the measurement of his words, and the substitution of foreign circumlocutions (with no precise associations) for the mother-tongue.[5] How simple it is to be dignified without ease, to be pompous without meaning! Surely, it is but a mechanical rule for avoiding what is low to be always pedantic and affected. It is clear you cannot use a vulgar English word, if you never use a common English word at all. A fine tact is shewn in adhering to those which are perfectly common, and yet never falling into any expres-

[2] See Johnson's "Preface to Shakespeare," earlier in this volume.

[3] Cited by Hazlitt in an earlier essay as well, but no source is known. At times, Hazlitt seemed to dignify especially striking phrases with the sense of quotation, even though he may have invented them himself.

[4] *Hamlet*, Act II, Sc. 2, l. 447. Hazlitt was evidently quoting from Pope's text of Shakespeare, which in this instance is inaccurate.

[5] Hazlitt's note: I have heard of such a thing as an author, who makes it a rule never to admit a monysyllable into his vapid verse. Yet the charm and sweetness of Marlow's lines depended often on their being made up almost entirely of monysyllables.

sions which are debased by disgusting circumstances, or which owe their signification and point to technical or professional allusions. A truly natural or familiar style can never be quaint or vulgar, for this reason, that it is of universal force and applicability, and that quaintness and vulgarity arise out of the immediate connection of certain words with coarse and disagreeable, or with confined ideas. The last form what we understand by *cant* or *slang* phrases.—To give an example of what is not very clear in the general statement. I should say that the phrase *To cut with a knife,* or *To cut a piece of wood,* is perfectly free from vulgarity, because it is perfectly common: but to *cut an acquaintance* is not quite unexceptionable, because it is not perfectly common or intelligible, and has hardly yet escaped out of the limits of slang phraseology. I should hardly therefore use the word in this sense without putting it in italics as a license of expression, to be received *cum grano salis.* All provincial or bye-phrases come under the same mark of reprobation—all such as the writer transfers to the page from his fire-side or a particular *coterie,* or that he invents for his own sole use and convenience. I conceive that words are like money, not the worse for being common, but that it is the stamp of custom alone that gives them circulation or value. I am fastidious in this respect, and would almost as soon coin the currency of the realm as counterfeit the King's English. I never invented or gave a new and unauthorised meaning to any word but one single one (the term *impersonal* applied to feelings) and that was in an abstruse metaphysical discussion to express a very difficult distinction. I have been (I know) loudly accused of revelling in vulgarisms and broken English.[6] I cannot speak to that point: but so far I plead guilty to the determined use of

6 The *Quarterly's* review of Volume I of *Table-Talk* said that "Mr. Hazlitt's character as a writer may, we think, be not inaptly designated by a term borrowed from the vocabulary of our translantic brethren, which, though cacophonous, is sufficiently expressive.... The word to which we allude, Slang-Whanger, is interpreted in the American dictionary to be 'One who makes use of political or other gabble, vulgarly called slang, that serves to amuse the rabble.' "

acknowledged idioms and common elliptical expressions. I am not sure that the critics in question know the one from the other, that is, can distinguish any medium between formal pedantry and the most barbarous solecism. As an author, I endeavour to employ plain words and popular modes of construction, as were I a chapman and dealer, I should common weights and measures.

The proper force of words lies not in the words themselves, but in their application. A word may be a fine-sounding word, of an unusual length, and very imposing from its learning and novelty, and yet in the connection in which it is introduced, may be quite pointless and irrelevant. It is not pomp or pretension, but the adaptation of the expression to the idea that clenches a writer's meaning:—as it is not the size or glossiness of the materials, but their being fitted each to its place, that gives strength to the arch; or as the pegs and nails are as necessary to the support of the building as the larger timbers, and more so than the mere shewy, unsubstantial ornaments. I hate any thing that occupies more space that it is worth. I hate to see a load of band-boxes go along the street, and I hate to see a parcel of big words without any thing in them. A person who does not deliberately dispose of all his thoughts alike in cumbrous draperies and flimsy disguises, may strike out twenty varieties of familiar everyday language, each coming somewhat nearer to the feeling he wants to convey, and at last not hit upon that particular and only one, which may be said to be identical with the exact impression in his mind. This would seem to shew that Mr. Cobbett is hardly right in saying that the first word that occurs is always the best.[7] It may be a very good one; and yet a better may present itself on reflection or from time to time. It should be suggested naturally, however, and spontaneously, from a fresh and lively conception of the subject. We seldom succeed by trying at im-

---

[7] "Use the first words that occur to you, and never attempt to *alter a thought*; for, that which has come of itself into your mind is likely to pass into that of another more readily and with more effect than anything which you can, by reflection, invent." Letter xxxiii, *A Grammar of the English Language.*

provement, or by merely substituting one word for another that we are not satisfied with, as we cannot recollect the name of a place or person by merely plaguing ourselves about it. We wander farther from the point by persisting in a wrong scent; but it starts up accidentally in the memory when we least expected it, by touching some link in the chain of previous association.

There are those who hoard up and make a cautious display of nothing but rich and rare phraseology;—ancient medals, obscure coins, and Spanish pieces of eight. They are very curious to inspect; but I myself would neither offer nor take them in the course of exchange. A sprinkling of archaisms is not amiss; but a tissue of obsolete expressions is more fit *for keep than wear.* I do not say I would not use any phrase that had been brought into fashion before the middle or the end of the last century; but I should be shy of using any that had not been employed by any approved author during the whole of that time. Words, like clothes, get old-fashioned, or mean and ridiculous, when they have been for some time laid aside. Mr. Lamb [8] is the only imitator of old English style I can read with pleasure; and he is so thoroughly imbued with the spirit of his authors, that the idea of imitation is almost done away. There is an inward unction, a marrowy vein both in the thought and feeling, an intuition, deep and lively, of his subject, that carries off any quaintness or awkwardness arising from an antiquated style and dress. The matter is completely his own, though the manner is assumed. Perhaps his ideas are altogether so marked and individual, as to require their point and pungency to be neutralised by the affection of a singular but traditional form of conveyance. Tricked out in the prevailing costume, they would probably seem more startling and out of the way. The old English authors, Burton, Fuller, Coryate, Sir Thomas Brown,[9] are a kind of mediators between

[8] Charles Lamb (1775-1834), author of the *Essays of Elia,* a close friend of Hazlitt, and one of the most distinguished English essayists.

[9] Burton, Fuller, Coryate, and Sir Thomas Brown (e) were prose writers of the Renaissance and seventeenth century.

us and the more eccentric and whimsical modern, reconciling
us to his peculiarities. I do not however know how far this is
the case or not, till he condescends to write like one of us.
I must confess that what I like best of his papers under the
signature of Elia (still I do not presume, amidst such excellence, to decide what is most excellent) is the account of
Mrs. Battle's Opinions on Whist, which is also the most free
from obsolete allusions and turns of expression—

'A well of native English undefiled.' 10

To those acquainted with his admired prototypes, these Essays
of the ingenious and highly gifted author have the same sort
of charm relish, that Erasmus's Colloquies 11 or a fine piece
of modern Latin have to the classical scholar. Certainly, I do
not know any borrowed pencil that has more power or felicity
of execution than the one of which I have here been speaking.

It is as easy to write a gaudy style without ideas, as it is to
spread a pallet of shewy colours, or to smear in a flaunting
transparency. 'What do you read?' 12—'Words, words.'—'What
is the matter?'—'*Nothing*,' it might be answered. The florid
style is the reverse of the familiar. The last is employed as
an unvarnished medium to convey ideas; the first is resorted
to as a spangled veil to conceal the want of them. When there
is nothing to be set down but words, it costs little to have
them fine. Look through the dictionary, and cull out a
florilegium, rival the *tulippomania.*13 *Rouge* high enough, and
never mind the natural complexion. The vulgar, who are not
in the secret, will admire the look of preternatural health and
vigour; and the fashionable, who regard only appearances,
will be delighted with the imposition. Keep to your sounding

10 One of the most famous lines of English verse (Spenser, *The Faerie
Queen,* Book IV, Canto III, 1. 32), here reshaped from its actual reading:
"Dan Chaucer, well of English undefyled."

11 The *Colloquia* of Desiderius Erasmus (1466-1536), written in Latin
and printed in 1519. The implication is that Lamb's style is as archaic
and artificial as the Latin of the Renaissance.

12 *Hamlet,* Act 2, Sc. 2, 1. 193.

13 Make an anthology of choice terms (flowery words), and go wild in
the process.

generalities, your tinkling phrases, and all will be well. Swell out an unmeaning truism to a perfect tympany of style. A thought, a distinction is the rock on which all this brittle cargo of verbiage splits at once. Such writers have merely *verbal* imaginations, that retain nothing but words. Or their puny thoughts have dragon-wings, all green and gold. They soar far above the vulgar failing of the *Sermo humi obrepens* [14]— their most ordinary speech is never short of an hyperbole, splendid, imposing, vague, incomprehensible, magniloquent, a cento of sounding common-places. If some of us, whose 'ambition is more lowly,' [15] pry a little too narrowly into nooks and corners to pick up a number of 'unconsidered trifles,' [16] they never once direct their eyes or lift their hands to seize on any but the most gorgeous, tarnished, thread-bare patch-work set of phrases, the left-off finery of poetic extravagance, transmitted down through successive generations of barren pretenders. If they criticise actors and actresses, a huddled phantasmagoria of feathers, spangles, floods of light, and oceans of sound float before their morbid sense, which they paint in the style of Ancient Pistol. Not a glimpse can you get of the merits or defects of the performers: they are hidden in a profusion of barbarous epithets and wilful rhodomontade. Our hypercritics are not thinking of these little fantoccini beings—

'That strut and fret their hour upon the stage'—[17]

but of tall phantoms of words, abstractions, *genera* and *species,* sweeping clauses, periods that unite the Poles, forced alliterations, astounding antitheses—

'And on their pens *Fustian* sits plumed.' [18]

---

[14] Horace, *Epistles II,* 1. 251. Hazlitt misquotes Horace, who wrote "Nec sermones ego mallem/repentes per humum..." As for me, I wouldn't prefer my "little conversations" that creep along the ground to epic narrations.

[15] Possibly paraphrased from *The Tempest,* Act I, Sc. 2, 1. 480-483.

[16] *A Winter's Tale,* Act IV, Sc. 3, 1. 26.

[17] *Macbeth,* Act V, Sc. 4, 1. 25.

[18] Ironic paraphrase of *Paradise Lost,* Book IV, 988-989.

If they describe kings and queens, it is an Eastern pageant.
The Coronation at either House is nothing to it. We get at
four repeated images—a curtain, a throne, a sceptre, and a
foot-stool. These are with them the wardrobe of a lofty
imagination; and they turn their servile strains to servile uses.
Do we read a description of pictures? It is not a reflection of
tones and hues which 'nature's own sweet and cunning hand
laid on,' [19] but piles of precious stones, rubies, pearls, em-
eralds, Golconda's mines,[20] and all the blazonry of art. Such
persons are in fact besotted with words, and their brains are
turned with the glittering, but empty and sterile phantoms of
things. Personifications, capital letters, seas of sunbeams,
visions of glory, shining inscriptions, the figures of a transparency, Britannia with her shield, or Hope leaning on an
anchor, make up their stock in trade. They may be considered as *hieroglyphical* writers. Images stand out in their
minds isolated and important merely in themselves, without
any ground-work of feeling—there is no context in their
imaginations. Words affect them in the same way, by the mere
sound, that is, by their possible, not by their actual application to the subject in hand. They are fascinated by first
appearances, and have no sense of consequences. Nothing
more is meant by them than meets the ear: they understand or
feel nothing more than meets their eye. The web and texture
of the universe, and of the heart of man, is a mystery to them:
they have no faculty that strikes a chord in unison with it.
They cannot get beyond the daubings of fancy, the varnish of
sentiment. Objects are not linked to feelings, words to things,
but images revolve in splendid mockery, words represent
themselves in their strange rhapsodies. The categories of such
a mind are pride and ignorance—pride in outside show, to
which they sacrifice every thing, and ignorance of the true
worth and hidden structure both of words and things. With a
sovereign contempt for what is familiar and natural, they are
the slaves of vulgar affectation—of a routine of high-flown

19 *Twelfth Night*, Act I, Sc. 5, l. 258.
20 Synonym for "a mine of wealth."

phrases. Scorning to imitate realities, they are unable to invent any thing, to strike out one original idea. They are not copyists of nature, it is true: but they are the poorest of all plagiarists, the plagiarists of words. All is far-fetched, dear-bought, artificial, oriental in subject and allusion: all is mechanical, conventional, vapid, formal, pedantic in style and execution. They startle and confound the understanding of the reader, by the remoteness and obscurity of their illustrations: they soothe the ear by the monotony of the same everlasting round of circuitous metaphors. They are the *mock-school* in poetry and prose. They flounder about between fustian in expression, and bathes in sentiment. They tantalise the fancy, but never reach the head nor touch the heart. Their Temple of Fame is like a shadowy structure raised by Dulness to Vanity, or like Cowper's description [21] of the Empress of Russia's palace of ice, as 'worthless as in shew 'twas glittering'—

'It smiled, and it was cold!'

21 William Cowper, *The Task*, Book V, 173-176.

Ralph Waldo Emerson

Ralph Waldo Emerson (1803-1882), after serving briefly as a Unitarian minister, turned his full energies to a career as essayist and lecturer. He has long stood at the center of American intellectual history, because of his influence (on Thoreau and Whitman, for example) and because of his ability to comprehend and embody basic ideals of the American mind. His prime intent is to unsettle, provoke, and suggest, and his manner of writing has as its prime aim the revelation of new possibilities in idea and phrase. Emerson was educated at Harvard. Principal works: Essays, First Series *(1841);* Representative Men *(1850);* English Traits *(1856);* Society and Solitude *(1870).*

SELF-RELIANCE [1]

Ne te quaesiveris extra.[2]

> Man is his own star; and the soul that can
> Render an honest and a perfect man,
> Commands all light, all influence, all fate;
> Nothing to him falls early or too late.
> Our acts our angels are, or good or ill,
> Our fatal shadows that walk by us still.

Epilogue to Beaumont and Fletcher's Honest Man's Fortune

> Cast the bantling on the rocks,
> Suckle him with the she-wolf's teat,

---

[1] From *Essays, First Series* (1841).
[2] Do not seek yourself outside yourself. Persius, *Satire* I, 7.

> Wintered with the hawk and fox,
> Power and speed be hands and feet.[3]

I read the other day some verses written by an eminent painter which were original not conventional. Always the soul hears an admonition in such lines, let the subject be what it may. The sentiment they instil is of more value than any thought they may contain. To believe your own thought, to believe that what is true for you in your private heart is true for all men,—that is genius. Speak your latent conviction, and it shall be universal sense; for always the inmost becomes the outmost—and our first thought is rendered back to us by the trumpets of the Last Judgment. Familiar as the voice of the mind is to each, the highest merit we ascribe to Moses, Plato and Milton is that they set at naught books and traditions, and spoke not what men, but what they thought. A man should learn to detect and watch that gleam of light which flashes across his mind from within, more than the lustre of the firmament of bards and sages. Yet he dismisses without notice his thought, because it is his. In every work of genius we recognize our own rejected thoughts; they come back to us with a certain alienated majesty. Great works of art have no more affecting lesson for us than this. They teach us to abide by our spontaneous impression with good-humored inflexibility then most when the whole cry of voices is on the other side. Else to-morrow a stranger will say with masterly good sense precisely what we have thought and felt all the time, and we shall be forced to take with shame our own opinion from another.

There is a time in every man's education when he arrives at the conviction that envy is ignorance; that imitation is suicide; that he must take himself for better for worse as his portion; that though the wide universe is full of good, no kernel of nourishing corn can come to him but through his toil bestowed on that plot of ground which is given to him to till. The power which resides in him is new in nature,

3 Written by Emerson.

and none but he knows what that is which he can do, nor does he know until he has tried. Not for nothing one face, one character, one fact, makes much impression on him, and another none. It is not without preëstablished harmony, this sculpture in the memory. The eye was placed where one ray should fall, that it might testify of that particular ray. Bravely let him speak the utmost syllable of his confession. We but half express ourselves, and are ashamed of that divine idea which each of us represents. It may be safely trusted as proportionate and of good issues, so it be faithfully imparted, but God will not have his work made manifest by cowards. It needs a divine man to exhibit anything divine. A man is relieved and gay when he has put his heart into his work and done his best; but what he has said or done otherwise shall give him no peace. It is a deliverance which does not deliver. In the attempt his genius deserts him; no muse befriends; no invention, no hope.

Trust thyself: every heart vibrates to that iron string. Accept the place the divine providence has found for you, the society of your contemporaries, the connexion of events. Great men have always done so, and confided themselves childlike to the genius of their age, betraying their perception that the Eternal was stirring at their heart, working through their hands, predominating in all their being. And we are now men, and must accept in the highest mind the same transcendent destiny; and not pinched in a corner, not cowards fleeing before a revolution, but redeemers and benefactors, pious aspirants to be noble clay under the Almighty effort let us advance on Chaos and the Dark.

What pretty oracles nature yields us on this text in the face and behavior of children, babes, and even brutes. That divided and rebel mind, that distrust of a sentiment because our arithmetic has computed the strength and means opposed to our purpose, these have not. Their mind being whole, their eye is as yet unconquered, and when we look in their faces, we are disconcerted. Infancy conforms to nobody; all conform to it; so that one babe commonly makes four or five out of the adults who prattle and play to it. So God has armed youth and puberty and manhood no less with its own piquancy and charm, and made it enviable and gracious and its claims not to be put by, if it will stand by itself. Do not think the youth has no force, because he cannot speak to you and me. Hark! in the next room who spoke so clear and emphatic? It seems he knows how to speak to his contemporaries. Good Heaven! it is he! it is that very lump of bashfulness and phlegm which for weeks has done nothing but eat when you were by, and now rolls out these words like bell-strokes. It seems he knows how to speak to his contemporaries. Bashful or bold then, he well knew how to make us seniors very unnecessary.

The nonchalance of boys who are sure of a dinner, and would disdain as much as a lord to do or say aught to conciliate one, is the healthy attitude of human nature. How is a boy the master of society; independent, irresponsible, looking out from his corner on such people and facts as pass by, he tries and sentences them on their merits, in the swift, summary way of boys, as good, bad, interesting, silly, eloquent, troublesome. He cumbers himself never about consequences, but interest; he gives an independent, genuine verdict. You must court him; he does not court you. But the man is as it were clapped into jail by his consciousness. As soon as he has once acted or spoken with eclat he is a committed person, watched by the sympathy or the hatred of hundreds, whose affections must now enter into his account. There is no Lethe for this.[4] Ah, that he could pass again into his neutral, godlike independence! Who can thus lose all pledge and, having observed, observe again from the same unaffected, unbiased, unbribable, unaffrighted innocence, must always engage the poet's and the man's regards. Of such an immortal youth the force would be felt. He would utter opinions on all passing affairs, which being seen to be not private but necessary, would sink like darts into the ear of men and put them in fear.

[4] He cannot be washed free of the memory of the judgment of others.

These are the voices which we hear in solitude, but they grow faint and inaudible as we enter into the world. Society everywhere is in conspiracy against the manhood of every one of its members. Society is a joint-stock company, in which the members agree, for the better securing of his bread to each shareholder, to surrender the liberty and culture of the eater. The virtue in most request is conformity. Self-reliance is its aversion. It loves not realities and creators, but names and customs.

Whoso would be a man, must be a nonconformist. He who would gather immortal palms must not be hindered by the name of goodness, but must explore if it be goodness. Nothing is at last sacred but the integrity of our own mind. Absolve you to yourself, and you shall have the suffrage of the world. I remember an answer which when quite young I was prompted to make to a valued adviser who was wont to importune me with the dear old doctrines of the church. On my saying, What have I to do with the sacredness of traditions, if I live wholly from within? my friend suggested,— "But these impulses may be from below, not from above." I replied, "They do not seem to me to be such; but if I am the devil's child, I will live then from the devil." No law can be sacred to me but that of my nature. Good and bad are but names very readily transferable to that or this; the only right is what is after my constitution; the only wrong what is against it. A man is to carry himself in the presence of all opposition as if every thing were titular and ephemeral but he. I am ashamed to think how easily we capitulate to badges and names, to large societies and dead institutions. Every decent and well-spoken individual affects and sways me more than is right. I ought to go upright and vital, and speak the rude truth in all ways. If malice and vanity wear the coat of philanthrophy, shall that pass? If an angry bigot assumes this bountiful cause of Abolition, and comes to me with his last news from Barbadoes, why should I not say to him, "Go love thy infant; love thy wood-chopper; be good-natured and modest; have that grace; and never varnish your hard, uncharitable ambition with this incredible tenderness for black folk a thousand miles off. Thy love afar is spite at home." Rough and graceless would be such greeting, but truth is handsomer than the affectation of love. Your goodness must have some edge to it,—else it is none. The doctrine of hatred must be preached, as the counteraction of the doctrine of love, when that pules and whines. I shun father and mother and wife and brother when my genius calls me. I would write on the lintels of the door-post, *Whim*. I hope it is somewhat better than whim at last, but we cannot spend the day in explanation. Expect me not to show cause why I seek or why I exclude company. Then, again, do not tell me, as a good man did to-day, of my obligation to put all poor men in good situations. Are they *my* poor? I tell thee, thou foolish philanthropist, that I grudge the dollar, the dime, the cent I give to such men as do not belong to me and to whom I do not belong. There is a class of persons to whom by all spiritual affinity I am bought and sold; for them I will go to prison if need be; but your miscellaneous popular charities; the education at college of fools; the building of meeting-houses to the vain end to which many now stand; alms to sots, and the thousandfold Relief Societies;—though I confess with shame I sometimes succumb and give the dollar, it is a wicked dollar, which by-and-by I shall have the manhood to withhold.

Virtues, are, in the popular estimate, rather the exception than the rule. There is the man *and* his virtues. Men do what is called a good action, as some piece of courage or charity, much as they would pay a fine in expiation of daily non-appearance on parade. Their works are done as an apology or extenuation of their living in the world,—as invalids and the insane pay a high board. Their virtues are penances. I do not wish to expiate, but to live. My life is not an apology, but a life. It is for itself and not for a spectacle. I much prefer that it should be of a lower strain, so it be genuine and equal, than that it should be glittering and unsteady. I wish it to be sound and sweet, and not to need diet and bleeding. My life should be unique; it should be an alms, a battle, a conquest, a medicine. I ask primary evidence that you are a man, and refuse this appeal from the man to his actions. I know that for myself it makes no difference whether I do or forbear those actions which are reckoned excellent. I cannot consent to pay for a privilege where I have intrinsic right. Few and mean as my gifts may be, I actually am, and do not need for my own assurance or the assurance of my fellows and secondary testimony.

What I must do is all that concerns me, not what the people think. This rule, equally arduous in actual and in intellectual life, may serve for the whole distinction between greatness and meanness. It is the harder because you will always find those who think they know what is your duty better than you know it. It is easy in the world to live after the world's opinion; it is easy in solitude to live after our own; but the great man is he who in the midst of the crowd keeps with perfect sweetness the independence of solitude.

The objection to conforming to usages that have become dead to you is that it scatters your force. It loses your time and blurs the impression of your character. If you maintain a dead church, contribute to a dead Bible Society, vote with a great party either for the Government or against it, spread your table like base housekeepers,—under all these screens I have difficulty to detect the precise man you are. And of course so much force is withdrawn from your proper life. But do your thing, and I shall know you. Do your work, and you shall reinforce yourself. A man must consider what a blindman's-buff is this game of conformity. If I know your sect I anticipate your argument. I hear a preacher announce for his text and topic the expediency of one of the institutions of his church. Do I not know beforehand that not possibly can he say a new and spontaneous word? Do I not know that with all this ostentation of examining the grounds of the institution he will do no such thing? Do I not know that he is pledged to himself not to look but at one side, the permitted side, not as a man, but as a parish minister? He is a retained attorney, and these airs of the bench are the emptiest affection. Well, most men have bound their eyes with one or another handkerchief, and attached themselves to some one of these communities of opinion. This conformity makes them not false in a few particulars, authors of a few lies, but false in all particulars. Their every truth is not quite true. Their two is not the real two, their four not the real four: so that every word they say chagrins us and we know not where to begin to set them right. Meantime nature is not slow to equip us in the prison-uniform of the party to which we adhere. We come to wear one cut of face and figure, and acquire by degrees the gentlest asinine expression. There is a mortifying experience in particular, which does not fail to wreak itself also in the general history; I mean "the foolish face of praise," the forced smile which we put on in company where we do not feel at ease, in answer to conversation which does not interest us. The muscles, not spontaneously moved but moved by a low usurping wilfulness, grow tight about the outline of the face, and make the most disagreeable sensation; a sensation of rebuke and warning which no brave young man will suffer twice.

For non-conformity the world whips you with its displeasure. And therefore a man must know how to estimate a sour face. The bystanders look askance on him in the public street or in the friend's parlor. If this aversion had its origin in contempt and resistance like his own he might well go home with a sad countenance; but the sour faces of the multitude, like their sweet faces, have no deep cause—disguise no god, but are put on and off as the wind blows and a newspaper directs. Yet is the discontent of the multitude more formidable than that of the senate and the college. It is easy enough for a firm man who knows the world to brook the rage of the cultivated classes. Their rage is decorous and prudent, for they are timid, as being very vulnerable themselves. But when to their feminine rage the indignation of the people is added, when the ignorant and the poor are aroused, when the unintelligent brute force that lies at the bottom of society is made to growl and mow, it needs the habit of magnanimity and religion to treat it godlike as a trifle of no concernment.

The other terror that scares us from self-trust is our consistency; a reverence for our past act or word because the eyes of others have no other data for computing our orbit than our past acts, and we are loath to disappoint them.

But why should you keep your head over your shoulder? Why drag about this monstrous corpse of your memory, lest you contradict somewhat you have stated in this or that public place? Suppose you should contradict yourself; what then? It seems to be a rule of wisdom never to rely on your memory alone, scarcely even in acts of pure memory, but to bring the past for judgment into the thousand-eyed present, and live ever in a new day. Trust your emotion. In your metaphysics you have denied personality to the Deity, yet when the devout motions of the soul come, yield to them heart and life, though they should clothe God with shape and color. Leave your theory, as Joseph his coat in the hand of the harlot, [5] and flee.

A foolish consistency is the hobgoblin of little minds, adored by little statesmen and philosophers and divines. With consistency a great soul has simply nothing to do. He may as well concern himself with his shadow on the wall. Out upon your guarded lips! Sew them up with packthread, do. Else if you would be a man speak what you think to-day in words as hard as cannon balls, and to-morrow speak what to-morrow thinks in hard words again, though it contradict every thing you said to-day. Ah, then, exclaim the aged ladies, you shall be sure to be misunderstood! Misunderstood! It is a right fool's word. Is it so bad then to be misunderstood? Pythagoras was misunderstood, and Socrates, and Jesus, and Luther, and Copernicus, and Galileo, and Newton, and every pure and wise spirit that ever took flesh. To be great is to be misunderstood.

I suppose no man can violate his nature. All the sallies of his will are rounded in by the law of his being, as the in-

[5] The tale of Joseph and Potiphar's wife, Genesis xxix.

equalities of Andes and Himmaleh [6] are insignificant in the curve of the sphere. Nor does it matter how you gauge and try him. A character is like an acrostic or Alexandrian stanza; —read it forward, backward, or across, it still spells the same thing. In this pleasing contrite wood-life which God allows me, let me record day by day my honest thought without prospect or retrospect, and I cannot doubt, it will be found symmetrical, though I mean it not and see it not. My book should smell of pines and resound with the hum of insects. The swallow over my window should interweave that thread or straw he carries in his bill into my web also. We pass for what we are. Character teaches above our wills. Men imagine that they communicate their virtue or vice only by overt actions, and do not see that virtue or vice emit a breath every moment.

Fear never but you shall be consistent in whatever variety of actions, so they be each honest and natural in their hour. For of one will, the actions will be harmonious, however unlike they seem. These varieties are lost sight of when seen at a little distance, at a little height of thought. One tendency unites them all. The voyage of the best ship is a zigzag line of a hundred tacks. This is only microscopic criticism. See the line from a sufficient distance, and it straightens itself to the average tendency. Your genuine action will explain itself and will explain your other genuine actions. Your conformity explains nothing. Act singly, and what you have already done singly will justify you now. Greatness always appeals to the future. If I can be great enough now to do right and scorn eyes, I must have done so much right before as to defend me now. Be it how it will, do right now. Always scorn appearances and you always may. The force of character is cumulative. All the foregone days of virtue work their health into this. What makes the majesty of the heroes of the senate and the field, which so fills the imagination? The consciousness of a train of great days and victories behind. There they all stand and shed an united light on the advancing actor. He is attended

6 The Himalayas.

as by a visible escort of angels to every man's eye. That is it which throws thunder into Chatham's voice, [7] and dignity into Washington's port, and America into Adam's eye. Honor is venerable to us because it is no ephemeris. It is always ancient virtue. We worship it to-day because it is not of to-day. We love it and pay it homage because it is not a trap for our love and homage, but is self-dependent, self-derived, and therefore of an old immaculate pedigree, even if shown in a young person.

I hope in these days we have heard the last of conformity and consistency. Let the words be gazetted and ridiculous henceforward. Instead of the gong for dinner, let us hear a whistle from the Spartan fife. Let us bow and apologize never more. A great man is coming to eat at my house. I do not wish to please him: I wish that he should wish to please me. I will stand here for humanity, and though I would make it kind, I would make it true. Let us affront and reprimand the smooth mediocrity and squalid contentment of the times, and hurl in the face of custom and trade and office, the fact which is the upshot of all history, that there is a great responsible Thinker and Actor moving wherever moves a man; that a true man belongs to no other time or place, but is the centre of things. Where he is, there is nature. He measures you and all men and all events. You are constrained to accept his standard. Ordinarily, every body in society reminds us of somewhat else, or of some other person. Character, reality, reminds you of nothing else; it takes place of the whole creation. The man must be so much that he must make all circumstances in-different—put all means into the shade. This all great men are and do. Every true man is a cause, a country, and an age; requires infinite spaces and numbers and time fully to ac-complish his thought;—and posterity seem to follow his steps as a procession. A man Caesar is born, and for ages after we have a Roman Empire. Christ is born, and millions of minds so grow and cleave to his genius that he is confounded with

[7] The reference is to William Pitt, first earl of Chatham (1708-1778), famous English statesman and orator.

virtue and the possible of man. An institution is the length-
ened shadow of one man; as, the Reformation, of Luther;
Quakerism, of Fox; Methodism, of Wesley; Abolition, of
Clarkson.[8] Scipio, Milton called "the height of Rome"; and
all history resolves itself very easily into the biography of a
few stout and earnest persons.

Let a man then know his worth, and keep things under
his feet. Let him not peep or steal, or skulk up and down with
the air of a charity-boy, a bastard, or an interloper in the
world which exists for him. But the man in the street, finding
no worth in himself which corresponds to the force which
built a tower or sculptured a marble god, feels poor when
he looks on these. To him a palace, a statue, or a costly book
have an alien and forbidding air, much like a gay equipage,
and seem to say like that, "Who are you, sir?" Yet they all are
his, suitors for his notice, petitioners to his faculties that they
will come out and take possession. The picture waits for my
verdict; it is not to command me, but I am to settle its claim
to praise. That popular fable of the sot who was picked up
dead drunk in the street, carried to the duke's house, washed
and dressed and laid in the duke's bed, and, on his waking,
treated with all obsequious ceremony like the duke, and
assured that he had been insane—owes its popularity to the
fact it symbolizes so well the state of man, who is in the world
a sort of sot, but now and then wakes up, exercises his reason
and finds himself a true prince.

Our reading is mendicant and sycophantic. In history our
imagination makes fools of us, plays us false. Kingdom and
lordship, power and estate, are a gaudier vocabulary than
private John and Edward in a small house and common day's
work: but the things of life are the same to both: the sum
total of both is the same. Why all this deference to Alfred
and Scanderbeg and Gustavus? [9] Suppose they were virtuous;
did they wear out virtue? As great a stake depends on your

8 Leader of the Abolitionist movement in England.
9 Alfred, Scanderbeg, and Gustavus were, respectively, Saxon, Albanian,
and Swedish national heroes and rulers.

private act to-day as followed their public and renowned steps. When private men shall act with original views, the lustre will be transferred from the actions of kings to those of gentlemen.

The world has indeed been instructed by its kings, who have so magnetized the eyes of nations. It has been taught by this colossal symbol the mutual reverence that is due from man to man. The joyful loyalty with which men have everywhere suffered the king, the noble, or the great proprietor to walk among them by a law of his own, make his own scale of men and things and reverse theirs, pay for benefits not with money but with honor, and represent the Law in his person, was the hieroglyphic by which they obscurely signified their consciousness of their own right and comeliness, the right of every man.

The magnetism which all original action exerts is explained when we inquire the reason of self-trust. Who is the Trustee? What is the aboriginal Self, on which a universal reliance may be grounded? What is the nature and power of that science-baffling star, without parallax, without calculable elements, which shoots a ray of beauty even into trivial and impure actions, if the least mark of independence appear? The inquiry leads us to that source, at once the essence of genius, the essence of virtue, and the essence of life, which we call Spontaneity or Instinct. We denote this primary wisdom as Intuition, whilst all later teachings are tuitions. In that deep force, the last fact behind which analysis cannot go, all things find their common origin. For the sense of being which in calm hours rises, we know not how, in the soul, is not diverse from things, from space, from light, from time, from man, but one with them and proceedeth obviously from the same source whence their life and being also proceedeth. We first share the life by which things exist and afterwards see them as appearances in nature and forget that we have shared their cause. Here is the fountain of action and the fountain of thought. Here are the lungs of that inspiration which giveth man wisdom, of that inspiration of man which cannot be

denied without impiety and atheism. We lie in the lap of immense intelligence, which makes us organs of its activity and
receivers of its truth. When we discern justice, when we discern truth, we do nothing of ourselves, but allow a passage
to its beams. If we ask whence this comes, if we seek to pry
into the soul that causes—all metaphysics, all philosophy
is at fault. Its presence or its absence is all we can affirm.
Every man discerns between the voluntary acts of his mind
and his involuntary perceptions. And to his involuntary perceptions he knows a perfect respect is due. He may err in the
expression of them, but he knows that these things are so,
like day and night, not to be disputed. All my wilful actions
and acquisitions are but roving;—the most trivial reverie, the
faintest native emotion, are domestic and divine. Thoughtless
people contradict as readily the statement of perceptions as
of opinions, or rather much more readily; for they do not distinguish between perception and notion. They fancy that I
choose to see this or that thing. But perception is not whimsical, but fatal. If I see a trait, my children will see it after
me, and in course of time all mankind,—although it may
chance that no one has seen it before me. For my perception
of it is as much a fact as the sun.

The relations of the soul to the divine spirit are so pure *transcendental*
that it is profane to seek to interpose helps. It must be that *philosophy*
when God speaketh he should communicate, not one thing,
but all things; should fill the world with his voice; should
scatter forth light, nature, time, souls, from the centre of the
present thought; and new date and new create the whole.
Whenever a mind is simple and receives a divine wisdom, then
old things pass away,—means, teachers, texts, temples fall; it
lives now, and absorbs past and future into the present hour.
All things are made sacred by relation to it,—one thing as
much as another. All things are dissolved to their centre by
their cause, and in the universal miracle petty and particular
miracles disappear. This is and must be. If therefore a man
claims to know and speak of God and carries you backward
to the phraseology of some old mouldered nation in another

country, in another world, believe him not. Is the acorn better than the oak which is its fulness and completion? Is the parent better than the child into whom he has cast his ripened being? Whence then this worship of the past? The centuries are conspirators against the sanity and majesty of the soul. Time and space are but physiological colors which the eye maketh, but the soul is light; where it is, is day; where it was, is night; and history is an impertinence and an injury if it be any thing more than a cheerful apologue or parable of my being and becoming.

Man is timid and apologetic; he is no longer upright; he dares not say "I think," "I am," but quotes some saint or sage. He is ashamed before the blade of grass or the blowing rose. These roses under my window make no reference to former roses or to better ones; they are for what they are; they exist with God to-day. There is no time to them. There is simply the rose; it is perfect in every moment of its existence. Before a leaf-bud has burst, its whole life acts; in the full-blown flower there is no more; in the leafless root there is no less. Its nature is satisfied and it satisfies nature in all moments alike. There is no time to it. But man postpones or remembers; he does not live in the present, but with reverted eye laments the past, or, heedless of the riches that surround him, stands on tiptoe to forsee the future. He cannot be happy and strong until he too lives with nature in the present, above time.

This should be plain enough. Yet see what strong intellects dare not yet hear God himself unless he speak the phraseology of I know not what David, or Jeremiah, or Paul. We shall not always set so great a price on a few texts, on a few lives. We are like children who repeat by rote the sentences of grandames and tutors, and, as they grow older, of the men of talents and character they chance to see,—painfully recollecting the exact words they spoke; afterwards, when they come into the point of view which those had who uttered these sayings, they understand them and are willing to let the words go; for at any time they can use words as good when occasion comes. So was it with us, so will it be, if we proceed. If we live truly, we shall see truly. It is as easy for the strong man to be strong, as it is for the weak to be weak. When we have new perception, we shall gladly disburthen the memory of its hoarded treasures as old rubbish. When a man lives with God, his voice shall be as sweet as the murmur of the brook and the rustle of the corn.

And now at last the highest truth on this subject remains unsaid; probably cannot be said; for all that we say is the far off remembering of the intuition. That thought, by what I can now nearest approach to say it, is this. When good is near you, when you have life in yourself,—it is not by any known or appointed way; you shall not discern the foot-prints of any other, you shall not see the face of man; you shall not hear any name;—the way, the thought, the good, shall be wholly strange and new. It shall exclude all other being. You take the way from man, not to man. All persons that ever existed are its fugitive ministers. There shall be no fear in it. Fear and hope are alike beneath it. It asks nothing. There is somewhat low even in hope. We are then in vision. There is nothing that can be called gratitude, nor properly joy. The soul is raised over passion. It seeth identity and eternal caus- ation. It is a perceiving that Truth and Right are. Hence it becomes a Tranquillity out of the knowing that all things go well. Vast spaces of nature; the Atlantic Ocean, the South Sea; vast intervals of time, years, centuries, are of no account. This which I think and feel underlay that former state of life and circumstances, as it does underlie my present and will always all circumstances, and what is called life and what is called death.

Life only avails, not the having lived. Power ceases in the instant of repose; it resides in the moment of transition from a past to a new state, in the shooting of the gulf, in the darting to an aim. This one fact the world hates, that the soul *becomes;* for that forever degrades the past; turns all riches to poverty, all reputation to a shame; confounds the saint with the rogue; shoves Jesus and Judas equally aside. Why then did we prate of self-reliance? Inasmuch as the soul is present there will be power not confident but agent. To talk of reliance is a poor external way of speaking. Speak rather of that which relies because it works and is. Who has more soul than I masters me, though he should not raise his finger. Round him I must revolve by the gravitation of spirits. Who has less I rule with like facility. We fancy it rhetoric when we speak of eminent virtue. We do not yet see that virtue is Height, and that a man or a company of men, plastic and permeable to principles, by the law of nature must overpower and ride all cities, nations, kings, rich men, poets, who are not.

This is the ultimate fact which we so quickly reach on this, as on every topic, the resolution of all into the ever-blessed ONE. Virtue is the governor, the creator, the reality. All things real are so by so much virtue as they contain. Hardship, husbandry, hunting, whaling, war, eloquence, personal weight, are somewhat, and engage my respect as examples of the soul's presence and impure action. I see the same law working in nature for conservation and growth. The poise of a planet, the bended tree recovering itself from the strong wind, the vital resources of every animal and vegetable, are also demonstrations of the self-sufficing and therefore self-relying soul. All history, from its highest to its trivial passages is the various record of this power.

Thus all concentrates; let us not rove; let us sit at home with the cause. Let us stun and astonish the intruding rabble of men and books and institutions by a simple declaration of the divine fact. Bid them take the shoes from off their feet, for God is here within. Let our simplicity judge them, and our docility to our own law demonstrate the poverty of nature and fortune beside our native riches.

But now we are a mob. Man does not stand in awe of man, nor is the soul admonished to stay at home, to put itself in communication with the internal ocean, but it goes abroad to beg a cup of water of the urns of men. We must go alone. Isolation must precede true society. I like the silent church before the service begins, better than any preaching. How far off, how cool, how chaste the persons look, begirt each one with a precinct or sanctuary. So let us always sit. Why should we assume the faults of our friend, or wife, or father, or child, because they sit around our hearth, or are said to have the same blood? All men have my blood and I have all men's. Not for that will I adopt their petulance or folly, even to the extent of being ashamed of it. But your isolation must not be mechanical, but spiritual, that is, must be elevation. At times the whole world seems to be in conspiracy to importune you with emphatic trifles. Friend, client, child, sickness, fear, want, charity, all knock at once at thy closet door and say, "Come out unto us."—Do not spill thy soul; do not all descend; keep thy state; stay at home in thine own heaven; come not for a moment into their facts, into their hubbub of conflicting appearances, but let in the light of thy law on their confusion. The power men possess to annoy me I give them by a weak curiosity. No man can come near me but through my act. "What we love that we have, but by desire we bereave ourselves of the love."

If we cannot at once rise to the sanctities of obedience and faith, let us at least resist our temptations, let us enter into the state of war and wake Thor and Woden, courage and constancy, in our Saxon breasts. This is to be done in our smooth times by speaking the truth. Check this lying hospitality and lying affection. Live no longer to the expectation of these deceived and deceiving people with whom we converse. Say to them, O father, O mother, O wife, O brother, O friend, I have lived with you after appearances hitherto. Henceforward I am the truth's. Be it known unto you that henceforward I obey no law less than the eternal law. I will have no covenants but proximities. I shall endeavor to nourish my parents, to support my family, to be the chaste husband of one wife,—but these relations I must fill after a new and unprecedented way. I appeal from your customs. I must be myself. I cannot break myself any longer for you, or you. If you can love me for what I am, we shall be happier. If you cannot, I will seek to deserve that you should. I must be myself. I will not hide my tastes or aversions. I will so trust that what is deep is holy, that I will do strongly before the sun and moon whatever inly rejoices me and the heart appoints. If you are noble, I will love you; if you are not, I will not hurt you and myself by hypocritical attentions. If you are true, but not in the same truth with me, cleave to your companions; I will seek my own. I do this not selfishly but humbly and truly. It is alike your interest, and mine, and all men's, however long we have dwelt in lies, to live in truth. Does this sound harsh to-day? You will soon love what is dictated by your nature as well as mine, and if we follow the truth it will bring us out safe at last.—But so may you give these friends pain. Yes, but I cannot sell my liberty and my power, to save their sensibility. Besides, all persons have their moments of reason, when they look out into the region of absolute truth; then will they justify me and do the same thing.

The populace think that your rejection of popular standards is a rejection of all standard, and mere antinomianism; and the bold sensualist will use the name of philosophy to gild his crimes. But the law of consciousness abides. There are two confessionals, in one or the other of which we must be shriven. You may fulfil your round of duties by clearing yourself in the *direct* or in the *reflex* way. Consider whether you have satisfied your relations to father, mother, cousin, neighbor, town, cat and dog; whether any of these can upbraid you. But I may also neglect this reflex standard and absolve me to myself. I have my own stern claims and perfect circle. It denies the name of duty to many offices that are called duties. But if I can discharge its debts it enables me to dispense with the popular code. If any one imagines that this law is lax, let him keep its commandment one day.

And truly it demands something godlike in him who has cast off the common motives of humanity and has ventured to trust himself for a task-master. High be his heart, faithful his will, clear his sight, that he may in good earnest be doctrine,

Set your own Standard

"To thine own self be true... and then thou canst not be false to any man"

Hamlet – Polonius' speech

It isn't incidental that Shakespeare put these words in the mouth of a fool.

Emerson restates one side of an old idea.

assume infallibility

Emerson = rely on yourself – vs. relying on society

society, law, to himself, that a simple purpose may be to him as strong as iron necessity is to others.

If any man consider the present aspects of what is called by distinction *society*, he will see the need of these ethics. The sinew and heart of man seem to be drawn out, and we are become timorous desponding whimperers. We are afraid of truth, afraid of fortune, afraid of death, and afraid of each other. Our age yields no great and perfect persons. We want men and women who shall renovate life and our social state, but we see that most natures are insolvent; cannot satisfy their own wants, have an ambition out of all proportion to their practical force, and so do lean and beg day and night continually. Our housekeeping is mendicant, our arts, our occupations, our marriages, our religion we have not chosen, but society has chosen for us. We are parlor soldiers. The rugged battle of fate, where strength is born, we shun.

If our young men miscarry in their first enterprises they lose all heart. If the young merchant fails, men say he is *ruined*. If the finest genius studies at one of our colleges, and is not installed in an office within one year afterwards, in the cities or suburbs of Boston or New York, it seems to his friends and to himself that he is right in being disheartened and in complaining the rest of his life. A sturdy lad from New Hampshire or Vermont, who in turn tries all the professions, who *teams it, farms it, peddles,* keeps a school, preaches, edits a newspaper, goes to Congress, buys a township, and so forth, in successive years, and always like a cat falls on his feet, is worth a hundred of these city dolls. He walks abreast with his days and feels no shame in not "studying a profession," for he does not postpone his life, but lives already. He has not one chance, but a hundred chances. Let a stoic arise who shall reveal the resources of man and tell men they are not leaning willows, but can and must detach themselves; that with the exercise of self-trust, new powers shall appear; that a man is the word made flesh, born to shed healing to the nations, that he should be ashamed of our compassion, and that the moment he acts from himself, tossing the laws, the books, idola-

tries and customs out of the window,—we pity him no more
but thank and revere him;—and that teacher shall restore the
life of man to splendor and make his name dear to all History.

It is easy to see that a greater self-reliance—a new respect
for the divinity in man—must work a revolution in all the
offices and relations of men; in their religion; in their education; in their pursuits; their modes of living; their association;
in their property; in their speculative views.

1. In what prayers do men allow themselves! That which
they call a holy office is not so much as brave and manly.
Prayer looks abroad and asks for some foreign addition to
come through some foreign virtue, and loses itself in endless
mazes of natural and supernatural, and mediatorial and miraculous. Prayer that craves a particular commodity—anything
less than all good, is vicious. Prayer is the contemplation of
the facts of life from the highest point of view. It is the soliloquy of a beholding and jubilant soul. It is the spirit of God
pronouncing his works good. But prayer as a means to effect
a private end is theft and meanness. It supposes dualism and
not unity in nature and consciousness. As soon as the man is
at one with God, he will not beg. He will then see prayer in
all action. The prayer of the farmer kneeling in his field to
weed it, the prayer of a rower kneeling with the stroke of his
oar, are true prayers heard throughout nature, though for
cheap ends. Caratach, in Fletcher's Bonduca, when admonished to inquire the mind of the god Audate, replies,

> His hidden meaning lies in our endeavors;
> Our valors are our best gods.

Another sort of false prayers are our regrets. Discontent is
the want of self-reliance: it is infirmity of will. Regret calami-
ties if you can thereby help the sufferer; if not, attend your
own work and already the evil begins to be repaired. Our
sympathy is just as base. We come to them who weep foolishly
and sit down and cry for company, instead of imparting to
them truth and health in rough electric shocks, putting them
once more in communication with the soul. The secret of

fortune is joy in our hands. Welcome evermore to gods and
men is the self-helping man. For him all doors are flung wide.
Him all tongues greet, all honors crown, all eyes follow with
desire. Our love goes out to him and embraces him because
he did not need it. We solicitously and apologetically caress
and celebrate him because he held on his way and scorned
our disapprobation. The gods love him because men hated
him. "To the persevering mortal," said Zoroaster, "the blessed
Immortals are swift." [10]

As men's prayers are a disease of the will, so are their creeds
a disease of the intellect. They say with those foolish Israel-
ites, "Let not God speak to us, lest we die. Speak thou, speak
any man with us, and we will obey." [11] Everywhere I am be-
reaved of meeting God in my brother, because he has shut his
own temple doors and recites fables merely of his brother's,
or his brother's God. Every new mind is a new classification.
If it prove a mind of uncommon activity and power, a Locke,
a Lavoisier, a Hutton, a Bentham, a Spurzheim, it imposes its
classification on other men, and lo! a new system. In proportion always to the depth of the thought, and so to the number
of the objects it touches and brings within reach of the pupil,
is his complacency. But chiefly is this apparent in creeds and
churches, which are also classification of some powerful mind
acting on the great elemental thought of Duty and man's relation to the Highest. Such is Calvinism, Quakerism, Sweden-
borgianism. The pupil takes the same delight in subordinating
every thing to the new terminology that a girl does who has
just learned botany in seeing a new earth and new seasons
thereby. It will happen for a time that the pupil will feel a
real debt to the teacher—will find his intellectual power has
grown by the study of his writings. This will continue until
he has exhausted his master's mind. But in all unbalanced
minds the classification is idolized, passes for the end and not
for a speedily exhaustible means, so that the walls of the system blend to their eye in the remote horizon with the walls

10 One of the "Chaldean oracles" attributed to Zoroaster.
11 Adapted from Exodus xx, 19.

of the universe; the luminaries of heaven seem to them hung
on the arch their master built. They cannot imagine how you
aliens have any right to see—how you can see; "It must be
somehow that you stole the light from us." They do not yet
perceive that light, unsystematic, indomitable, will break into
any cabin, even into theirs. Let them chirp awhile and call it
their own. If they are honest and do well, presently their
neat new pinfold will be too strait and low, will crack, will
lean, will rot and vanish, and the immortal light, all young
and joyful, million-orbed, million-colored, will beam over
the universe as on the first morning.

2. It is for want of self-culture that the idol of Travelling,
the idol of Italy, of England, of Egypt, remains for all educated Americans. They who made England, Italy, or Greece
venerable in the imagination, did so not by rambling round
creation as a moth round a lamp, but by sticking fast where
they were, like an axis of the earth. In manly hours we feel
that duty is our place and that the merry men of circumstance
should follow as they may. The soul is no traveller: the wise
man stays at home with the soul, and when his necessities, his
duties, on any occasion call him from his house, or into foreign
lands, he is at home still and is not gadding abroad from
himself, and shall make men sensible by the expression of his
countenance that he goes, the missionary of wisdom and virtue, and visits cities and men like a sovereign and not like an
interloper or a valet.

I have no churlish objection to the circumnavigation of the
globe for the purposes of art, of study, and benevolence, so
that the man is first domesticated, or does not go abroad with
the hope of finding somewhat greater than he knows. He who
travels to be amused or to get somewhat which he does not
carry, travels away from himself, and grows old even in youth
among old things. In Thebes, in Palmyra, his will and mind
have become old and dilapidated as they. He carries ruins to
ruins.

Travelling is a fool's paradise. We owe to our first journeys
the discovery that place is nothing. At home I dream that at

Naples, at Rome, I can be intoxicated with beauty and lose my sadness. I pack my trunk, embrace my friends, embark on the sea and at last wake up in Naples, and there beside me is the stern Fact, the sad self, unrelenting, identical, that I fled from. I seek the Vatican and the palaces. I affect to be intoxicated with sights and suggestions, but I am not intoxicated. My giant goes with me wherever I go.

3. But the rage of travelling is itself only a symptom of a deeper unsoundness affecting the whole intellectual action. The intellect is vagabond, and the universal system of education fosters restlessness. Our minds travel when our bodies are forced to stay at home. We imitate; and what is imitation but the travelling of the mind? Our houses are built with foreign taste; our shelves are garnished with foreign ornaments; our opinions, our tastes, our whole minds, lean, and follow the Past and the Distant, as the eyes of a maid follow her mistress. The soul created the arts wherever they have flourished. It was in his own mind that the artist sought his model. It was an application of his own thought to the thing to be done and the conditions to be observed. And why need we copy the Doric or the Gothic model? Beauty, convenience, grandeur of thought and quaint expression are as near to us as to any, and if the American artist will study with hope and love the precise thing to be done by him, considering the climate, the soil, the length of the day, the wants of the people, the habit and form of the government, he will create a house in which all these will find themselves fitted, and taste and sentiment will be satisfied also.

Insist on yourself; never imitate. Your own gift you can present every moment with the cumulative force of a whole life's cultivation; but of the adopted talent of another you have only an extemporaneous half possession. That which each can do best, none but his Maker can teach him. No man yet knows what it is, nor can, till that person has exhibited it. Where is the master who could have taught Shakspeare? Where is the master who could have instructed Franklin, or Washington, or Bacon, or Newton? Every great man is an unique. The Scipionism of Scipio is precisely that part he could not borrow. If anybody will tell me whom the great man imitates in the original crisis when he performs a great act, I will tell him who else than himself can teach him. Shakspeare will never be made by the Study of Shakspeare. Do that which is assigned thee and thou canst not hope too much or dare too much. There is at this moment, there is for me an utterance bare and grand as that of the colossal chisel of Phidias, or trowel of the Egyptians, or the pen of Moses or Dante, but different from all these. Not possibly will the soul, all rich, all eloquent, with thousand-cloven tongue, deign to repeat itself; but if I can hear what these patriarchs say, surely I can reply to them in the same pitch of voice; for the ear and the tongue are two organs of one nature. Dwell up there in the simple and noble regions of thy life, obey thy heart and thou shalt reproduce the Foreworld again.

4. As our Religion, our Education, our Art look abroad, so does our spirit of society. All men plume themselves on the improvement of society, and no man improves.

Society never advances. It recedes as fast on one side as it gains on the other. Its progress is only apparent like the workers of a treadmill. It undergoes continual changes; it is barbarous, it is civilized, it is Christianized, it is rich, it is scientific; but this change is not amelioration. For every thing that is given something is taken. Society acquires new arts and loses old instincts. What a contrast between the well-clad, reading, writing, thinking American, with a watch, a pencil and a bill of exchange in his pocket, and the naked New Zealander, whose property is a club, a spear, a mat and an undivided twentieth of a shed to sleep under. But compare the health of the two men and you shall see that his aboriginal strength, the white man has lost. If the traveller tell us truly, strike the savage with a broad axe and in a day or two the flesh shall unite and heal as if you struck the blow into soft pitch, and the same blow shall send the white to his grave.

The civilized man has built a coach, but has lost the use of his feet. He is supported on crutches, but lacks so much support of muscle. He has got a fine Geneva watch, but he has lost the skill to tell the hour by the sun. A Greenwich nautical almanac he has, and so being sure of the information when he wants it, the man in the street does not know a star in the sky. The solstice he does not observe; the equinox he knows as little; and the whole bright calendar of the year is without a dial in his mind. His note-books impair his memory; his libraries overload his wit; the insurance-office increases the number of accidents; and it may be a question whether machinery does not encumber; whether we have not lost by refinement some energy, by a Christianity entrenched in establishments and forms some vigor of wild virtue. For every stoic was a stoic; but in Christendom where is the Christian?

There is no more deviation in the moral standard than in the standard of height or bulk. No greater men are now than ever were. A singular equality may be observed between the great men of the first and of the last ages; nor can all the science, art, religion, and philosophy of the nineteenth century avail to educate greater men than Plutarch's heroes, three or four and twenty centuries ago. Not in time is the race progressive. Phocion, Socrates, Anaxagoras, Diogenes, are great men, but they leave no class.[12] He who is really of their class will not be called by their name, but be wholly his own man, and in turn the founder of a sect. The arts and inventions of each period are only its costumes and do not invigorate men. The harm of the improved machinery may compensate its good. Hudson and Behring accomplished so much in their fishing-boats as to astonish Parry and Franklin, whose equipment exhausted the resources of science and art.[13] Galileo, with an opera-glass, discovered a more splendid series of facts than any one since. Columbus found the New World in an undecked boat. It is curious to see the periodical disuse and perishing of means and machinery which were introduced with loud laudation a few years or centuries before. The great

12 They are unique.
13 Parry and Franklin, nineteenth-century explorers, are here contrasted with the under-equipped early explorers Hudson and Behring.

genius returns to essential man. We reckoned the improvements of the art of war among the triumphs of science, and yet Napoleon conquered Europe by the Bivouac, which consisted of falling back on naked valor and disencumbering it of all aids. The Emperor held it impossible to make a perfect army, says Las Cases, "without abolishing our arms, magazines, commissaries and carriages, until, in imitation of the Roman custom, the soldier should receive his supply of corn, grind it in his hand-mill and bake his bread himself."

Society is a wave. The wave moves onward, but the water of which it is composed does not. The same particle does not rise from the valley to the ridge. Its unity is only phenomenal. The persons who make up a nation to-day, die, and their experience with them.

And so the reliance on Property, including the reliance on governments which protect it, is the want of self-reliance. Men have looked away from themselves and at things so long that they have come to esteem what they call the soul's progress, namely, the religious, learned and civil institutions as guards of property, and they deprecate assaults on these, because they feel them to be assaults on property. They measure their esteem of each other by what each has, and not by what each is. But a cultivated man becomes ashamed of his property, ashamed of what he has, out of new respect for his being. Especially he hates what he has if he sees that it is accidental, —came to him by inheritance, or gift, or crime; then he feels that it is not having; it does not belong to him, has no root in him, and merely lies there because no revolution or no robber takes it away. But that which a man is, does always by necessity acquire, and what the man acquires, is permanent and living property, which does not wait the beck of rulers, or mobs, or revolutions, or fire, or storm, or bankruptcies, but perpetually renews itself wherever the man is put. "Thy lot or portion of life," said the Caliph Ali, "is seeking after thee; therefore be at rest from seeking after it." Our dependence on these foreign goods leads us to our slavish respect for numbers. The political parties meet in numerous conventions; the greater the concourse and with each new uproar of announcement. The delegation from Essex! The Democrats from New Hampshire! The Whigs of Maine! the young patriot feels himself stronger than before by a new thousand of eyes and arms. In like manner the reformers summon conventions and vote and resolve in multitude. But not so O friends! will the God deign to enter and inhabit you, but by a method precisely the reverse. It is only as a man puts off from himself all external support and stands alone that I see him to be strong and to prevail. He is weaker by every recruit to his banner. Is not a man better than a town? Ask nothing of men, and, in the endless mutation, thou only firm column must presently appear the upholder of all that surrounds thee. He who knows that power is in the soul, that he is weak only because he has looked for good out of him and elsewhere, and, so perceiving, throws himself unhesitatingly on his thought, instantly rights himself, stands in the erect position, commands his limbs, works miracles; just as a man who stands on his feet is stronger than a man who stands on his head.

So use all that is called Fortune. Most men gamble with her, and gain all, and lose all, as her wheel rolls. But do thou leave as unlawful these winnings, and deal with Cause and Effect, the chancellors of God. In the Will work and acquire, and thou hast chained the wheel of Chance, and shalt always drag her after thee. A political victory, a rise of rents, the recovery of your sick or the return of your absent friend, or some other quite external event raises your spirit, and you think good days are preparing for you. Do not believe it. It can never be so. Nothing can bring you peace but yourself. Nothing can bring you peace but the triumph of principles.

John Stuart Mill

JOHN STUART MILL *(1806-1873) held a clerkship in the India House from 1823 onward, which gave him leisure for extensive writing on philosophy and political economy. He was a passionate libertarian, but his passions never clouded the clear, deliberate movement of his richly stocked intelligence. He was educated by his father in a regime which Mill later described in his* Autobiography. *Principal works:* System of Logic *(1843);* Principles of Political Economy *(1848);* Essay on Liberty *(1859);* Utilitarianism *(1861);* Autobiography *(1873).*

OF THE LIBERTY OF
THOUGHT AND DISCUSSION[1]

The time, it is to be hoped, is gone by, when any defense would be necessary of the "liberty of the press" as one of the securities against corrupt or tyrannical government. No argument, we may suppose, can now be needed, against permitting a legislature or an executive, not identified in interest with the people, to prescribe opinions to them, and determine what doctrines or what arguments they shall be allowed to hear. This aspect of the question, besides, has been so often and so triumphantly enforced by preceding writers, that it needs not be specially insisted on in this place. Though the law of England, on the subject of the press, is as servile to this day as it was in the time of the Tudors, there is little danger of

1 This selection comprises Chapter II of *Essay on Liberty* (1859).

its being actually put in force against political discussion, except during some temporary panic, when fear of insurrection drives ministers and judges from their propriety; [2] and, speaking generally, it is not, in constitutional countries, to be apprehended, that the government, whether completely responsible to the people or not, will often attempt to control the expression of opinion, except when in doing so it makes itself the organ of the general intolerance of the public. Let us suppose, therefore, that the government is entirely at one with the people, and never thinks of exerting any power of coercion unless in agreement with what it conceives to be their voice. But I deny the right of the people to exercise such coercion, either by themselves or by their government. The power itself is illegitimate. The best government has no more

[2] Mill's note: These words had scarcely been written, when, as if to give them an emphatic contradiction, occurred the Government Press Prosecutions of 1858. That ill-judged interference with the liberty of public discussion has not, however, induced me to alter a single word in the text, nor has it at all weakened my conviction that, moments of panic excepted, the era of pains and penalties for political discussion has, in our own country, passed away. For, in the first place, the prosecutions were not persisted in; and, in the second, they were never, properly speaking, political prosecutions. The offense charged was not that of criticizing institutions, or the acts or persons of rulers, but of circulating what was deemed an immoral doctrine, the lawfulness of Tyrannicide. If the arguments of the present chapter are of any validity, there ought to exist the fullest liberty of professing and discussing, as a matter of ethical conviction, any doctrine, however immoral it may be considered. It would, therefore, be irrelevant and out of place to examine here, whether the doctrine of Tyrannicide deserves that title. I shall content myself with saying that the subject has been at all times one of the open questions of morals; that the act of a private citizen in striking down a criminal, who, by raising himself above the law, has placed himself beyond the reach of legal punishment or control, has been accounted by whole nations, and by some of the best and wisest of men, not a crime, but an act of exalted virtue; and that, right or wrong, it is not of the nature of assassination, but of civil war. As such, I hold that the instigation to it, in a specific case, may be a proper subject of punishment, but only if an overt act has followed, and at least a probable connection can be established between the act and the instigation. Even then, it is not a foreign government, but the very government assailed, which alone, in the exercise of self-defense, can legitimately punish attacks directed against its own existence.

title to it than the worst. It is as noxious, or more noxious, when exerted in accordance with public opinion, than when in opposition to it. If all mankind minus one, were of one opinion, and only one person were of the contrary opinion, mankind would be no more justified in silencing that one person, than he, if he had the power, would be justified in silencing mankind. Were an opinion a personal possession of no value except to the owner; if to be obstructed in the enjoyment of it were simply a private injury, it would make some difference whether the injury was inflicted only on a few persons or on many. But the peculiar evil of silencing the expression of an opinion is, that it is robbing the human race; posterity as well as the existing generation; those who dissent from the opinion, still more than those who hold it. If the opinion is right, they are deprived of the opportunity of exchanging error for truth: if wrong, they lose, what is almost as great a benefit, the clearer perception and livelier impression of truth, produced by its collision with error.

It is necessary to consider separately these two hypotheses, each of which has a distinct branch of the argument corresponding to it. We can never be sure that the opinion we are endeavoring to stifle is a false opinion; and if we were sure, stifling it would be an evil still.

First: the opinion which it is attempted to suppress by authority may possibly be true. Those who desire to suppress it, of course deny its truth; but they are not infallible. They have no authority to decide the question for all mankind, and exclude every other person from the means of judging. To refuse a hearing to an opinion, because they are sure that it is false, is to assume that *their* certainty is the same thing as *absolute* certainty. All silencing of discussion is an assumption of infallibility. Its condemnation may be allowed to rest on this common argument, not the worse for being common.

Unfortunately for the good sense of mankind, the fact of their fallibility is far from carrying the weight in their practical judgment, which is always allowed to it in theory; for while every one well knows himself to be fallible, few think it necessary to take any precautions against their own fallibility, or admit the supposition that any opinion, of which they feel very certain, may be one of the examples of the error to which they acknowledge themselves to be liable. Absolute princes, or others who are accustomed to unlimited deference, usually feel this complete confidence in their own opinions on nearly all subjects. People more happily situated, who sometimes hear their opinions disputed, and are not wholly unused to be set right when they are wrong, place the same unbounded reliance only on such of their opinions as are shared by all who surround them, or to whom they habitually defer: for in proportion to a man's want of confidence in his own solitary judgment, does he usually repose, with implicit trust, on the infallibility of "the world" in general. And the world, to each individual, means the part of it with which he comes in contact; his party, his sect, his church, his class of society: the man may be called, by comparison, almost liberal and large-minded to whom it means anything so comprehensive as his own country or his own age. Nor is his faith in this collective authority at all shaken by his being aware that other ages, countries, sects, churches, classes, and parties have thought, and even now think, the exact reverse. He devolves upon his own world the responsibility of being in the right against the dissentient worlds of other people; and it never troubles him that mere accident has decided which of these numerous worlds is the object of his reliance, and that the same causes which make him a Churchman in London, would have made him a Buddhist or a Confucian in Pekin. Yet it is as evident in itself, as any amount of argument can make it, that ages are no more infallible than individuals; every age having held many opinions which subsequent ages have deemed not only false but absurd; and it is as certain that many opinions, now general, will be rejected by future ages, as it is that many, once general, are rejected by the present.

The objection likely to be made to this argument would probably take some such form as the following. There is no

greater assumption of infallibility in forbidding the propagation of error, than in any other thing which is done by public
authority on its own judgment and responsibility. Judgment
is given to men that they may use it. Because it may be used
erroneously, are men to be told that they ought not to use it at
all? To prohibit what they think pernicious, is not claiming
exemption from error, but fulfilling the duty incumbent on
them, although fallible, of acting on their conscientious conviction. If we were never to act on our opinions, because those
opinions may be wrong, we should leave all our interests un-
cared for, and all our duties unperformed. An objection which
applies to all conduct, can be no valid objection to any conduct in particular. It is the duty of governments, and of individuals, to form the truest opinions they can; to form them
carefully, and never impose them upon others unless they are
quite sure of being right. But when they are sure (such rea-
soners may say), it is not conscientiousness but cowardice to
shrink from acting on their opinions, and allow doctrines
which they honestly think dangerous to the welfare of mankind, either in this life or in another, to be scattered abroad
without restraint, because other people, in less enlightened
times, have persecuted opinions now believed to be true. Let
us take care, it may be said, not to make the same mistake:
but governments and nations have made mistakes in other
things, which are not denied to be fit subjects for the exercise
of authority: they have laid on bad taxes, made unjust wars.
Ought we therefore to lay on no taxes, and, under whatever
provocation, make no wars? Men, and governments, must act
to the best of their ability. There is no such thing as absolute
certainty, but there is assurance sufficient for the purposes of
human life. We may, and must, assume our opinion to be true
for the guidance of our own conduct: and it is assuming no
more when we forbid bad men to pervert society by the propagation of opinions which we regard as false and pernicious.

I answer, that it is assuming very much more. There is the
greatest difference between presuming an opinion to be true,
because, with every opportunity for contesting it, it has not

been refuted, and assuming its truth for the purpose of not permitting its refutation. Complete liberty of contradicting and disproving our opinion, is the very condition which justifies us in assuming its truth for purposes of action; and on no other terms can a being with human faculties have any rational assurance of being right.

When we consider either the history of opinion, or the ordinary conduct of human life, to what is it to be ascribed that the one and the other are no worse than they are? Not certainly to the inherent force of the human understanding; for, on any matter not self-evident, there are ninety-nine persons totally incapable of judging of it, for one who is capable; and the capacity of the hundredth person is only comparative; for the majority of the eminent men of every past generation held many opinions now known to be erroneous, and did or approved numerous things which no one will now justify. Why is it, then, that there is on the whole a preponderance among mankind of rational opinions and rational conduct? If there really is this preponderance—which there must be unless human affairs are, and have always been, in an almost desperate state—it is owing to a quality of the human mind, the source of everything respectable in man either as an intellectual or as a moral being, namely, that his errors are corrigible. He is capable of rectifying his mistakes, by discussion and experience. Not by experience alone. There must be discussion, to show how experience is to be interpreted. Wrong opinions and practices gradually yield to fact and argument: but facts and arguments, to produce any effect on the mind, must be brought before it. Very few facts are able to tell their own story, without comments to bring out their meaning. The whole strength and value, then, of human judgment, depending on the one property, that it can be set right when it is wrong, reliance can be placed on it only when the means of setting it right are kept constantly at hand. In the case of any person whose judgment is really deserving of confidence, how has it become so? Because he has kept his mind open to criticism of his opinions and conduct. Because it has been his practice to listen to all that could be said against him; to profit by as much of it as was just, and expound to himself, and upon occasion to others, the fallacy of what was fallacious. Because he has felt, that the only way in which a human being can make some approach to knowing the whole of a subject, is by hearing what can be said about it by persons of every variety of opinion, and studying all modes in which it can be looked at by every character of mind. No wise man ever acquired his wisdom in any mode but this; nor is it in the nature of human intellect to become wise in any other manner. The steady habit of correcting and completing his own opinion by collating it with those of others, so far from causing doubt and hesitation in carrying it in to practice, is the only stable foundation for a just reliance on it: for, being cognizant of all that can, at least obviously, be said against him, and having taken up his position against all gainsayers— knowing that he has sought for objections and difficulties, instead of avoiding them, and has shut out no light which can be thrown upon the subject from any quarter—he has a right to think his judgment better than that of any person, or any multitude, who have not gone through a similar process.

It is not too much to require that what the wisest of mankind, those who are best entitled to trust their own judgment, find necessary to warrant their relying on it, should be submitted to by that miscellaneous collection of a few wise and many foolish individuals, called the public. The most intolerant of churches, the Roman Catholic Church, even at the canonization of a saint, admits, and listens patiently to, a "devil's advocate." The holiest of men, it appears, cannot be admitted to posthumous honors, until all that the devil could say against him is known and weighed. If even the Newtonian philosophy were not permitted to be questioned, mankind could not feel as complete assurance of its truth as they now do. The beliefs which we have most warrant for, have no safeguard to rest on, but a standing invitation to the whole world to prove them unfounded. If the challenge is not accepted, or is accepted and the attempt fails, we are far enough from certainty still; but we have done the best that the existing state of human reason admits of; we have neglected nothing that could give the truth a chance of reaching us: if the lists are kept open, we may hope that if there be a better truth, it will be found when the human mind is capable of receiving it; and in the meantime we may rely on having attained such approach to truth, as is possible in our own day. This is the amount of certainty attainable by a fallible being, and this the sole way of attaining it.

Strange it is, that men should admit the validity of the arguments for free discussion, but object to their being "pushed to an extreme"; not seeing that unless the reasons are good for an extreme case, they are not good for any case. Strange that they should imagine that they are not assuming infallibility, when they acknowledge that there should be free discussion on all subjects which can possibly be *doubtful*, but think that some particular principle or doctrine should be forbidden to be questioned because it is so *certain*, that is, because *they are certain* that it is certain. To call any proposition certain, while there is any one who would deny its certainty if permitted, but who is not permitted, is to assume that we ourselves, and those who agree with us, are the judges of certainty, and judges without hearing the other side.

In the present age—which has been described as "destitute of faith, but terrified at scepticism"—in which people feel sure, not so much that their opinions are true, as that they should not know what to do without them—the claims of an opinion to be protected from public attack are rested not so much on its truth, as on its importance to society. There are, it is alleged, certain beliefs, so useful, not to say indispensable to well-being, that it is as much the duty of governments to uphold those beliefs, as to protect any other of the interests of society. In a case of such necessity, and so directly in the line of their duty, something less than infallibility may, it is maintained, warrant, and even bind, governments, to act on their own opinion, confirmed by the general opinion of mankind. It is also often argued, and still oftener thought, that none but bad men would desire to weaken these salutary beliefs; and there can be nothing wrong, it is thought, in restraining bad men, and prohibiting what only such men would wish to practice. This mode of thinking makes the justification of restraints on discussion not a question of the truth of doctrines, but of their usefulness; and flatters itself by that means to escape the responsibility of claiming to be an infallible judge of opinions. But those who thus satisfy themselves, do not perceive that the assumption of infallibility is merely shifted from one point to another. The usefulness of an opinion is itself matter of opinion: as disputable, as open to discussion, and requiring discussion as much, as the opinion itself. There is the same need of an infallible judge of opinions to decide an opinion to be noxious, as to decide it to be false, unless the opinion condemned has full opportunity of defending itself. And it will not do to say that the heretic may be allowed to maintain the utility or harmlessness of his opinion, though forbidden to maintain its truth. The truth of an opinion is part of its utility. If we would know whether or not it is desirable that a proposition should be believed, is it possible to exclude the consideration of whether or not it is true? In the opinion, not of bad men, but of the best men, no belief which is contrary to truth can be really useful: and can you prevent such men from urging that plea, when they are charged with culpability for denying some doctrine which they are told is useful, but which they believe to be false? Those who are on the side of received opinions, never fail to take all possible advantage of this plea; you do not find *them* handling the question of utility as if it could be completely abstracted from that of truth: on the contrary, it is, above all, because their doctrine is the "truth," that the knowledge or the belief of it is held to be so indispensable. There can be no fair discussion of the question of usefulness, when an argument so vital may be employed on one side, but not on the other. And in point of fact, when law or public feeling do not permit the truth of an opinion to be disputed, they are just as little tolerant of a denial of its usefulness. The utmost they allow is an extenua-

tion of its absolute necessity, or of the positive guilt of rejecting it.

In order more fully to illustrate the mischief of denying a
hearing to opinions because we, in our own judgment, have
condemned them, it will be desirable to fix down the discussion to a concrete case; and I choose, by preference, the cases
which are least favorable to me—in which the argument
against freedom of opinion, both on the score of truth and on
that of utility, is considered the strongest. Let the opinions
impugned be the belief in a God and in a future state, or any
of the commonly received doctrines of morality. To fight the
battle on such ground, gives a great advantage to an unfair
antagonist; since he will be sure to say (and many who have
no desire to be unfair will say it internally), Are these the doctrines which you do not deem sufficiently certain to be taken
under the protection of law? Is the belief in a God one of the
opinions, to feel sure of which, you hold to be assuming infal-
liability? But I must be permitted to observe, that it is not the
feeling sure of a doctrine (be it what it may) which I call an
assumption of infallibility. It is the undertaking to decide that
question *for others*, without allowing them to hear what can
be said on the contrary side. And I denounce and reprobate
this pretension not the less, if put forth on the side of my most
solemn convictions. However positive any one's persuasion
may be, not only of the falsity but of the pernicious consequences—not only of the pernicious consequences, but (to
adopt expressions which I altogether condemn) the immorality
and impiety of an opinion; yet if, in pursuance of that private
judgment, though backed by the public judgment of his
country or his contemporaries, he prevents the opinion from
being heard in its defense, he assumes infallibility. And so far
from the assumption being less objectionable or less dangerous because the opinion is called immoral or impious, this is
the case of all others in which it is most fatal. These are
exactly the occasions on which the men of one generation commit those dreadful mistakes, which excite the astonishment
and horror of posterity. It is among such that we find the

instances memorable in history, when the arm of the law has been employed to root out the best men and the noblest doctrines; with deplorable success as to the men, though some of the doctrines have survived to be (as if in mockery) invoked, in defense of similar conduct towards those who dissent from *them*, or from their received interpretation.

Mankind can hardly be too often reminded, that there was once a man named Socrates, between whom and the legal authorities and public opinion of his time, there took place a memorable collision. Born in an age and country abounding in individual greatness, this man has been handed down to us by those who best knew both him and the age, as the most virtuous man in it; while *we* know him as the head and prototype of all subsequent teachers of virtue, the source equally of the lofty inspiration of Plato and the judicious utilitarianism of Aristotle, *"i maëstri di color che sanno,"* [3] the two headsprings of ethical as of all other philosophy. This acknowledged master of all the eminent thinkers who have since lived —whose fame, still growing after more than two thousand years, all but outweighs the whole remainder of the names which make his native city illustrious—was put to death by his countrymen, after a judicial conviction, for impiety and immorality. Impiety, in denying the gods recognized by the State; indeed his accuser asserted (see the *Apologia*) that he believed in no gods at all. Immorality, in being, by his doctrines and instructions, a "corruptor of youth." Of these charges the tribunal, there is every ground for believing, honestly found him guilty, and condemned the man who probably of all then born had deserved best of mankind, to be put to death as a criminal.

To pass from this to the only other instance of judicial iniquity, the mention of which, after condemnation of Socrates, would not be an anti-climax: the event which took place on Calvary rather more than eighteen hundred years

---

[3] Dante, *Inferno*, Canto IV, 131. In Dante, the line refers only to Aristotle, "the master of those who know," but Mill brings Plato into a category that Dante reserved for Aristotle alone.

ago. The man who left on the memory of those who witnessed his life and conversation, such an impression of his moral grandeur, that eighteen subsequent centuries have done homage to him as the Almighty in person, was ignominiously put to death, as what? As a blasphemer. Men did not merely mistake their benefactor; they mistook him for the exact contrary of what he was, and treated him as that prodigy of impiety, which they themselves are now held to be, for their treatment of him. The feelings with which mankind now regard these lamentable transactions, especially the later of the two, render them extremely unjust in their judgment of the unhappy actors. These were, to all appearance, not bad men—not worse than men commonly are, but rather the contrary; men who possessed in a full, or somewhat more than a full measure, the religious, moral, and patriotic feelings of their time and people: the very kind of men who, in all times, our own included, have every chance of passing through life blameless and respected. The high-priest who rent his garments when the words were pronounced, which, according to all the ideas of his country, constituted the blackest guilt, was in all probability quite as sincere in his horror and indignation, as the generality of respectable and pious men now are in the religious and moral sentiments they profess; and most of those who now shudder at his conduct, if they had lived in his time, and been born Jews, would have acted precisely as he did. Orthodox Christians who are tempted to think that those who stoned to death the first martyrs must have been worse men than they themselves are, ought to remember that one of those persecutors was Saint Paul.

Let us add one more example, the most striking of all, if the impressiveness of an error is measured by the wisdom and virtue of him who falls into it. If ever any one, possessed of power, had grounds for thinking himself the best and most enlightened among his contemporaries, it was the Emperor Marcus Aurelius. Absolute monarch of the whole civilized world, he preserved through life not only the most unblemished justice, but what was less to be expected from his Stoical breeding, the tenderest heart. The few failings which are attributed to him, were all on the side of indulgence: while his writings, the highest ethical product of the ancient mind, differ scarcely perceptibly, if they differ at all, from the most characteristic teachings of Christ. This man, a better Christian in all but the dogmatic sense of the word, than almost any of the ostensibly Christian sovereigns who have since reigned, persecuted Christianity. Placed at the summit of all the previous attainments of humanity, with an open, <u>unfettered</u> intellect, and a character which led him of himself to embody in his moral writings the Christian ideal, he yet failed to see that Christianity was to be a good and not an evil to the world, with his duties to which he was so deeply penetrated. Existing society he knew to be in a deplorable state. But such as it was, he saw, or thought he saw, that it was held together, and prevented from being worse, by belief and reverence of the received divinities. As a ruler of mankind, he deemed it his duty not to suffer society to fall in pieces; and saw not how, if its existing ties were removed, any others could be formed which could again knit it together. The new religion openly aimed at dissolving these ties: unless, therefore, it was his duty to adopt that religion, it seemed to be his duty to put it down. Inasmuch then as the theology of Christianity did not appear to him true or of divine origin; inasmuch as this strange history of a crucified God was not credible to him, and a system which purported to rest entirely upon a foundation to him so wholly unbelievable, could not be forseen by him to be that renovating agency which, after all abatements, it has in fact proved to be; the gentlest and most amiable of philosophers and rulers, under a solemn sense of duty, authorized the persecution of Christianity. To my mind this is one of the most tragical facts in all history. It is a bitter thought, how different a thing the Christianity of the world might have been, if the Christian faith had been adopted as the religion of the empire under the auspices of Marcus Aurelius instead of those of Constantine. But it would be equally unjust to him and false to truth, to deny, that no one plea which can be urged for punishing anti-Christian teaching, was wanting to Marcus Aurelius for punishing, as he did, the propagation of Christianity. No Christian more firmly believes that Atheism is false, and tends to the dissolution of society, than Marcus Aurelius believed the same things of Christianity; he who, of all men then living might have been thought the most capable of appreciating it. Unless any one who approves of punishment for the promulgation of opinions, flatters himself that he is a wiser and better man than Marcus Aurelius—more deeply versed in the wisdom of his time, more elevated in this intellect above it—more earnest in his search for truth, or more singleminded in his devotion to it when found;—let him abstain from that assumption of the joint infallibility of himself and the multitude, which the great Antoninus made with so unfortunate a result.

Aware of the impossibility of defending the use of punishment for restraining irreligious opinions, by any argument which will not justify Marcus Antoninus, the enemies of religious freedom, when hard pressed, occasionally accept this consequence, and say, with Dr. Johnson, that the persecutors of Christianity were in the right; that persecution is an ordeal through which truth ought to pass, and always passes successfully, legal penalties being, in the end, powerless against truth, though sometimes beneficially effective against mischievous errors. This is a form of the argument for religious intolerance, sufficiently remarkable not to be passed without notice.

A theory which maintains that truth may justifiably be persecuted because persecution cannot possibly do it any harm, cannot be charged with being intentionally hostile to the reception of new truths; but we cannot commend the generosity of its dealing with the persons to whom mankind are indebted for them. To discover to the world something which deeply concerns it, and of which it was previously ignorant; to prove to it that it had been mistaken on some vital point of temporal or spiritual interest, is as important a service as a human being can render to his fellow creatures, and in certain cases, as in those of the early Christians and of the Reformers, those

who think with Dr. Johnson believe it to have been the most
precious gift which could be bestowed on mankind. That the
authors of such splendid benefits should be requited by
martyrdom; that their reward should be to be dealt with as
the vilest of criminals, is not, upon this theory, a deplorable
error and misfortune, for which humanity should mourn in
sack-cloth and ashes, but the normal and justifiable state of
things. The propounder of a new truth, according to this doctrine, should stand, as stood, in the legislation of the Locrians,
the proposer of a new law, with a halter round his neck, to be
instantly tightened if the public assembly did not, on hearing
his reasons, then and there adopt his proposition. People who
defend this mode of treating benefactors, cannot be supposed
to set much value on the benefit; and I believe this view of
the subject is mostly confined to the sort of persons who think
that new truths may have been desirable once, but that we
have had enough of them now.

But, indeed, the dictum that truth always triumphs over
persecution, is one of those pleasant falsehoods which men repeat after one another till they pass into commonplaces, but
which all experience refutes. History teems with instances of
truth put down by persecution. If not suppressed for ever, it
may be thrown back for centuries. To speak only of religious
opinions: the Reformation broke out at least twenty times before Luther, and was put down. Arnold of Brescia was put
down. Fra Dolcino was put down. Savonarola was put down.
The Albigeois were put down. The Vaudois were put down.
The Lollards were put down. The Hussites were put down.
Even after the era of Luther, wherever persecution was persisted in, it was successful. In Spain, Italy, Flanders, the
Austrian empire, Protestantism was rooted out; and, most
likely, would have been so in England, had Queen Mary lived,
or Queen Elizabeth died. Persecution has always succeeded,
save where the heretics were too strong a party to be effectually
persecuted. No reasonable person can doubt that Christianity
might have been extirpated in the Roman Empire. It spread,
and became predominant, because the persecutions were only

occasional, lasting but a short time, and separated by long intervals of almost undisturbed propagandism. It is a piece of idle sentimentality that truth, merely as truth, has any inherent power denied to error, of prevailing against the dungeon and the stake. Men are not more zealous for truth than they often are for error, and a sufficient application of legal or even of social penalities will generally succeed in stopping the propagation of either. The real advantage which truth has, consists in this, that when an opinion is true, it may be extinguished once, twice, or many times, but in the course of ages there will generally be found persons to rediscover it, until some one of its reappearances falls on a time when from favorable circumstances it escapes persecution until it has made such head as to withstand all subsequent attempts to suppress it.

It will be said, that we do not now put to death the introducers of new opinions: we are not like our fathers who slew the prophets, we even build sepulchres to them. It is true we no longer put heretics to death; and the amount of penal infliction which modern feeling would probably tolerate, even against the most obnoxious opinions, is not sufficient to extirpate them. But let us not flatter ourselves that we are yet free from the stain even of legal persecution. Penalties for opinion, or at least for its expression, still exist by law; and their enforcement is not, even in these times, so unexampled as to make it at all incredible that they may some day be revived in full force. In the year 1857, at the summer assizes of the county of Cornwall, an unfortunate man, said to be of unexceptionable conduct in all relations of life, was sentenced to twenty-one months' imprisonment, for uttering, and writing on a gate, some offensive words concerning Christianity. Within a month of the same time, at the Old Bailey, two persons, on ~English Court~ two separate occasions, were rejected as jurymen, and one of them grossly insulted by the judge and by one of the counsel, because they honestly declared that they had no theological belief; and a third, a foreigner, for the same reason, was denied justice against a thief. This refusal of redress took place in virtue of the legal doctrine, that no person can be allowed to give evidence in a court of justice, who does not profess belief in a God (any god is sufficient) and in a future state; which is equivalent to declaring such persons to be outlaws, excluded from the protection of the tribunals; who may not only be robbed or assaulted with impunity, if no one but themselves, or persons of similar opinions, be present, but any one else may be robbed or assaulted with impunity, if the proof of the fact depends on their evidence. The assumption on which this is grounded is that the oath is worthless, of a person who does not believe in a future state; a proposition which betokens much ignorance of history in those who assent to it (since it is historically true that a large proportion of infidels in all ages have been persons of distinguished integrity and honor); and would be maintained by no one who had the smallest conception how many of the persons in greatest repute with the world, both for virtues and for attainments, are well known, at least to their intimates, to be unbelievers. The rule, besides, is suicidal, and cuts away its own foundation Under pretense that atheists must be liars, it admits the testimony of all atheists who are willing to lie, and rejects only those who brave the obloquy of publicly confessing a detested creed rather than affirm a falsehood. A rule thus self-convicted of absurdity so far as regards its professed purpose, can be kept in force only as a badge of hatred, a relic of persecution; a persecution, too, having the peculiarity, that the qualification for undergoing it, is the being clearly proved not to deserve it. The rule, and the theory it implies, are hardly less insulting to believers than to infidels. For if he who does not believe in a future state, necessarily lies, it follows that they who do believe are only prevented from lying, if prevented they are, by the fear of hell. We will not do the authors and abettors of the rule the injury of supposing, that the conception which they have formed of Christian virtue is drawn from their own consciousness.

These, indeed, are but rags and remnants of persecution, and may be thought to be not so much an indication of the wish to persecute, as an example of that very frequent infirmity of English minds, which makes them take a preposterous pleasure in the assertion of a bad principle, when they are no longer bad enough to desire to carry it really into practice. But unhappily there is no security in the state of the public mind, that the suspension of worse forms of legal persecution, which has lasted for about the space of a generation, will continue. In this age the quiet surface of routine is as often ruffled by attempts to resuscitate past evils, as to introduce new benefits. What is boasted of at the present time as the revival of religion, is always, in narrow and uncultivated minds, at least as much the revival of bigotry; and where there is the strong permanent leaven of intolerance in the feelings of a people, which at all times abides in the middle classes of this country, it needs but little to provoke them into actively persecuting those whom they have never ceased to think proper objects of persecution.[4] For it is this—it is the opinions

4 Mill's note: Ample warning may be drawn from the large infusion of the passions of a persecutor, which mingled with the general display of the worst parts of our national character on the occasion of the Sepoy insurrection. The ravings of fanatics or charlatans from the pulpit may be unworthy of notice; but the heads of the Evangelical party have announced as their principal for the government of Hindoos and Mohammedans, that no schools be supported by public money in which the Bible is not taught, and by necessary consequence that no public employment be given to any but real or pretended Christians. An under-Secretary of State, in a speech delivered to his constituents on November 12, 1857, is reported to have said: "Toleration of their faith" (the faith of a hundred millions of British subjects), "the superstition which they called religion, by the British Government, had the effect of retarding the ascendancy of the British name, and preventing the salutary growth of Christianity. . . . Toleration was the great corner-stone of the religious liberties of this country; but do not let them abuse that precious word toleration. As he understood it, it meant the complete liberty to all, freedom of worship, *among Christians, who worshipped upon the same foundation.* It meant toleration of all sects and denominations of *Christians who believed in the one mediation.*" I desire to call attention to the fact, that a man who has been deemed fit to fill a high office in the government of this country, under a liberal Ministry, maintains the doctrine that all who do not believe in the divinity of Christ are beyond the pale of toleration. Who, after this imbecile display, can indulge the illusion that religious persecution has passed away, never to return?

men entertain, and the feelings they cherish, respecting those who disown the beliefs they deem important, which makes this country not a place of mental freedom. For a long time past, the chief mischief of the legal penalties is that they strengthen the social stigma. It is that stigma which is really effective, and so effective is it, that the profession of opinions which are under the ban of society is much less common in England, than is, in many other countries, the avowal of those which incur risk of judicial punishment. In respect to all persons but those whose pecuniary circumstances make them independent of the goodwill of other people, opinion, on this subject, is as efficacious as law; men might as well be imprisoned, as excluded from the means of earning their bread. Those whose bread is already secured, and who desire no favors from men in power, or from bodies of men, or from the public, have nothing to fear from the open avowal of any opinions, but to be ill-thought of and ill-spoken of, and this it ought not to require a very heroic mold to enable them to bear. There is no room for any appeal *ad misericordiam* in behalf of such persons. But though we do not now inflict so much evil on those who think differently from us, as it was formerly our custom to do, it may be that we do ourselves as much evil as ever by our treatment of them. Socrates was put to death, but the Socratic philosophy rose like the sun in heaven, and spread its illumination over the whole intellectual firmament. Christians were cast to the lions, but the Christian church grew up a stately and spreading tree, overtopping the older and less vigorous growths, and stifling them by its shade. Our merely social intolerance kills no one, roots out no opinions, but induces men to disguise them, or to abstain from any active effort for their diffusion. With us, heretical opinions do not perceptibly gain, or even lose, ground in each decade or generation; they never blaze out far and wide, but continue to smolder in the narrow cricles of thinking and studious persons among whom they originate, without ever lighting up the general affairs of mankind with either a true or a deceptive light. And thus is kept up a state of things very satisfactory to some minds, because, without the unpleasant process of fining or imprisoning anybody, it maintains all prevailing opinions outwardly undisturbed, while it does not absolutely interdict the exercise of reason by dissentients afflicted with the malady of thought. A convenient plan for having peace in the intellectual world, and keeping all things going on therein very much as they do already. But the price paid for this sort of intellectual pacification, is the sacrifice of the entire moral courage of the human mind. A state of things in which a large portion of the most active and inquiring intellects find it advisable to keep the general principles and grounds of their convictions within their own breasts, and attempt, in what they address to the public, to fit as much as they can of their own conclusions to premises which they have internally renounced, cannot send forth the open, fearless characters, and logical, consistent intellects who once adorned the thinking world. The sort of men who can be looked for under it, are either mere conformers to commonplace, or time-servers for truth, whose arguments on all great subjects are meant for their hearers, and are not those which have convinced themselves. Those who avoid this alternative, do so by narrowing their thoughts and interest to things which can be spoken of without venturing within the region of principles, that is, to small practical matters, which would come right of themselves, if but the minds of mankind were strengthened and enlarged, and which will never be made effectually right until then: while that which would strengthen and enlarge men's minds, free and daring speculation on the highest subjects, is abandoned.

Those in whose eyes this reticence on the part of heretics is no evil, should consider in the first place, that in consequence of it there is never any fair and thorough discussion of heretical opinions; and that such of them as could not stand such a discussion, though they may be prevented from spreading, do not disappear. But it is not the minds of heretics that are deteriorated most, by the ban placed on all inquiry which does not end in the orthodox conclusions. The greatest harm done is to those who are not heretics, and whose whole mental development is cramped, and their reason cowed, by the fear of heresy. Who can compute what the world loses in the multitude of promising intellects combined with timid characters, who dare not follow out any bold, vigorous, independent train of thought, lest it should land them in something which would admit of being considered irreligious or immoral? Among them we may occasionally see some man of deep conscientiousness, and subtle and refined understanding, who spends a life in sophisticating with an intellect which he cannot silence, and exhausts the resources of ingenuity in attempting to reconcile the promptings of his conscience and reason with orthodoxy, which yet he does not, perhaps, to the end succeed in doing. No one can be a great thinker who does not recognize, that as a thinker it is his first duty to follow his intellect to whatever conclusions it may lead. Truth gains more even by the errors of one who, with due study and preparation, thinks for himself, than by the true opinions of those who only hold them because they do not suffer themselves to think. Not that it is solely, or chiefly, to form great thinkers, that freedom of thinking is required. On the contrary, it is as much and even more indispensable, to enable average human beings to attain the mental stature which they are capable of. There have been, and may again be, great individual thinkers, in a general atmosphere of mental slavery. But there never has been, nor ever will be, in that atmosphere, an intellectually active people. When any people has made a temporary approach to such a character, it has been because the dread of heterodox speculation was for a time suspended. Where there is a tacit convention that principles are not to be disputed; where the discussion of the greatest questions which can occupy humanity is considered to be closed, we cannot hope to find that generally high scale of mental activity which has made some periods of history so remarkable. Never when controversy avoided the subjects which are large and important enough to kindle enthusiasm, was the mind of a people stirred up from its foundations, and the impulse given which raised even persons of the most ordinary intellect to something of the dignity of thinking beings. Of such we have had an example in the condition of Europe during the times immediately following the Reformation; another, though limited to the Continent and to a more cultivated class, in the speculative movement of the latter half of the eighteenth century; and a third, of still briefer duration, in the intellectual fermentation of Germany during the Goethian and Fichtean period. These periods differed widely in the particular opinions which they developed; but were alike in this, that during all three the yoke of authority was broken. In each, an old mental despotism had been thrown off, and no new one had yet taken its place. The impulse given at these three periods has made Europe what it now is. Every single improvement which has taken place either in the human mind or in institutions, may be traced distinctly to one or other of them. Appearances have for some time indicated that all three impulses are wellnigh spent; and we can expect no fresh start, until we again assert our mental freedom.

Let us now pass to the second division of the argument, and dismissing the supposition that any of the received opinions may be false, let us assume them to be true, and examine into the worth of the manner in which they are likely to be held, when their truth is not freely and openly canvassed. However unwillingly a person who has a strong opinion may admit the possibility that his opinion may be false, he ought to be moved by the consideration that however true it may be, if it is not fully, frequently, and fearlessly discussed, it will be held as a dead dogma, not a living truth.

There is a class of persons (happily not quite so numerous as formerly) who think it enough if a person assents undoubtingly to what they think true, though he has no knowledge whatever of the grounds of the opinion, and could not make a tenable defense of it against the most superficial objections. Such persons, if they can once get their creed taught from authority, naturally think that no good, and some harm, comes of its being allowed to be questioned. Where their influence prevails, they make it nearly impossible for the received opinion to be rejected wisely and considerately, though it may still be rejected rashly and ignorantly; for to shut out discussion entirely is seldom possible, and when it once gets in, beliefs not grounded on conviction are apt to give way before the slightest semblance of an argument. Waiving, however, this possibility—assuming that the true opinion abides in the mind, but abides as a prejudice, a belief independent of, and proof against, argument—this is not the way in which truth ought to be held by a rational being. This is not knowing the truth. Truth, thus held, is but one superstition the more accidentally clinging to the words which enunciate a truth.

If the intellect and judgment of mankind ought to be cultivated, a thing which Protestants at least do not deny, on what can these faculties be more appropriately exercised by any one, than on the things which concern him so much that it is considered necessary for him to hold opinions on them? If the cultivation of the understanding consists in one thing more than in another, it is surely in learning the grounds of one's own opinions. Whatever people believe, on subjects on which it is of the first importance to believe rightly, they ought to be able to defend against at least the common objections. But, some one may say, "Let them be *taught* the grounds of their opinions. It does not follow that opinions must be merely parroted because they are never heard controverted. Persons who learn geometry do not simply commit the theorems to memory, but understand and learn likewise the demonstrations; and it would be absurd to say that they remain ignorant of the grounds of geometrical truths, because they never hear any one deny, and attempt to disprove them." Undoubtedly: and such teaching suffices on a subject like mathematics, where there is nothing at all to be said on the wrong side of the question. The peculiarity of the evidence of mathematical truths is, that all the argument is on one side. There are no objections, and no answers to objections. But on every subject on which difference of opinion is possible, the truth depends on a balance to be struck between two sets of conflicting reasons. Even in natural philosophy, there is always some other explanation possible of the same facts; some geocentric theory instead of heliocentric, some phlogiston instead of oxygen; and it has to be shown why that other theory cannot be the true one: and until this is shown, and until we know how it is shown, we do not understand the grounds of our opinion. But when we turn to subjects infinitely more complicated, to morals, religion, politics, social relations, and the business of life, three-fourths of the arguments for every disputed opinion consist in dispelling the appearances which favor some opinion different from it. The greatest orator, save one, of antiquity, has left it on record that he always studied his adversary's case with as great, if not with still greater, intensity than even his own. What Cicero practiced as the means of forensic success, requires to be imitated by all who study any subject in order to arrive at the truth. He who knows only his own side of the case, knows little of that. His reasons may be good, and no one may have been able to refute them. But if he is equally unable to refute the reasons on the opposite side; if he does not so much as know what they are, he has no ground for preferring either opinion. The rational position for him would be suspension of judgment, and unless he contents himself with that, he is either led by authority, or adopts, like the generality of the world, the side to which he feels most inclination. Nor is it enough that he should hear the arguments of adversaries from his own teachers, presented as they state them, and accompanied by what they offer as refutations. That is not the way to do justice to the arguments, or bring them into real contact with his own mind. He must be able to hear them from persons who actually believe them; who defend them in earnest, and do their very utmost for them. He must know them in their most plausible and persuasive form; he must feel the whole force of the difficulty which the true view of the subject has to encounter and dispose of; else he will never really possess himself of the portion of truth which meets and removes that difficulty. Ninety-nine in a hundred of what are called edu-

cated men are in this condition; even of those who can argue
fluently for their opinions. Their conclusion may be true, but
it might be false for anything they know: they have never
thrown themselves into the mental position of those who think
differently from them, and considered what such persons may
have to say; and consequently they do not, in any proper sense
of the word, know the doctrine which they themselves profess.
They do not know those parts of it which explain and justify
the remainder; the considerations which show that a fact
which seemingly conflicts with another is reconcilable with it,
or that, of two apparently strong reasons, one and not the
other ought to be preferred. All that part of the truth which
turns the scale, and decides the judgment of a completely
informed mind, they are strangers to; nor is it ever really
known, but to those who have attended equally and impartially to both sides, and endeavored to see the reasons of
both in the strongest light. So essential is this discipline to a
real understanding of moral and human subjects, that if
opponents of all important truths do not exist, it is indispensable to imagine them, and supply them with the strongest
arguments which the most skillful devil's advocate can con-
jure up.

To abate the force of these considerations, an enemy of free
discussion may be supposed to say, that there is no necessity
for mankind in general to know and understand all that can
be said against or for their opinions by philosophers and
theologians. That it is not needful for common men to be able
to expose all the misstatements or fallacies of an ingenious
opponent. That it is enough if there is always somebody capable of answering them, so that nothing likely to mislead
uninstructed persons remains unrefuted. That simple minds,
having been taught the obvious grounds of the truths inculcated in them, may trust to authority for the rest, and being
aware that they have neither knowledge nor talent to resolve
every difficulty which can be raised, may repose in the assurance that all those which have been raised have been or can
be answered, by those who are specially trained to the task.

Conceding to this view of the subject the utmost that can be claimed for it by those most easily satisfied with the amount of understanding of truth which ought to accompany the belief of it; even so, the argument for free discussion is no way weakened. For even this doctrine acknowledges that mankind ought to have a rational assurance that all objections have been satisfactorily answered; and how are they to be answered if that which requires to be answered is not spoken? or how can the answer be known to be satisfactory, if the objectors have no opportunity of showing that it is unsatisfactory? If not the public, at least the philosophers and theologians who are to resolve the difficulties, must make themselves familiar with those difficulties in their most puzzling form; and this cannot be accomplished unless they are freely stated, and placed in the most advantageous light which they admit of. The Catholic Church has its own way of dealing with this embarrassing problem. It makes a broad separation between those who can be permitted to receive its doctrines on conviction, and those who must accept them on trust. Neither, indeed, are allowed any choice as to what they will accept; but the clergy, such at least as can be fully confided in, may admissibly and meritoriously make themselves acquainted with the arguments of opponents, in order to answer them, and may, therefore, read heretical books; the laity, not unless by special permission, hard to be obtained. This discipline recognizes a knowledge of the enemy's case as beneficial to the teachers, but finds means, consistent with this, of denying it to the rest of the world: thus giving to the *élite* more mental culture, though not more mental freedom, than it allows to the mass. By this device it succeeds in obtaining the kind of mental superiority which its purposes require; for though culture without freedom never made a large and liberal mind, it can make a clever *nisi prius* advocate of a cause. But in countries professing Protestantism, this resource is denied; since Protestants hold, at least in theory, that the responsibility for the choice of a religion must be borne by each for himself, and cannot be thrown off upon teachers. Besides, in the present state of the world, it is practically impossible that writings which are read by the instructed can be kept from the uninstructed. If the teachers of mankind are to be cognizant of all that they ought to know, everything must be free to be written and published without restraint.

If, however, the mischievous operation of the absence of free discussion, when the received opinions are true, were confined to leaving men ignorant of the grounds of those opinions, it might be thought that this, if an intellectual, is no moral evil, and does not affect the worth of the opinions, regarded in their influence on the character. The fact, however, is, that not only the grounds of the opinion are forgotten in the absence of discussion, but too often the meaning of the opinion itself. The words which convey it, cease to suggest ideas, or suggest only a small portion of those they were originally employed to communicate. Instead of a vivid conception and a living belief, there remain only a few phrases retained by rote; or, if any part, the shell and husk only of the meaning is retained, the finer essence being lost. The great chapter in human history which the fact occupies and fills, cannot be too earnestly studied and meditated on.

It is illustrated in the experience of almost all ethical doctrines and religious creeds. They are all full of meaning and vitality to those who originate them, and to the direct disciples of the originators. Their meaning continues to be felt in undiminished strength, and is perhaps brought out into even fuller consciousness, so long as the struggle lasts to give the doctrine or creed an ascendancy over other creeds. At last it either prevails, and becomes the general opinion, or its progress stops; it keeps possession of the ground it has gained, but ceases to spread further. When either of these results has become apparent, controversy on the subject flags, and gradually dies away. The doctrine has taken its place, if not as a received opinion, as one of the admitted sects or divisions of opinion: those who hold it have generally inherited, not adopted it; and conversion from one of these doctrines to another, being now an exceptional fact, occupies little place in the thoughts of their professors. Instead of being, as at first, constantly on the alert either to defend themselves against the world, or to bring the world over to them, they have subsided into acquiescence, and neither listen, when they can help it, to arguments against their creed, nor trouble dissentients (if there be such) with arguments in its favor. From this time may usually be dated the decline in the living power of the doctrine. We often hear the teachers of all creeds lamenting the difficulty of keeping up in the minds of believers a lively apprehension of the truth which they nominally recognize, so that it may penetrate the feelings, and acquire a real mastery over the conduct. No such difficulty is complained of while the creed is still fighting for its existence: even the weaker combatants then know and feel what they are fighting for, and the difference between it and other doctrines; and in that period of every creed's existence, not a few persons may be found, who have realized its fundamental principles in all the forms of thought, have weighed and considered them in all their important bearings, and have experienced the full effect on the character, which belief in that creed ought to produce in a mind thoroughly imbued with it. But when it has come to be an hereditary creed, and to be received passively, not actively—when the mind is no longer compelled, in the same degree as at first, to exercise its vital powers on the questions which its belief presents to it, there is a progressive tendency to forget all of the belief except the formularies, or to give it a dull and torpid assent, as if accepting it on trust dispened with the necessity of realizing it in consciousness, or testing it by personal experience; until it almost ceases to connect itself at all with the inner life of the human being. Then are seen the cases, so frequent in this age of the world as almost to form the majority, in which the creed remains as it were outside the mind, encrusting and petrifying it against all other influences addressed to the higher parts of our nature; manifesting its power by not suffering any fresh and living conviction to get in, but itself doing nothing for the mind or heart, except standing sentinel over them to keep them vacant.

EXCELLENT EXAMPLE

To what an extent doctrines intrinsically fitted to make the deepest impression upon the mind may remain in it as dead beliefs, without being ever realized in the imagination, the feelings, or the understanding, is exemplified by the manner in which the majority of believers hold the doctrines of Christianity. By Christianity I here mean what is accounted such by all churches and sects—the maxims and precepts contained in the New Testament. These are considered sacred, and accepted as laws, by all professing Christians. Yet it is scarcely too much to say that not one Christian in a thousand guides or tests his individual conduct by reference to those laws. The standard to which he does refer it, is the custom of his nation, his class, or his religious profession. He has thus, on the one hand, a collection of ethical maxims, which he believes to have been vouchsafed to him by infallible wisdom as rules for his government; and on the other, a set of everyday judgments and practices, which go a certain length with some of those maxims, not so great a length with others, stand in direct opposition to some, and are, on the whole, a compromise between the Christian creed and the interests and suggestions of worldly life. To the first of these standards he gives his homage; to the other his real allegiance. All Christians believe that the blessed are the poor and humble, and those who are ill-used by the world; that it is easier for a camel to pass through the eye of a needle than for a rich man to enter the kingdom of heaven; that they should judge not, lest they be judged; that they should swear not at all; that they should love their neighbor as themselves; that if one take their cloak, they should give him their coat also; that they should take no thought for the morrow; that if they would be perfect, they should sell all that they have and give it to the poor. They are not insincere when they say that they believe these things. They do believe them, as people believe what they have always heard lauded and never discussed. But in the sense of that living belief which regulates conduct, they believe these doctrines just up to the point to which it is usual to act upon them. The doctrines in their integrity are serviceable to pelt adversaries with; and it is understood that they are to be put forward (when possible) as the reasons for whatever people do that they think laudable. But any one who reminded them that the maxims require an infinity of things which they never even think of doing, would gain nothing but to be classed among those very unpopular characters who affect to be better than other people. The doctrines have no hold on ordinary believers—are not a power in their minds. They have an habitual respect for the sound of them, but no feeling which spreads from the words to the things signified, and forces the mind to take *them* in, and make them conform to the formula. Whenever conduct is concerned, they look round for Mr. A and B to direct them how far to go in obeying Christ.

Now we may be well assured that the case was not thus, but far otherwise, with the early Christians. Had it been thus, Christianity never would have expanded from an obscure sect of the despised Hebrews into the religion of the Roman empire. When their enemies said, "See how these Christians love one another" (a remark not likely to be made by anybody now), they assuredly had a much livelier feeling of the meaning of their creed than they have ever had since. And to this cause, probably, it is chiefly owing that Christianity now makes so little progress in extending its domain, and after eighteen centuries, is still nearly confined to Europeans and the descendants of Europeans. Even with the strictly religious, who are much in earnest about their doctrines, and attach a greater amount of meaning to many of them than people in general, it commonly happens that the part which is thus comparatively active in their minds is that which was made by Calvin, or Knox, or some such person much nearer in character to themselves. The sayings of Christ co-exist passively in their minds, producing hardly any effect beyond what is caused by mere listening to words so amiable and bland. There are many reasons, doubtless, why doctrines which are the badge of a sect retain more of their vitality than those common to all recognized sects, and why more pains are taken by teachers to keep their meaning alive; but one reason certainly is, that the peculiar doctrines are more questioned, and have to be oftener defended against open gainsayers. Both teachers and learners go to sleep at their post, as soon as there is no enemy in the field.

The same thing holds true, generally speaking, of all traditional doctrines—those of prudence and knowledge of life, as well as morals or religion. All languages and literatures are full of general observations on life, both as to what it is, and how to conduct oneself in it; observations which everybody knows, which everybody repeats, or hears with acquiescence, which are received as truisms, yet of which most people first truly learn the meaning, when experience, generally of a painful kind, has made it a reality to them. How often, when smarting under some unforeseen misfortune or disappointment, does a person call to mind some proverb or common saying, familiar to him all his life, the meaning of which, if he had ever before felt it as he does now, would have saved him from the calamity. There are indeed reasons for this, other than the absence of discussion: there are many truths of which the full meaning *cannot* be realized, until personal experience has brought it home. But much more of the meaning even of these would have been understood, and what was understood would have been far more deeply impressed on the mind, if the man had been accustomed to hear it argued *pro* and *con* by people who did understand it. The fatal tendency of mankind to leave off thinking about a thing when it is no longer doubtful, is the cause of half their errors. A contemporary author has well spoken of "the deep slumber of a decided opinion."

But what! (it may be asked) Is the absence of unanimity an indispensable condition of true knowledge? Is it necessary that some part of mankind should persist in error, to enable any to realize the truth? Does a belief cease to be real and vital as soon as it is generally received—and is a proposition never thoroughly understood and felt unless some doubt of it remains? As soon as mankind have unanimously accepted a truth, does the truth perish within them? The highest aim and best result of improved intelligence, it has hitherto been thought, is to unite mankind more and more in the acknowledgment of all important truths: and does the intelligence only last as long as it has not achieved its object? Do the fruits of conquest perish by the very completeness of the victory?

I affirm no such thing. As mankind improve, the number of doctrines which are no longer disputed or doubted will be constantly on the increase: and the well-being of mankind may almost be measured by the number and gravity of the truths which have reached the point of being uncontested. The cessation, on one question after another, of serious controversy, is one of the necessary incidents of the consolidation of opinion; a consolidation as salutary in the case of true opinions, as it is dangerous and noxious when the opinions are erroneous. But though this gradual narrowing of the bounds of diversity of opinion is necessary in both senses of the term, being at once inevitable and indispensable, we are not therefore obliged to conclude that all its consequences must be beneficial. The loss of so important an aid to the intelligent and living apprehension of a truth, as is afforded by the necessity of explaining it to, or defending it against, opponents, though not sufficient to outweigh, is no trifling drawback from, the benefit of its universal recognition. Where this advantage can no longer be had, I confess I should like to see the teachers of mankind endeavoring to provide a substitute for it; some contrivance for making the difficulties of the question as present to the learner's consciousness, as if they were pressed upon him by a dissentient champion, eager for his conversion.

But instead of seeking contrivances for this purpose, they have lost those they formerly had. The Socratic dialectics, so magnificently exemplified in the dialogues of Plato, were a contrivance of this description. They were essentially a negative discussion of the great questions of philosophy and life, directed with consummate skill to the purpose of convincing any one who had merely adopted the commonplaces of received opinion, that he did not understand the subject—that he as yet attached no definite meaning to the doctrines he professed; in order that, becoming aware of his ignorance, he might be put in the way to attain a stable belief, resting on a clear apprehension both of the meaning of doctrines and of their evidence. The school disputations of the middle ages had a somewhat similar object. They were intended to make sure that the pupil understood his own opinion, and (by necessary correlation) the opinion opposed to it, and could enforce the grounds of the one and confute those of the other. These last-mentioned contests had indeed the incurable defect, that the premises appealed to were taken from authority, not from reason; and, as a discipline to the mind, they were in every respect inferior to the powerful dialectics which formed the intellects of the "Socratici viri": [5] but the modern mind owes far more to both than it is generally willing to admit, and the present modes of education contain nothing which in the smallest degree supplies the place either of the one or of the other. A person who derives all his instruction from teachers or books, even if he escape the besetting temptation of contenting himself with cram, is under no compulsion to hear both sides; accordingly it is far from a frequent accomplishment, even among thinkers, to know both sides; and the weakest part of what everybody says in defense of his opinion, is what he intends as a reply to antagonists. It is the fashion of the present time to disparage negative logic—that which points out weaknesses in theory or errors in practice, without establishing positive truths. Such negative criticism would indeed be poor enough as an ultimate result; but as a means to attaining any positive knowledge or conviction worthy the name, it cannot be valued too highly; and until people are again systematically trained to it, there will be few great thinkers, and a low general average of intellect, in any but the mathematical and physical departments of speculation. On any other subject no one's opinions deserve the name of knowledge, except so far as he has either had forced upon him by others, or gone through of himself, the same mental process which would have been required of him in carrying on an

[5] Philosophical men.

active controversy with opponents. That, therefore, which when absent, it is so indispensable, but so difficult, to create, how worse than absurd it is to forgo, when spontaneously offering itself! If there are any persons who contest a received opinion, or who will do so if law or opinion will let them, let us thank them for it, open our minds to listen to them, and rejoice that there is some one to do for us what we otherwise ought, if we have any regard for either the certainty or the vitality of our convictions, to do with much greater labor for ourselves.

It still remains to speak of one of the principal causes which make diversity of opinion advantageous, and will continue to do so until mankind shall have entered a stage of intellectual advancement which at present seems at an incalculable distance. We have hitherto considered only two possibilities: that the received opinion may be false, and some other opinion, consequently, true; or that, the received opinion being true, a conflict with the opposite error is essential to a clear apprehension and deep feeling of its truth. But there is a commoner case than neither of these; when the conflicting doctrines, instead of being one true and the other false, share the truth between them; and the nonconforming opinion is needed to supply the remainder of the truth, of which the received doctrine embodies only a part. Popular opinions, on subjects not palpable to sense, are often true, but seldom or never the whole truth. They are a part of the truth; sometimes a greater, sometimes a smaller part, but exaggerated, distorted, and disjoined from the truths by which they ought to be accompanied and limited. Heretical opinions, on the other hand, are generally some of these suppressed and neglected truths, bursting the bonds which kept them down, and either seeking reconciliation with the truth contained in the common opinion, or fronting it as enemies, and setting themselves up, with similar exclusiveness, as the whole truth. The latter case is hitherto the most frequent, as, in the human mind, one-sidedness has always been the rule, and many-sidedness the exception. Hence, even in revolutions of opinion, one part of the truth usually sets while another rises. Even progress, which ought to superadd, for the most part only substitutes, one partial and incomplete truth for another; improvement consisting chiefly in this, that the new fragment of truth is more wanted, more adapated to the needs of the time, than that which it displaces. Such being the partial character of prevailing opinions, even when resting on a true foundation, every opinion which embodies somewhat of the portion of truth which the common opinion omits, ought to be considered precious, with whatever amount of error and confusion that truth may be blended. No sober judge of human affairs will feel bound to be indignant because those who force on our notice truths which we should otherwise have overlooked, overlook some of those which we see. Rather, he will think that so long as popular truth is one-sided, it is more desirable than otherwise that unpopular truth should have one-sided asserters too; such being usually the most energetic, and the most likely to compel reluctant attention to the fragment of wisdom which they proclaim as if it were the whole.

Thus, in the eighteenth century, when nearly all the instructed, and all those of the uninstructed who were led by them, were lost in admiration of what is called civilization, and of the marvels of modern science, literature, and philosophy, and while greatly overrating the amount of unlikeness between the men of modern and those of ancient times, indulged the belief that the whole of the difference was in their own favor; with what a salutary shock did the paradoxes of Rousseau explode like bombshells in the midst, dislocating the compact mass of one-sided opinion, and forcing its elements to recombine in a better form and with additional ingredients. Not that the current opinions were on the whole farther from the truth than Rousseau's were; on the contrary, they were nearer to it; they contained more of positive truth, and very much less of error. Nevertheless there lay in Rousseau's doctrine, and has floated down the stream of opinion along with it, a considerable amount of exactly those truths which the popular opinion wanted; and these are the deposit which was left behind when the flood subsided. The superior worth of simplicity of life, the enervating and demoralizing effect of the trammels and hypocrisies of artificial society, are ideas which have never been entirely absent from cultivated minds since Rousseau wrote; and they will in time produce their due effect, though at present needing to be asserted as much as ever, and to be asserted by deeds, for word, on this subject, have nearly exhausted their power.

In politics, again, it is almost a commonplace, that a party of order or stability, and a party of progress or reform, are both necessary elements of a healthy state of political life; until the one or the other shall have so enlarged its mental grasp as to be a party equally of order and of progress, knowing and distinguishing what is fit to be preserved from what ought to be swept away. Each of these modes of thinking derives its utility from the deficiencies of the other; but it is in a great measure the opposition of the other that keeps each within the limits of reason and sanity. Unless opinions favorable to democracy and to aristocracy, to property and to equality, to co-operation and to competition, to luxury and to abstinence, to sociality and individuality, to liberty and discipline, and all the other standing antagonisms of practical life, are expressed with equal freedom, and enforced and defended with equal talent and energy, there is no chance of both elements obtaining their due; one scale is sure to go up, and the other down. Truth, in the great practical concerns of life, is so much a question of the reconciling and combining of opposites, that very few have minds sufficiently capacious and impartial to make the adjustment with an approach to correctness, and it has to be made by the rough process of a struggle between combatants fighting under hostile banners. On any of the great open questions just enumerated, if either of the two opinions had a better claim than the other, not merely to be tolerated, but to be encouraged and countenanced, it is the one which happens at the particular time and place to be in a minority. That is the opinion which, for the time being, repre-

sents the neglected interests, the side of human well-being
which is in danger of obtaining less than its share. I am aware
that there is not, in this country, any intolerance of differences
of opinion on most of these topics. They are adduced to show,
by admitted and multiplied examples, the universality of the
fact, that only through diversity of opinion is there, in the existing state of human intellect, a chance of fair play to all sides
of the truth. When there are persons to be found, who form
an exception to the apparent unanimity of the world on any
subject, even if the world is in the right, it is always probable
that dissentients have something worth hearing to say for
themselves, and that truth would lose something by their
silence.

It may be objected, "But *some* received principles, especially
on the highest and most vital subjects, are more than half-
truths. The Christian morality, for instance, is the whole truth
on that subject, and if any one teaches a morality which varies
from it, he is wholly in error." As this is of all cases the most
important in practice, none can be fitter to test the general
maxim. But before pronouncing what Christian morality is
or is not, it would be desirable to decide what is meant by
Christian morality. If it means the morality of the New Testament, I wonder that any one who derives his knowledge of
this from the book itself, can suppose that it was announced,
or intended, as a complete doctrine of morals. The Gospel always refers to a pre-existing morality, and confines its precepts
to the particulars in which that morality was to be corrected,
or superseded by a wider and higher; expressing itself, moreover, in terms most general, often impossible to be interpreted
literally, and possessing rather the impressiveness of poetry
or eloquence than the precision of legislation. To extract from
it a body of ethical doctrine, has never been possible without
eking it out from the Old Testament, that is, from a system
elaborate indeed, but in many respects barbarous, and intended
only for a barbarous people. St. Paul, a declared enemy to this
Judaical mode of interpreting the doctrine and filling up the
scheme of his Master, equally assumes a pre-existing morality,

namely that of the Greeks and Romans; and his advice to Christians is in a great measure a system of accommodation to that; even to the extent of giving an apparent sanction to slavery. What is called Christian, but should rather be termed theological, morality, was not the work of Christ or the Apostles, but is of much later origin, having been gradually built up by the Catholic church of the first five centuries, and though not implicitly adopted by moderns and Protestants, has been much less modified by them than might have been expected. For the most part, indeed, they have contented themselves with cutting off the additions which had been made to it in the middle ages, each sect supplying the place by fresh additions, adapted to its own character and tendencies. That mankind owe a great debt to this morality, and to its early teachers, I should be the last person to deny; but I do not scruple to say of it, that it is, in many important points, incomplete and one-sided, and that unless ideas and feelings, not sanctioned by it, had contributed to the formation of European life and character, human affairs would have been in a worse condition than they now are. Christian morality (so called) has all the characters of a reaction; it is, in great part, a protest against Paganism. Its ideal is negative rather than positive; passive rather than active; Innocence rather than Nobleness; Abstinence from Evil, rather than energetic Pursuit of Good: in its precepts (as has been well said) "thou shalt not" predominates unduly over "thou shalt." In its horror of sensuality, it made an idol of asceticism, which has been gradually compromised away into one of legality. It holds out the hope of heaven and the threat of hell, as the appointed and appropriate motives to a virtuous life: in this falling far below the best of the ancients, and doing what lies in it to give to human morality an essentially selfish character, by disconnecting each man's feelings of duty from the interests of his fellow-creatures, except so far as a self-interested inducement is offered to him for consulting them. It is essentially a doctrine of passive obedience; it inculcates submission to all authorities found established; who indeed are not to be actively obeyed when they command what religion forbids, but who are not to be resisted, far less rebelled against, for any amount of wrong to ourselves. And while, in the morality of the best Pagan nations, duty to the State holds even a disproportionate place, infringing on the just liberty of the individual; in purely Christian ethics, that grand department of duty is scarcely noticed or acknowledged. It is in the Koran, not the New Testament, that we read the maxim—"A ruler who appoints any man to an office, when there is in his dominions another man better qualified for it, sins against God and against the State." What little recognition the idea of obligation to the public obtains in modern morality, is derived from Greek and Roman sources, not from Christian; as, even in the morality of private life, whatever exists of magnanimity, high-mindedness, personal dignity, even the sense of honor, is derived from the purely human, not the religious part of our education, and never could have grown out of a standard of ethics in which the only worth, professedly recognized, is that of obedience.

I am as far as any one from pretending that these defects are necessarily inherent in the Christian ethics, in every manner in which it can be conceived, or that the many requisites of a complete moral doctrine which it does not contain, do not admit of being reconciled with it. Far less would I insinuate this of the doctrines and precepts of Christ himself. I believe that the sayings of Christ are all, that I can see any evidence of their having been intended to be; that they are irreconcilable with nothing which a comprehensive morality requires; that everything which is excellent in ethics may be brought within them, with no greater violence to their language than has been done to it by all who have attempted to deduce from them any practical system of conduct whatever. But it is quite consistent with this, to believe that they contain, and were meant to contain, only a part of the truth; that many essential elements of the highest morality are among the things which are not provided for, nor intended to be provided for, in the recorded deliverances of the Founder of Christianity, and which have been entirely thrown aside in the system of ethics erected on the basis of those deliverances by the Christian Church. And this being so, I think it a great error to persist in attempting to find in the Christian doctrine that complete rule for our guidance, which its author intended it to sanction and enforce, but only partially to provide. I believe, too, that this narrow theory is becoming a grave practical evil, detracting greatly from the value of the moral training and instruction, which so many well-meaning persons are now at length exerting themselves to promote. I much fear that by attempting to form the mind and feelings on an exclusively religious type, and discarding those secular standards (as for want of a better name they may be called) which heretofore co-existed with and supplemented the Christian ethics, receiving some of its spirit, and infusing into it some of theirs, there will result, and is even now resulting, a low, abject, servile type of character, which, submit itself as it may to what it deems the Supreme Will, is incapable of rising to or sympathizing in the conception of Supreme Goodness. I believe that other ethics than any which can be evolved from exclusively Christian sources, must exist side by side with Christian ethics to produce the moral regeneration of mankind; and that the Christian system is no exception to the rule, that in an imperfect state of the human mind, the interests of truth require a diversity of opinions. It is not necessary that in ceasing to ignore the moral truths not contained in Christianity, men should ignore any of those which it does contain. Such prejudice, or oversight, when it occurs, is altogether an evil; but it is one from which we cannot hope to be always exempt, and must be regarded as the price paid for an inestimable good. The exclusive pretension made by a part of the truth to be the whole, must and ought to be protested against; and if a reactionary impulse should make the protestors unjust in their turn, this one-sidedness, like the other, may be lamented, but must be tolerated. If Christians would teach infidels to be just to Christianity, they should themselves be just to infidelity. It can do truth no service to blink the fact, known to all who have the most ordinary acquaintance with literary history, that a large portion of the noblest and most valuable moral teaching has been the work, not only of men who did not know, but of man who knew and rejected, the Christian faith.

I do not pretend that the most unlimited use of the freedom of enunciating all possible opinions would put an end to the evils of religious or philosophical sectarianism. Every truth which men of narrow capacity are in earnest about, is sure to be asserted, inculcated, and in many ways even acted on, as if no other truth existed in the world, or at all events none that could limit or qualify the first. I acknowledge that the tendency of all opinions to become sectarian is not cured by the freest discussion, but is often heightened and exacerbated thereby; the truth which ought to have been, but was not, seen, being rejected all the more violently because proclaimed by persons regarded as opponents. But it is not on the impassioned partisan, it is on the calmer and more disinterested bystander, that this collision of opinions works its salutary effect. Not the violent conflict between parts of the truth, but the quiet suppression of half of it, is the formidable evil; there is always hope when people are forced to listen to both sides; it is when they attend only to one that errors harden into prejudices, and truth itself ceases to have the effect of truth, by being exaggerated into falsehood. And since there are few mental attributes more rare than that judicial faculty which can sit in intelligent judgment between two sides of a question, of which only one is represented by an advocate before it, truth has no chance but in proportion as every side of it, every opinion which embodies any fraction of the truth, not only finds advocates, but is so advocated as to be listened to.

We have now recognized the necessity to the mental well-being of mankind (on which all their other well-being depends) of freedom of opinion, and freedom of the expression of opinion, on four distinct grounds; which we will now briefly recapitulate.

First, if any opinion is compelled to silence, that opinion

may, for aught we can certainly know, be true. To deny this is to assume our own infallibility.

Secondly, though the silenced opinion be an error, it may, and very commonly does, contain a portion of truth; and since the general or prevailing opinion on any subject is rarely or never the whole truth, it is only by the collision of adverse opinions that the remainder of the truth has any chance of being supplied.

Thirdly, even if the received opinion be not only true, but the whole truth; unless it is suffered to be, and actually is, vigorously and earnestly contested, it will, by most of those who receive it, be held in the manner of a prejudice, with little comprehension or feeling of its rational grounds. And not only this, but, fourthly, the meaning of the doctrine itself will be in danger of being lost, or enfeebled, and deprived of its vital effect on the character and conduct: the dogma becoming a mere formal profession, inefficacious for good, but cumbering the ground, and preventing the growth of any real and heart-felt conviction, from reason or personal experience.

Before quitting the subject of freedom of opinion, it is fit to take some notice of those who say, that the free expression of all opinions should be permitted, on condition that the manner be temperate, and do not pass the bounds of fair discussion. Much might be said on the impossibility of fixing where these supposed bounds are to be placed; for if the test be offense to those whose opinion is attacked, I think experience testifies that this offense is given whenever the attack is telling and powerful, and that every opponent who pushes them hard, and whom they find it difficult to answer, appears to them, if he shows any strong feeling on the subject, an intemperate opponent. But this, though an important consideration in a practical point of view, merges in a more fundamental objection. Undoubtedly the manner of asserting an opinion, even though it be a true one, may be very objectionable, and may justly incur severe censure. But the principal offenses of the kind are such as it is mostly impossible, unless by accidental self-betrayal, to bring home to conviction. The gravest of them is, to argue sophistically, to suppress facts or arguments, to misstate the elements of the case, or misrepresent the opposite opinion. But all this, even to the most aggravated degree, is so continually done in perfect good faith, by persons who are not considered, and in many other respects may not deserve to be considered, ignorant or incompetent, that it is rarely possible on adequate grounds conscientiously to stamp the misrepresentation as morally culpable; and still less could law presume to interfere with this kind of controversial misconduct. With regard to what is commonly meant by intemperate discussion, namely invective, sarcasm, personality, and the like, the denunciation of these weapons would deserve more sympathy if it were ever proposed to interdict them equally to both sides; but it is only desired to restrain the employment of them against the prevailing opinion: against the unprevailing they may not only be used without general disapproval, but will be likely to obtain for him who uses them the praise of honest zeal and righteous indignation. Yet whatever mischief arises from their use, is greatest when they are employed against the comparatively defenseless; and whatever unfair advantage can be derived by an opinion from this mode of asserting it, accrues almost exclusively to received opinions. The worst offense of this kind which can be committed by a polemic, is to stigmatize those who hold the contrary opinion as bad and immoral men. To calumny of this sort, those who hold any unpopular opinion are peculiarly exposed, because they are in general few and uninfluential, and nobody but themselves feels much interested in seeing justice done them; but this weapon is, from the nature of the case, denied to those who attack a prevailing opinion: they can neither use it with safety to themselves, nor, if they could, would it do anything but recoil on their own cause. In general, opinions contrary to those commonly received can only obtain a hearing by studied moderation of language, and the most cautious avoidance of unnecessary offense, from which they hardly ever deviate even in a slight degree without losing ground: while unmeasured vituperation employed on the side of the prevailing opinion, really does deter people from professing contrary opinions, and from listening to those who profess them. For the interest, therefore, of truth and justice, it is far more important to restrain this employment of vituperative language than the other; and, for example, if it were necessary to choose, there would be much more need to discourage offensive attacks on infidelity, than on religion. It is, however, obvious that law and authority have no business with restraining either, while opinion ought, in every instance, to determine its verdict by the circumstances of the individual case; condemning every one, on whichever side of the argument he places himself, in whose mode of advocacy either want of candor, or malignity, bigotry, or intolerance of feeling manifest themselves; but not inferring these vices from the side which a person takes, though it be the contrary side of the question to our own: and giving merited honor to every one, whatever opinion he may hold, who has calmness to see and honesty to state what his opponents and their opinions really are, exaggerating nothing to their discredit, keeping nothing back which tells, or can be supposed to tell, in their favor. This is the real morality of public discussion: and if often violated, I am happy to think that there are many controversialists who to a great extent observe it, and a still greater number who conscientiously strive towards it.

Henry David Thoreau

HENRY DAVID THOREAU *(1817-1862) displays in his writing a style that shows the welding together of the philosopher and naturalist, the idea constantly implied in the observation, and the declared idea always forcing him back to the world of data. His prose, like Whitman's poetry, embodies a man, a complex of feeling and perception and judgment, rather than a book schemed in outline. His effort is to unsettle, alarm, even to outrage received opinion. His style seeks out the haunting or gnomic phrase. The essay here reproduced, first published in 1849, is one of the most effective short essays ever written, and the issues it raised have echoed through the entire world. Thoreau was educated at Harvard College and in the woods of New England. Principal works:* A Week on the Concord and Merrimack Rivers *(1849);* Walden; or Life in the Woods *(1854);* Journals *(posthumously published, 1906).*

ON THE DUTY OF CIVIL DISOBEDIENCE

I heartily accept the motto, "That government is best which governs least"; and I should like to see it acted up to more rapidly and systematically. Carried out, it finally amounts to this, which also I believe—"That government is best which governs not at all"; and when men are prepared for it, that will be the kind of government which they will have. Govern-

ment is at best but an expedient; but most governments
are usually, and all governments are sometimes, inexpedient.
The objections which have been brought against a standing
army, and they are many and weighty, and deserve to prevail,
may also at last be brought against a standing government.
The standing army is only an arm of the standing government. The government itself, which is only the mode which
the people have chosen to execute their will, is equally liable
to be abused and perverted before the people can act through
it. Witness the present Mexican war, the work of comparatively a few individuals using the standing government as
their tool; for, in the outset, the people would not have consented to this measure.

literal meaning of words

This American government—what is it but a tradition,
though a recent one, endeavoring to transmit itself unim-
paired to posterity, but each instant losing some of its integrity? It has not the vitality and force of a single living
man; for a single man can bend it to his will. It is a sort
of wooden gun to the people themselves. But it is not the less
necessary for this; for the people must have some complicated
machinery or other, and hear its din, to satisfy that idea of
government which they have. Governments show thus how
successfully men can be imposed on, even impose on themselves, for their own advantage. It is excellent, we must all
allow. Yet this government never of itself furthered any
enterprise, but by the alacrity with which it got out of its way.
It does not keep the country free. *It* does not settle the West.
It does not educate. The character inherent in the American
people has done all that has been accomplished; and it would
have done somewhat more, if the government had not sometimes got in its way. For government is an expedient by
which men would fain succeed in letting one another alone;
and, as has been said, when it is most expedient, the governed are most let alone by it. Trade and commerce, if they
were not made of india-rubber, would never manage to
bounce over the obstacles which legislators are continually
putting in their way; and, if one were to judge these men

wholly by the effects of their actions and not partly by their
intentions, they would deserve to be classed and punished
with those mischievous persons who put obstructions on the
railroads.

But, to speak practically and as a citizen, unlike those
who call themselves no-government men, I ask for, not at
once no government, but *at once* a better government. Let
every man make known what kind of government would
command his respect, and that will be one step toward obtaining it.

After all, the practical reason why, when the power is
once in the hands of the people, a majority are permitted,
and for a long period continue, to rule is not because they
are most likely to be in the right, nor because this seems
fairest to the minority, but because they are physically the
strongest. But a government in which the majority rule in
all cases cannot be based on justice, even as far as men understand it. Can there not be a government in which majorities do not virtually decide right and wrong, but conscience?—in which majorities decide only those questions
to which the rule of expediency is applicable? Must the citizen ever for a moment, or in the least degree, resign his
conscience to the legislator? Why has every man a conscience,
then? I think that we should be men first, and subjects afterwards. It is not desirable to cultivate a respect for the law,
so much as for the right. The only obligation which I have a
right to assume is to do at any time what I think right. It
is truly enough said that a corporation has no conscience;
but a corporation of conscientious men is a corporation *with*
a conscience. Law never made men a whit more just; and,
by means of their respect for it, even the well-disposed are
daily made the agents of injustice. A common and natural
result of an undue respect for law is, that you may see a file
of soldiers, colonel, captain, corporal, privates, powder-
monkeys, and all, marching in admirable order over hill
and dale to the wars, against their wills, ay, against their

common sense and consciences, which makes it very steep marching indeed, and produces a palpitation of the heart. They have no doubt that it is a damnable business in which they are concerned; they are all peaceably inclined. Now, what are they? Men at all? or small movable forts and magazines, at the service of some unscrupulous man in power? Visit the Navy-Yard, and behold a marine, such a man as an American government can make, or such as it can make a man with its black arts—a mere shadow and reminiscence of humanity, a man laid out alive and standing, and already, as one may say, buried under arms with funeral accompaniments, though it may be,—

> "Not a drum was heard, not a funeral note,
>   As his corse to the rampart we hurried;
> Not a soldier discharged his farewell shot
>   O'er the grave where our hero was buried." [1]

The mass of men serve the state thus, not as men mainly, but as machines, with their bodies. They are the standing army, and the militia, jailers, constables, *posse comitatus*, etc. In most cases there is no free exercise whatever of the judgment or of the moral sense; but they put themselves on a level with wood and earth and stones; and wooden men can perhaps be manufactured that will serve the purpose as well. Such command no more respect than men of straw or a lump of dirt. They have the same sort of worth only as horses and dogs. Yet such as these even are commonly esteemed good citizens. Others—as most legislators, politicians, lawyers, ministers, and office-holders—serve the state chiefly with their heads; and, as they rarely make any moral distinctions, they are as likely to serve the devil, without *intending* it, as God. A very few—as heroes, patriots, martyrs, reformers in the great sense, and *men*—serve the state with their consciences also, and so necessarily resist it for the most part; and they are commonly treated as enemies by it. A wise man will only

---

[1] Charles Wolfe, "Burial of Sir John Moore at Corunna" (1817).

be useful as a man, and will not submit to be "clay," and "stop a hole to keep the wind away," [2] but leave that office to his dust at least:—

> "I am too high-born to be propertied,
>   To be a secondary at control,
>   Or useful serving-man and instrument
>   To any sovereign state throughout the world." [3]

He who gives himself entirely to his fellow-men appears to them useless and selfish; but he who gives himself partially to them is pronounced a benefactor and philanthropist.

How does it become a man to behave toward this American government today? I answer, that he cannot without disgrace be associated with it. I cannot for an instant recognize that political organization as *my* government which is the *slave's* government also.

All men recognize the right of revolution; that is, the right to refuse allegiance to, and to resist, the government, when its tyranny or its inefficiency are great and unendurable. But almost all say that such is not the case now. But such was the case, they think, in the Revolution of '75. If one were to tell me that this was a bad government because it taxed certain foreign commodities brought to its ports, it is most probable that I should not make an ado about it, for I can do without them. All machines have their friction; and possibly this does enough good to counter-balance the evil. At any rate, it is a great evil to make a stir about it. But when the friction comes to have its machine, and oppression and robbery are organized, I say, let us not have such a machine any longer. In other words, when a sixth of the population of a nation which has undertaken to be the refuge of liberty are slaves, and a whole country is unjustly overrun and conquered by a foreign army, and subjected to military law, I think that it is not too soon for honest men to rebel and revolutionize. What makes this duty the more urgent is the

2 *Hamlet,* Act V, Sc. 1, ll. 236-237.
3 *King John,* Act V, Sc. 2, ll. 79-82.

fact that the country so overrun is not our own, but ours is the invading army.

Paley,[4] a common authority with many on moral questions, in his chapter on the "Duty of Submission to Civil Government," resolves all civil obligation into expediency; and he proceeds to say that "so long as the interest of the whole society requires it, that is, so long as the established government cannot be resisted or changed without public inconveniency, it is the will of God . . . that the established government be obeyed—and no longer. This principle being admitted, the justice of every particular case of resistance is reduced to a computation of the quantity of the danger and grievance on the one side, and of the probability and expense of redressing it on the other." Of this, he says, every man shall judge for himself. But Paley appears never to have contemplated those cases to which the rule of expediency does not apply, in which a people, as well as an individual, must do justice, cost what it may. If I have unjustly wrested a plank from a drowning man, I must restore it to him though I drown myself.[5] This, according to Paley, would be inconvenient. But he that would save his life, in such a case, shall lose it.[6] This people must cease to hold slaves, and to make war on Mexico, thought it cost them their existence as a people.

In their practice, nations agree with Paley; but does any one think that Massachusetts does exactly what is right at the present crisis?

> "A drab of state, a cloth-o'-silver slut,
>   To have her train borne up, and her soul trail in the dirt."

Practically speaking, the opponents to a reform in Massachusetts are not a hundred thousand politicians at the South, but a hundred thousand merchants and farmers here, who are more interested in commerce and agriculture than they

4 Rev. William Paley, *Principles of Moral and Political Philosophy* (1785).
5 Cicero, *De Officiis*, III.
6 Luke ix, 24; Matthew x, 39.

are in humanity, and are not prepared to do justice to the slave and to Mexico, *cost what it may.* I quarrel not with far-off foes, but with those who, near at home, coöperate with, and do the bidding of, those far away, and without whom the latter would be harmless. We are accustomed to say, that the mass of men are unprepared; but improvement is slow, because the few are not materially wiser or better than the many. It is not so important that many should be as good as you, as that there be some absolute goodness somewhere; for that will leaven the whole lump.[7] There are thousands who are *in opinion* opposed to slavery and to the war, who yet in effect do nothing to put an end to them; who, esteeming themselves children of Washington and Franklin, sit down with their hands in their pockets, and say that they know not what to do, and do nothing; who even postpone the question of freedom to the question of free trade, and quietly read the prices-current along with the latest advices from Mexico, after dinner, and, it may be, fall asleep over them both. What is the price-current of an honest man and patriot today? They hesitate, and they regret, and sometimes they petition; but they do nothing in earnest and with effect. They will wait, well disposed, for others to remedy the evil, that they may no longer have it to regret. At most, they give only a cheap vote, and a feeble countenance and God-speed, to the right, as it goes by them. There are nine hundred and ninety-nine patrons of virtue to one virtuous man. But it is easier to deal with the real possessor of a thing than with the temporary guardian of it.

All voting is a sort of gaming, like checkers or backgammon, with a slight moral tinge to it, a playing with right and wrong, with moral questions; and betting naturally accompanies it. The character of the voters is not staked. I cast my vote, perchance, as I think right; but I am not vitally concerned that right should prevail. I am willing to leave it to the majority. Its obligation, therefore, never exceeds that of expediency. Even voting *for the right* is *doing* nothing for it.

7 First Corinthians v, 6.

It is only expressing to men feebly your desire that it should prevail. A wise man will not leave the right to the mercy of chance, nor wish it to prevail through the power of the majority. There is but little virtue in the action of masses of men. When the majority shall at length vote for the abolition of slavery, it will be because they are indifferent to slavery, or because there is but little slavery left to be abolished by their vote. *They* will then be the only slaves. Only *his* vote can hasten the abolition of slavery who asserts his own freedom by his vote.

I hear of a convention to be held at Baltimore, or elsewhere, for the selection of a candidate for the Presidency, made up chiefly of editors, and men who are politicians by profession; but I think, what is it to any independent, intelligent, and respectable man what decision they may come to? Shall we not have the advantage of his wisdom and honesty, nevertheless? Can we not count upon some independent votes? Are there not many individuals in the country who do not attend conventions? But no: I find that the respectable man, so called, has immediately drifted from his position, and despairs of his country, when his country has more reason to despair of him. He forthwith adopts one of the candidate thus selected as the only *available* one, thus proving that he is himself *available* for any purposes of the demagogue. His vote is of no more worth than that of any unprincipled foreigner or hireling native, who may have been bought. O for a man who is a *man*, and, as my neighbor says, has a bone in his back which you cannot pass your hand through! Our statistics are at fault: the population has been returned too large. How many *men* are there to a square thousand miles in this country? Hardly one. Does not America offer any inducement for men to settle here? The American has dwindled into an Odd Fellow—one who may be known by the development of his organ of gregariousness, and a manifest lack of intellect and cheerful self-reliance; whose first and chief concern, on coming into the world, is to see that the almshouses are in good repair; and, *latin*

before yet he has lawfully donned the <u>virile</u> garb, to collect
a fund for the support of the widows and orphans that may
be; who, in short, ventures to live only by the aid of the
Mutual Insurance company, which has promised to bury
him decently.

It is not a man's duty, as a matter of course, to devote
himself to the eradication of any, even the most enormous,
wrong; he may still properly have other concerns to engage
him; but it is his duty, at least, to wash his hands of it, and,
if he gives it no thought longer, not to give it practically his
support. If I devote myself to other pursuits and contemplations, I must first see, at least, that I do not pursue them
sitting upon another man's shoulders. I must get off him
first, that he may pursue his contemplations too. See what
gross inconsistency is tolerated. I have heard some of my
townsmen say, "I should like to have them order me out to
help put down an insurrection of the slaves, or to march to
Mexico;—see if I would go"; and yet these very men have
each, directly by their allegiance, and so indirectly, at least,
by their money, furnished a substitute. The soldier is applauded who refuses to serve in an unjust war by those who
do not refuse to sustain the unjust government which makes
the war; is applauded by those whose own act and authority
he disregards and sets at naught; as if the state were penitent
to that degree that it hired one to scourge it while it sinned,
but not to that degree that it left off sinning for a moment.
Thus, under the name of Order and Civil Government, we
are all made at last to pay homage to and support our own
meanness. After the first blush of sin comes its indifference;
and from immoral it becomes, as it were, *un*moral, and not
quite unnecessary to that life which we have made.

The broadest and most prevalent error requires the most
disinterested virtue to sustain it. The slight reproach to which
the virtue of patriotism is commonly liable, the noble are
most likely to incur. Those who, while they disapprove of
the character and measures of a government, yield to it their
allegiance and support are undoubtedly its most conscientious

supporters, and so frequently the most serious obstacles to reform. Some are petitioning the State to dissolve the Union, to disregard the requisitions of the President. Why do they not dissolve it themselves—the union between themselves and the State—and refuse to pay their quota into its treasury? Do not they stand in the same relation to the State that the States does to the Union? And have not the same reasons prevented the State from resisting the Union which have prevented them from resisting the State?

How can a man be satisfied to entertain an opinion merely, and enjoy *it?* Is there any enjoyment in it, if his opinion is that he is aggrieved? If you are cheated out of a single dollar by your neighbor, you do not rest satisfied with knowing that you are cheated, or with saying that you are cheated, or even with petitioning him to pay you your due; but you take effectual steps at once to obtain the full amount, and see that you are never cheated again. Action from principle, the perception and the performance of right, changes things and relations; it is essentially revolutionary, and does not consist wholly with anything which was. It not only divides States and churches, it divides families; ay, it divides the *individual,* separating the diabolical in him from the divine.

Unjust laws exist; shall we be content to obey them, or shall we endeavor to amend them, and obey them until we have succeeded, or shall we transgress them at once? Men generally, under such a government as this, think that they ought to wait until they have persuaded the majority to alter them. They think that, if they should resist, the remedy would be worse than the evil. But it is the fault of the government itself that the remedy *is* worse than the evil. *It* makes it worse. Why is it not more apt to anticipate and provide for reform? Why does it not cherish its wise minority? Why does it cry and resist before it is hurt? Why does it not encourage its citizens to be on the alert to point out its faults, and *do* better than it would have them? Why does it always crucify Christ, and excommunicate Copernicus and Luther, and pronounce Washington and Franklin rebels?

One would think, that a deliberate and practical denial of its authority was the only offence never contemplated by government; else, why has it not assigned its definite, its suitable and proportionate, penalty? If a man who has no property refuses but once to earn nine shillings for the State, he is put in prison for a period unlimited by any law that I know, and determined only by the discretion of those who placed him there; but if he should steal ninety times nine shillings from the State, he is soon permitted to go at large again.

If the injustice is part of the necessary friction of the machine of government, let it go, let it go: perchance it will wear smooth—certainly the machine will wear out. If the injustice has a spring, or a pulley, or a rope, or a crank, exclusively for itself, then perhaps you may consider whether the remedy will not be worse than the evil; but if it is of such a nature that it requires you to be the agent of injustice to another, then, I say, break the law. Let your life be a counter friction to stop the machine. What I have to do is to see, at any rate, that I do not lend myself to the wrong which I condemn.

As for adopting the ways which the State has provided for remedying the evil, I know not of such ways. They take too much time, and a man's life will be gone. I have other affairs to attend to. I came into this world, not chiefly to make this a good place to live it, but to live in it, be it good or bad. A man has not everything to do, but something; and because he cannot do *everything*, it is not necessary that he should do *something* wrong. It is not my business to be petitioning the Governor or the Legislature any more than it is theirs to petition me; and if they should not hear my petition, what should I do then? But in this case the State has provided no way; its very Constitution is the evil. This may seem to be harsh and stubborn and unconciliatory; but it is to treat with the utmost kindness and consideration the only spirit that can appreciate or deserves it. So is all change for the better, like birth and death, which convulse the body.

I do not hesitate to say, that those who call themselves Abolitionists should at once effectually withdraw their support, both in person and property, from the government of Massachusetts, and not wait till they constitute a majority of one, before they suffer the right to prevail through them. I think that it is enough if they have God on their side, without waiting for that other one. Moreover, any man more right than his neighbors constitutes a majority of one already.

I meet this American government, or its representative, the State government, directly, and face to face, once a year—no more—in the person of its tax-gatherer; this is the only mode in which a man situated as I am necessarily meets it; and it then says distinctly, Recognize me; and the simplest, the most effectual, and, in the present posture of affairs, the indispensablest mode of treating with it on this head, of expressing your little satisfaction with and love for it, is to deny it then. My civil neighbor, the tax-gatherer, is the very man I have to deal with—for it is, after all, with men and not with parchment that I quarrel—and he has voluntarily chosen to be an agent of the government. How shall he ever know well what he is and does as an officer of the government, or as a man, until he is obliged to consider whether he shall treat me, his neighbor, for whom he has respect, as a neighbor and well-disposed man, or as a maniac and disturber of the peace, and see if he can get over this obstruction to his neighborliness without a ruder and more impetuous thought or speech corresponding with his action. I know this well, that if one thousand, if one hundred, if ten men whom I could name—if ten *honest* men only—ay, if *one* HONEST man, in this State of Massachusetts, *ceasing to hold slaves*, were actually to withdraw from this copartnership, and be locked up in the county jail therefor, it would be the abolition of slavery in America. For it matters not how small the beginning may seem to be: what is once well done is done forever. But we love better to talk about it: that we say is our mission. Reform keeps many scores of newspapers in its service, but not one man. If my esteemed neighbor, the State's ambassador,[8] who will devote his days to the settlement of the

8 In 1844 Samuel Hoar, the statesman of Concord, was sent to Charleston, South Carolina, on behalf of Negro seamen from Massachusetts threatened with arrest and slavery on entering the port, and was rudely expelled from Charleston.

question of human rights in the Council Chamber, instead of being threatened with the prisons of Carolina, were to sit down the prisoner of Massachusetts, that State which is so anxious to foist the sin of slavery upon her sister—though at present she can discover only an act of inhospitality to be the ground of a quarrel with her—the Legislature would not wholly waive the subject the following winter.

Under a government which imprisons any unjustly, the true place for a just man is also a prison. The proper place to-day, the only place which Massachusetts has provided for her freer and less desponding spirits, is in her prisons, to be put out and locked out of the State by her own act, as they have already put themselves out by their principles. It is there that the fugitive slave, and the Mexican prisoner on parole, and the Indian come to plead the wrongs of his race should find them; on that separate, but more free and honorable, ground, where the State places those who are not *with* her, but *against* her—the only house in a slave State in which a free man can abide with honor. If any think that their influence would be lost there, and their voices no longer afflict the ear of the State, that they would not be as an enemy within its walls, they do not know by how much truth is stronger than error, nor how much more eloquently and effectively he can combat injustice who has experienced a little in his own person. Cast your whole vote, not a strip of paper merely, but your whole influence. A minority is powerless while it conforms to the majority; it is not even a minority then; but it is irresistible when it clogs by its whole weight. If the alternative is to keep all just men in prison, or give up war and slavery, the State will not hesitate which to choose. If a thousand men were not to pay their tax-bills this year, that would not be a violent and bloody measure, as it would be to pay them, and enable the State to commit violence and shed innocent blood. This is, in fact, the definition of a peaceable revolution, if any such is possible. If the tax-gatherer, or any other public officer, asks me, as one has done, "But what shall I do?" my answer is, "If you really wish to do anything, resign your office." When the subject has refused allegiance, and the officer has resigned his office, then the revolution is accomplished. But even suppose blood should flow. Is there not a sort of blood shed when the conscience is wounded? Through this wound a man's real manhood and immortality flow out, and he bleeds to an everlasting death. I see this blood flowing now.

I have contemplated the imprisonment of the offender, rather than the seizure of his goods—though both will serve the same purpose—because they who assert the purest right, and consequently are most dangerous to a corrupt State, commonly have not spent much time in accumulating property. To such the State renders comparatively small service, and a slight tax is wont to appear exorbitant, particularly if they are obliged to earn it by special labor with their hands. If there were one who lived wholly without the use of money, the State itself would hesitate to demand it of him. But the rich man—not to make any invidious comparison—is always sold to the institution which makes him rich. Absolutely speaking, the more money, the less virtue; for money comes between a man and his objects, and obtains them for him; and it was certainly no great virtue to obtain it. It puts to rest many questions which he would otherwise be taxed to answer; while the only new question which it puts is the hard but superfluous one, how to spend it. Thus his moral ground is taken from under his feet. The opportunities of living are diminished in proportion as what are called the "means" are increased. The best thing a man can do for his culture when he is rich is to endeavor to carry out those schemes which he entertained when he was poor. Christ answered the Herodians according to their condition. "Show me the tribute-money," said he;—and one took a penny out of his pocket;—if you use money which has the image of Caesar on it, and which he has made current and valuable, that is, *if you are men of the State,* and gladly enjoy the advantages of Caesar's government, they pay him back some of his own when he demands it. "Render therefore to Caesar that which is Caesar's, and to God those things which are God's"—leaving them no wiser than before as to which was which; for they did not wish to know.

When I converse with the freest of my neighbors, I perceive

that, whatever they may say about the magnitude and seriousness of the question, and their regard for the public tranquillity, the long and the short of the matter is, that they cannot
spare the protection of the existing government, and they
dread the consequences to their property and families of disobedience to it. For my own part, I should not like to think
that I ever rely on the protection of the State. But, if I deny
the authority of the State when it presents its tax-bill, it will
soon take and waste all my property, and so harass me and my
children without end. This is hard. This makes it impossible
for a man to live honestly, and at the same time comfortably,
in outward respects. It will not be worth the while to accumu-
late property; that would be sure to go again. You must hire
or squat somewhere, and raise but a small crop, and eat that
soon. You must live within yourself, and depend upon yourself
always tucked up and ready for a start, and not have many
affairs. A man may grow rich in Turkey even, if he will be in
all respects a good subject of the Turkish government. Con-
fucius said: "If a state is governed by the principles of reason,
poverty and misery are subjects of shame; if a state is not governed by the principles of reason, riches and honors are the
subjects of shame." No: until I want the protection of Massachusetts to be extended to me in some distant Southern port,
where my liberty is endangered, or until I am bent solely on
building up an estate at home by peaceful enterprise, I can
afford to refuse allegiance to Massachusetts, and her right to
my property and life. It costs me less in every sense to incur
the penalty of disobedience to the State than it would to obey.
I should feel as if I were worth less in that case.

Some years ago, the State met me in behalf of the Church,
and commanded me to pay a certain sum toward the support
of a clergyman whose preaching my father attended, but never
I myself. "Pay," it said, "or be locked up in the jail." I declined to pay.[9] But, unfortunately, another man saw fit to pay
it. I did not see why the schoolmaster should be taxed to sup-

9 On returning to Concord after leaving college, Thoreau refused to
subscribe to the Church.

port the priest, and not the priest the schoolmaster; for I was not the State's schoolmaster, but I supported myself by voluntary subscription. I did not see why the lyceum should not present its tax-bill, and have the State to back its demand, as well as the Church. However, at the request of the selectmen, I condescended to make some such statement as this in writing:—"Know all men by these presents, that I, Henry Thoreau, do not wish to be regarded as a member of any incorporated society which I have not joined." This I gave to the town clerk; and he has it. The State, having thus learned that I did not wish to be regarded as a member of that church, has never made a like demand on me since; though it said that it must adhere to its original presumption that time. If I had known how to name them, I should then have signed off in detail from all the societies which I never signed on to; but I did not know where to find a complete list.

I have paid no poll-tax for six years. I was put into a jail once on this account, for one night; and, as I stood considering the walls of solid stone, two or three feet thick, the door of wood and iron, a foot thick, and the iron grating which strained the light, I could not help being struck with the foolishness of that institution which treated me as if I were mere flesh and blood and bones to be locked up. I wondered that it should have concluded at length that this was the best use it could put me to, and had never thought to avail itself of my services in some way. I saw that, if there was a wall of stone between me and my townsmen, there was a still more difficult one to climb or break through before they could get to be as free as I was. I did not for a moment feel confined, and the walls seemed a great waste of stone and mortar. I felt as if I alone of all my townsmen had paid my tax. They plainly did not know how to treat me, but behaved like persons who are underbred. In every threat and in every compliment there was a blunder; for they thought that my chief desire was to stand the other side of that stone wall. I could not but smile to see how industriously they locked the door on my meditations, which followed them out again without let or hindrance, and

*stone
walls
do not
a prison
make.*

they were really all that was dangerous. As they could not reach me, they had resolved to punish my body; just as boys, if they cannot come at some person against whom they have a spite, will abuse his dog. I saw that the State was half-witted, that it was timid as a lone woman with her silver spoons, and that it did not know its friends from its foes, and I lost all my remaining respect for it, and pitied it.

Thus the State never intentionally confronts a man's sense, intellectual or moral, but only his body, his senses. It is not armed with superior wit or honesty, but with superior physical strength. I was not born to be forced. I will breathe after my own fashion. Let us see who is the strongest. What force has a multitude? They only can force me who obey a higher law than I. They force me to become like themselves. I do not hear of *men* being *forced* to live this way or that by masses of men. What sort of life were that to live? When I meet a government which says to me, "Your money or your life," why should I be in haste to give it my money? It may be in a great strait, and not know what to do: I cannot help that. It must help itself; do as I do. It is not worth the while to snivel about it. I am not responsible for the successful working of the machinery of society. I am not the son of the engineer. I perceive that, when an acorn and a chestnut fall side by side, the one does not remain inert to make way for the other, but both obey their own laws, and spring and grow and flourish as best they can, till one, perchance, overshadows and destroys the other. If a plant cannot live according to its nature, it dies; and so a man.

The night in prison was novel and interesting enough. The prisoners in their shirt-sleeves were enjoying a chat and the evening air in the doorway, when I entered. But the jailer said, "Come, boys, it is time to lock up"; and so they dispersed, and I heard the sound of their steps returning into the hollow apartments. My room-mate was introduced to me by the jailer as "a first-rate fellow and a clever man." When the door was locked, he showed me where to hang my hat, and how he managed matters there. The rooms were whitewashed once a month; and this one, at least, was the whitest, most simply furnished, and probably the neatest apartment in the town. He naturally wanted to know where I came from, and what brought me there; and, when I had told him, I asked him in my turn how he came there, presuming him to be an honest man, of course; and, as the world goes, I believe he was. "Why," said he, "they accuse me of burning a barn, but I never did it." As near as I could discover, he had probably gone to bed in a barn when drunk, and smoked his pipe there; and so a barn was burnt. He had the reputation of being a clever man, had been there some three months waiting for his trial to come on, and would have to wait as much longer; but he was quite domesticated and contented, since he got his board for nothing, and thought that he was well treated.

He occupied one window, and I the other; and I saw that if one stayed there long, his principal business would be to look out the window. I had soon read all the tracts that were left there, and examined where former prisoners had broken out, and where a grate had been sawed off, and heard the history of the various occupants of that room; for I found that even here there was a history and a gossip which never circulated beyond the walls of the jail. Probably this is the only house in the town where verses are composed, which are afterward printed in a circular form, but not published. I was shown quite a long list of verses which were composed by some young men who had been detected in an attempt to escape, who avenged themselves by singing them.

I pumped my fellow-prisoner as dry as I could, for fear I should never see him again; but at length he showed me which was my bed, and left me to blow out the lamp.

It was like travelling into a far country, such as I had never expected to behold, to lie there for one night. It seemed to me that I never had heard the town clock strike before, nor the evening sounds of the village; for we slept with the windows open, which were inside the grating. It was to see my native village in the light of the Middle Ages, and our Concord was turned into a Rhine stream, and visions of knights and castles passed before me. They were the voices of old burghers that I heard in the streets. I was an involuntary spectator and auditor of whatever was done and said in the kitchen of the adjacent village inn—a wholly new and rare experience to me. It was a closer view of my native town. I was fairly inside of it. I never had seen its institutions before. This is one of its peculiar institutions; for it is a shire town. I began to comprehend what its inhabitants were about.

In the morning, our breakfasts were put through the hole in the door, in small oblong-square tin pans, made to fit, and holding a pint of chocolate, with brown bread, and an iron spoon. When they called for the vessels again, I was green enough to return what bread I had left; but my comrade seized it, and said that I should lay that up for lunch or dinner. Soon after he was let out to work at haying in a neighboring field, whither he went every day, and would not be back till noon; so he bade me good-day, saying that he doubted if he should see me again.

When I came out of prison—for some one interfered, and paid that tax—I did not perceive that great changes had taken place on the common, such as he observed who went in a youth and emerged a tottering and gray-headed man; and yet a change had to my eyes come over the scene—the town, and State, and country—greater than any that mere time could effect. I saw yet more distinctly the State in which I lived. I saw to what extent the people among whom I lived could be trusted as good neighbors and friends; that their friendship was for summer weather only; that they did not greatly propose to do right; that they were a distinct race from me by their prejudices and superstitions, as the Chinamen and Malays are; that in their sacrifices to humanity they ran no risks, not even to their property; that after all they were not so noble but they treated the thief as he had treated them, and hoped, by a certain outward observance and a few prayers, and by walking in a particular straight though useless path from time to time, to save their souls. This may be to judge my neighbors harshly; for I believe that many of them are not aware that they have such an institution as the jail in the village.

It was formerly the custom in our village, when a poor debtor came out of jail, for his acquaintances to salute him, looking through their fingers, which were crossed to represent the grating of a jail window, "How do ye do?" My neighbors did not thus salute me, but first looked at me, and then at one another, as if I had returned from a long journey. I was put into jail as I was going to the shoemaker's to get a shoe which was mended. When I was let out the next morning, I proceeded to finish my errand, and, having put on my mended shoe, joined a huckleberry party, who were impatient to put themselves under my conduct; and in half an hour—for the horse was soon tackled—was in the midst of a huckleberry field, on one of our highest hills, two miles off, and then the State was nowhere to be seen.

This is the whole history of "My Prisons."

I have never declined paying the highway tax, because I am as desirous of being a good neighbor as I am of being a bad subject; and as for supporting schools, I am doing my part to educate my fellow-countrymen now. It is for no particular item in the tax-bill that I refuse to pay it. I simply wish to refuse allegiance to the State, to withdraw and stand aloof from it effectually. I do not care to trace the course of my dollar, if I could, till it buys a man or a musket to shoot one with—the dollar is innocent—but I am concerned to trace the effects of my allegiance. In fact, I quietly declare war with the State, after my fashion, though I will still make what use and get what advantage of her I can, as is usual in such cases.

If others pay the tax which is demanded of me, from a sympathy with the State, they do but what they have already done in their own case, or rather they abet injustice to a greater extent than the State requires. If they pay the tax from a mistaken interest in the individual taxed, to save his property, or prevent his going to jail, it is because they have not considered

wisely how far they let their private feelings interfere with
the public good.

This, then, is my position at present. But one cannot be too
much on his guard in such a case, lest his action be biased by
obstinacy or an undue regard for the opinions of men. Let him
see that he does only what belongs to himself and to the hour.

I think sometimes, Why, this people mean well, they are
only ignorant; they would do better if they knew how: why
give your neighbors this pain to treat you as they are not
inclined to? But I think again, This is no reason why I should
do as they do, or permit others to suffer much greater pain
of a different kind. Again, I sometimes say to myself, When
many millions of men, without heat, without ill will, without
personal feeling of any kind, demand of you a few shillings
only, without the possibility, such is their constitution, of
retracting or altering their present demand, and without the
possibility, on your side, of appeal to any other millions, why
expose yourself to this overwhelming brute force? You do not
resist cold and hunger, the winds and the waves, thus obsti-
nately; you quietly submit to a thousand similar necessities.
You do not put your head into the fire. But just in proportion
as I regard this as not wholly a brute force, but partly a human
force, and consider that I have relations to those millions as
to so many millions of men, and not of mere brute or inanimate things, I see that appeal is possible, first and instantane-
ously, from them to the Maker of them, and, secondly, from
them to themselves. But if I put my head deliberately into the
fire, there is no appeal to fire or to the Maker of fire, and I
have only myself to blame. If I could convince myself that I
have any right to be satisfied with men as they are, and to
treat them accordingly, and not according, in some respects,
to my requisitions and expectations of what they and I ought
to be, then, like a good Mussulman and fatalist, I should
endeavor to be satisfied with things as they are, and say it is
the will of God. And, above all, there is this difference between resisting this and a purely brute or natural force, that
I can resist this with some effect; but I cannot expect, like

Orpheus, to change the nature of the rocks and trees and beasts.

I do not wish to quarrel with any man or nation. I do not wish to split hairs, to make fine distinctions, or set myself up as better than my neighbors. I seek rather, I may say, even an excuse for conforming the laws of the land. I am but too ready to conform to them. Indeed, I have reason to suspect myself on this head; and each year, as the tax-gatherer comes round, I find myself disposed to review the acts and positions of the general and State governments, and the spirit of the people, to discover a pretext for conformity.

> "We must affect our country as our parents,
> And if at any time we alienate
> Our love or industry from doing it honor,
> We must respect effects and teach the soul
> Matter of conscience and religion,
> And not desire of rule or benefit."

I believe that the State will soon be able to take all my work of this sort out of my hands, and then I shall be no better a patriot than my fellow-countrymen. Seen from a lower point of view, the Constitution, with all its faults, is very good; the law and the courts are very respectable; even this State and this American government are, in many respects, very admirable, and rare things, to be thankful for, such as a great many have described them; but seen from a point of view a little higher, they are what I have described them; seen from a higher still, and the highest, who shall say what they are, or that they are worth looking at or thinking of at all?

However, the government does not concern me much, and I shall bestow the fewest possible thoughts on it. It is not many moments that I live under a government, even in this world. If a man is thought-free, fancy-free, imagination-free, that which *is not* never for a long time appearing *to be* to him, unwise rulers or reformers cannot fatally interrupt him.

I know that most men think differently from myself; but those whose lives are by profession devoted to the study of these or kindred subjects content me as little as any. Statesmen and legislators, standing so completely within the institution, never distinctly and nakedly behold it. They speak of moving society, but have no resting-place without it. They may be men of a certain experience and discrimination, and have no doubt invented ingenious and even useful systems, for which we sincerely thank them; but all their wit and usefulness lie within certain not very wide limits. They are wont to forget that the world is not governed by policy and expediency. Webster never goes behind government, and so cannot speak with authority about it. His words are wisdom to those legislators who contemplate no essential reform in the existing government; but for thinkers, and those who legislate for all time, he never once glances at the subject. I know of those whose serene and wise speculations on this theme would soon reveal the limits of his mind's range and hospitality. Yet, compared with the cheap professions of most reformers, and the still cheaper wisdom and eloquence of politicians in general, his are almost the only sensible and valuable words, and we thank Heaven for him. Comparatively, he is always strong, original, and, above all, practical. Still, his quality is not wisdom, but prudence. The lawyer's truth is not Truth, but consistency or a consistent expediency. Truth is always in harmony with herself, and is not concerned chiefly to reveal the justice that may consist with wrong-doing. He well deserves to be called, as he has been called, the Defender of the Constitution. There are really no blows to be given by him but defensive ones. He is not a leader, but a follower. His leaders are the men of '87. "I have never made an effort," he says, "and never propose to make an effort; I have never countenanced an effort, and never mean to countenance an effort, to disturb the arrangement as originally made, by which the various States came into the Union." Still thinking of the sanction which the Constitution gives to slavery, he says, "Because it was a part of the original compact—let it stand." Notwithstanding his special acuteness and ability, he is unable to take a fact out of its merely political relations, and behold it as it lies absolutely to be disposed of by the intellect—what, for instance, it behooves a man to do here in America today with regard to slavery—but ventures, or is driven, to make some such desperate answer as the following, while professing to speak absolutely, and as a private man—from which what new and similar code of social duties might be inferred? "The manner," says he, "in which the governments of those States where slavery exists are to regulate it is for their own consideration, under their responsibility to their constituents, to the general laws of propriety, humanity, and justice, and to God. Associations formed elsewhere, springing from a feeling of humanity, or any other cause, have nothing whatever to do with it. They have never received any encouragement from me, and they never will." [10]

They who know of no purer sources of truth, who have traced up its stream no higher, stand, and wisely stand, by the Bible and the Constitution, and drink at it there with reverence and humility; but they who behold where it comes trickling into this lake or that pool, gird up their loins once more, and continue their pilgrimage towards its fountain-head.

No man with a genius for legislation has appeared in America. They are rare in the history of the world. There are orators, politicians, and eloquent men, by the thousand; but the speaker has not yet opened his mouth to speak who is capable of settling the much-vexed questions of the day. We love eloquence for its own sake, and not for any truth which it may utter, or any heroism it may inspire. Our legislators have not yet learned the comparative value of free trade and of freedom, of union, and of rectitude, to a nation. They have no genius or talent for comparatively humble questions of taxation and finance, commerce and manufactures and agriculture. If we were left solely to the wordy wit of legislators in Congress for our guidance, uncorrected by the seasonable experience and the effectual complaints of the people, America would not long retain her rank among the nations. For eigh-

[10] Thoreau's note: These extracts have been inserted since the lecture was read.

teen hundred years, though perchance I have no right to say it, the New Testament has been written; yet where is the legislator who has wisdom and practical talent enough to avail himself of the light which it sheds on the science of legislation?

The authority of government, even such as I am willing to submit to—for I will cheerfully obey those who know and can do better than I, and in many things even those who neither know nor can do so well—is still an impure one: to be strictly just, it must have the sanction and consent of the governed. It can have no pure right over my person and property but what I concede to it. The progress from an absolute to a limited monarchy, from a limited monarchy to a democracy, is a progress toward a true respect for the individual. Even the Chinese philosopher was wise enough to regard the individual as the basis of the empire. Is a democracy, such as we know it, the last improvement possible in government? Is it not possible to take a step further towards recognizing and organizing the rights of man? There will never be a really free and enlightened State until the State comes to recognize the individual as a higher and independent power, from which all its own power and authority are derived, and treats him accordingly. I please myself with imagining a State at least which can afford to be just to all men, and to treat the individual with respect as a neighbor; which even would not think it inconsistent with its own repose if a few were to live aloof from it, not meddling with it, nor embraced by it, who fulfilled all the duties of neighbors and fellow-men. A State which bore this kind of fruit, and suffered it to drop off as fast as it ripened, would prepare the way for a still more perfect and glorious State, which also I have imagined, but not yet anywhere seen.

Matthew Arnold

MATTHEW ARNOLD *(1822-1888) was a distinguished poet and critic whose occupation as an inspector of schools brought him into contact with the detailed problems of civilization in the growing industrial world of the nineteenth century. In his later years, he became one of the most searching analysts of the relation between tradition and modernity in education, politics, literature, and religion. Arnold was educated at Rugby, where his father Thomas Arnold was headmaster, and at Balliol College, Oxford. His poems have been collected in various editions. Principal prose works:* Essays in Criticism *(1865 and 1888);* Culture and Anarchy *(1869);* Literature and Dogma *(1873).*

LITERATURE AND SCIENCE [1]

Practical people talk with a smile of Plato and of his absolute ideas; [2] and it is impossible to deny that Plato's ideas do often seem unpractical and impracticable, and especially when one views them in connexion with the life of a great work-a-day world like the United States.[3] The necessary staple of the life of such a world Plato regards with disdain; handicraft and trade and the working professions he regards with disdain; but what becomes of the life of an industrial modern community if you take handicraft and trade and the working

[1] From *Discourses in America* (1885).

[2] Arnold is here referring to the arguments made by Plato for the existence of a world of ideal forms (see *Republic*, X).

[3] This essay was one of a series of lectures given by Arnold on his American tour of 1883-1884.

309

unpractical — not practical
impracticable — not practicable

professions out of it? The base mechanic arts and handi-
crafts, says Plato, bring about a natural weakness in the
principle of excellence in a man, so that he cannot govern
the ignoble growths in him, but nurses them, and cannot
understand fostering any other. Those who exercise such arts
and trades, as they have their bodies, he says, marred by
their vulgar businesses, so they have their souls, too, bowed
and broken by them. And if one of these uncomely people
has a mind to seek self-culture and philosophy, Plato compares him to a bald little tinker, who has scraped together
money, and has got his release from service, and has had a
bath, and bought a new coat and is rigged out like a bridegroom about to marry the daughter of his master who has
fallen into poor and helpless estate.

Nor do the working professions fare any better than trade
at the hands of Plato. He draws for us an inimitable picture
of the working lawyer, and of his life of bondage; he shows
how this bondage from his youth up has stunted and warped
him, and made him small and crooked of soul, encompassing
him with difficulties which he is not man enough to rely on
justice and truth as means to encounter, but has recourse,
for help out of them, to falsehood and wrong. And so, says
Plato, this poor creature is bent and broken, and grows up
from boy to man without a particle of soundness in him,
although exceedingly smart and clever in his own esteem.

One cannot refuse to admire the artist who draws these
pictures. But we say to ourselves that his ideas show the
influence of a primitive and obsolete order of things, when
the warrior caste and the priestly caste were alone in honour,
and the humble work of the world was done by slaves. We
have now changed all that; the modern majority [4] consists
in work, as Emerson declares; and in work, we may add, principally of such plain and dusty kind as the work of cultivators
of the ground, handicraftsmen, men of trade and business,

---

[4] Emerson wrote *majesty* (in his essay on *Literary Ethics*), and this
would certainly make more sense in Arnold's context.

men of the working professions. Above, all is this true in a
great industrious community such as that of the United States.

Now education, many people go on to say, is still mainly
governed by the ideas of men like Plato, who lived when
the warrior caste and the priestly or philosophical class were
alone in honour, and the really useful part of the community
were slaves. It is an education fitted for persons of leisure
in such a community. This education passed from Greece
and Rome to the feudal communities of Europe, where also
the warrior caste and the priestly caste were alone held in
honour, and where the really useful and working part of the
community, though not nominally slaves as in the pagan
world, were practically not much better off than slaves, and
not more seriously regarded. And how absurd it is, people
end by saying, to inflict this education upon an industrious
modern community, where very few indeed are persons of
leisure, and the mass to be considered has not leisure, but
is bound, for its own great good, and for the great good of
the world at large, to plain labour and to industrial pursuits,
and the education in question tends necessarily to make
men dissatisfied with these pursuits and unfitted for them!

That is what is said. So far I must defend Plato, as to plead
that his view of education and studies is in the general, as
it seems to me, sound enough, and fitted for all sorts and
conditions of men, whatever their pursuits may be. 'An intelligent man,' says Plato, 'will prize those studies which result
in his soul getting soberness, righteousness, and wisdom, and
will less value the others.' I cannot consider *that* a bad description of the aim of education, and of the motives which
should govern us in the choice of studies, whether we are
preparing ourselves for a hereditary seat in the English House
of Lords or for the pork trade in Chicago.

Still I admit that Plato's world was not ours, that his scorn
of trade and handicraft is fantastic, that he had no conception
of a great industrial community such as that of the United
States, and that such a community must and will shape its

education to suit its own needs. If the usual education handed down to it from the past does not suit it, it will certainly before long drop this and try another. The usual education in the past has been mainly literary. The question is whether the studies which were long supposed to be the best for all of us are practically the best now; whether others are not better. The tyranny of the past, many think, weighs on us injuriously in the predominance given to letters in education. The question is raised whether, to meet the needs of our modern life, the predominance ought not now to pass from letters to science; and naturally the question is nowhere raised with more energy than here in the United States. The design of abasing what is called 'mere literary instruction and education,' and of exalting what is called 'sound, extensive, and practical scientific knowledge,' is, in this intensely modern world of the United States, even more perhaps than in Europe, a very popular design, and makes great and rapid progress.

I am going to ask whether the present movement for ousting letters from their old predominance in education, and for transferring the predominance in education to the natural sciences, whether this brisk and flourishing movement ought to prevail, and whether it is likely that in the end it really will prevail. An objection may be raised which I will anticipate. My own studies have been almost wholly in letters, and my visits to the field of the natural sciences have been very slight and inadequate, although those sciences have always strongly moved by curiosity. A man of letters, it will perhaps be said, is not competent to discuss the comparative merits of letters and natural science as means of education. To this objection I reply, first of all, that his incompetence, if he attempts the discussion but is really incompetent for it, will be abundantly visible; nobody will be taken in; he will have plenty of sharp observers and critics to save mankind from that danger. But the line I am going to follow is, as you will soon discover, so extremely simple, that perhaps it may be followed without failure even by one who for a more ambitious line of discussion would be quite incompetent.

Some of you may possibly remember a phrase of mine which has been the object of a good deal of comment; an observation to the effect that in our culture, the aim being *to know ourselves and the world,* we have, as the means to this end, *to know the best which has been thought and said in the world.*[5] A man of science, who is also an excellent writer and the very prince of debaters, Professor Huxley,[6] in a discourse at the opening of Sir Josiah Mason's college at Birmingham, laying hold of this phrase, expanded it by quoting some more words of mine, which are these: 'The civilised world is to be regarded as now being, for intellectual and spiritual purposes, one great confederation, bound to a joint action and working to a common result; and whose members have for their proper outfit a knowledge of Greek, Roman, and Eastern antiquity, and of one another. Special local and temporary advantages being put out of account, that modern nation will in the intellectual and spiritual sphere make most progress, which most thoroughly carries out this programme.'

Now on my phrase, thus enlarged, Professor Huxley remarks that when I speak of the above-mentioned knowledge as enabling us to know ourselves and the world, I assert *literature* to contain the materials which suffice for thus making us know ourselves and the world. But it is not by any means clear, says he, that after having learnt all which ancient and modern literatures have to tell us, we have laid a sufficiently broad and deep foundation for that criticism of life, that knowledge of ourselves and the world, which constitutes culture. On the contrary, Professor Huxley declares that he finds himself 'wholly unable to admit that either nations or individuals will really advance, if their outfit draws nothing from the stores of physical science. An army without weapons of precision, and with no particular

5 From Arnold's essay "The Function of Criticism at the Present Time."
6 Thomas Henry Huxley (1825-1895), noted writer on scientific subjects and early popularizer of Darwin's theories.

base of operations, might more hopefully enter upon a campaign on the Rhine, than a man, devoid of a knowledge of what physical science has done in the last century, upon a criticism of life.

This shows how needful it is for those who are to discuss any matter together, to have a common understanding as to the sense of the terms they employ,—how needful, and how difficult. What Professor Huxley says, implies just the reproach which is so often brought against the study of *belles lettres,* as they are called: that the study is an elegant one, but slight and ineffectual; a smattering of Greek and Latin and other ornamental things, of little use for any one whose object is to get at truth, and to be a practical man. So, too, M. Renan [7] talks of the 'superficial humanism' of a school-course which treats us as if we were all going to be poets, writers, preachers, orators, and he opposes this humanism to positive science, or the critical search after truth. And there is always a tendency in those who are remonstrating against the predominance of letters in education, to understand by letters *belles lettres,* and by *belles lettres* a superficial humanism, the opposite of science or true knowledge.

But when we talk of knowing Greek and Roman antiquity, for instance, which is the knowledge people have called the humanities, I for my part mean a knowledge which is something more than a superficial humanism, mainly decorative. 'I call all teaching *scientific,*' says Wolf, the critic of Homer, 'which is systematically laid out and followed up to its original sources. For example: a knowledge of classical antiquity is scientific when the remains of classical antiquity are correctly studied in the original languages.' There can be no doubt that Wolf is perfectly right; that all learning is scientific which is systematically laid out and followed up to its original sources, and that a genuine humanism is scientific.

When I speak of knowing Greek and Roman antiquity, therefore, as a help to knowing ourselves and the world, I

7 Ernest Renan (1823-1892), French historian, famous for his application of historical method to the origins of Christianity.

mean more than a knowledge of so much vocabulary, so much grammar, so many portions of authors in the Greek and Latin languages. I mean knowing the Greeks and Romans, and their life and genius, and what they were and did in the world; what we get from them, and what is its value. That, at least, is the ideal; and when we talk of endeavouring to know Greek and Roman antiquity, as a help to knowing ourselves and the world, we mean endeavouring so to know them as to satisfy this ideal, however much we may still fall short of it.

The same also as to knowing our own and other modern nations, with the like aim of getting to understand ourselves and the world. To know the best that has been thought and said by the modern nations, is to know, says Professor Huxley, 'only what modern *literatures* have to tell us; it is the criticism of life contained in modern literature.' And yet 'the distinctive character of our times,' he urges, 'lies in the vast and constantly increasing part which is played by natural knowledge.' And how, therefore, can a man, devoid of knowledge of what physical science has done in the last century, enter hopefully upon a criticism of modern life?

Let us, I say, be agreed about the meaning of the terms we are using I talk of knowing the best which has been thought and uttered in the world; Professor Huxley says this means knowing *literature*. Literature is a large word; it may mean everything written with letters or printed in a book. Euclid's *Elements* and Newton's *Principia* are thus literature. All knowledge that reaches us through books is literature. But by literature Professor Huxley means *belles lettres*. He means to make me say, that knowing the best which has been thought and said by the modern nations is knowing their *belles lettres* and no more. And this is no sufficient equipment, he argues, for a criticism of modern life. But as I do not mean, by knowing ancient Rome, knowing merely more or less of Latin *belles lettres*, and taking no account of Rome's military, and political, and legal, and administrative work in the world; and as, by knowing ancient Greece, I under-

stand knowing her as the giver of Greek art, and the guide
to a free and right use of reason and to scientific method,
and the founder of our mathematics and physics and as-
tronomy and biology,—I understand knowing her as all this,
and not merely knowing certain Greek poems, and histories,
and treatises, and speeches,—so as to the knowledge of modern
nations also. By knowing modern nations, I mean not merely
knowing their *belles lettres,* but knowing also what has been
done by such men as Copernicus, Galileo, Newton, Darwin.
'Our ancestors learned,' says Professor Huxley, 'that the earth
is the centre of the visible universe, and that man is the
cynosure of things terrestrial; and more especially was it
inculcated that the course of nature had no fixed order, but
that it could be, and constantly was, altered.' But for us now,
continues Professor Huxley, 'the notions of the beginning
and the end of the world entertained by our forefathers are
no longer credible. It is very certain that the earth is not
the chief body in the material universe, and that the world
is not subordinated to man's use. It is even more certain that
nature is the expression of a definite order, with which nothing interferes.' 'And yet,' he cries, 'the purely classical education advocated by the representatives of the humanists in
our day gives no inkling of all this!'
In due place and time I will just touch upon that vexed
question of classical education; but at present the question
is as to what is meant by knowing the best which modern
nations have thought and said. It is not knowing their *belles
lettres* merely which is meant. To know Italian *belles lettres*
is not to know Italy, and to know English *belles lettres* is
not to know England. Into knowing Italy and England there
comes a great deal more, Galileo and Newton, amongst it.
The reproach of being a superficial humanism, a tincture of
belles lettres, may attach rightly enough to some other disciplines; but to the particular discipline recommended when
I proposed knowing the best that has been thought and said
in the world, it does not apply. In that best I certainly in-

clude what in modern times has been thought and said by
the great observers and knowers of nature.

There is, therefore, really no question between Professor
Huxley and me as to whether knowing the great results of
the modern scientific study of nature is not required as a
part of our culture, as well as knowing the products of literature and art. But to follow the processes by which those
results are reached, ought, say the friends of physical science,
to be made the staple of education for the bulk of mankind.
And here there does arise a question between those whom
Professor Huxley calls with playful sarcasm 'the Levites of
culture,' [8] and those whom the poor humanist is sometimes
apt to regard as its Nebuchadnezzars.[9]

The great results of the scientific investigation of nature
we are agreed upon knowing, but how much of our study
are we bound to give to the processes by which those results
are reached? The results have their visible bearing on human
life. But all the processes, too, all the items of fact, by which
those results are reached and established, are interesting. All
knowledge is interesting to a wise man, and the knowledge
of nature is interesting to all men. It is very interesting to
know, that, from the albuminous white of the egg, the
chick in the egg gets the materials for for its flesh, bones,
blood, and feathers; while, from the fatty yolk of the egg,
it gets the heat and energy which enable it at length to
break its shell and begin the world. It is less interesting,
perhaps, but still it is interesting, to know that when a taper
burns, the wax is converted into carbonic acid and water.
Moreover, it is quite true that the habit of dealing with
facts, which is given by the study of nature, is, as the friends
of physical science praise it for being, an excellent discipline.
The appeal, in the study of nature, is constantly to observa-

[8] Custodians of rituals and customs. Huxley accuses the Humanists of
being obsessed with arid habits. Arnold, in turn, accuses the scientists
of having destructive motives.

[9] Nebuchadnezzar was the king of Babylon who captured Jerusalem.

tion and experiment; not only is it said that the thing is so, but we can be made to see that it is so. Not only does a man tell us that when a taper burns the wax is converted into carbonic acid and water, as a man may tell us, if he likes, that Charon is punting his ferry-boat on the river Styx, or that Victor Hugo is a sublime poet, or Mr. Gladstone the most admirable of statesmen; but we are made to see that the conversion into carbonic acid and water does actually happen. This reality of natural knowledge it is, which makes the friends of physical science contrast it, as a knowledge of things, with the humanist's knowledge, which is, say they, a knowledge of words. And hence Professor Huxley is moved to lay it down that, 'for the purpose of attaining real culture, an exclusively scientific education is at least as effectual as an exclusively literary education.' And a certain President of the Section for Mechanical Science in the British Association is, in Scripture phrase, 'very bold,' and declares that if a man, in his mental training, 'has substituted literature and history for natural science, he has chosen the less useful alternative.' But whether we go these lengths or not, we must all admit that in natural science the habit gained of dealing with facts is a most valuable discipline, and that every one should have some experience of it.

More than this, however, is demanded by the reformers. It is proposed to make the training in natural science the main part of education, for the great majority of mankind at any rate. And here, I confess, I part company with the friends of physical science, with whom up to this point I have been agreeing. In differing from them, however, I wish to proceed with the utmost caution and diffidence. The small-ness of my own acquaintance with the disciplines of natural science is ever before my mind, and I am fearful of doing these disciplines an injustice. The ability and pugnacity of the partisans of natural science makes them formidable persons to contradict. The tone of tentative inquiry, which befits a being of dim faculties and bounded knowledge is the tone I would wish to take and not to depart from. At present it

pugnacious - disposition to fighting belligerent

seems to me, that those who are for giving to natural knowledge, as they call it, the chief place in the education of the
majority of mankind, leave one important thing out of their
account: the constitution of human nature. But I put this
forward on the strength of some facts not at all recondite, *characterized*
very far from it; facts capable of being stated in the simplest *by profound*
possible fashion, and to which, if I so state them, the man of *scholarship*
science will, I am sure, be willing to allow their due weight.

Deny the facts altogether, I think, he hardly can. He can
hardly deny, that when we set ourselves to enumerate the
powers which go to the building up of human life, and say that
they are the power of conduct, the power of intellect and
knowledge, the power of beauty, and the power of social
life and manners,—he can hardly deny that this scheme,
though drawn in rough and plain lines enough, and not
pretending to scientific exactness, does yet give a fairly true
representation of the matter. Human nature is built up
by these powers; we have the need for them all. When we
have rightly met and adjusted the claims of them all, we
shall then be in a fair way for getting soberness and righteousness, with wisdom. This is evident enough, and the friends
of physical science would admit it.

But perhaps they may not have sufficiently observed another thing: namely, that the several powers just mentioned
are not isolated, but there is, in the generality of mankind, a
perpetual tendency to relate them one to another in divers
ways. With one such way of relating them I am particularly
concerned now. Following our instinct for intellect and
knowledge, we acquire pieces of knowledge; and presently, *relate knowledge*
in the generality of men, there arises the desire to relate *to sense of*
these pieces of knowledge to our sense for conduct, to our *beauty and*
sense for beauty,—and there is weariness and dissatisfaction *that of*
if the desire is baulked. Now in this desire lies, I think, the *conduct*
strength of that hold which letters have upon us.

All knowledge is, as I said just now, interesting; and even
items of knowledge which from the nature of the case cannot
well be related, but must stand isolated in our thoughts,

have their interest. Even lists of exceptions have their interest. If we are studying Greek accents, it is interesting to know that *pais* and *pas,* and some other monosyllables of the same form of declension, do not take the circumflex upon the last syllable of the genitive plural, but vary, in this respect, from the common rule. If we are studying physiology, it is interesting to know that the pulmonary artery carries dark blood and the pulmonary vein carries bright blood, departing in this respect from the common rule for the division of labour between the veins and the arteries. But every one knows how we seek naturally to combine the pieces of our knowledge together, to bring them under general rules, to relate them to principles; and how unsatisfactory and tiresome it would be to go on for ever learning lists of exceptions, or accumulating items of fact which must stand isolated.

Well, that same need of relating our knowledge, which operates here within the sphere of our knowledge itself, we shall find operating, also, outside that sphere. We experience, as we go on learning and knowing,—the vast majority of us experience,—the need of relating what we have learnt and known to the sense which we have in us for conduct, to the sense which we have in us for beauty.

A certain Greek prophetess [10] of Mantineia in Arcadia, Diotima by name, once explained to the philosopher Socrates that love, and impulse, and bent of all kinds, is, in fact, nothing else but the desire in men that good should for ever be present to them. This desire for good, Diotima assured Socrates, is our fundamental desire of which fundamental desire every impulse in us is only some one particular form. And therefore this fundamental desire it is, I suppose,—this desire in men that good should be for ever present to them,—which acts in us when we feel the impulse for relating our knowledge to our sense for conduct and to our sense for beauty. At any rate, with men in general the

10 See Plato, *Symposium.*

instinct exists. Such is human nature. And the instinct, it will be admitted, is innocent, and human nature is preserved by our following the lead of its innocent instincts. Therefore, in seeking to gratify this instinct in question, we are following the instinct of self-preservation in humanity.

But, no doubt, some kinds of knowledge cannot be made to directly serve the instinct in question, cannot be directly related to the sense for beauty, to the sense for conduct. These are instrument-knowledges; they lead on to other knowledges, which can. A man who passes his life in instrument-knowledges is a specialist. They may be invaluable as instruments to something beyond, for those who have the gift thus to employ them; and they may be disciplines in themselves wherein it is useful for every one to have some schooling. But it is inconceivable that the generality of men should pass all their mental life with Greek accents or with formal logic. My friend Professor Sylvester, who is one of the first mathematicians in the world, holds transcendental doctrines as to the virtue of mathematics, but those doctrines are not for common men. In the very Senate House and heart of our English Cambridge I once ventured, though not without an apology for my profaneness, to hazard the opinion that for the majority of mankind a little of mathematics, even, goes a long way. Of course this is quite consistent with their being of immense importance as an instrument to something else; but it is the few who have the aptitude for thus using them, not the bulk of mankind.

The natural sciences do not, however, stand on the same footing with these instrument-knowledges. Experience shows us that the generality of men will find more interest in learning that, when a taper burns, the wax is converted into carbonic acid and water, or in learning the explanation of the phenomenon of dew, or in learning how the circulation of the blood is carried on, than they find in learning that the genitive plural of *pais* and *pas* does not take the circumflex on the termination. And one piece of natural knowledge is added to another, and others are added to that, and at last we come to propositions so interesting as Mr. Darwin's famous proposition that 'our ancestor was a hairy quadruped furnished with a tail and pointed ears, probably arboreal in his habits.' [11] Or we come to propositions of such reach and magnitude as those which Professor Huxley delivers, when he says that the notions of our forefathers about the beginning and the end of the world were all wrong, and that nature is the expression of a definite order with which nothing interferes.

Interesting, indeed, these results of science are, important they are, and we should all of us be acquainted with them. But what I now wish you to mark is, that we are still, when they are propounded to us and we receive them, we are still in the sphere of intellect and knowledge. And for the generality of men there will be found, I say, to arise, when they have duly taken in the proposition that their ancestor was 'a hairy quadruped furnished with a tail and pointed ears, probably arboreal in his habits,' there will be found to arise an invincible desire to relate this proposition to the sense in us for conduct, and to the sense in us for beauty. But this the men of science will not do for us, and will hardly even profess to do. They will give us other pieces of knowledge, other facts, about other animals and their ancestors, or about plants, or about stones, or about stars; and they may finally bring us to those great 'general conceptions of the universe, which are forced upon us all,' says Professor Huxley, 'by the progress of physical science.' But still it will be *knowledge* only which they give us; knowledge not put for us into relation with our sense for conduct, our sense for beauty, and touched with emotion by being so put; not thus put for us, and therefore, to the majority of mankind, after a certain while, unsatisfying, wearying.

Not to the born naturalist, I admit. But what do we mean by a born naturalist? We mean a man in whom the zeal for observing nature is so uncommonly strong and eminent, that it marks him off from the bulk of mankind. Such a man will

11 *The Descent of Man* (1871), Part II, Chap. xxi.

pass his life happily in collecting natural knowledge and reasoning upon it, and will ask for nothing, or hardly anything, more. I have heard it said that the sagacious and admirable naturalist whom we lost not very long ago, Mr. Darwin, once owned to a friend that for his part he did not experience the necessity for two things which most men find so necessary to them,—religion and poetry; science and the domestic affections, he thought, were enough. To a born naturalist, I can well understand that this should seem so. So absorbing is his occupation with nature, so strong his love for his occupation, that he goes on acquiring natural knowledge and reasoning upon it, and has little time or inclination for thinking about getting it related to the desire in man for conduct, the desire in man for beauty. He relates it to them for himself as he goes along, so far as he feels the need; and he draws from the domestic affections all the additional solace necessary. But then Darwins are extremely rare. Another great and admirable master of natural knowledge, Faraday,[12] was a Sandemanian. That is to say, he related his knowledge to his instinct for conduct and to his instinct for beauty, by the aid of that respectable Scottish sectary, Robert Sandeman, And so strong, in general, is the demand of religion and poetry to have their share in a man, to associate themselves with his knowing, and to relieve and rejoice it, that, probably, for one man amongst us with the disposition to do as Darwin did in this respect, there are at least fifty with the disposition to do as Faraday.

Education lays hold upon us, in fact, by satisfying this demand. Professor Huxley holds up to scorn mediaeval education, with its neglect of the knowledge of nature, its poverty even of literary studies, its formal logic devoted to 'showing how and why that which the Church said was true must be true.' But the great mediaeval Universities were not brought into being, we may be sure, by the zeal for giving a jejune and *void of interest, uninteresting*

12 Michael Faraday (1791-1867), great physicist and chemist. The Sandemanian sect of Protestant Christianity followed Robert Sandeman, who, in turn, took his ideas from his strongly dissenting father-in-law, John Glas. *Vapid -dull, spiritless, having lost its life, zest, spirit*

contemptible education. Kings have been their nursing fathers, and queens have been their nursing mothers, but not for this. The mediaeval Universities came into being, because the supposed knowledge, delivered by Scripture and the Church, so deeply engaged men's hearts, by so simply, easily, and powerfully relating itself to their desire for conduct, their desire for beauty. All other knowledge was dominated by this supposed knowledge and was subordinated to it, because of the surpassing strength of the hold which it gained upon the affections of men, by allying itself profoundly with their sense for conduct, their sense for beauty.

But now, says Professor Huxley, conceptions of the universe fatal to the notions held by our forefathers have been forced upon us by physical science. Grant to him that they are thus fatal, that the new conceptions must and will soon become current everywhere, and that every one will finally perceive them to be fatal to the beliefs of our forefathers. The need of humane letters, as they are truly called, because they serve the paramount desire in men that good should be for ever present to them,—the need of humane letters, to establish a relation between the new conceptions, and our instinct for beauty, our instinct for conduct, is only the more visible. The Middle Age could do without humane letters, as it could do without the study of nature, because its supposed knowledge was made to engage its emotions so powerfully. Grant that the supposed knowledge disappears, its power of being made to engage the emotions will of course disappear along with it,—but the emotions themselves, and their claim to be engaged and satisfied, will remain. Now if we find by experience that humane letters have an undeniable power of engaging the emotions, the importance of humane letters in a man's training becomes not less, but greater, in proportion to the success of modern science in extirpating what it calls 'mediaeval thinking.'

Have humane letters, then, have poetry and eloquence, the power here attributed to them of engaging the emotions, and do they exercise it? And if they have it and exercise it, *how* do they exercise it, so as to exert an influence upon man's sense for conduct, his sense for beauty? Finally, even if they both can and do exert an influence upon the senses in question, how are they to relate to them the results,—the modern results,—of natural science? All these questions may be asked. First, have poetry and eloquence the power of calling out the emotions? The appeal is to experience. Experience shows that for the vast majority of men, for mankind in general, they have the power. Next do they exercise it? They do. But then, *how* do they exercise it so as to affect man's sense for conduct, his sense for beauty? And this is perhaps a case for applying the Preacher's words: 'Though a man labour to seek it out, yet he shall not find it; yea, farther, though a wise man think to know it, yet shall he not be able to find it.' [13] Why should it be one thing, in its effect upon the emotions, to say, 'Patience is a virtue,' and quite another thing, in its effect upon the emotions, to say with Homer,

τλητὸν γὰρ Μοῖραι θυμὸν θέσαν ἀνθρώποισιν—

'for an enduring heart have the destinies appointed to the children of men?' [14] Why should it be one thing, in its effect upon the emotions, to say with the philosopher Spinoza, *Felicitas in eo consistit quod homo suum esse conservare potest*—'Man's happiness consists in his being able to preserve his own essence,' [15] and quite another thing, in its effect upon the emotions, to say with the Gospel, 'What is a man advantaged, if he gain the whole world, and lose himself, forfeit himself?' [16] How does this difference of effect arise? I cannot tell, and I am not much concerned to know; the important thing is that it does arise, and that we can profit by it. But how, finally, are poetry and eloquence to exercise the power of relating the modern results of natural science to man's instinct for conduct, his instinct for beauty? And here again

13 Ecclesiastes viii, 17.
14 *Iliad*, XXIV, 49.
15 Spinoza, *Ethics*, IV, Prop. xviii.
16 Luke ix, 25. Slightly modified.

I answer that I do not know *how* they will exercise it, but
that they can and will exercise it I am sure. I do not mean
that modern philosophical poets and modern philosophical
moralists are to come and relate for us, in express terms, the
results of modern scientific research to our instinct for conduct, our instinct for beauty. But I mean that we shall find,
as a matter of experience, if we know the best that has been
thought and uttered in the world, we shall find that the art
and poetry and eloquence of men who lived, perhaps, long
ago, who had the most limited natural knowledge, who had
the most erroneous conceptions about many important matters,
we shall find that this, art, and poetry, and eloquence, have
in fact not only the power of refreshing and delighting us,
they have also the power,—such is the strength and worth, in
essentials, of their authors' criticism of life,—they have a forti-
fying, and elevating, and quickening, and suggestive power,
capable of wonderfully helping us to relate the results of modern science to our need for conduct, our need for beauty.
Homer's conceptions of the physical universe were, I imagine,
grotesque; but really, under the shock of hearing from modern science that 'the world is not subordinated to man's use,'
and that man is not the cynosure of things terrestrial,' I could,
for my own part, desire no better comfort than Homer's line
which I quoted just now,

τλητὸν γὰρ Μοῖραι θυμὸν θέσαν ἀνθρώποισιν—

'for an enduring heart have the destinies appointed to the
children of men!'
    And the more that men's minds are cleared, the more that
the results of science are frankly accepted, the more that poetry
and eloquence come to be received and studied as what in
truth they really are,—the criticism of life by gifted men, alive
and active with extraordinary power at an unusual number
of points;—so much the more will the value of humane letters,
and of art also, which is an utterance having a like kind of
power with theirs, be felt and acknowledged, and their place
in education be secured.

unjustly descriminating

Let us therefore, all of us, avoid indeed as much as possible any invidious comparison between the merits of humane letters, as means of education, and the merits of the natural sciences. But when some President of a Section for Mechanical Science insists on making the comparison, and tells us that 'he who in his training has substituted literature and history for natural science has chosen the less useful alternative,' let us make answer to him that the student of humane letters only, will, at least, know also the great general conceptions brought in by modern physical science; for science, as Professor Huxley says, forces them upon us all. But the student of the natural sciences only, will, by our very hypothesis, know nothing of humane letters; not to mention that in setting himself to be perpetually accumulating natural knowledge, he sets himself to do what only specialists have in general *graciously* the gift for doing genially. And so he will probably be unsatisfied, or at any rate incomplete, and even more incomplete than the student of humane letters only.

I once mentioned in a school-report, how a young man in one of our English training colleges having to paraphrase the passage in *Macbeth* beginning,

'Can'st thou not minister to a mind diseased?' [17]

turned this line into, 'Can you not wait upon the lunatic?' And I remarked what a curious state of things it would be, if every pupil of our national schools knew, let us say, that the moon is two thousand one hundred and sixty miles in diameter, and thought at the same time that a good paraphrase for

'Can'st thou not minister to a mind diseased?'

was, 'Can you not wait upon the lunatic?' If one is driven to choose, I think I would rather have a young person ignorant about the moon's diameter, but aware that 'Can you not wait

[17] *Macbeth*, Act V, Sc. 3, l. 40. It is hard to imagine what Arnold would have said if he could have seen a current "modernized" text in which the line reads "Can't you take care of a sick mind?"

upon the lunatic?' is bad, than a young person whose education had been such as to manage things the other way.

Or to go higher than the pupils of our national schools. I have in my mind's eye a member of our British Parliament who comes to travel here in America, who afterwards relates his travels, and who shows a really masterly knowledge of the geology of this great country and of its mining capabilities, but who ends by gravely suggesting that the United States should borow a prince from our Royal Family, and should make him their king, and should create a House of Lords of great landed proprietors after the pattern of ours; and then America, he thinks, would have her future happily and perfectly secured. Surely, in this case, the President of the Section for Mechanical Science would himself hardly say that our member of Parliament, by concentrating himself upon geology and mineralogy, and so on, and not attending to literature and history, had 'chosen the more useful alternative.'

If then there is to be separation and option between humane letters on the one hand, and the natural sciences on the other, the great majority of mankind, all who have not exceptional and overpowering aptitudes for the study of nature, would do well, I cannot but think, to choose to be educated in humane letters rather than in the natural sciences. Letters will call out their being at more points, will make them live more.

I said that before I ended I would just touch on the question of classical education, and I will keep my word. Even if literature is to retain a large place in our education, yet Latin and Greek, say the friends of progress, will certainly have to go. Greek is the grand offender in the eyes of these gentlemen. The attackers of the established course of study think that against Greek, at any rate, they have irresistible arguments. Literature may perhaps be needed in education, they say; but why on earth should it be Greek literature? Why not French or German? Nay, 'has not an Englishman models in his own literature of every kind of excellence?' As before, it is not on any weak pleadings of my own that I rely for convincing the gainsayers; it is on the constitution of human nature itself, and on the instinct of self-preservation in humanity. The instinct for beauty is set in human nature, as surely as the instinct for knowledge is set there, or the instinct for conduct. If the instinct for beauty is served by Greek literature and art as it is served by no other literature and art, we may trust to the instinct of self-preservation in humanity for keeping Greek as part of our culture. We may trust to it for even making the study of Greek more prevalent than it is now. Greek will come, I hope, some day to be studied more rationally than at present; but it will be increasingly studied as men increasingly feel the need in them for beauty, and how powerfully Greek art and Greek literature can serve this need. Women will again study Greek, as Lady Jane Grey did; I believe that in that chain of forts, with which the fair host of the Amazons are now engirdling our English universities, I find that here in America, in colleges like Smith College in Massachusetts, and Vassar College in the State of New York, and in the happy families of the mixed universities out West, they are studying it already.

Defuit una mihi symmetria prisca,

—'The antique symmetry was the one thing wanting to me,' said Leonardo da Vinci; and he was an Italian. I will not presume to speak for the Americans, but I am sure that, in the Englishman, the want of this admirable symmetry of the Greeks is a thousand times more great and crying than in any Italian. The results of the want show themselves most glaringly, perhaps, in our architecture, but they show themselves, also, in all our art. *Fit details strictly combined, in view of a large general result nobly conceived;* that is just the beautiful *symmetria prisca* of the Greeks, and it is just where we English fail, where all our art fails. Striking ideas we have, and well-executed details we have; but that high symmetry which, with satisfying and delightful effect, combines them, we seldom or never have. The glorious beauty of the Acropolis at Athens did not come from single fine things stuck about on that hill,

a statue here, a gateway there;—no, it arose from all things
being perfectly combined for a supreme total effect. What
must not an Englishman feel about our deficiencies in this
respect, as the sense for beauty, whereof this symmetry is an
essential element, awakens and strengthen within him! what
will not one day be his respect and desire for Greece and its
symmetria prisca, when the scales drop from his eyes as he
walks the London streets, and he sees such a lesson in meanness as the Strand,[18] for instance, in its true deformity! But
here we are coming to our friend Mr. Ruskin's province,[19]
and I will not intrude upon it, for he is its very sufficient
guardian.

And so we at last find, it seems, we find flowing in favour
of the humanities the natural and necessary stream of things,
which seemed against them when we started. The 'hairy
quadruped furnished with a tail and pointed ears, probably
arboreal in his habits,' this good fellow carried hidden in his
nature, apparently, something destined to develop into a
necessity for humane letters. Nay, more; we seem finally to
be even led to the further conclusion that our hairy ancestor
carried in his nature, also, a necessity for Greek.

And therefore, to say the truth, I cannot really think that
humane letters are in much actual danger of being thrust out
from their leading place in education, in spite of the array
of authorities against them at this moment. So long as human
nature is what it is, their attractions will remain irresistible.
As with Greek, so with letters generally: they will some day
come, we may hope, to be studied more rationally, but they
will not lose their place. What will happen will rather be that
there will be crowded into education other matters besides,
far too many; there will be, perhaps, a period of unsettlement
and confusion and false tendency; but letters will not in the
end lose their leading place. If they lose it for a time, they
will get it back again. We shall be brought back to them by

[18] A commercial street in the city of London, not notable for its beauty.
[19] Ruskin was an extremely active writer on architecture and a critic
of the drift of urban England.

our wants and aspirations. And a poor humanist may possess his soul in patience, neither strive nor cry, admit the energy and brilliancy of the partisans of physical science, and their present favour with the public, to be far greater than his own, and still have a happy faith that the nature of things works silently on behalf of the studies which he loves, and that, while we shall all have to acquaint ourselves with the great results reached by modern science, and to give ourselves as much training in its disciplines as we can conveniently carry, yet the majority of men will always require humane letters; and so much the more, as they have the more and the greater results of science to relate to the need in man for conduct, and to the need in him for beauty.

Gilbert Keith Chesterton

GILBERT KEITH CHESTERTON *(1874-1936) was an ex-*
tremely prolific essayist and novelist and one of the
most various and unpredictable of the great English
essayists. He delighted in paradox, and the result
was often mere cleverness. But when a subject (like
Dickens) fitted in the categories of paradox, he could
then write with a fitting brilliance. Chesterton was
educated at St. Paul's School. Principal works: The
Man Who Was Thursday *(1908);* The Innocence of
Father Brown *(1911);* What's Wrong with the World
(1910); Autobiography *(1936).*

THE DICKENS PERIOD [1]

Much of our modern difficulty, in religion and other things,
arises merely from this, that we confuse the word "indefinable" with the word "vague." If some one speaks of a spiritual
fact as "indefinable" we promptly picture something misty,
a cloud with indeterminate edges. But this is an error even
in commonplace logic. The thing that cannot be defined is the
first thing; the primary fact. It is our arms and legs, our pots
and pans, that are indefinable. The indefinable is the indis-
putable. The man next door is indefinable, because he is too
actual to be defined. And there are some to whom spiritual
things have the same fierce and practical proximity; some to
whom God is too actual to be defined.

But there is a third class of primary terms. There are

[1] Introductory chapter to *Charles Dickens: the Last of the Great Men*
(1906).

332

popular expressions which every one uses and no one can explain; which the wise man will accept and reverence, as he reverences desire or darkness or any elemental thing. The prigs of the debating club will demand that he should define his terms. And being a wise man he will flatly refuse. This first inexplicable term is the most important term of all. The word that has no definition is the word that has no substitute. If a man falls back again and again on some such word as "vulgar" or "manly" do not suppose that the word means nothing because he cannot say what it means. If he could say what the word means he would say what it means instead of saying the word. When the Game Chicken (that fine thinker) kept on saying to Mr. Toots,[2] "It's mean. That's what it is— it's mean," he was using language in the wisest possible way. For what else could he say? There is no word for mean except mean. A man must be very mean himself before he comes to defining meanness. Precisely because the word is indefinable, the word is indispensable.

In everyday talk, or in any of our journals, we may find the loose but important phrase, "Why have we no great men to-day? Why have we no great men like Thackeray, or Carlyle, or Dickens?" Do not let us dismiss this expression, because it appears loose or arbitrary. "Great" does means something, and the test of its actuality is to be found by noting how instinctively and decisively we do apply it to some men and not to others; above all how instinctively and decisively we do apply it to four or five men in the Victorian era, four or five men of whom Dickens was not the least. The term is found to fit a definite thing. Whatever the word "great" means, Dickens was what it means. Even the fastidious and unhappy who cannot read his books without a continuous critical exasperation, would use the word of him without stopping to think. They feel that Dickens is a great writer even if he is not a good writer. He is treated as a classic; that is, as a king who may now be deserted, but who cannot now

---

2 In *Dombey and Son.*

be dethroned. The atmosphere of this word clings to him; and the curious thing is that we cannot get it to cling to any of the men of our own generation. "Great" is the first adjective which the most supercilious modern critic would apply to Dickens. And "great" is the last adjective that the most supercilious modern critic would apply to himself. We dare not claim to be great men, even when we claim to be superior to them.

Is there, then, any vital meaning in the idea of "greatness" or in our laments over its absence in our own time? Some people say, indeed, that this sense of mass is but a mirage of distance, and that men always think dead men great and live men small. They seem to think that the law of perspective in the mental world is the precise opposite to the law of perspective in the physical world. They think that figures grow larger as they walk away. But this theory cannot be made to correspond with the facts. We do not lack great men in our own day because we decline to look for them in our own day; on the contrary, we are looking for them all day long. We are not, as a matter of fact, mere examples of those who stone the prophets and leave it to their posterity to build their sepulchres. If the world would only produce our perfect prophet, solemn, searching, universal, nothing would give us keener pleasure than to build his sepulchre. In our eagerness we might even bury him alive. Nor is it true that the great men of the Victorian era were not called great in their own time. By many they were called great from the first. Charlotte Brontë held this heroic language about Thackeray. Ruskin held it about Carlyle. A definite school regarded Dickens as a great man from the first days of his fame: Dickens certainly belonged to this school.

In reply to this question, "Why have we no great men today?" many modern explanations are offered. Advertisement, cigarette-smoking, the decay of religion, the decay of agriculture, too much humanitarianism, too little humanitarianism, the fact that people are educated insufficiently, the fact that they are educated at all, all these are reasons given. If I give my own explanation, it is not for its intrinsic value; it is because my answer to the question, "Why have we no great men?" is a short way of stating the deepest and most catastrophic difference between the age in which we live and the early nineteenth century; the age under the shadow of the French Revolution, the age in which Dickens was born.

The soundest of the Dickens critics, a man of genius, Mr. George Gissing, opens his criticism by remarking that the world in which Dickens grew up was a hard and cruel world. He notes its gross feeding, its fierce sports, its fighting and foul humour, and all this he summarizes in the words hard and cruel. It is curious how different are the impressions of men. To me this old English world seems infinitely less hard and cruel than the world described in Gissing's own novels. Coarse external customs are merely relative, and easily assimilated. A man soon learnt to harden his hands and harden his head. Faced with the world of Gissing, he can do little but harden his heart. But the fundamental difference between the beginning of the nineteenth century and the end of it is a difference simple but enormous. The first period was full of evil things, but it was full of hope. The second period, the *fin de siècle,* was even full (in some sense) of good things. But it was occupied in asking what was the good of good things. Joy itself became joyless; and the fighting of Cobbett was happier than the feasting of Walter Pater. The men of Cobbett's day were sturdy enough to endure and inflict brutality; but they were also sturdy enough to alter it. This "hard and cruel" age was, after all, the age of reform. The gibbet stood up black above them; but it was black against the dawn.

This dawn, against which the gibbet and all the old cruelties stood out so black and clear, was the developing idea of liberalism, the French Revolution. It was a clear and a happy philosophy. And only against such philosophies do evils appear evident at all. The optimist is a better reformer than the pessimist; and the man who believes life to be excellent is the man who alters it most. It seems a paradox, yet the reason of it is very plain. The pessimist can be enraged at evil. But only the optimist can be surprised at it. From the reformer is required a simplicity of surprise. He must have the faculty of a violent and virgin astonishment. It is not enough that he should think injustice distressing; he must think injustice *absurd,* an anomaly in existence, a matter less for tears than for a shattering laughter. On the other hand, the pessimists at the end of the century could hardly curse even the blackest thing; for they could hardly see it against its black and eternal background. Nothing was bad, because everything was bad. Life in prison was infamous—like life anywhere else. The fires of persecution were vile—like the stars. We perpetually find this paradox of a contented discontent. Dr. Johnson takes too sad a view of humanity, but he is also too satisfied a Conservative. Rousseau takes too rosy a view of humanity, but he causes a revolution. Swift is angry, but a Tory. Shelley is happy, and a rebel. Dickens, the optimist, satirizes the Fleet, and the Fleet is gone.[3] Gissing, the pessimist, satirizes Suburbia, and Suburbia remains.

Mr. Gissing's error, then, about the early Dickens period we may put thus: in calling it hard and cruel he omits the wind of hope and humanity that was blowing through it. It may have been full of inhuman institutions, but it was full of humanitarian people. And this humanitarianism was very much the better (in my view) because it was a rough and even rowdy humanitarianism. It was free from all the faults that cling to the name. It was, if you will, a coarse humanitarianism. It was a shouting, fighting, drinking philanthropy —a noble thing. But, in any case, this atmosphere was the atmosphere of the Revolution; and its main idea was the idea of human equality. I am not concerned here to defend the egalitarian idea against the solemn and babyish attacks made upon it by the rich and learned of to-day. I am merely concerned to state one of its practical consequences. One of the actual and certain consequences of the idea that all men are

[3] The Fleet Prison, treated by Dickens in *Pickwick Papers* and *Barnaby Rudge.*

equal is immediately to produce very great men. I would say superior men, only that the hero thinks of himself as great, but not as superior. This has been hidden from us of late by a foolish worship of sinister and exceptional men, men without comradeship, or any infectious virtue. This type of Caesar does exist. There is a great man who makes every man feel small. But the real great man is the man who makes every man feel great.

The spirit of the early century produced great men, because it believed that men were great. It made strong men by encouraging weak men. Its education, its public habits, its rhetoric, were all addressed towards encouraging the greatness in everybody. And by encouraging the greatness in everybody, it naturally encouraged superlative greatness in some. Superiority came out of the high rapture of equality. It is precisely in this sort of passionate unconsciousness and bewildering community of thought that men do become more than themselves. No man by taking thought can add one cubit to his stature; but a man may add many cubits to his stature by not taking thought. The best men of the Revolution were simply common men at their best. This is why our age can never understand Napoleon. Because he was something great and triumphant, we suppose that he must have been something extraordinary, something inhuman. Some say he was the Devil; some say he was the Superhuman. Was he a very, very bad man? Was he a good man with some greater moral code? We strive in vain to invent the mysteries behind that immortal mask of brass. The modern world with all its subtleness will never guess his strange secret; for his strange secret was that he was very like other people.

And almost without exception all the great men have come out of this atmosphere of equality. Great men may make despotisms; but democracies make great men. The other main factory of heroes besides a revolution is a religion. And a religion, again, is a thing which, by its nature, does not think of men as more or less valuable, but of men as all intensely and painfully valuable, a democracy of eternal danger. For

religion all men are equal, as all pennies are equal, because
the only value in any of them is that they bear the image of
the King. This fact has been quite insufficiently observed in
the study of religious heroes. Piety produces intellectual
greatness precisely because piety in itself is quite indifferent
to intellectual greatness. The strength of Cromwell was that
he cared for religion. But the strength of religion was that
it did not care for Cromwell; did not care for him, that is,
any more than for anybody else. He and his footman were
equally welcomed to warm places in the hospitality of hell.
It has often been said, very truly, that religion is the thing
that makes the ordinary man feel extraordinary; it is an
equally important truth that religion is the thing that makes
the extraordinary man feel ordinary.

Carlyle killed the heroes;[4] there have been none since his
time. He killed the heroic (which he sincerely loved) by
forcing upon each man this question: "Am I strong or weak?"
To which the answer from any honest man whatever (yes,
from Caesar or Bismarck) would certainly be "weak." He
asked for candidates for a definite aristocracy, for men who
should hold themselves consciously above their fellows. He
advertised for them, so to speak; he promised them glory; he
promised them omnipotence. They have not appeared yet.
They never will. For the real heroes of whom he wrote had
appeared out of an ecstasy of the ordinary. I have already
instanced such a case as Cromwell. But there is no need to
go through all the great men of Carlyle. Carlyle himself was
as great as any of them; and if ever there was a typical child
of the French Revolution, it was he. He began with the
wildest hopes from the Reform Bill, and although he soured
afterwards, he had been made and moulded by those hopes.
He was disappointed with Equality; but Equality was not
disappointed with him. Equality is justified of all her children.

But we, in the post-Carlylean period, have become fastidious
about great men. Every man examines himself, every man

---

4 Carlyle's *On Heroes, Hero-Worship, and the Heroic in History* (1841)
was one of the most influential books of the nineteenth century.

examines his neighbours, to see whether they or he quite come up to the exact line of greatness. The answer is, naturally, "No." And many a man calls himself contentedly "a minor poet" who would then have been inspired to be a major prophet. We are hard to please and of little faith. We can hardly believe that there is such a thing as a great man. They could hardly believe there was such a thing as a small one. But we are always praying that our eyes may behold greatness, instead of praying that our hearts may be filled with it. Thus, for instance, the Liberal party (to which I belong) was, in its period of exile, always saying, "O for a Gladstone!" and such things. We were always asking that it might be strengthened from above, instead of ourselves strengthening it from below, with our hope and our anger and our youth. Every man was waiting for a leader. Every man ought to be waiting for a chance to lead. If a god does come upon the earth, he will descend at the sight of the brave. Our protestations and litanies are of no avail; our new moons and our sabbaths are an abomination. The great man will come when all of us are feeling great, not when all of us are feeling small. He will ride in at some splendid moment when we all feel that we could do without him.

We are then able to answer in some manner the question, "Why have we no great men?" We have no great men chiefly because we are always looking for them. We are connoisseurs of greatness, and connoisseurs can never be great; we are fastidious, that is, we are small. When Diogenes went about with a lantern looking for an honest man, I am afraid he had very little time to be honest himself. And when anybody goes about on his hands and knees looking for a great man to worship, he is making sure that one man at any rate shall not be great. Now, the error of Diogenes is evident. The error of Diogenes lay in the fact that he omitted to notice that every man is both an honest man and a dishonest man. Diogenes looked for his honest man inside every crypt and cavern; but he never thought of looking inside the thief. And there is where the Founder of Christianity found the honest man; He found him on a gibbet and promised him Paradise. Just as Christianity looked for the honest man inside the thief, democracy looked for the wise man inside the fool. It encouraged the fool to be wise. We can call this thing sometimes optimism, sometimes equality; the nearest name for it is encouragement. It had its exaggerations—failure to understand original sin, notions that education would make all men good, the childlike yet pedantic philosophies of human perfectibility. But the whole was full of a faith in the infinity of human souls, which is in itself not only Christian but orthodox; and this we have lost amid the limitations of a pessimistic science. Christianity said that any man could be a saint if he chose; democracy, that any man could be a citizen if he chose. The note of the last few decades in art and ethics has been that a man is stamped with an irrevocable psychology, and is cramped for perpetuity in the prison of his skull. It was a world that expected everything of everybody. It was a world that encouraged anybody to be anything. And in England and literature its living expression was Dickens.

We shall consider Dickens in many other capacities, but let us put this one first. He was the voice in England of this humane intoxication and expansion, this encouraging of anybody to be anything. His best books are a carnival of liberty, and there is more of the real spirit of the French Revolution in "Nicholas Nickleby" than in "A Tale of Two Cities." His work has the great glory of the Revolution, the bidding of every man to be himself; it has also the revolutionary deficiency; it seems to think that this mere emancipation is enough. No man *encouraged* his characters as much as Dickens. "I am an affectionate father," he says, "to every child of my fancy." He was not only an affectionate father, he was an ever-indulgent father. The children of his fancy are spoilt children. They shake the house like heavy and shouting schoolboys; they smash the story to pieces like so much furniture. When we moderns write stories our characters are better controlled. But, alas! our characters are rather easier to control. We are in no danger from the gigantic gambols of

creatures like Mantalini and Micawber.[5] We are in no danger
of giving our readers too much Weller or Wegg.[6] We have not
got it to give. When we experience the ungovernable sense of
life which goes along with the old Dickens sense of liberty,
we experience the best of the revolution. We are filled with
the first of all democratic doctrines, that all men are interesting; Dickens tried to make some of his people appear dull
people, but he could not keep them dull. He could not make
a monotonous man. The bores in his books are brighter than
the wits in other books.

I have put this position first for a defined reason. It is
useless for us to attempt to imagine Dickens and his life unless
we are able at least to imagine this old atmosphere of a democratic optimism—a confidence in common men. Dickens depends upon such a comprehension in a rather unusual manner,
a manner worth explanation, or at least remark.

The disadvantage under which Dickens has fallen, both as
an artist and a moralist, is very plain. His misfortune is that
neither of the two last movements in literary criticism has
done him any good. He has suffered alike from his enemies,
and from the enemies of his enemies. The facts to which I
refer are familiar. When the world first awoke from the mere
hypnotism of Dickens, from the direct tyranny of his temperament, there was, of course, a reaction. At the head of it came
the Realists, with their documents, like Miss Flite.[7] They
declared that scenes and types in Dickens were wholly impossible (in which they were perfectly right), and on this rather
paradoxical ground objected to them as literature. They were
not "like life," and there, they thought, was an end of the
matter. The Realists for a time prevailed. But Realists did not
enjoy their victory (if they enjoyed anything) very long. A
more symbolic school of criticism soon arose. Men saw that it
was necessary to give a much deeper and more delicate mean-

[5] Madame Mantalini in *Nicholas Nickleby* and Mr. Micawber in *David Copperfield*.
[6] Samuel Weller in *Pickwick Papers* and Silas Wegg in *Our Mutual Friend*.
[7] In *Bleak House*.

ing to the expression "like life." Streets are not life, cities
and civilizations are not life, faces even and voices are not
life itself. Life is within, and no man hath seen it at any time.
As for our meals, and our manners, and our daily dress, these
are things exactly like sonnets; they are random symbols of
the soul. One man tries to express himself in books, another
in boots; both probably fail. Our solid houses and square
meals are in the strict sense fiction. They are things made up
to typify our thoughts. The coat a man wears may be wholly
fictitious; the movement of his hands may be quite unlike life.

This much the intelligence of men soon perceived. And by
this much Dickens's fame should have greatly profited. For
Dickens is "like life" in the truer sense, in the sense that he
is akin to the living principle in us and in the universe; he is
like life, at least in this detail, that he is alive. His art is like
life, because, like life, it cares for nothing outside itself, and
goes on its way rejoicing. Both produce monsters with a kind
of carelessness, like enormous by-products; life producing the
rhinoceros, and art Mr. Bunsby.[8] Art indeed copies life in
not copying life, for life copies nothing. Dickens's art is like
life because, like life, it is irresponsible, because, like life, it
is incredible.

Yet the return of this realization has not greatly profited
Dickens, the return of romance has been almost useless to
this great romantic. He has gained as little from the fall of
the Realists as from their triumph; there has been a revolution, there has been a counter revolution, there has been no
restoration. And the reason of this brings us back to that
atmosphere of popular optimism of which I spoke. And the
shortest way of expressing the more recent neglect of Dickens
is to say that for our time and taste he exaggerates the wrong
thing.

Exaggeration is the definition of Art. That both Dickens
and the moderns understood Art is, in its inmost nature,
fantastic. Time brings queer revenges, and while the Realists

8 Captain John Bunsby in *Dombey and Son.*

were yet living, the art of Dickens was justified by Aubrey Beardsley.[9] But men like Aubrey Beardsley were allowed to be fantastic, because the mood which they overstrained and overstated was a mood which their period understood. Dickens overstrains and overstates a mood our period does not understand. The truth he exaggerates is exactly this old Revolution sense of infinite opportunity and boisterous brotherhood. And we resent his undue sense of it, because we ourselves have not even a due sense of it. We feel troubled with too much where we have too little; we wish he would keep it within bounds. For we are all exact and scientific on the subjects we do not care about. We all immediately detect exaggeration in an exposition of Mormonism or a patriotic speech from Paraguay. We all require sobriety on the subject of the sea serpent. But the moment we begin to believe a thing ourselves, that moment we begin easily to overstate it; and the moment our souls become serious, our words become a little wild. And certain moderns are thus placed towards exaggeration. They permit any writer to emphasize doubts, for instance, for doubts are their religion, but they permit no man to emphasize dogmas. If a man be the mildest Christian, they smell "cant"; but he can be a raving windmill of pessimism, and they call it "temperament." If a moralist paints a wild picture of immorality, they doubt its truth, they say that devils are not so black as they are painted. But if a pessimist paints a wild picture of melancholy, they accept the whole horrible psychology, and they never ask if devils are as blue as they are painted.

It is evident, in short, why even those who admire exaggeration do not admire Dickens. He is exaggerating the wrong thing. They know what it is to feel a sadness so strange and deep that only impossible characters can express it: they do not know what it is to feel a joy so vital and violent that only impossible characters can express that. They know that the soul can be so sad as to dream naturally of the blue faces of the corpses of Baudelaire: they do not know that the soul

9 Aubrey Vincent Beardsley (1872-1898), an artist of the 1890's.

can be so cheerful as to dream naturally of the blue face of Major Bagstock.[10] They know that there is a point of depression at which one believes in Tintagiles: [11] they do not know that there is a point of exhilaration at which one believes in Mr. Wegg. To them the impossibilities of Dickens seem much more impossible than they really are, because they are already attuned to the opposite impossibilities of Maeterlinck. For every mood there is an appropriate impossibility—a decent and tactful impossibility—fitted to the frame of mind. Every train of thought may end in an ecstasy, and all roads lead to Elfland. But few now walk far enough along the street of Dickens to find the place where the cockney villas grow so comic that they become poetical. People do not know how far mere good spirits will go. For instance, we never think (as the old folk-lore did) of good spirits reaching to the spiritual world. We see this in the complete absence from modern, popular supernaturalism of the old popular mirth. We hear plenty to-day of the wisdom of the spiritual world; but we do not hear, as our fathers did, of the folly of the spiritual world, of the tricks of the gods, and the jokes of the patron saints. Our popular tales tell us of a man who is so wise that he touches the supernatural, like Dr Nikola; but they never tell us (like the popular tales of the past) of a man who was so silly that he touched the supernatural like Bottom the Weaver. We do not understand the dark and transcendental sympathy between fairies and fools. We understand a devout occultism, an evil occultism, a tragic occultism, but a farcical occultism is beyond us. Yet a farcical occultism is the very essence of "A Midsummer Night's Dream." It is also the right and credible essence of "A Christmas Carol." Whether we understand it depends upon whether we can understand that exhilaration is not a physical accident, but a mystical fact; that exhilaration can be infinite, like sorrow; that a joke can be so big that it breaks the roof of the stars. By simply going on being ab-

10 A character in *Dombey and Son.*

11 The famous castle in Cornwall where the various fabulous episodes of the Arthurian legends were set.

surd, a thing can become godlike; there is but one step from the ridiculous to the sublime.

Dickens was great because he was immoderately possessed with all this; if we are to understand him at all we must also be moderately possessed with it. We must understand this old limitless hilarity and human confidence, at least enough to be able to endure it when it is pushed a great deal too far. For Dickens did push it too far; he did push the hilarity to the point of incredible character-drawing; he did push the human confidence to the point of an unconvincing sentimentalism. You can trace, if you will, the revolutionary joy till it reaches the incredible Sapsea epitaph; you can trace the revolutionary hope till it reaches the repentance of Dombey. There is plenty to carp at in this man if you are inclined to carp; you may easily find him vulgar if you cannot see that he is divine; and if you cannot laugh with Dickens, undoubtedly you can laugh at him.

I believe myself that this braver world of his will certainly return; for I believe that it is bound up with realities, like morning and the spring. But for those who beyond remedy regard it as an error, I put this appeal before any other observations on Dickens. First let us sympathize, if only for an instant, with the hopes of the Dickens period, with that cheerful trouble of change. If democracy has disappointed you, do not think of it as a burst bubble, but at least as a broken heart, an old love affair. Do not sneer at the time when the creed of humanity was on its honeymoon; treat it with the dreadful reverence that is due to youth. For you, perhaps, a drearier philosophy has covered and eclipsed the earth. The fierce poet of the Middle Ages wrote, "Abandon hope all ye who enter here," over the gates of the lower world.[12] The emancipated poets of to-day have written it over the gates of this world. But if we are to understand the story which follows, we must erase that apocalyptic writing, if only for an hour. We must recreate the faith of our fathers, if only as an

12 Dante, *Inferno*, Canto III, 1. 9.

artistic atmosphere. If, then, you are a pessimist, in reading this story, forego for a little the pleasures of pessimism. Dream for one mad moment that the grass is green. Unlearn that sinister learning that you think so clear; deny that deadly knowledge that you think you know. Surrender the very flower of your culture; give up the very jewel of your pride; abandon hopelessness, all ye who enter here.